# THE RISE AND FALL OF THE SOVIET UNION

**Recent Titles in**
**Bibliographies and Indexes in World History**

The American Field Service Archives of World War I, 1914-1917
*L. D. Geller, compiler*

An Annotated Bibliography of Latin American Sport: Pre-Conquest to the Present
*Joseph L. Arbena, compiler*

Modern Italian History: An Annotated Bibliography
*Frank J. Coppa and William Roberts, compilers*

Colonial British Caribbean Newspapers: A Bibliography and Directory
*Howard S. Pactor, compiler*

France under the German Occupation, 1940-1944: An Annotated Bibliography
*Donna Evleth, compiler*

A World in Turmoil: An Integrated Chronology of the Holocaust and World War II
*Hershel Edelheit and Abraham J. Edelheit*

First-Person Accounts of Genocidal Acts Committed in the Twentieth Century: An Annotated Bibliography
*Samuel Totten*

A Catalogue of Audio and Video Collections of Holocaust Testimony—Second Edition
*Joan Ringelheim, compiler*

A Guide to East Asian Collections in North America
*Thomas H. Lee, compiler*

World Racism and Related Inhumanities: A Country-by-Country Bibliography
*Meyer Weinberg, compiler*

A Selected Bibliography of Modern Historiography
*Attila Pók, editor*

# THE RISE AND FALL OF THE SOVIET UNION

## A Selected Bibliography of Sources in English

EDITED BY
ABRAHAM J. EDELHEIT
AND
HERSHEL EDELHEIT

Bibliographies and Indexes in World History, Number 27

**Greenwood Press**
Westport, Connecticut • London

**Library of Congress Cataloging-in-Publication Data**

The Rise and fall of the Soviet Union : a selected bibliography of sources in English / edited by Abraham J. Edelheit and Hershel Edelheit.
p. cm.—(Bibliographies and indexes in world history, ISSN 0742-6852 ; no. 27)
Includes bibliographical references and index.
ISBN 0-313-28625-6 (alk. paper)
1. Soviet Union—History—Bibliography. I. Edelheit, Abraham J. II. Edelheit, Hershel. III. Series.
Z2510.3.R57 1992
[DK266]
016.94708—dc20 92-24470

British Library Cataloguing in Publication Data is available.



Library of Congress Catalog Card Number: 92-24470
ISBN: 0-313-28625-6
ISSN: 0742-6852

First published in 1992

Greenwood Press, 88 Post Road West, Westport, CT 06881
An imprint of Greenwood Publishing Group, Inc.

Printed in the United States of America

The paper used in this book complies with the Permanent Paper Standard issued by the National Information Standards Organization (Z39.48-1984).

10 9 8 7 6 5 4 3 2 1

To the Memory of

Abraham Jacob and Pesha Rachel Edelheit

Joseph and Fannie Rashbaum

Samuel and Ann Edelheit

and to the

Thousands of Dissidents of all Persuasions in the
Former Soviet Union

To the Millions of Victims
Who Perished Under Stalinist Oppression and Terror

and to the

Victims Everywhere Who Lived
(and to those that are still living)
Under the Yoke of Totalitarianism and Dictatorship

We Humbly Dedicate This Book

# Contents

# Preface

On December 25, 1991 the Union of Soviet Socialist Republics (USSR) ceased to exist, replaced by the new Confederation of Independent States. A new era began as the red flag was lowered from the Kremlin's walls for the last time -- and the Russian Republic's tricolor went up for the first time in seventy-four years. This new era was the denouement of events that began in August 1991: a half-hearted military *coup* led by a junta of hardcore Communists and high-ranking Red Army officers sought to unseat the legitimate government of Soviet President Mikhail S. Gorbachev, but the plotters lost their nerve in face of popular support for the democratic movement, in the guise of both USSR President Gorbachev and Russian Republic President Boris N. Yeltsin. In three days, the people's voice overcame military might and the *coup* collapsed. Yet, the coup must be seen in context, for it was the last gasp response to the massive changes that had swept Eastern Europe from mid-1989 onward. In three years the Cold War had ended, Germany was reunited, and the Soviet sattelite states cast off their Communist governments in a series of popular uprisings that truly shook the world.

The revolutions of 1989 and the events that followed were unprecedented. To be sure, dissidents had always argued that popular sentiment in Eastern Europe supported freedom and democracy. Then too, a popular book by Soviet dissident Andrei

Amalrik asked if the Soviet Union could last even until George Orwell's famous turning point, 1984. Still, few had anticipated so rapid a change and no one thought it likely that the USSR could simply disintegrate almost overnight. Anti-Communist pundits always assumed that the state Vladimir Lenin and Joseph Stalin created would ultimately fall; they assumed, however, that a cataclysm of global proportions would precipitate the collapse of communism. Instead, the people demanded the opportunity to control their own destinies. Their voices were heard most resoundingly at the barricades in Moscow, Leningrad (now Petrograd), and other Soviet cities, where hundreds of thousands turned their own bodies into a human fence that prevented the *coup*'s leaders from taking over the offices of President Yeltsin, the first leader ever elected in free elections in Soviet history.

In the months following the rise of the Commonwealth, the former Soviet republics suffered from continuing economic dislocations in addition to increasingly severe ethnic tensions. In Georgia and in the disputed Nagorno-Kabakh region (bordering Armenia and Azerbaijan) -- areas where tensions were already discernable for some time -- violence escalated into even higher levels. Where violence did not immediately ensue, relations between and within the Republics remains strained, making it impossible to predict the outcome of current trends and the direction that the Commonwealth's leaders are taking them in.

To place these events in their proper context requires an understanding of nearly a century of Russian and Soviet history. Yet, to gain such information, readers need access to an often bewildering array of sources in a multiplicity of languages. The sheer amount of material is itself daunting. Since 1972 more than 10,000 books on the Soviet Union have appeared in English alone, while all publications on the subject published since 1917 in all languages would increase that total at least tenfold. Readers, especially non-experts, have found that accessing timely information under such circumstances is a nearly herculean task. The present bibliography is designed to help such readers by providing them with a brief guide to the available literature on the subject, limited to works that have appeared in English.

We make no claims about the comprehensiveness of the present bibliography. Instead we have emphasized quality, consciously attemptimg to cite and annotate the best books on Soviet history, politics, and culture including those that have become standards in the field of Sovietology. A selection of articles from twenty-eight scholarly periodicals covering the same subjects is also included. Although materials from almost every era of Soviet history are presented, the data has been skewed toward more recent events by citing a plurality of materials that have appeared since the 1970s. The annotations concentrate on content, but also include comments on methodologies used by the different authors when appropriate. Some of the more interesting articles have also been annotated, especially when they present opinions on controversial topics.

Cross-references have been included for works dealing with more than one topic, although general surveys -- potentially relevant to every section of the book -- have not been cross-refered. In general, citations have been placed according to primary subject rather than first relevant section/subsection.

In almost all cases Russian and other foreign terms as well as names have been transliterated on the basis of the *Webster's Collegiate Dictionary*, ninth edition. Definitions for all such terms will be found in the glossary at the end of the book. We have made a number of minor changes in titles, primarily to accord with standard American usage. Thus, we have consistently used defense, rather than the British defence and collectivization rather than collectivisation.

All of the chapters are subdivided into large thematic or chronological sections; in some cases further subdivisions have been deemed appropriate. It is interesting to note that some aspects of Soviet history appear to have attracted more attention than others. In particular, political history predominates in the periodical literature, perhaps a reflection of the intense ideological battles that prevailed during the Cold War. The second largest body of literature refers to the Soviet economy by far. Albeit, studies on Soviet culture, science and technology, national minorities, and social issues have also been included. In addition to the table of contents, the Author/Title and Subject indexes should help readers find books and articles on topics of interest.

In completing this bibliography we have benefitted from the assistance of the following institutions: The New York Public Library, The Brooklyn Public Library, and The Library of Congress. Thanks go to Karin Vanderveer and Allen Wollman for their technical assistance in preparing the manuscript. Our special thanks are reserved for Rabbi Amos and Helen Edelheit, David and Phyllis Edelheit, and Ann D. Edelheit -- wife and mother -- for their continuing support and encouragement of our joint scholarly pursuits; to Ms. Nita Romer and the editorial staff of Greenwood Publishing Group who have made this project possible. Nevertheless, we alone bear responsibility for any errors contained herein.

# Index of Periodicals

*American Historical Review*
*American Review of the Soviet Union*
*Annals*
*Commentary*
*Comparative Studies in Society and History*
*Current History*
*Foreign Affairs*
*Foreign Policy*
*History of Political Economy*
*History of World War II*
*Holocaust and Genocide Studies*
*Holocaust Studies Annual*
*International Affairs*
*International History Review*
*International Journal*
*Journal of Contemporary History*
*Journal of International Affairs*
*Labour Monthly*
*Midstream*
*Military History*
*Problems of Communism*
*Russian Review*
*Slavic Review*
*Soviet Economy*

# 1

# Reference Works

## A. RESEARCH GUIDES

1. Birkos, Alexander S. (comp.): *Soviet cinema: directors and films*. Hamden, CT: Archon Books, 1976. 344 p.

An annotated cinematography of the Soviet Union, citing films and documentaries produced in the USSR from 1918 to 1975. Includes a directory of major Soviet film studios and a brief bibliography.

2. Bourguina, Anna and Michael Jakobson (comps.): *Guide to the Boris I. Nicolaevsky collection in the Hoover Institution archives*. Stanford, CA: Hoover Institution Press, 1989. 755 p.

Guide to the Hoover Institute's archival holdings on the Russian Revolutions, the Civil War, and Russian collaborators with the Nazis during World War II.

3. de Mowbray, Stephen: *Key facts in Soviet history: volume I 1917 to 22 June 1941*. Boston, MA: G. K. Hall, 1990. 386 p.

4. Diller, Daniel C. (ed.): *The Soviet Union* (third edition). Washington, DC: Congressional Quarterly, 1990. 352 p.

Up to date handbook covering every aspect of Russian and Soviet history and politics.

5. Edelheit, Hershel and Abraham J. Edelheit: *A world in turmoil: an integrated chronology of the Holocaust and World War II*. Westport, CT: Greenwood Press, 1991. 450 p.

Extensively covers the period between January 30, 1933 and May 14, 1948. Primary focus is on events in Europe, America, and the Middle East. Heavy concentration on World War II and the Holocaust in Nazi-occupied Soviet territory.

6. Feldbrugge, F. J. M. (ed.): *Encyclopedia of Soviet law* (2 vols.). Dobbs Ferry, NY: Oceana Publications, 1974. 772 p.

Alphabetically arranged description of the Soviet legal system.

7. Galler, Meyer (comp.): *Soviet prison camp speech: a survivor's glossary supplement*. Hayward, CA: Soviet Studies, 1977. 102 p.

The original *Soviet prison camp speech: a survivor's glossary* was published in 1972 by the University of Wisconsin Press. During the interim hundreds of new terms came to light. This supplement contains an additional 900 entries, and an introduction to the original. Of special interest is its section on *samizdat* literature.

8 . Gilbert, Martin: *Russian History Atlas*. London: Weidenfeld and Nicolson, 1972. 175 p.

9. Grimsted, Patricia K.: *A handbook for archival research in the USSR*. New York: International Research and Exchange Board / Washington, DC: Kennan Institute for Advanced Russian Studies, 1989. 430 p.

10. ---: "A new Soviet directory of archives and manuscript repositories: a major contribution in light of recent reference aids." *Slavic Review*, v. 45 # 3 (Fall, 1986): 534-544.

11. Horak, Stephan M.: *Guide to the study of the Soviet nationalities: non-Russian peoples of the USSR*. Littleton, CO: Libraries Unlimited, 1982. 265 p.

12. Jackson, George (ed.): *Dictionary of the Russian Revolution*. Westport, CT: Greenwood Press, 1989. 704 p.

Contains 300 entries on all aspects of the revolutions, although the lion's share of information is on Russia and the Ukraine.

13. Kish, George: *Economic atlas of the Soviet Union*. Ann Arbor: University of Michigan Press, 1971. 90 p.

Offers graphic data on the Soviet economy in the 1960s.

14. Krasnov, Vladislav: *Soviet defectors: the KGB wanted list*. Stanford, CA: The Hoover Institution Press, 1985. 264 p.

A biographic compilation of 470 Soviet defectors between 1945 and 1969.

15. Laird, Roy D. and Betty A. Laird: *A Soviet lexicon: important concepts, terms, and phrases*. Lexington, MA: Lexington Books/D.C. Heath, 1988. 201 p.

A "must-have" guide for students of Soviet politics. Deals with such concepts as *apparatchik, stukach, glasnost*, and *perestroika*. In total, some 800 terms dealing with all aspects of the Soviet system are listed and defined.

16. Lerman, Antony (ed.): *The Jewish communities of the world: a contemporary guide* (fourth edition). New York: Facts On File, 1989. 206 p.

The Jewish community of the USSR is reviewed on pp. 163-169.

17. Lewytzkyi, Borys (ed.): *The Soviet Union: figures, facts, data*. Munich/New York: K. G. Saur, 1979. 614 p.

18. Maxwell, Robert: *Information USSR: an authorative encyclopedia about the Union of Soviet Socialist Republics*. New York: Macmillan Publishing, 1962. 982 p.

19. Milner-Gulland, Robin and Nikolai Dejevsky: *Cultural Atlas of*

*Russia*. New York: Facts on File, 1989. 240 p.

20. Parker, W. H.: *An historical geography of Russia*. London: University of London Press, 1968. 416 p.

21. O'Relley, Z. Edward: *Soviet-type economic systems: a guide to information sources*. Detroit, MI: Gale, 1978. 228 p.

English language guide, with a base of some 1,200 entries. Among the most important topics covered are: economic organization; structural policies; planning theories; market prices and inflation; capital and investment; wages; and consumer welfare.

22. Prokhorov, A. M. (ed. in chief): *The Great Soviet encyclopedia* (32 vols.). New York: Macmillan Publishing, 1973.

23. Rahr, Alexander (comp.): *A biographical directory of 100 leading Soviet officials*. Boulder, CO: Westview Press in cooperation with Radio Liberty, 1990. 250 p.

24. *Religious prisoners in the USSR*. Keston, UK: Keston College/ Greenfire Press, 1987. 160 p.

Lists 296 prisoners incarcerated in Soviet prisons for religious activities. Among the prisoners are Jews, Muslims, Hare Krishna, and members of all Christian denominations.

25. Shaw, Warren and David Pryce (comps.): *The World Almanac of the Soviet Union from 1905 to the present*. New York: World Almanac Publishing House, 1990. 360 p.

Combines a general chronology of Soviet history with an encyclopedic compilation of data. Especially useful as a first source for student research.

26. Sobolewski, Jury (ed): *Abridged list of some Byelorussian intellectuals liquidated by Soviet Russia*. New York: Committee for Independence of Byelorussia, 1956. 15 p.

Stalinist era executions of Belorussian nationalist leaders.

27. Zickel, Raymond E.: *The Soviet Union: a country study*. Washington, DC: U.S. Government Printing Office, 1991. 1,068 p.

Massive, fully illustrated reference compendium on the USSR.

## B. BIBLIOGRAPHIES

28. Dossick, Jesse J. (comp): *Doctoral research on Russia and the Soviet Union, 1960-1975*. New York: Garland, 1976. 345 p.

Classified bibliography of 3,150 disserations completed in the universities of the United States, Canada, and Great Britain.

29. Edelheit, Abraham J. and Hershel Edelheit (eds): *The Jewish world in modern times: a selected annotated bibliography*. Boulder, CO: Westview Press, 1988. 569 p.

Chapter 12 lists sources on Jews in Russia and the USSR.

30. Egan, David R. and Melinda A Egan (eds): *V. I. Lenin: an annotated bibliography of English language sources to 1980*. Metuchan, NJ: Scarecrow Press, 1982. 482 p.

31. Fiene, Donald M. (comp.): *Alexander Solzhenitsyn: an international bibliography of writings by and about him*. Ann Arbor, MI: Ardis Publishers, 1973. 148 p.

Comprehensive bibliography listing 2,465 citations in thirty-eight languages, on materials either written by the Nobel Prize-winning novelist or about him through May 1973.

32. Fluk, Louise R.: *Jews in the Soviet Union: an annotated bibliography*. New York: Institute of Human Relations, The American Jewish Committee, 1975. 44 p.

A concise selective bibliography of scholarly (and some popular) books and articles on Soviet Jewry published in English between January 1967 and September 1974.

33. Green, William C.: *Soviet nuclear weapons policy: a research and bibliographic guide*. Boulder, CO: Westview Press, 1987. 399 p.

Critical bibliography interspersed with analytical chapters explaining Soviet and Western nuclear policy.

34. Hecht, David: "The history of Russia and eastern Europe: a survey of scholarly and related writings (1966-1970)." *Annals*, v. 417 (January, 1975): 120-141.

35. Jones, David L. (comp.): *Books in English on the Soviet Union, 1917-1970*. New York: Garland, 1973. 331 p.

Unannotated listing of 4,485 books published on Russian and Soviet subjects since the Revolutions.

36. Kanet, Roger E.: *Soviet and East European foreign policy: a bibliography of English and Russian-language publications, 1967-1971*. Santa Barbara, CA: ABC-Clio, 1974. 208 p.

Unannotated listing of 3,327 citations, largely culled from American periodicals.

37. Korsch, Boris (ed.): *Soviet publications on Judaism, Zionism, and the State of Israel, 1948-1988*. New York: Garland Publishing, 1989. 168 p.

38. Luckert, Yelena (ed.): *Soviet Jewish history: an annotated bibliography, 1917 to 1990*. New York: Garland Publishing, 1992. 200 p.

39. Rocca, Raymond and John Dziak (eds.): *Bibliography on Soviet intelligence and security services*. Boulder, CO: Westview Press, 1985. 203 p.

40. Smith, Myron J., Jr. (ed.): *The Soviet air and strategic rocket forces, 1939-1980: a guide to sources in English*. Santa Barbara, CA: ABC-Clio, 1981. 321 p.

Number 10 in the ABC-Clio "War and Peace" bibliography series.

Includes a brief chronology and citations from a wide range of sources in English.

41. ---: *The Soviet navy, 1941-1978: a guide to sources in English.* Santa Barbara, CA: ABC-Clio, 1980. 211 p.

42. Wynar, Bohdan S. (ed.): *Ukraine: A bibliographic guide to English-language publications.* Englewood, CO: Libraries Unlimited/Ukrainian Academy Press, 1990. 406 p.

Annotated bibliography listing 1,084 items from the 1950s to 1989.

## C. COLLECTIONS OF PRIMARY SOURCES

43. Andropov, Yury V.: *Speeches and writings* (second edition). New York: Oxford University Press, 1983. 370 p.

Collection of Andropov's speeches, part of a series of anthologies on the writings of major world leaders, under the general editorship of Robert Maxwell. Yuri V. Andropov was the sixth Chairman and General Secretary of the CPSU.

44. Degras, Jane (ed.): *Soviet documents on foreign policy.* London: Oxford University Press, 1951/1953. 1,561 p.

A compedium of important documents translated into English, ending with the Great Patriotic War. Divided into three parts, Volume I covers 1917-1924; Volume II: 1925-1932; Volume III: 1933-1941.

45. Gorbachev, Mikhail S.: *Speeches and writings.* Oxford: Pergamon Press, 1986. 359 p.

Latest in the series of anthologies on leaders of the world published by Pergamon Press. Includes a brief introduction by Robert Maxwell.

46. Lenin, Vladimir I.: *Complete collected works* (45 vols.). Chicago, IL: Imported Publications, 1980.

47. Pomper, Philip with Yuri Felshtinsky: *Trotsky's notebooks, 1933-1935* (English/Russian). New York: Columbia University Press, 1986. 175 p.

Provides the text and translation of two of Trotsky's notebooks, including passages of his planned biography on Lenin and various studies on Marxism, Darwin, and logic. Never before available to readers in any language, the notebooks provide insight into Trotsky's ideological development in exile.

48. Schechter, J. L. and V. V. Luchkov (eds. and translators): *Khrushchev remembers: the glasnost tapes*. Boston, MA: Little, Brown, 1990. 219 p.

Transcripts of tape recordings made by former Soviet Premier Nikita S. Khrushchev while writing his memoirs in the mid 1960s (see # 2013). At the time, the subjects covered were considered too controversial and Khrushchev deleted those passages. They are reproduced here in full for the first time. The foreword is by Strobe Talbott, who edited the first volume of Khrushchev's memoirs.

49. Walsh, Warren B. (ed.): *Readings in Russian history*. Syracuse, NY: Syracuse University Press, 1950. 638 p.

50. Wyndham, Francis and David King (comp.): *Trotsky: a documentary*. New York: Frederick A. Praeger, 1972. 204 p.

Collection of documents, photographs, posters, and cartoons offering a biography of Trotsky. The text is based on Leon Trotsky's writings.

# 2

# Background Studies

## A. THE DECLINE OF THE TSARIST AUTOCRACY

51. Armstrong, John A.: "Tsarist and Soviet elite administrators." *Slavic Review*, v. 31 # 1 (March, 1972): 1-28.

> # 353. Baron, S. W.: *The Russian Jews under Tsars and Soviets.*

52. Bushnell, John: "The Tsarist officer corps, 1881-1914: customs, duties, inefficiency." *American Historical Review*, v. 86 # 4 (October, 1981): 753-780.

> # 104. Crankshaw, E.: *The shadow of the winter palace.*

53. de Custine, Astolphe: *Empire of the Czar: a journey through eternal Russia.* Garden City, NY: Doubleday, 1989. 633 p.

> # 480. Deriabin, P.: *Watchdogs of terror.*

54. Emmons, Terence: "The *Deseda* circle, 1899-1905." *Slavic Review*, v. 32 # 3 (September, 1973): 461-490.

Movement for Constitutional Reform. Many members later joined the *Kadets* or the "Right" Socialist Revolutionaries.

55. Fallows, Thomas: "Politics and the war effort in Russia: the union of *Zemstvos* and the organization of the food supply, 1914-1916." *Slavic Review*, v. 37 # 1 (March, 1978): 70-90.

56. Florinsky, Michael T.: *Russia: a history and an interpretation* (2 vols.). New York: Macmillan Publishing, 1953. 1,587 p.

General history of the Russian empire from foundation to the revolutions of 1917.

> # 364. Gitelman, Z.: *A century of ambivalence.*

> # 483. Hingley, R.: *The Russian secret police.*

57. Judge, Edward H.: *Repression and reform in Imperial Russia, 1902-1904*. Syracuse, NY: Syracuse University Press, 1983. 299 p.

Biographical investigation into the last attempt to reform the Tsarist empire before the revolutions. When Viacheslav Plevhe was appointed minister of the interior in 1902, he sought to deal with the empire's manifold problems. Judge reviews Plevhe's policies in a thematic way, with independent chapters dedicated to peasants, industrial workers, police repression, national minorities, and the Far Eastern question. Judge also offers a critical evaluation of Plevhe, seeing him as a non-ideologue who sought to repair the empire, not replace it.

> # 112. Kochan, L.: *Russia in revolution.*

> # 145. Mazour, A. G.: *Russia: Tsarist and Communist.*

58. Mosse, Werner E.: "Russian bureaucracy at the end of the *Ancien Regime*: the Imperial State Council, 1897-1915." *Slavic Review*, v. 39 # 4 (December, 1980): 616-632.

59. Peled, Yoav and Gershon Shafir: "From caste to exclusion: the dynamics of modernization in the Russian Pale of Settlement." *Studies in Contemporary Jewry*, v. 3 (1987): 98-114.

> # 604. Pushkarev, S. et al: *Christianity and government.*

60. Raeff, Marc: *Plans for political reform in Imperial Russia, 1730-1905*. Englewood Cliffs, NJ: Prentice-Hall, 1966. 159 p.

Collects all the crucial documents in Russian constitutional developments from the failed efforts to create a constitutional monarchy in 1730 to the abortive effort to reform the empire after the Revolution of 1905. For almost two centuries Russian reformers sought to curb caprice and arbitrariness in the Tsarist autocracy: in almost every case the reformers failed to impose their ideas upon an imperial system which still maintained belief in divine-right monarchy. Raeff's introduction places the documents into context, while his annotated bibliography offers students a guide for further research.

61. Rice, Christopher: "'Land and freedom' in the factories of Petersburg: the SRs and the workers curia elections to the Second *Duma*, January 1907." *Soviet Studies*, v. 36 # 1 (January, 1984): 87-107.

62. Rogger, Hans: *Jewish policies and right-wing politics in Imperial Russia*. Basingstoke, UK: Macmillan, in association with St. Antony's College, Oxford, 1986. 289 p.

Collection of six articles on antisemitism in Imperial Russia. Seeks to explain why Russian antisemitism at the turn of the twentieth century was more virulent than the antisemitic agitation in Western and Central Europe at the same time. Rogger notes that a measure of pragmatism was always included in Tsarist policy. General xenophobia and a specific tradition of Jew hatred prevented Jewish emancipation from becoming an option in Russian-Jewish relations.

63. Samuel, Maurice: *Blood accusation: the strange history of the Beiliss case*. New York: Alfred A. Knopf, 1966. 286 p.

Investigates the blood libel trial of Mendel Beiliss, a simple laborer from Kiev who, in 1911, was falsely accused of ritual murder. The Tsarist government attempted to use the trial as a means of pillorying both Russian Jewry and the democratic movement. As such, the government's tactics failed: after all the testimony was heard a jury found Beiliss innocent of all charges.

> # 232. Senn, A.: *Russian political and diplomatic history.*

64. Seth, Ronald: *The Russian terrorists: the story of Narodniki.* London: Barrie, 1966. 303 p.

65. Seton-Watson, Hugh: *The Russian empire: 1801-1917.* Oxford: Clarendon Press, 1967. 813 p.

Broad objective survey of the Russian empire in the nineteenth and twentieth centuries. As with Seton-Watson's other works, the book is carefully documented and contains a wealth of details. Unlike other historians, Seton-Watson also pays careful attention to the empire's peripheries -- the Caucasus, Central Asia, Finland, and the Baltic regions.

66. Snow, George E.: "The Kokovstov Commission: an abortive attempt at labor reform in Russia in 1905." *Slavic Review*, v. 31 # 4 (December, 1972): 780-796.

67. Stavrou, Theofanis (ed.): *Russia under the last Tsar.* Minneapolis: Minnesota University Press, 1969. 265 p.

Collection of Stavrou's essays on the reign of Tsar Nicholas II. The lion's share of attention is on constitutional developments during Nicholas II's reign. Other essays probe scientific development, the rise of radicalism, and foreign policy from 1894 to 1914.

> # 381. Szajkowski, Z.: *Sourcebook of Russian antisemitism.*

68. Turnbull, Daniel: "The defeat of popular representation, December 1904: Prince Mirskii, Witte, and the imperial family." *Slavic Review*, v. 48 # 1 (Spring, 1989): 54-70.

> # 152. Ulam, A. B.: *Russia's failed revolutions.*

69. Weissman, Neil B.: "Rural crime in Tsarist Russia: the question of hooliganism, 1905-1914." *Slavic Review*, v. 37 # 2 (June, 1978): 228-240.

## B. COMMUNISM IN THEORY AND PRACTICE

70. Arendt, Hannah: *The origins of totalitarianism* (New Edition). San Diego, CA: A Harvest/HBJ Book, 1973. 527 p. [PB]

Perhaps the best-known and most influential single volume on totalitarianism. Based on a comparative study of Nazism and Stalinism, Arendt's is also the first effort to integrate Jewish history into the general course of European developments. Also includes a fascinating study of imperialism and its impact on the totalitarianization of Europe. Arendt argues that totalitarianism originated with the rise of mass politics at the end of the nineteenth century. By the beginning of the twentieth century the masses had been politicized but, in some cases lacked both the opportunity for political action and a clear democratic tradition. Thus, they were ripe for an apocalyptic visionary who could win their support by the force of his rhetoric. Arendt also notes the differences between the Nazi and the Soviet models of totalitarianism, and offers insights into the relationship between totalitarian and non-totalitarian states.

71. Barfield, Rodney: "Lenin's utopianism: *State and Revolution.*" *Slavic Review*, v. 30 # 1 (March, 1971): 45-56.

72. Bobroff, Anne: "The Bolsheviks and working women, 1905-20." *Soviet Studies*, v. 26 # 4 (October, 1974): 540-567.

73. Crozier, Brian and Arthur Seldon: *Socialism: the grand delusion*. New York: Universe Books, 1986. 208 p.

Polemical investigation into socialism. After exploring Marxist social theories, the authors compare them to reality. Far from the noble slogans that Socialists have offered, when socialism was put into practice economic failure and socio-political stagnation resulted. Inauspiciously, the polemical elements in the book often crowd out the insights that both authors do provide.

74. Day, Richard B.: "Laws and lawlessness in Marxist political economy." *International Journal*, v. 32 # 1 (Winter, 1976/1977): 100-127.

75. Elwood, Ralph C.: "Lenin and *Pravda*, 1912-1914." *Slavic Review*, v. 31 # 2 (June, 1972): 355-380.

76. Evans, Alfred B.: "Rereading Lenin's *State and Revolution*." *Slavic Review*, v. 46 # 1 (Spring, 1987): 1-19.

77. Gerschenkron, Alexander: "Soviet Marxism and absolutism." *Slavic Review* v. 30 # 4 (December, 1971): 853-869.

> # 1943. Hobson, C.: *Trotskyism and the dilemma of socialism*.

78. *The Individual and Communism*. Moscow: Novosti Press Agency Publishing House, n.d. 114 p. [PB]

Philosophical investigation of the meaning of Marxism-Leninism for the individual living in the Communist bloc. Discusses economic, intellectual, and ethical issues in separate chapters while offering an interesting insight into Communist Party thinking on morality and education.

79. Joll, James: *The Anarchists*. Boston: Little, Brown, 1964. 303 p.

This carefully documented survey of the history of the Anarchist movement from the French Revolution to the Spanish Civil War emphasizes the fact that not all anarchists were "bomb throwers." Some were serious and sensitive critics of modern social organization. On the other hand, Joll reminds us, advocates of "propaganda by deeds" have often captured headlines and imaginations. Investigates the relationship between anarchism and syndicalism which ironically led to Fascism. Joll concludes that the Anarchist movement was important, although its revolution could never succeed since by definition Anarchists could never establish a government.

80. ---: *The Second International 1889-1914*. London: Routledge & Kegan Paul, 1974. 224 p.

Investigates the history of the Second Socialist International from its founding in 1889 until the outbreak of World War I. Marxist in orientation -- and therefore in theory committed to revolution -- in reality the International came to see its role in European politics in the evolutionary, that is social democratic mold. Joll's review of the ideological struggles within the International and between Socialists and Anarchists is of special interest. He notes that World War I irreversably rent the International assunder: it was a schism between those still committed to revolution (Lenin and the Bolsheviks) and those committed to reformism (Ebert and the *Sozialdemokratische Partei Deutschlands,* SPD).

81. Kingston-Mann, Esther: "Marxism and Russian rural development: problems of evidence, experience, and culture." *American Historical Review*, v. 86 # 4 (October, 1981): 731-752.

82. ---: "Proletarian theory and peasant practice: Lenin 1901-04." *Soviet Studies*, v. 26 # 4 (October, 1974): 522-539.

83. Kolakowski, Lezek: "Totalitarianism and the lie." *Commentary*, v. 75 # 5 (May, 1983): 33-38.

84. Krapivensky, S.: *The revolution and its moral mission.* Moscow: Novosti Press Agency Publishing House, n.d. 88 p.

Ideological defense of communism that views the morality of Communist party actions. Divided into three sections, with the first organized around a series of accusations and responses -- most of the former being patently specious. In the last two sections Krapivensky expounds on Marxist-Leninist ideas of morality. Meant as party propaganda, the booklet sheds light on the means used to justify Communist party actions.

85. Lane, David: *The roots of Russian communism.* University Park: Pennsylvania State University Press, 1975. 240 p.

Sociological history of the rank and file of the All Russian Social Democratic Party, precursor to both the Mensheviks and the Bolsheviks, from 1898 to 1907. Lane has carefully reconstructed all available data to provide a clear picture of the "typical" party member: in terms of age, occupation, education, and nationality. Lane also offers some interesting insights into personality differences within the Social Democratic Party -- Mensheviks tended to be older, urban dwellers, and minority nationalities (Jews, Ukrainians, and Belorussians, among others) while Bolsheviks tended to be younger, town dwellers, and Russians.

86. Laqueur, W.: "Is there now, or has there ever been, such a thing as totalitarianism." *Commentary*, v. 80 # 4 (October, 1985): 29-35.

87. Lenin, V. I.: "Features of the labor movement." *Labour Monthly*, v. 16 # 1 (January, 1934): 32-35.

88. Leontyev, L.: *Fundamentals of Marxist political economy*. Moscow: Novosti Press Agency Publishing House, n.d. 155 p. [PB]

Booklet examining theoretical issues relating to communism, primarily from the perspective of economics. The booklet's four chapters are actually arranged as a series of questions with paragraph length answers examining the methods of Marxist-Leninist "political economics"; the origins and development of capitalism; Socialist theory; and the development of socialism into its ultimate form, communism.

89. Löwenthal, Richard: "Communism as an historical force." *International Journal*, v. 32 # 1 (Winter, 1976/1977): 1-19.

> # 445. Makepeace, R.: *Marxist ideology and Soviet criminal law*.

90. Malia, Martin: *Alexander Herzen and the birth of Russian socialism, 1812-1855*. Cambridge, MA: Harvard University Press, 1961. 486 p.

Biography of the father of Russian socialism. Malia deals with all of Herzen's many activities: publicist, visionary, and revolutionary. The only comprehensive biography on Herzen available to date, Malia concludes that his socialism was always grounded on democratic principles and on the concept of national self-determination for all nationalities in the Russian empire.

91. Minayev, L. and L. Fyodorov: *Struggle for Socialism in the world* (translated from Russian by John Weir). Moscow: Progress Publishers, n.d. 125 p. [PB]

Brief investigation into the theory and practice of national liberation movements, as viewed from the perspective of the Communist party. Posits that world capitalism remains in crisis and will soon collapse in the face of a Marxist-Leninist world revolution. The irony is, of course, that the opposite has occurred: the economic bankruptcy of communism directly led to the decline of the Soviet Union and the retrenchment of Marxism-Leninism.

92. Puddington, Arch: "Totalitarianism today." *Commentary*, v. 78 # 6 (December, 1984): 31-39

Reviews the state of Marxism-Leninism throughout the world.

93. *Right-wing revisionism today* (translated from Russian by Jim Riordan). Moscow: Progress Publishers, 1976. 554 p.

Investigation into revisionism, the brand of socialism that emphasizes evolution rather than revolution. Historically, revisionism is most commonly associated with the name of Eduard Bernstein, a German-Jewish Socialist who broke with Marxism in the 1890s. In this book revisionism is associated with all movements that seek to reform communism -- such as the Czech reform movement associated with Alexander Dubcek. Despite the obvious ideological prejudices, the book contains many interesting insights into Communist party thinking before *glasnost*.

94. Roberts, James W.: "Lenin's theory of imperialism in Soviet usage." *Soviet Studies*, v. 29 # 3 (July, 1977): 353-372.

95. Scanlan, James P.: *Marxism in the USSR: a critical survey of current Soviet thought*. Ithaca, NY: Cornell University Press, 1985. 362 p.

Surveys the current state of Marxist-Leninist philosophy in the Soviet Union. After the first chapter, which introduces the subject and provides an overview of Marxist philosophical systems, the remaining seven chapters are thematic. Scanlan notes the numerous contradictions among Soviet philosophers, creating opposing schools of Marxist-Leninist thought which use the same terminology to arrive at contradictory ends.

96. Spirkin, Alexander: *Theoretical questions of Communist strategy and tactics*. Moscow: Novosti Press Agency Publishing House, n.d. 80 p. [PB]

Brief primer on ideological issues, focused primarily on class struggle and social revolution.

97. Suslov, Mikhail: *The CPSU -- the party of creative Marxism*. Moscow: Novosti Press Agency Publishing House, 1972. 71 p.

Three essays on the Communist party written by Mikhail Suslov, one of the most important ideologues of communism in the twentieth century. A politburo member for much of his career, Suslov was able to survive the crucial turns in Soviet policy during the Stalin years and thereafter. In this work, Suslov investigates the relationship between the Communist party, Marxism, and the human condition.

98. Talmon, J. L.: *The origins of totalitarian democracy*. New York: Frederick A. Praeger, Publisher, 1960. 366 p. [PB]

Classic analysis of the ideologies active in Europe from the mid-eighteenth century to the French Revolution. Brings into focus the division between liberal and totalitarian democracy. Talmon defines the former as an ideology that emphasizes individual rights. The latter is an ideology that emphasizes the creation of a salvationist new order that will result in a perfect world. Talmon's *Political messianisn: the romantic phase* (see # 99), follows up on the ideas reviewed here.

99. ---: *Political messianism: the romantic phase*. Boulder, CO: Westview Press, 1985. 607 p. [PB]

Sequel to *The origins of totalitarian democracy* (see # 98). Here, Talmon follows the ideological origins of modern totalitarianism from 1815 to 1848. He includes Marxism in his characterization of the movements of that era that he considers messianic -- all of which had an apocalyptic vision of a revolution that would overturn contemporary society besides a utopian vision of the post-revolutionary world. Beyond generalities, however, the ideologies that Talmon surveys may be divided into two groups. The first group Talmon characterizes as messianic nationalists, since all placed their emphasis on attaining national unification (in the case of Germany and Italy) or independence (Poland). Talmon characterizes the second group as messianic socialists. Both groups came to the fore during the revolutions of 1848 and proved how mass democracy could be manipulated to create an authoritarian or totalitarian state.

100. Tyagunenko, V.: *Bypassing capitalism*. Moscow: Novosti Press Agency Publishing House, n.d. 80 p.

Popularized essays seeking to place Communist development into historical context. Specifically, Tyagunenko attempts to explain the discordant fact that communism has, contrary to Marxist theory, sprouted in countries that were not originally capitalist. Of course, that paradox also animated Lenin's revisions of Marx. The experience of the national liberation movements, however, elucidates the utopian elements in Marx's "scientific" socialism.

101. White, James D.: "The first *Pravda* and the Russian Marxist tradition." *Soviet Studies*, v. 26 # 2 (April, 1974): 181-204.

102. Wolfe, Bertram D.: *Marxism: one hundred years in the life of a doctrine*. Boulder, CO: Westview Press, 1985. 404 p. [PB]

Investigates the doctrines of Marxism as presented in Marx's major ideological works. Three themes dealt with by Marx in different ways at different times animate Wolfe's study: the question of nationalism versus internationalism; the question of revolution versus evolution; and the question of democracy versus dictatorship. Each of these shows a tension within what was ostensibly a scientific body of literature. In turn, the inconsistencies of Marxist thought bring Wolfe to a serious question: what happens to Marxist theory when the workers -- having gained class consciousness -- decide to reject salvation?

## C. RUSSIA'S DRIFT TO REVOLUTION

103. Ascher, Abraham: *The Revolution of 1905: Russia in disarray.* Stanford, CA: Stanford University Press, 1988. 412 p.

Analytical review of the Revolution of 1905. Although offering few new insights, Ascher has succeeded in presenting an incisive overview of an amorphous period that has often been misunderstood. The revolution, which began as a spontaneous popular uprising, is also placed into chronological context. Ascher surveys both the well-known events in the major cities and the less well-known course of the revolt in the provinces. He points to considerable confusion within government circles, then busy prosecuting the disastrous war against Japan and within the opposition, critically divided and unable to take effective action at the decisive moment. The book is thus a primer on a critical period of Russian history.

> # 285. Atkinson, D.: *The end of the Russian land commune.*

> # 72. Bobroff, A.: "The Bolsheviks and working women."

104. Crankshaw, Edward: *The shadow of the winter palace: Russia's drift to revolution, 1825-1917.* New York: Viking Press, 1976. 429 p.

Panoramic history of imperial Russia from the failed Decembrist plot of 1825 to the outbreak of World War I in August 1914. Particularly interesting is Crankshaw's explanation of the combination of terror and reform the Tsarist government used to control an unruly population. In many ways, the Tsarist system parallels recent Communist party efforts to hold back democratic reforms.

105. Elwood, R. C.: "The congress that never was: Lenin's attempt to call a 'Sixth' Party Congress in 1914." *Soviet Studies*, v. 31 # 3 (July, 1979): 343-363.

> # 1939. ---: "Trotsky's questionaire."

106. Engelstein, Laura: *Moscow, 1905: working-class organization and political conflict*. Stanford, CA: Stanford University Press, 1982. 308 p.

Social history of revolutionary Russia, focusing on Moscow's working-class during the Revolution of 1905. Divided into two parts: part I offers a detailed study of the working class and includes a number of novel interpretations. Part II concentrates on the revolution and is largely derived from previously known sources. The first part of the book is an important reference tool for readers interested in social history and the Russian working class.

107. Haimson, Leopold H.: *The Russian Marxists and the origins of bolshevism*. Cambridge, MA: Harvard University Press, Russian Research Center Studies, 1955. 246 p.

108. Hamm, Michael F.: "Kharkov's progressive *Duma*, 1910-1914: a study in Russian municipal reform." *Slavic Review*, v. 40 # 1 (Spring, 1981): 17-36.

109. ---: "Liberal politics in wartime Russia: an analysis of the progressive bloc." *Slavic Review*, v. 33 # 3 (September, 1974): 453-468.

Surveys performence of the *Kadet* party in the Fourth *Duma* (1914-1915).

110. Kelly, Aileen: "Self-censorship and the Russian intelligentsia, 1905-1914." *Slavic Review*, v. 46 # 2 (Summer, 1987): 193-213.

111. Kerensky, Alexander: "Russia on the eve of World War I." *Russian Review*, v. 5 # 1 (Fall, 1945): 10-30.

112. Kochan, Lionel: *Russia in revolution, 1890-1918*. New York: New American Library, 1966. 352 p.

Surveys twenty-eight turbulent years of Russian history: a period that coincides with the reign of Nicholas II, the last tsar of the Romanov dynasty. Kochan has divided the work into three parts: Part I surveys conditions in the empire in the last years of the nineteenth and first years of the twentieth centuries; Part II offers a detailed study of the Revolution of 1905 and the subsequent counter-revolution; and Part III surveys the developments within government and opposition circles from 1908 to 1918. This last part ends with the Bolshevik *putsch* and the start of the Russian Civil War. Of special importance is the way Kochan integrates social and economic trends into the political history of that crucial era.

113. Lincoln, W. Bruce: *In war's dark shadow: the Russians before the Great War.* New York: Dial Press, 1983. 557 p.

Vivid history of the Romanov dynasty's declining years. Explains the background to Russian participation in World War I and thus places the disasters during the War into their proper context. Although he does not deal with the 1917 Revolutions, Lincoln does help to explain the causes for tsarism's collapse. He carefully documents the beginning of the end, with the Revolution of 1905 and then the successful counter-revolution of 1905 and 1906.

> # 643. ---: *Passage through armageddon.*

> # 1950. Loe, M. L.: "Maksim Gorkii and the *sreda* circle."

114. Melnçon, Michael: "'Marching together!': left bloc activities in the Russian revolutionary movement, 1900 to February 1917." *Slavic Review*, v. 49 # 2 (Summer, 1990): 239-252.

> # 650. Nelson, H. W.: *Leon Trotsky and the art of insurrection.*

115. Offord, Derek: *The Russian revolutionary movement in the 1880s.* New York: Cambridge University Press, 1986. 213 p.

Investigates the history of Russian revolutionaries from the collapse of the *Narodniki* in 1882 to the rise of Marxism in the mid-1890s. Traces the numerous setbacks experienced by the revolutionaries during an era of heavy-handed governmental control. Under the circumstances, Offord concludes that the revolutionaries' most important achievement was keeping the spirit of resistance to Tsarist autocracy alive in an important interregnum period.

116. Perrie, Maureen: "The social composition and structure of the Socialist-Revolutionary Party before 1917." *Soviet Studies*, v. 24 # 2 (October, 1972): 223-250.

117. Pinchuk, Ben-Cion: *The Octobrists in the Third Duma, 1907-1912*. Seattle: University of Washington Press, 1974. 232 p.

Evaluates the role of the *Octobrists*, the democratic groups that briefly merged after the Revolution of 1905. *Octobrists* actually represented a number of different sub-groups that disagreed on many issues: some were capitalists, others Socialists; some sought the creation of a constitutional monarchy, others a republic; and still others saw no need to fundamentally change the Tsarist system but sought only reforms. What unified the *Octobrists* was their adherence to the October 17, 1905 manifesto that created the semblance of a constitutional democracy in Russia. The *Octobrists* remained the largest party in the *Duma*, but more than anything else that reality showed just how much of a sham the Tsarist reforms were: the Tsar paid no attention to the *Octobrists* and his ministers behaved as if the *Duma* barely existed. Under the circumstances, Pinchuk correctly notes the failure of moderate reform; only a revolution could fundamentally change the regime.

118. Raun, Toivo V.: "The Revolution of 1905 in the Baltic provinces and Finland." *Slavic Review* v. 43 # 3 (Fall, 1984): 453-467.

119. Read, Christopher: *Religion, revolution, and the Russian intelligentsia, 1900-1912*. London: Macmillan, 1979. 256 p.

Reviews the religious and philosophical currents among the Russian intelligentsia just before World War I. Read concentrates on the *Vekhists*, ex-Marxists who after 1905 turned to pietistic religious practices as a means to bridge the gap between ideology and reality. Staunch critics of Russian society, by 1909 the *Vekhists* had developed into a group of mystical anarchists. Bridging the gap between traditional religious groups and modern revolutionary movements, the *Vekhists* were strongly anti-Bolshevik but still reflected the intense unrest at the end of the Tsarist era.

> # 61. Rice, Ch.: "Freedom in the factories of Petersburg."

120. Rosenthal, Bernice G.: "The transmutation of the symbolist ethos: mystical anarchism and the Revolution of 1905." *Slavic Review*, v. 36 # 4 (December, 1977): 608-627.

121. Sablinsky, Walter: *The road to bloody Sunday: father Gapon and the St. Petersburg massacre of 1905*. Princeton, NJ: Princeton University Press, 1976. 414 p.

Biographical history of the Revolution of 1905 that concentrates on the events of January 9, 1905, now known as "Bloody Sunday." Primary focus is on father Georgii Gapon, the Russian Orthodox priest who led the protest march that day. According to Sablinsky, Gapon combined traditional piety with an innovative spirit that catapulted him to the forefront of the workers' movement.

122. Salisbury, Harrison E.: *Black night, white snow: Russia's revolutions, 1905-1917*. New York: Da Capo Press, 1977. 746 p. [PB]

Panoramic history of revolutionary Russia from 1905 to 1917. Salisbury begins with the Russo-Japanese War disasters, viewing them in the context of a declining Tsarist system. The Revolution of 1905 proved to be abortive, as a counter-revolution successfully overturned all the concessions forced on Nicholas II. Thereafter, revolutionary activity only increased, until the accumulated frustrations of a regime no longer responsive to its citizens combined with failures at the front in World War I to cause a new revolution. Salisbury carefully reconstructs the rise and fall of Alexander Kerensky's provisional government as well as the Bolshevik *putsch*. Although the book may be categorized as political history, Salisbury also discusses the key actors' personalities in this well executed historical investigation.

123. Schwarz, Solomon M.: *The Russian Revolution of 1905: the workers' movement and the formation of bolshevism and menshevism* (translated from Russian by Gertrude Vakar). Chicago: University of Chicago Press, 1967. 361 p.

Probes the controversies that led to the split in the All-Russian Social Democratic Party. Schwarz, a Bolshevik who later became a Menshevik, possess a unique perspective that permits him to elucidate behind-the-scenes aspects of the schism within Russian Marxism not usually noted by other historians.

124. Senese, Donald: "S. M. Kravchinski and the National Front

against Autocracy." *Slavic Review*, v. 34 # 3 (September, 1975): 506-522.

Post-1905 efforts to gain freedom of the press.

> # 65. Seton-Watson, H.: *The Russian empire.*

125. Shanin, Teodor: "Socio-economic mobility and the rural history of Russia 1905-1930." *Soviet Studies*, v. 23 # 2 (October, 1971): 222-235.

> # Solzhenitsyn, A.: *August 1914.*

> # 67. Stavrou, T.: *Russia under the last Tsar.*

126. Suny, Ronald G.: "A journeyman for the revolution: Stalin and the labor movement in Baku, June 1907-May 1908." *Soviet Studies*, v. 23 # 3 (January, 1972): 373-394.

127. ---: "Labor and liquidators: revolutionaries and the 'reaction' in Baku, May 1908-April 1912." *Slavic Review*, v. 34 # 2 (June, 1975): 319-340.

128. Swain, G. R.: "Bolsheviks and metal workers on the eve of the First World War." *Journal of Contemporary History*, v. 16 # 2 (April, 1981): 273-291.

129. Trotsky, Leon: *1905* (translated from Russian by Anya Bostock). New York: Random House, 1971. 488 p.

Tendentious but very interesting review of the Revolution of 1905, available in English for the first time. Trotsky plays up the Bolshevik role in 1905, but still provides interesting insight into the history -- and historiography -- of the revolution.

> # 703. Ulam, A. B.: *The Bolsheviks.*

130. Ulam, Adam B.: *In the name of the people: prophets and conspirators in revolutionary Russia*. New York: Viking Press, 1977. 418 p.

Saga of the revolutionary movements in modern Russia, covering the period from the 1820s to 1918. Divides the Russian revolutionaries chronologically, elucidating both their actions and their ideology in each period. Inter alia, Ulam reflects on the distinctions between resistance to tyranny and crime as well as between fanaticism and insanity. Well written and carefully documented, the book can be a useful introduction to Russian history for specialists and lay readers alike.

131. Wildman, Allan K.: *The making of a workers' revolution: Russian social democracy, 1891-1903*. Chicago: Chicago University Press, 1967. 271 p.

Focuses on the tension between rank and file members of the Socialist movement and their leaders; the former were largely proletarians while the latter were intellectuals. Contacts between the two were ambivalent, even though each group needed the other: the intellectuals needed workers to carry out their revolutionary ideas and the workers needed intellectuals to lead the revolution.

132. Zipperstein, Steven J.: "The politics of relief: the transformation of Russian Jewish communal life during the First World War." *Studies in Contemporary Jewry*, v. 4 (1988): 22-40.

133. Zuckerman, Frederic S.: "Vladimir Burtsev and the Tsarist political police in conflict, 1907-1914." *Journal of Contemporary History*, v. 12 # 1 (January, 1977): 193-219.

# 3

# Overviews of Soviet History

## A. SURVEYS

### 1. Historical Overviews

134. Belasco, Milton J. and Harold E. Hammond: *The Soviet Union: history, culture, people*. New York: Globe Book, 1981. 234 p. [PB]

Brief textbook surveying Russian and Soviet history written for junior and senior high school students.

135. Brzezinski, Zbigniew: *The grand failure: the birth and death of communism in the twentieth century*. New York: Charles Scribner's Sons, 1989. 278 p.

Extensive investigation which, in many ways, predicted the downfall of communism. The author, a respected political scientist who served as U.S. President Jimmy Carter's Chief National Security Advisor, cites four factors that according to his predictions would lead to the fall of communism: first, the decline of belief in communism; second, the sustained failure of Communist economics; third, the return of nationalism as a force for change in the Soviet Union; fourth, the inability to change the system without replacing it altogether. Many insights into aspects of Soviet history are interspersed throughout the book, ending with a prediction visualizing a post-Communist Europe. Although many of Brzezinski's specific prediction may not yet have been borne out, his broad analysis has proven to be substantially correct.

136. Cohen, Stephen F.: *Rethinking the Soviet experience: politics and history since 1917*. New York: Oxford University Press, 1985. 222 p. [PB]

Brief survey of Sovietology focused primarily on the issues that have animated scholarly research on the USSR, including methods used. Argues for a mildly revisionist viewpoint, although the author does not propose changing all conventional wisdom. Most significantly, Cohen argues for a return to historical analysis as part and parcel of political science. The book's last chapter concentrates on the possibility of reform within the Soviet Union.

137. Daniels, Robert V.: *Russia: the roots of confrontation*. Cambridge, MA: Harvard University Press, 1985. 411 p.

Survey of Russian history attempting to place it into a global context. Examines the different paths that Russian history has taken and uses the understanding of the past as a means to explain current policies. The chapters are thematic and discuss a wide range of subthemes. Forcefully argues that Russia will ultimately follow a convergent path with the West.

138. Gross, Jan T.: "A note on the nature of Soviet totalitarianism." *Soviet Studies*, v. 34 # 3 (July, 1982): 367-376.

139. Heller, Mikhail and Aleksandr M. Nekrich: *Utopia in power: the history of the Soviet Union from 1917 to the present*. New York: Summit Books, 1986. 877 p.

Comprevensive survey of Soviet history from the revolutions to the eve of Mikhail Gorbachev's rise to power in 1985. As both authors were born, raised, and educated in the Soviet Union, the book reads like an insider's account. Careful documentation adds a wealth of new details to facts that were previously known outside of the Soviet Union only in outline form. Additionally, the authors investigate the ideological and utopian roots of Communist totalitarianism. This analysis allows a useful comparative history with other twentieth century totalitarian regimes, notably Nazi Germany. As a general survey, the work may be used as a textbook for both students and interested laypeople. Although not treated with as much detail as in the area of Soviet political history, Heller and Nekrich summarize the development of Soviet culture and literature. Other topics, including the status of religion and of Russian nationalism in the Soviet Union, are similarly treated in the context of unfolding political and diplomatic history.

140. Hirszowicz, Maria: "Is there a ruling class in the USSR? -- a comment." *Soviet Studies*, v. 28 # 2 (April, 1976): 262-273.

141. Kerst, Kenneth A.: "CPSU history re-revised." *Problems of Communism*, v. 26 # 3 (May/June, 1977): 17-32.

142. Laqueur, Walter: *The fate of the revolution: interpretations of Soviet history from 1917 to the present*. New York/London: Collier Macmillan Publishers, 1987. 285 p.

Historiographical survey of Russian history from the 1917 revolutions to the mid-1980s. The chapters are written as independent but interconnected essays on specific subjects in Soviet history and hisoriography. Chapter Seven is a particularly interesting chapter which surveys the twists and turns in Soviet historiography. Offering insightful comments on almost every page, the book is especially useful as a guide to both issues and methodologies used in academic Sovietology.

143. --- and Leopold Labedz (eds.): *The state of Soviet studies*. Cambridge, MA: M.I.T. Press, 1965. 177 p.

Anthology of historiographical studies on the Soviet Union. Originally published as two special issues of the London magazine *Survey*, the essays assess Western knowledge of the Soviet Union and the methodologies used in academic Sovietology.

CONTENTS: W. Laqueur: In search of Russia / A. Ulam: USA:

some critical reflections / R. F. Byrnes: USA: work at the universities / P. Wiles: Western research into the Soviet economy / A. Gerschenkron: Study of the Soviet economy in the USA / V. Frank, B. Kerblay, J. Hacker: Soviet studies in Western Europe: 1. Britain; 2. France; 3. Germany / G. Lichtheim: Western Marxist literature 1953-1963 / E. Kamenka: Soviet philosophy in Western eyes / G. Struve: Western writing on Soviet literature / B. Morris: World communism / A. Adams: The hybrid art of Sovietology / R. Conquest: In defence of Kremlinology / A. Nove: The uses and abuses of Kremlinology / T. H. Rigby: Crypto-politics / F. Griffiths: The origins of peaceful co-existence / L. Labedz: Soviet studies, the press, and the public.

144. Lourie, Richard: *Russia speaks: an oral history from the revolution to the present*. New York: Harper Collins Publishers, 1991. 396 p.

Survey of Russian history based on anecdotes the author collected over numerous trips to the Soviet Union. Arranged chronologically from the Revolution to the rise of Mikhail S. Gorbachev. Despite the interesting tidbits that some of the anecdotes provide, the book is light on their analysis, thus directing it more toward general readers than to serious scholars.

> # 421. Malia, M. E.: *The Soviet tragedy*.

145. Mazour, Anatole G.: *Russia: Tsarist and Communist*. Princeton, NJ: D. Van Nostrand, 1962. 995 p.

Survey of Russian history from earliest times to the rise of Nikita S. Khrushchev. Two-thirds of the book is focused on the Tsarist period, the remainder on the era since World War I. Five chapters investigate Russian cultural history. Given the broad descriptive nature of the book, it is most useful as an introductory review for high school and college students.

146. Nenarokov, Albert P.: *Russia in the twentieth century: the view of a Soviet historian*. New York: William Morrow, 1968. 309 p.

Tendentious, but interesting, survey that covers half-a-century of

Soviet history. Although the factual basis of the book appears somewhat shaky, it does offer some insight into the way Soviet historians viewed their craft in the mid-1960s. With its broad outlines, laypeople will also find the book useful. This edition includes forewords by *cosmonaut* Herman Titov and by the editor of *Soviet Life,* Georgi Isachenko.

147. Ponomarev, B. N. (ed.): *History of the Communist Party of the Soviet Union.* New York: International Publishers, 1939. 364 p.

148. Schapiro, Leonard: *The Communist Party of the Soviet Union.* New York: Vintage Books, 1971. 686 p. [PB]

Comprehensive history of the CPSU from its origins in the controversy between Revolutionary and Revisionist Marxists in 1899 to the years immediately after Nikita Khrushchev's fall. Based on an intensive study of all available primary and secondary sources, this highly readable volume is still the standard to which all others are compared. This edition includes four appendixes which detail the key actors in Communist party history from 1917 to 1966.

149. Seton-Watson, Hugh: *From Lenin to Khrushchev: the history of world communism.* Boulder, CO: Westview Press, 1986. 432 p.

Survey of Soviet history and politics from the revolutions to the post-Stalin era. Primary attention is given to the operation of the Communist Party in Russia and the rest of the world. Of special importance is Seton-Watson's review of the Nazi-Soviet pact, that places Josef Stalin's deal with Adolf Hitler into a global context. Carefully documented and based on an extensive bibliography, the book serves as a model of detailed political analysis. Scrutinizing Communist strategy and tactics, Seton-Watson offers ample insight for both scholars and laypeople interested in Soviet history and politics. This edition is a reprint of a 1961 volume, published by Frederick A. Praeger.

150. Thompson, John: *Russia and the Soviet Union: an historical introduction* (second edition). Boulder, CO: Westview Press, 1990. 315 p.

Historical survey of Imperial Russia and the Soviet Union from ancient times to Mikhail S. Gorbachev. Organized around the key eras in Russian history, with special emphasis on the leaders of each era. Given the general nature of the work, the focus on developments in the late 1980s and early 1990s is too brief. Nevertheless, Thompson does permit a broader understanding of Soviet history's place in the continuum of Russia's millenial story.

151. Treadgold, Donald W.: *Twentieth century Russia* (seventh edition). Boulder, CO: Westview Press, 1989. 593 p.

Textbook covering the history of the Soviet Union from the Revolution to Gorbachev. Divided chronologically, Treadgold emphasizes political rather than social or intellectual history. A subtheme of the book is the transformation of Bolshevism from a minor protest ideology to the ruling ideology of the Soviet state. Treadgold also views the ideological decline of communism. Broadly analytical, this is one of the standard reference sources and is especially useful for college courses on Soviet history.

152. Ulam, Adam B.: *Russia's failed revolutions: from the Decembrists to the dissidents*. New York: Basic Books, 1981. 453 p.

Surveys the struggle for freedom in the Russian empire and Soviet Union. Ulam deals with four broad revolutionary eras: the 1820s, exemplified by the Decembrist uprising; the 1870s, exemplified by *Narodnik* terrorism; the early twentieth century, exemplified by the Revolutions of 1905 and 1917; and contemporary Russia, exemplified by the dissidents. Ulam notes the many missed opportunities to bring democracy to Russia: his conclusion that revolutionary idealists have consistently failed to consider nationalism is amply borne out by the collapse of the Soviet Union after the revolution of 1989-1991.

153. Urban, Michael E. and John McClure: "The folklore of state socialism: semiotics and the study of the Soviet state." *Soviet Studies*, v. 35 # 4 (October, 1983): 471-486.

154. Wesson, Robert G.: *The Russian dilemma: a political and geo-political view*. New Brunswick, NJ: Rutgers University Press,

1974. 228 p.

Broad geopolitical investigation of the state of the Soviet Union. Wesson begins by analyzing the USSR's geographic position. With a mildly revisionist orientation, Wesson notes that the USSR -- and the Warsaw Pact -- are little more than the old Russian Empire spread to its logical borders. That realization, however, allows Wesson to evaluate the economic, political, and ideological fractures that he predicted would tear the USSR apart. Although much of his analysis was based on very broad generalizations -- often adduced from other secondary sources -- Wesson's basic predictions proved essentially correct.

155. ---: "The USSR: oligarchy or dictatorship?" *Slavic Review*, v. 31 # 2 (June, 1972): 314-322.

**2. The Soviet Political System**

> # 51. Armstrong, J. A.: "Tsarist and Soviet elite administrators."

156. Best, Harry: *The Soviet state and its inception*. New York: Philosophical Library, 1950. 448 p.

157. Black, Cyril E.: *Understanding Soviet politics: the perspective of Russian history*. Boulder, CO: Westview Press, 1986. 308 p.

This collection of essays written by one of the foremost American Sovietologists has been arranged to confront one central theme: the specific historical circumstances that shaped the USSR's political history from 1917 to 1967. Black seeks to put the Soviet Union into a comparative perspective, as he does for example regarding Russian and Soviet foreign policy. Also charts the origins of the Cold War as seen by Bulgarian Communists specifically and by the Communist bloc generally.

> # 336. Breslauer, G. W.: "The Soviet political establishment."

158. Clark, Willian A.: "Token representation in the CPSU Central Committee." *Soviet Studies*, v. 43 # 5 (1991): 913-932.

159. Colton, Timothy J.: "Moscow's party organization." *Problems of Communism*, v. 37 # 1 (January/February, 1988): 30-59.

160. Connor, Walter D.: "Dissent in a complex society: the Soviet case." *Problems of Communism*, v. 22 # 2 (March/April, 1973): 40-52.

> #214. Dallin, A.: "Soviet foreign policy and domestic politics."

161. Fainsod, Merle: *How Russia is ruled*. Cambridge, MA: Harvard University Press, 1967. 679 p.

Classic review of Soviet government and politics. The book literally covers every aspect of Soviet governance. Part I reviews the subject from a historical and chronological perspective. Part II is thematic, and reviews the Soviet decision making process, the continual problem of succession, and the issue of popular input into the Communist party. The first edition became a standard reference work and the new edition, written by Jerry F. Hough (published in 1979), remains the most detailed study on Soviet politics to date.

162. Gill, Graeme: "Institutionalism and revolution: rules and the Soviet political system." *Soviet Studies*, v. 37 # 2 (April, 1985): 212-226.

163. Guins, George C.: "Claims and realities of Soviet Socialism." *Russian Review*, v. 11 # 3 (July, 1952): 138-147.

164. Hammer, Darrell P.: *The USSR: the politics of oligarchy*. Hinsdale, IL: Dryden Press, 1974. 452 p.

Multi-dimensional survey of Soviet politics. Hammer begins by analyzing the lowest levels of Soviet government, working his way up to the national level. At each level Hammer analyzes both influences on, and implications of, governmental policy. Central to the analysis is the concept of "democratic centralism": the idea that debate is permissible at any level of government only until a higher level decides the party line.

165. Heller, Michael: "The price of revolution." (translated from

Russian by M. Callaway). *Midstream*, v. 28 # 4 (April, 1982): 7-11.

166. Hill, Ronald J.: "The CPSU in a Soviet election campaign." *Soviet Studies*, v. 28 # 4 (October, 1976): 590-598.

167. Hodnett, Grey: "Succession contingencies in the Soviet Union." *Problems of Communism*, v. 24 # 2 (March/April, 1975): 1-21.

168. Hough, Jerry F.: "Political participation in the Soviet Union." *Soviet Studies*, v. 28 # 1 (January, 1976): 3-20.

169. Huskey, Eugene: "Specialists in the Soviet Communist party apparatus: legal professionals as party functionaries." *Soviet Studies*, v. 40 3 4 (October, 1988): 538-555.

170. Jaworskyj, Michael (ed.): *Soviet political thought: an anthology*. Baltimore, MD: The John Hopkins University Press, 1968. 621 p.

Anthology of Soviet political theory. After an extensive introduction explaining Marxist political theory, Jaworskyj offers selections from a veritible panoply of Soviet political thinkers. Among the better known ideologues represented in the collection are Vladimir Lenin, Joseph Stalin, Nikita Khrushchev, and Mikhail Suslov. Also quite useful are Jaworskyj's selections from lesser known ideologues -- most of whose writings were previously unavailable to English reading audiences.

> # 223. Keeble, C.: *The Soviet state*.

171. Kress, John H.: "Representation of positions on the CPSU *Politburo*." *Slavic Review*, v. 39 # 2 (June, 1980): 218-238.

172. Kutafin, O. and M. Shafir: *The Soviet parliament: how it works*. Moscow: Novosti Press Agency Publishing House, 1972. 120 p. [PB]

Polemical guide to the Soviet parliamentary system. Reviews the operational technique of the Supreme Soviet and its two chambers (the Soviet of the Union and the Soviet of the Nationalities). The standing parliamentary committees are also reviewed. Finally the book places the workings of legislative action within the context of the Soviet system. The polemical nature of the work derives from what the authors have not mentioned: that the Supreme Soviet was, in reality, little more than a rubberstamp for decisions made in the *Politburo* of the Communist party. That anomalous situation derived from the fact that the Soviet system was -- after Lenin silenced the constituent assembly -- a single party dictatorship.

173. Kux, Ernst: "Contradiction in Soviet socialism." *Problems of Communism*, v. 33 # 6 (November/December, 1984): 1-27.

174. Little, D. Richard: "Legislative authority in the Soviet political system." *Slavic Review*, v. 30 # 1 (March, 1971): 57-73.

175. Löwenhardt, John: *Decision making in Soviet Politics*. New York: St. Martin's Press, 1981. 238 p.

Studies the Soviet government's decision making process in the late 1950s and 1960s as a means of analyzing Soviet politics. Based on detailed study of ten major decisions made after Stalin's death. Löwenhardt concludes that the Communist party is basically conservative in its decision making process, although individual initiative can sometimes produce fundamental changes in policy.

176. Matthews, Mervyn (comp.): *Soviet government: a selection of official documents on internal policies*. New York: Talpinger, 1974. 472 p.

Collection of documents on domestic politics in the Soviet Union. All of the documents originate with official sources, only a few of which have been published in English before. Divided into four parts: State Administration, Law and Police, The Peasantry, and Labor Legislation.

177. Meyer, Alfred G.: *The Soviet political system: an interpretation*. New York: Random House, 1964. 494 p.

Compares the government system in the Soviet Union to a Western business corporation. Primarily focuses on the bureaucratic mentality in both forms of governance. Oriented toward lay readers, Meyer uncovers no new information but does offer an interesting analogy which helps further understanding of the Soviet government structure.

178. Mote, Max E.: *Soviet local and republic elections*. Stanford, CA: Hoover Institution of War, Revolution, and Peace, 1965. 123 p.

Extensively documented description of the 1963 elections in Leningrad based on official sources, press accounts, and private interviews.

> # 432. Oliver, J. H. "Turnover and family circles."

179. Roeder, Philip G.: "Electoral avoidance in the Soviet Union." *Soviet Studies*, v. 41 # 3 (July, 1989): 462-483.

180. Simes, Dimitri K.: "The Soviet succession: domestic and international dimensions." *Journal of International Affairs*, v. 32 # 2 (Fall/Winter, 1978): 211-221.

181. Solovyov, Vladimir and Elena Klepikova: *Behind the high Kremlin walls* (translated from Russian by Guy Daniels). New York: Dodd, Meed, 1986. 248 p.

Investigation into the power politics behind the Kremlin's walls. Based on interviews with Communist party insiders, dissidents, and Western experts. The authors have utilized numerous published sources as well as their secret political diary which they smuggled out of the Soviet Union. The book thus offers an insight into Soviet politics that is rarely available to readers with access to public sources alone. It also offers an insight into Soviet perceptions, and misperceptions, of life in the West. The chapter on Gorbachev explains much about the meaning of *glasnost* and provides the background to the failed August 1991 *coup*. The authors note that although committed to reform -- "communism with a human face," as it were -- Gorbachev rejected *a priori* the total elimination of communism from Soviet life.

> #97 Suslov, M.: *The CPSU*.

182. Taubman, William: *Governing Soviet cities: bureaucratic politics and urban development in the USSR*. New York: Frederick A. Praeger, 1973. 167 p.

Examines Soviet local government in both theory and practice. Taubman attempts to place the administration of localities into context: by studying the governmental bureaucracy in twenty Soviet cities he also elucidates the role of cities in Soviet society as well.

183. Towster, Julian: *Political power in the USSR, 1917-1947: the theory and structure of government in the Soviet state*. New York: Oxford University Press, 1948. 443 p.

184. Unger, Aryeh L.: *Constitutional development in the USSR: a guide to the Soviet constitutions*. New York: Pica Press, 1982. 310 p.

Analyzes each of the four major constitutions adopted in the Soviet Union (1918, 1924, 1936, and 1977). Each of the four are reproduced in full English translation and Unger provides extensive commentary on each. Notes the fundamental difference between the Soviet constitutions and those of Western democracies: unlike the latter, the former are not based on a concept of inalienable rights, the assumption of political equality, nor of separation of powers.

185. Urban, Michael E. and Russell B. Reed: "Regionalism in a systems perspective: explaining elite circulation in a Soviet republic." *Slavic Review*, v. 48 # 3 (Fall, 1989): 413-431.

186. Voslensky, Michael: *Nomenklatura: the Soviet ruling class, an insider's report* (translated from Russian by Eric Musbacher). New York: Doubleday, 1990. 472 p.

Important investigation of the *nomenklatura*, members of the Soviet bureaucracy and Party apparat who enjoy some privileges within Soviet society. In effect, the *nomenklatura* ran the Soviet Union and Voslensky identifies its members as an independent class -- ironically in what is supposed to be a classless society. Follows up on Merle Fainsod's *How Russia is ruled* (see # 161) and adds important insight into the governmental system of the USSR.

187. Wolfe, Bertram D.: *Revolution and reality: essays on the origin and fate of the Soviet system*. Chapel Hill: The University of North Carolina Press, 1981. 401 p.

Collection of Wolfe's essays on communism and totalitarianism. Half the essays focus on Leninist and Stalinist Russia. Wolfe believed that historical research had to be combined with intense moral concern; he thus attempted to warn the West of the consequences of despotism, whether of the right or left. Additionally, Wolfe rejects the theory of convergence -- that capitalism and communism are essentially identical political systems and that they will eventually meet in a democratic middle ground.

### 3. Social Issues

188. Andrusz, Gregory D.: "A note on the financing of housing in the Soviet Union." *Soviet Studies*, v. 42 # 3 (July, 1990): 555-570.

On housing shortages in the Soviet republics and CPSU efforts since the Twenty-seventh Party Congress to end it.

189. Bush, Keith: "Enviromental problems in the USSR." *Problems of Communism*, v. 21 # 4 (July/August, 1972): 21-31.

190. Cohn, Helen D.: "Population policy in the USSR." *Problems of Communism*, v. 22 # 4 (July/August, 1973): 41-55.

191. Connor, Walter D.: "Alcohol and Soviet society." *Slavic Review*, v. 30 # 3 (September, 1971): 570-588.

192. Controy, Mary S.: "Abuse of drugs other than alcohol and tobacco in the Soviet Union." *Soviet Studies*, v. 42 # 3 (July, 1990): 447-480.

193. Gidwitz, Betsy: "Labor unrest in the Soviet Union." *Problems of Communism*, v. 31 # 6 (November/December, 1982): 25-42.

Posits that to avoid strikes and labor unrest, the Kremlin uses the carrot-and-stick method of discipline, by combining immediate material concessions with repression.

194. Hough, Jerry F.: *The Soviet Union and social science theory*. Cambridge, MA: Harvard University Press, 1977. 275 p.

Investigates the methodologies used by academic Sovietologists to study the USSR. Written as both an introduction to and critique of methodologies, the work is most important for students and serious scholars. Hough places special emphasis on the study of different conceptual models used to explain the Soviet experience: he also rejects the use of any one model, noting that the USSR is a complex and nuanced society that requires a broad range of approaches to give a complete analysis.

195. Inkeles, Alex: *Social change in Soviet Russia*. Cambridge, MA: Harvard University Press, 1968. 393 p.

196. Jones, Anthony, Walter D. Connor, and David E. Powell (eds.): *Soviet social problems*. Boulder, CO: Westview Press, 1991. 318 p.

Anthology reviewing the Soviet Union's pressing social problems. Each essay is written by a recognized authority and is framed as a complete entity. Covers the subject thematically, primarily from a sociological perspective. Raises a series of questions regarding the ability of the Soviet system to cope with the manifold problems given the rapid changeover in the Commonwealth of Independent States since the democratic revolution, while the likelihood of intense social conflict in the near future remains.

CONTENTS: Paul Hollander: Politics and social problems / E. Mickiewicz: Ethnic differentiation and political communication / M. I. Goldman: Polution in the Soviet Union: the growth of environmentalism and its consequences / P. R. Josephson: Atomic culture in the USSR: before and after Chernobyl / M. G. Field: Soviet health problems and the convergence hypothesis / J. M. Kramer: Drug abuse in the USSR / W. D. Connor: Equality of opportunity / V. Treml: Drinking and alcohol abuse in the USSR in the 1980s / M. Matthews: *Perestroika* and the rebirth of charity / D. E. Powell: Aging and the elderly / P. Juviler: No end of a problem: *perestroika* for the family / A. Jones: Problems in the schools / R. B. Dobson: Youth problems in the Soviet Union / L. I. Shelley: Crime in the Soviet Union / A. S. Sanjian: Prostitution, the press, and agenda-building in the Soviet policy process / L. Graham: Adapting to new technologies.

197. Komarov, Boris (pseud.): *The destruction of nature in the Soviet Union*. White Plains, NY: M. E. Sharpe, 1980. 150 p.

First *samizdat* work detailing environmental policy in the USSR. Komarov notes that Soviet industry is not only inefficient, but dirty as well: for each equivalent unit produced, Soviet factories pollute twice as much as Western ones. A Russian language edition was covertly circulated briefly in the USSR but did not generate any changes in Soviet environmental regulation.

198. Kramer, John M.: "Drug abuse in the Soviet Union." *Problems of Communism*, v. 37 # 2 (March/April, 1988): 28-40.

199. Lapidus, Gail W.: *State and society in the Soviet Union*. Boulder, CO: Westview Press, 1989. 256 p.

Collection of essays on aspects of social life in the Soviet Union. Two main themes are represented in the essays: the revival of ethno-nationalism in post-Brezhnev Russia and the status of women in an ostensibly egalitarean society. The conclusion unites the essays, thus placing Lapidus' data into a comprehendable context.

200. Lewis, J. Patrick: "Communications output in the USSR: a study of the Soviet telephone system." *Soviet Studies*, v. 28 # 3 (July, 1976): 406-417.

201. Lublin, Nancy: "Women in Soviet Central Asia: progress and contradictions." *Soviet Studies*, v. 33 # 2 (April, 1981): 182-203.

202. Madison, Bernice Q.: "Social services for families and children in the Soviet Union since 1967." *Slavic Review*, v. 31 # 4 (December, 1972): 831-852.

203. Matthews, Mervyn: *Poverty in the Soviet Union: the life-styles*

*of the underpriviliged in recent years*. Cambridge: Cambridge University Press, 1986. 227 p.

Reviews the problems of poverty and homelessness in the Soviet Union from the 1960s onward.

204. Mickiewicz, Ellen: "Regional variation in female recruitment and advancement in the Communist party of the Soviet Union." *Slavic Review*, v. 36 # 3 (September, 1977): 441-454.

205. Morton, Henry W.: "Who gets what, when and how?: housing in the Soviet Union." *Soviet Studies*, v. 32 # 2 (January, 1980): 235-259.

206. Murphy, Patrick: "Soviet *Shabashniki*: material incentives at work." *Problems of Communism*, v. 34 # 6 (November/December, 1985): 48-57.

Deals with the problems of migrant workers within the Soviet Union.

207. Pravda, Alex: "Is there a Soviet working class?" *Problems of Communism*, v. 31 # 6 (November/December, 1982): 1-24.

Examines the realities beneath the political myth of a Soviet working class.

208. Sanjian, Andrea S.: "Social problem, political issues: marriage and divorce in the USSR." *Soviet Studies*, v. 43 # 4 (1991): 629-650.

> # 1646. Segal, B. M.: *The drunken society*.

209. Shenfield, Stephan: "A note on data quality in the Soviet family budget survey." *Soviet Studies*, v. 35 # 4 (October, 1983): 561-568.

210. Simis, Konstantin M.: *USSR: the corrupt society*. New York: Simon & Schuster, 1982. 256 p.

Exposé of bribery as a way of life in the Soviet Union. Documents corruption on all levels of Soviet society, without any effort to evaluate the specific examples cited. Simis concludes that the only way to rid the Soviet Union of corruption is to rid it of the centralized Soviet form of government.

211. Staats, Steven J.: "Corruption in the Soviet system." *Problems of Communism*, v. 21 # 1 (January/February, 1972): 40-47.

212. Stolee, Margaret K.: "Homeless children in the USSR, 1917-1957." *Soviet Studies*, v. 40 # 1 (January, 1988): 64-83.

> # 882. Thruston, R. W.: "Soviet family during the Great Terror."

> # 1156. Treml, V. G.: "Alcohol in the USSR."

213. Treml, Vladimir G.: "Death from alcohol poisoning in the USSR." *Soviet Studies*, v. 34 # 4 (October, 1982): 487-505.

### 4. Soviet Foreign Policy

> # 384. Behbehani, H. S.: *The Soviet Union and Arab nationalism.*

214. Dallin, Alexander: "Soviet foreign policy and domestic politics: a framework for analysis." *Journal of International Affairs*, v. 23 # 2 (1969): 250-265.

215. Dmtryshyn, Basil and Frederick Cox (eds.): *The Soviet Union and the Middle East: a documentary record of Afghanistan, Iran, and Turkey, 1917-1985.* Princeton, NJ: The Press, Inc., 1987. 708 p.

Massive documentary detailing the currents of Soviet foreign policy in the northern Middle East and Persian Gulf. Beside the authors' introduction, which offers a general overview of Soviet foreign policy, the chapters are arranged by country and then subdivided chronologically. Thanks to the book's generous size, a wide range of documents are included offering both the student and scholar access to primary sources on an important region of world interest.

> # 598. Fletcher, W. C.: *Religion and Soviet foreign policy.*

216. Goren, Roberta: *The Soviet Union and terrorism* (edited by Jillian Becker). London: Allen & Unwin, 1984. 232 p.

Surveys Soviet involvement in international terrorism. Beginning with the ideological roots of Soviet support for "national liberation" movements, Goren pieces together the evidence for Soviet support for terrorist movements throughout the world.

> # 440. Grzybowski, K.: *Soviet public international law.*

217. Guan-Fu, Gu: "Soviet aid to the Third World, an analysis of its strategy." *Soviet Studies*, v. 35 # 1 (January, 1983): 71-89.

218. Guins, George C.: "East and West in Soviet Ideology." *Russian Review*, v. 8 # 4 (October, 1949): 271-283.

219. Hammond, Thomas T.: "Moscow and Communist takeovers." *Problems of Communism*, v. 25 #1 (January/February, 1976): 48-67.

220. Hook, Sidney (comp. and ed.): *World communism: key documentary material.* Princeton, NJ: D. Van Nostrand, 1962. 255 p. [PB]

Anthology investigating Communist ideology regarding foreign relations. Includes reprinted documents exemplifying both Communist theory and practice. The documents, originating from many different sources, are divided broadly into three chronological eras: Lenin's, Stalin's, and Khrushchev's Russia. An important section reviews the history of the Communist Party USA. Hook's introduction places the documents into their proper context, each of which has its own introductory and explainatory notes appended.

221. Iman, Zafar: "Soviet treaties with Third World countries." *Soviet Studies*, v. 35 # 1 (January, 1983): 53-70.

222. Jones, Ellen and B. L. Woodbury: "Chernobyl and *glasnost*." *Problems of Communism*, v. 35 # 6 (November/December, 1986): 28-38.

223. Keeble, Curtis (ed.): *The Soviet state: the domestic roots of*

*Soviet foreign policy*. Boulder, CO: Westview Press, 1985. 244 p.

Collection of essays investigating the determinant of Soviet foreign policy. Historical, ideological, and economic factors are all considered, although history is not the work's central focus. Part Three examines the makers of Soviet foreign policy, including the Communist Party, the military, and the foreign policy apparatus. Each chapter is written by an expert in the field and Keeble's insightful analysis of the implications of domestic politics for Soviet foreign relations binds the essays together. Published in cooperation with The Royal Institute of International Affairs, London.

CONTENTS: H. Seton-Watson: The historical roots / D. Lane: The societal dimension / A. McAuley: Nation and nationalism in Central Asia / J. Lawrence: Religion in the USSR / D. Dyker: Soviet industry in its international context / A. Nove: Soviet agriculture: problems and prospects / A. Smith: International trade and resources / E. Moreton: Comrade colossus: the impact of Soviet military industry on the Soviet economy / S. Kirby: Siberia: heartland and framework / P. Frank: The CPSU local *apparat* / M. Mackintosh: The military role in Soviet decision-making / A. Brown: The foreign policy making process / C. Keeble: The implications for foreign policy.

224. Killen, Linda R.: *The Soviet Union and the United States: a new look at the Cold War*. Boston: Twayne Publishers, 1989. 194 p. [PB]

Investigates the means by which the United States and the Soviet Union engaged in limited ideological conflict during the era known as the Cold War. Traces United States/USSR relations from the 1917 revolutions to the rise of Gorbachev. Also reviews specific areas of conflict: the Far East, the Middle East, and Latin America. Killen's approach is basically sound, although her attempt to prove that both the U.S. and the USSR are equally guilty of causing the Cold War is hard to sustain. A brief chronology and glossary round out this introductory text.

225. Kramer, John M.: "Chernobyl and Eastern Europe." *Problems of Communism*, v. 35 # 6 (November/December, 1986): 38-58.

226. Marantz, Paul: "Changing Soviet conceptions of East-West relations." *International Journal*, v. 37 # 2 (Spring, 1982): 220-240.

227. Marples, David R.: "Chernobyl and Ukraine." *Problems of Communism*, v. 35 # 6 (November/December, 1986): 117-127.

> # 467 MccGwire, M.: *Military objectives in Soviet foreign policy*.

228. Nichol, Jim: "The question of legitimate representation of the Soviet Union in signing interstate treaties: a research note." *Soviet Studies*, v. 42 # 2 (April, 1990): 241-354.

229. Ra'anan, Uri: "Soviet decision making and international relations." *Problems of Communism*, v. 29 # 6 (November/December, 1980): 41-47.

230. Rush, Myron (ed.): *The international situation and Soviet foreign policy: key reports by Soviet leaders from the Revolution to the present*. Columbus, OH: C. E. Merrill, 1969. 358 p.

Anthology of basic Soviet sources on foreign relations. The documents originate from every strata of the Soviet Union's foreign policy apparat. Since almost all of the documents are translated into English for the first time here, the anthology can be especially useful for English-speaking students and researchers.

231. Schapiro, Leonard: "The international department of the CPSU: key to Soviet policy." *International Journal*, v. 32 # 1 (Winter, 1976/1977): 41-55.

232. Senn, Alfred E.: *Readings in Russian political and diplomatic history*. Homewood, IL: The Dorsey Press, 1966. 490 p.

Two volume anthology of Russian and Soviet diplomatic history. Volume I deals with the Tsarist period; Volume II, with the Soviet period. The documents represent a wide range of sources. Many of the selections have previously appeared in English, although brought together for the first time here. The primary difficulty with the book is its inadequate introduction, leaving the documents with a somewhat restricted historical context. Still, the book is useful for college courses on Russian and Soviet politics.

233. Thronton, Judith: "Chernobyl and Soviet energy." *Problems of Communism*, v. 35 # 6 (November/December, 1986): 1-16.

234. Ulam, Adam B.: *Expansion and coexistence: Soviet foreign policy 1917-1973*. New York: Praeger, 1974. 797 p.

Interpretative history of Soviet foreign policy written as a college text. Since the book is not based on abstractions, but rather on specific events, leaders, and trends the material within is also useful for lay readers interested in the broad sweep of Soviet foreign relations.

235. Wallace, William V.: "Sino-Soviet relations: an interpretation." *Soviet Studies*, v. 35 # 4 (October, 1983): 457-470.

236. Wesson, Robert G.: *Soviet foreign policy in perspective*. Homewood, IL: The Dorsey Press, 1969. 472 p.

Chronologically organized study of Soviet foreign policy, attempting to distinguish between Marxist theory and Soviet practice. Wesson pays special attention to CPSU relations with Communist parties throughout the world.

237. Zimmerman, William: "Elite perspectives and the explanation of Soviet foreign policy." *Journal of International Affairs*, v. 24 # 1 (1970): 84-98.

### 5. The Soviet Economy

238. Abouchar, Alan: "Ineficiency and reform in the Soviet economy." *Soviet Studies*, v. 25 # 1 (July, 1973): 66-76.

239. Adirim, I.: "Current development and dissemination of computer technology in the Soviet economy." *Soviet Studies*, v. 43 # 4 (1991): 651-668.

240. Ash, Ehiel and Robert Strittmatter: *Accounting in the Soviet*

*Union*. Westport, CT: Praeger Publishers, 1991.

Focuses on the techniques used in industrial accounting in the USSR. Given the nature of the Soviet economy, Ash and Strittmatter place special emphasis on how accountancy and analysis impact upon short- and long-range planning. In particular, they note that consistent bookkeeping and careful financial reporting are vital to Moscow's central control. Interestingly, the same general lessons hold true in capitalist systems although both the techniques and results are vastly different.

241. Bergson, Abram: "On Soviet real investment growth." *Soviet Studies*, v. 39 # 3 (July, 1989): 406-424.

242. ---: "Toward a new growth model." *Problems of Communism*, v. 22 # 2 (March/April, 1973): 1-9.

243. Berliner, Joseph S.: "Managing the USSR economy: alternative models." *Problems of Communism*, v. 32 #1 (January/February, 1983): 40-56.

244. ---: *Soviet industry: from Stalin to Gorbachev*. Ithaca, NY: Cornell University Press, 1988. 306 p.

Collection of Berliner's essays on Soviet economic policy since Stalin. Two major themes animate Berliner's research: technological progress and managerial expertise. In his opinion this division has caused much of the tension within Soviet economic policy for the last half century. By and large Berliner concludes the managers have continued to emerge victorious, thus explaining the failure of all economic reform propsals previous to Gorbachev's. Indeed, we may now note that bureaucratic tendencies nearly overwhelmed Gorbachev's program as well and certainly they explain the waffling on reform which characterized the last eighteen months of Gorbachev's rule.

245. Bialer, Seweryn: "The politics of stringency in the USSR." *Problems of Communism*, v. 29 # 3 (May/June, 1980): 19-33.

246. Birman, Igor: "The imbalance of the Soviet economy." *Soviet*

*Studies*, v. 40 # 2 (April, 1988): 210-221.

Response by Steven Rosefielde in same issue, pp. 222-244 and a rejoinder to both by Alec Nove in v. 40 # 4 (October, 1988): 640-643.

247. Broderson, Arvid: *The Soviet worker.* New York: Random House, 1966. 278 p.

Discusses the worker's place in the Soviet Union.

248. Brus, Wlodzimierz: "Utopianism and realism in the evolution of the Soviet economic system." *Soviet Studies*, v. 40 # 3 (July, 1988): 434-443.

249. Clarke, Roger A.: "The study of Soviet-type economies: some trends and conclusions." *Soviet Studies*, v. 35 # 4 (October, 1983): 525-532.

250. Conyngham, William J.: "Technology and decision making: some aspects of the development of OGAS." *Slavic Review*, v. 39 # 3 (September, 1980): 426-445.

251. Dobb, Maurice: *Soviet economic development since 1917* (revised edition). New York: International Publishers, 1968.

Soviet economic development as seen from a Marxist perspective.

252. Dodge, Norton T.: *Women in the Soviet economy*. Baltimore, MD: The John Hopkins University Press, 1966. 331 p.

Study sponsored by the National Science Foundation detailing the role Soviet women play in economic, scientific, and technical development.

253. Elliot, John: "Marx and contemporary models of Socialist economy." *History of Political Economy*, v. 8 # 2 (Summer, 1976): 151-184.

254. Feiwel, George R.: *The Soviet quest for economic efficiency:*

*issues, controversies, and reforms*. New York: Praeger, 1967. 421 p.

Traces Soviet efforts to increase the efficiency of its centrally planned economy. Also reviews Marxist theories about industrial efficiency and compares the theory with actual Soviet practice. Notes that efficiency has been elusive, partly because of the inherent difficulty in predicting future trends and partly due to the lack of economic incentives that developed out of Soviet collective economics.

255. Friedgut, Theodore H.: *Political participation in the USSR*. Princeton, NJ: Princeton University Press, 1979. 353 p.

Important study on the ways that Soviet citizens have participated in their political system. Written as a corrective to narrowly construed studies attempting to impose Western standards on the Soviet system. Friedgut argues that since the Soviet Union was a one party state, political participation primarily was expressed in organizational terms but not necessarily those of the Communist party or its organs. Indeed, according to this argument, participation -- in a committee or group -- ultimately becomes an end in itself with the participants taking on many attributes generally associated with members of a political party. Of special importance is Friedgut's comparative perspective and his perspicacious analysis of Soviet local politics.

256. Hanson, Philip: *The consumer in the Soviet economy*. London: Macmillan, 1969. 249 p.

257. ---: "Soviet real investment growth: a reply to Bergson." *Soviet Studies*, v. 39 # 3 (July, 1987): 425-430.

258. ---: *Trade and technology in Soviet-Western relations*. New York: Columbia University Press, 1981. 271 p.

Comprehensive analysis of the implications of Soviet imports on East-West relations. Hanson carefully cites statistical data; too often, he cautions, the data cited has been inaccurate and hastily drawn. Hanson concludes that technology transfer has not been as important an element in East-West trade as would have otherwise been expected. He does predict an increase of such transfers, however, and cautions on the need for a more systematic U.S. policy on the subject.

259. Kaser, Michael: *Soviet economics*. New York: McGraw-Hill, 1970. 256 p.

Broad, interpretive history designed for college students examining Soviet economic development since 1917. Kaser uses a variety of primary and secondary sources to explain the ideology, mechanics, and goals of the Soviet economy.

260. Katsnelinboigen, Aron: *Soviet economic thought and political power in the USSR*. Elmsford, NY: Pergamon Press, 1980. 228 p.

Charts the development of economic theory in the Soviet Union, both as an academic discipline and a political battleground. Katsnelinboigen, who taught economics at Moscow University, notes that even within the rigid sphere of Marxism-Leninism considerable disputes arose within the academic and political elite over economic questions.

261. Kontorovich, Vladimir: "Inflation in the Soviet investment and capital stock series." *Soviet Studies*, v. 41 # 2 (April, 1989): 318-329.

> # 374. Kort, M.: "Soviet economy and the plight of Soviet Jewry."

262. Kushrinsky, Fyodor I.: "Inflation Soviet style." *Problems of Communism*, v. 33 # 1 (January/February, 1984): 48-53.

263. ---: "The new role of normatives in Soviet economic planning." *Soviet Studies*, v. 41 # 4 (October, 1989): 526-542.

264. Malle, Silvana: "Planned and unplanned mobility in the Soviet Union under the threat of labor shortage." *Soviet Studies*, v. 39 # 3 (July, 1987): 357-387.

265. Miller, Robert F.: "The future of the Soviet *kolkhoz*." *Problems of Communism*, v. 25 # 2 (March/April, 1976): 34-50.

> # 431 ---: "Role of the Communist party in Soviet research."

266. North, Robert N.: "Soviet northern development: the case of NW Siberia." *Soviet Studies*, v. 24 # 2 (October, 1972): 171-199.

267. Nove, Alec: "'Allocational efficiency' -- can it be so?" *Soviet Studies*, v. 43 # 3 (1991): 575-580.

Response to article by Robert Whitesell (see # 1898).

268. ---: "The Soviet model and underdeveloped countries." *International Affairs*, v. 37 # 1 (January, 1961): 29-38.

269. ---: "Soviet real investment growth: are investment volume statistics overstated? a reply to Bergson." *Soviet Studies*, v. 39 # 3 (July, 1987): 431-433.

270. Plokker, Karin: "The development of individual and cooperative labor activity in the Soviet Union." *Soviet Studies*, v. 42 # 3 (July, 1990): 403-428.

271. Porket, J. L.: "The Soviet model of industrial democracy." *Annals*, v. 431 (May, 1977): 123-132.

> # 1964. Remington, T. F.: "The foundation of Soviet planning."

272. Rosefielde, Stephen: "The illusion of material progress: the analytics of Soviet economic growth revisited." *Soviet Studies*, v. 43 # 4 (1991): 597-612.

273. Roucek, Libor: "Private enterprise in Soviet political debates." *Soviet Studies*, v. 40 # 1 (January, 1988): 46-63.

274. Rumer, Boris: "Soviet estimates of the rate of inflation." *Soviet Studies*, v. 41 # 2 (April, 1989): 298-317.

275. ---: "Soviet investment policy: unresolved problems." *Problems of Communism*, v. 31 # 5 (September/October, 1982): 53-68.

Soviet economic policies in the late 1970s and early 1980s.

276. ---: "Structural imbalance in the Soviet economy." *Problems of Communism*, v. 33 # 4 (July/August, 1984): 24-32.

277. Schroeder, Gertrude: "Consumer problems and prospects." *Problems of Communism*, v. 22 # 2 (March/April, 1973): 10-24.

> # 1149. Shapiro, J. P.: "Soviet consumer in the Brezhnev era."

278. Siegelbaum, Lewis H.: "Soviet norm determination in theory and practice, 1917-1941." *Soviet Studies*, v. 36 # 1 (January, 1984): 45-65.

279. Skursky, Roger: "The buyers' market and Soviet consumer goods distribution." *Slavic Review*, v. 31 # 4 (December, 1972): 817-830.

280. Slider, Darrell: "The brigade system in Soviet industry: an effort to restructure the labor force." *Soviet Studies*, v. 39 # 3 (July, 1987): 388-405.

281. Sutton, Anthony C.: *Western technology and Soviet economic development, 1917-1965* (3 vols.). Stanford, CA: Stanford University Press, 1968-1973. 1,201 p.

Three volume assessment of the impact of Western technology transfers on the Soviet economy. Each volume is organized as an independent whole covering a specific time frame. Volume I covers the period from 1917 to 1930; Volume II, from 1930 to 1945; and Volume III, from 1945 to 1965. In each period technology transfers are categorized by economic sector thus allowing Sutton to guage the impact of such transfers in a specific context.

282. Von Brabant, Jozef M.: "The USSR and Socialist economic integration: a comment." *Soviet Studies*, v. 36 # 1 (January, 1984): 127-138.

283. Weitzman, Phillip: "Soviet long-term consumption planning: distribution according to rational need." *Soviet Studies*, v. 26 # 3 (July, 1974): 305-321.

284. Wilhelm, John H.: "The Soviet Union has an administered, not a planned, economy." *Soviet Studies*, v. 37 # 1 (January, 1985): 118-130.

### 6. Soviet Agriculture

285. Atkinson, Dorothy: *The end of the Russian land commune, 1905-1930*. Stanford, CA: Stanford University Press, 1983. 457 p.

Political and economic study of the decline of peasant communes in revolutionary, Leninist, and Stalinist Russia. The book is divided into five chronological sections and ends with the beginning of the collectivization campaign of 1929. Although not a historical study, Atkinson does provide some background insights.

286. Clayton, Elizabeth: "Productivity in Soviet agriculture." *Slavic Review*, v. 39 # 3 (September, 1980): 446-458.

287. Després, Laure and Ksenya Khinchuk: "Hidden sector in Soviet agriculture: a study of the military *sovkhozy* and auxiliary farms." *Soviet Studies*, v. 42 # 2 (April, 1990): 269-294.

288. Gray, Kenneth R. (ed.): *Soviet agriculture: comparative perspectives*. Ames: Iowa State University Press, 1990. 284 p.

A special study of the Kennan Institute for Advanced Russian Studies, examining the economic aspects of agriculture within the Soviet state. Special emphasis is placed on the failure of agricultural production to keep pace with Soviet population growth, leading to continuing shortages, and on efforts to reform the USSR's system of collective farming.

CONTENTS: Lung-Fai Wong and V. Ruttan: A comparative analysis of agricultural trends in centrally planned economies / F. Dovring: Costs of agricultural growth and development: a cross-national analysis focusing on the USSR / I. Stebelsky: Soviet food imbalances and their prospective / K. R. Gray: Soviet Utilization of food: focus on meat and dairy processing / K. M. Brooks: Soviet agricultural policy and pricing under Gorbachev / D. Van Atta:

Toward a Soviet "responsibility system"? recent developments in the agricultural collective contract / C. Nechemias: Recent changes in Soviet rural housing policy / P. R. Craumer: Trends in Soviet dryland farming and soil conservation practices with comparison to North American developments / V. Litvin: Scientific and technical information concerning agriculture in the USSR / E. M. Jacobs: A content analysis of writings on foreign agricultural experience / M. L. Wyzan: The Bulgarian experience with centrally planned agriculture: lessons for Soviet reformers? / K. E. Wädekin: Private agriculture in Socialist countries: implications for the USSR / A. Nove: Can the USSR learn from the Hungarian and Chinese agricultural experiences?

289. Kaplan, Cynthia S.: *The party and agricultural crisis management in the USSR*. Ithaca, NY: Cornell University Press, 1987. 203 p.

Investigates Communist party involvement in Soviet farming on the local level. Special emphasis is on the economic impact of Communist policies.

290. Kroll, Heidi: "The role of contracts in the Soviet economy." *Soviet Studies*, v. 40 # 3 (July, 1988): 349-366.

291. Linz, Susan J.: "Managerial autonomy in Soviet farms." *Soviet Studies*, v. 40 # 2 (April, 1988): 175-195.

292. Litvin, Valentin: *The Soviet agro-industrial complex: structure and performance*. Boulder, CO: Westview Press, 1987. 151 p.

Describes the entire food production system in the USSR: from the farms that produce the food, to the transportation system that brings it to the cities, and finally, the markets which sell the food to Soviet citizens. Notes the great inefficiency at almost every level of food production and the efforts -- most recently by Mikhail S. Gorbachev -- to reform the means for food production and distribution.

293. Millar, James R.: "The prospects for Soviet agriculture." *Problems of Communism*, v. 26 # 3 (May/June, 1977): 1-16.

> #265. Miller, R. F.: "The future of the Soviet *kolkhoz*."

294. Potichnyj, Peter J.: *Soviet agricultural trade unions, 1917-1970*. Toronto: Toronto University Press, 1972. 258 p.

Chronological and systematic investigation of the history of trade unions in the Soviet Union. This makes for some repetition as opposed to a study by union or region, but allows Potichnyj a broad comparative perspective. Of special importance is the way that Potichnyj integrates statistical data and uses it to support his assertions.

295. Strauss, Erich: *Soviet agriculture in perspective: a study of its successes and failures*. New York: F. A. Praeger, 1969. 328 p.

296. Wädekin, Karl-Eugen: "Soviet agriculture's dependence on the West." *Foreign Affairs*, v. 60 # 4 (Spring, 1982): 882-903.

297. Wolf, Thomas A.: "Soviet market power and pricing behavior in Western export markets." *Soviet Studies*, v. 34 # 4 (October, 1982): 529-546.

## B. ETHNIC AND NATIONAL MINORITIES

### 1. Overviews

298. Anderson, Barbara A. and Brian D. Silver: "Growth and diversity of the population of the Soviet Union." *Annals*, v. 510 (July, 1990): 155-177.

299. ---: "'Permanent' and 'present' populations in Soviet statistics." *Soviet Studies*, v. 37 # 3 (July, 1985): 386-402.

Investigates the results of 1959, 1970, and 1979 censuses.

300. Armstrong, John A.: "Soviet nationalities policies." *Soviet Jewish Affairs*, v. 15 # 1 (1985): 57-71.

301. Bahry, Donn and Carol Nechemias: "Half full or half empty? the debate over Soviet regional equality." *Slavic Review*, v. 40 # 3 (Fall, 1981): 366-383.

302. Chamberlin, William H.: "Soviet race and nationality policies." *Russian Review*, v. 5 # 1 (Fall, 1945): 3-9.

303. Conquest, Robert: *The nation killers: the Soviet deportation of nationalities*. New York: Macmillan Publishing, 1970. 222 p.

Deals with the forced transfer of nationalities by Soviet authorities since the Stalin era. In all, Conquest estimates, nearly two million members of ten different nationalities were deported to Siberia, virtually depopulating some 62,000 square miles of territory. As of the revised edition (first edition was published by St. Martin's Press, 1960 under the title *The Soviet deportation of nationalities*), no compensation had been offered to the deportees, although Jews (who are not mentioned in the book) and Volga Germans have been permitted to emigrate from the USSR.

304. --- (ed.): *Soviet nationalities policy in practice*. New York: Frederick A. Praeger, Publisher / London: The Bodley Head, 1967. 160 p.

Anthology surveying Soviet nationalities policy in both theory and practice. Begins with Lenin's 1903 Party platform that established which groups would be accepted as nationalities and which would not be so considered. Since 1917 the former have had some form of autonomy while the latter have been encouraged to assimilate. Conquest correctly concludes that the nationalities problem is the key obstacle in contemporary Soviet political relations.

305. Dellenbrant, Jan Ake: *Soviet regional policy: a quantitative inquiry into the social and political development of the Soviet republics*. Atlantic Highlands, NJ: Humanities Press, 1980. 192 p.

Brief quantitative analysis of Soviet development during the late 1950s and 1960s. Notes that the Soviet Union made great strides in those two decades, particularly in raising its standard of living. Still, Dellenbrandt notes that development has been uneven: the

European republics were way ahead of the Asian ones and remained so throughout. The clear division helps to explain much about inter-republic tensions with the emergence of the Commonwealth of Independent States.

306. Desfosses, Helen: "Demography, ideology, and politics in the USSR." *Soviet Studies*, v. 28 # 2 (April, 1976): 244-256.

307. Dunlop, John B.: *The faces of contemporary Russian nationalism*. Princeton, NJ: Princeton University Press, 1983. 363 p.

Deals with the renaissance of Russian nationalism resulting from the decline of Soviet ideology in the post-Brezhnev years. Divides Russian nationalists into two types: the *Vozrozhdentsy* and the National Bolsheviks. While Dunlop views the former as essentially liberal, he categorizes the National Bolsheviks as neo-Fascist in orientation. Dunlop, however, uses the term National Bolshevism more loosely than most other scholars, leading to potential confusion of terminology. Inter alia also deals with the Jewish question, noting that not all Russian nationalists are antisemitic. His prediction that emigration would be the primary solution for Jewish national needs in a new Russia has been largely vindicated.

308. Feshbach, Murray: "Between the lines of the 1979 census." *Problems of Communism*, v. 31 # 1 (January/February, 1982): 27-37.

309. Fisher, Wesley A.: "Ethnic consciousness and intermarriage: correlates of endogamy among the major Soviet nationalities." *Soviet Studies*, v. 29 # 3 (July, 1977): 395-408.

310. Hajda, Lubomyr and Mark Beissinger (eds.): *The nationalities factor in Soviet politics and society*. Boulder, CO: Westview Press, 1990. 331 p.

Anthology of scholarly studies on the history and evolution of the nationalities problem in the Soviet Union. Also investigates the growing tension between ethnic groups -- as exemplified by the interethnic violence in Armenia and Azerbijan. Most significantly, the authors assess possible future avenues of development within a volatile issue in contemporary Soviet (now Russian) politics.

CONTENTS: R. Szporluk: The imperial legacy and the Soviet nationalities problem / S. L. Burg: Nationality elites and political change in the Soviet Union / G. E. Schroeder: Nationalities and the Soviet economy / T. Rakowska-Harmstone: Nationalities and the Soviet military / B. A. Anderson and B. D. Silver: Some factors in the linguistic and ethnic Russification of Soviet nationalities: is everyone becoming Russian? / P. A. Goble: Readers, writers, and republics: the structural basis of non-Russian literary politics / B. R. Bociurkiw: Nationalities and Soviet religious policies / R. Solchanyk: Ukraine, Belorussia, and Moldavia: imperial integration, Russification, and the struggle for national survival / R. J. Misiunas: The Baltic Republics: stagnation and strivings for soverignty / R. G. Suny: / Transcaucasia: cultural cohesion and ethnic revival in a multinational society / M. B. Olcott: Central Asia: the reformers challenge a traditional society / D. R. Spechler: Russian nationalism and Soviet politics / M. Beissinger and L. Hadja: Nationalism and reform in Soviet politics.

311. Hammer, Darrell P.: *Russian nationalism and Soviet politics*. Boulder, CO: Westview Press, 1990. 200 p.

Examines the political impact of Russian nationalism as an opposition movement in Soviet politics of the Gorbachev era. Also reviews Stalin's use of nationalism -- especially during World War II -- to justify broad Communist policies which led to distorted Marxist-Leninst doctrine and allowed ultra-nationalist ideologies a chance to return to prominence. Hammer's last chapter analyzes the implications of the resurgent Russian nationalism for the world and should be read by all interested in understanding global politics in the post-Soviet era.

312. Heitman, Sidney: *The third Soviet emigration: Jewish, German, and Armenian emigration from the USSR since World War II*. Fort Collins: Colorado State University, 1986. 114 p.

Comparative report on emigration from the Soviet Union compiled for the United States State Department Office of Long Range

Assessment and Research. Includes both legal and practical aspects of emigration as well as a sociological study on the émigrés. Well documented with materials in the United States, USSR, and Israel.

313. Hooson, David: "The outlook for regional development in the Soviet Union." *Slavic Review*, v. 31 # 3 (September, 1972): 535-554.

314. Jones, Ellen and Fred W. Grupp: "Measuring nationality trends in the Soviet Union: a research note." *Slavic Review*, v. 41 # (Spring, 1982): 112-122.

315. ---: "Modernization and ethnic equalization in the USSR." *Soviet Studies*, v. 36 # 2 (April, 1984): 159-184.

316. Karklins, Rasma: "A note on 'nationality' and 'native tongue' as census categories in 1979." *Soviet Studies*, v. 32 # 3 (July 1980): 415-422.

317. Katz, Zev: "The new nationalism in the USSR." *Midstream*, v. 19 # 2 (February, 1973): 3-13.

318. Kozlov, Viktor: *The peoples of the Soviet Union* (translated from Russian by Pauline M. Tiffen). Bloomington: Indiana University Press, 1988. 262 p.

Demographic and sociological study into Russian nationalities, written by one of the foremost ethnographic researchers in the Soviet Union. Includes a detailed analysis of the data from every census taken in Russia between 1897 and 1979. The chapters are organized thematically and discuss issues such as urbanization, demographic processes, and ethnic transformation. Provides an interesting look into the social aspect of Russia's multiple nationalities. Kozlov appears, however, to have erred when he predicted a lessening of ethnic diversity in the Soviet Union's future: given the collapse of the Soviet Union and its replacement by ethno-national republics, in addition to violent flare ups of inter-ethnic tensions (e.g. in Baku in January 1990), the opposite conclusion appears to hold true.

319. Kreindler, Isabelle: "The Soviet deported nationalities: a

summary and an update." *Soviet Studies*, v. 38 # 3 (July, 1986): 387-405.

> # 1679. Lapidus, G. W.: "Gorbachev and the national question."

320. Manning, Clarence A.: "The Soviet Union and the Slavs." *Russian Review*, v. 5 # 2 (Spring, 1946): 3-9.

321. Meissner, Boris: "The Soviet concept of nation and the right of national self-determination." *International Journal*, v. 32 # 1 (Winter, 1976/ 1977): 56-81.

Deals with Lenin's conception of self-determination and Stalin's definition of nation.

322. Miller, John H.: "Cadres policy in nationality areas: recruitment of CPSU first and second secretaries in non-Russian republics of the USSR." *Soviet Studies*, v. 29 # 1 (January, 1977): 3-36.

323. Nahaylo, Bohdan and Victor Swoboda: *Soviet disunion: a history of the nationalities problem in the USSR*. New York: The Free Press, 1990. 432 p.

Chronologically organized history of the national minorities problem in the Soviet Union. Notes that almost half of the Soviet population are members of national minorities. Draws a wide range of documents to reconstruct the often stormy history of their treatment. Especially saddening are the chapters on the Stalinist era. Nahaylo and Swoboda conclude with a discussion of Gorbachev's policy and prediction that *glasnost* without *perestroika* will not solve the problem. Instead, the authors propose returning to a truer form of federalism by the adoption of Lenin's "national contract."

> # 1483. Olcott, M. B.: "Andropov and the national question."

324. Parming, Tönu: "Population processes and the nationality issue in the Soviet Baltic." *Soviet Studies*, v. 32 # 3 (July, 1980): 398-414.

325. Pinkus, Binyamin: "The extra-territorial national minorities in the Soviet Union, 1917-39: Jews, Germans and Poles." *Studies in Contemporary Jewry*, v. 3 (1987): 72-97.

326. Rakowska-Harmstone, Teresa: "The dialectics of nationalism in the USSR." *Problems of Communism*, v. 23 # 3 (May/June, 1974): 1-22.

327. Ruble, Blair A.: "Ethnicity in Soviet cities." *Soviet Studies*, v. 41 # 3 (July, 1989): 401-414.

328. Segal, Boris M.: "Friendship of nationalities in Soviet society." *Midstream*, v. 26 # 3 (March, 1980): 5-9.

329. Silver, Brian D.: "The status of national minority languages in Soviet education: an assessment of recent changes." *Soviet Studies*, v. 26 # 1 (January, 1974): 28-40.

330. Solchanyk, Roman: "Russian language and Soviet politics." *Soviet Studies*, v. 34 # 1 (January, 1982): 23-42.

331. Szporluk, Roman: "Nationalities and the Russian problem in the USSR: an historical outline." *Journal of International Affairs*, v. 27 # 1 (1973): 22-40.

332. ---: "West Ukraine and west Belorussia: historical tradition, social communication, and linguistic assimilation." *Soviet Studies*, v. 31 # 1 (January, 1979): 76-98.

333. Tillett, Lowell: *The great friendship: Soviet historians on the non-Russian nationalities*. Chapel Hill: University of North Carolina Press, 1969. 468 p.

Historiographical investigation of the myth of "friendship of Soviet nationalities" propounded by Soviet historians. The book is arranged thematically and is based on a careful study of hundreds of Soviet sources. Tillet also criticizes those Western authors who -- before World War II -- accepted Soviet propaganda. Tillet's observation that far from multi-national harmony, intense hatred seethed just beneath the surface in the USSR has been amply borne out by border conflicts within the emerging Commonwealth of Independent States.

> #185. Urban, M.: "Regionalism in a systems perspective."

334. Vardys, V. S.: "Geography and nationalities in the USSR: a commentary." *Slavic Review*, v. 31 # 3 (September, 1972): 564-570.

335. Wixman, Ronald: *The peoples of the USSR: an ethnographic handbook.* London: Macmillan, 1984. 246 p.

Briefly offers data on a wide range of topics related to Soviet national minorities. Includes cultural and literary information but no historical background. Most useful for the compilation of quantifiable data, mostly originating with Soviet sources.

### 2. Russians

336. Breslauer, George W.: "Is there a generation gap in the Soviet political establishment? demand articulation by RSFSR provincial party first secretaries." *Soviet Studies*, v. 36 # 1 (January, 1984): 1-25.

> # 307. Dunlop, J. B.: *Faces of contemporary Russian nationalism.*

337. Dunn, Stephen and Ethel Dunn: *The peasants of central Russia.* New York: Holt, Rinehart & Winston, 1967. 139 p.

Important anthropological study based on Soviet sources. The Dunns seek to describe the peasants lifestyle in the Don and Volga River basisns.

> # 311. Hammer, D. P.: *Russian nationalism and Soviet politics.*

338. Lewin, Moshe: *Russian peasants and Soviet power* (translated from French by Irene Nove and John Biggart). London: Alen & Unwin, 1968. 539 p.

339. Nechemias, Carol: "Regional differentiation of living standards

in the RSFSR: the issue of inequality." *Soviet Studies*, v. 32 # 3 (July, 1980): 366-378.

340. Rywkin, Michael: *Russia in Central Asia*. New York: Crowell-Collier/Collier Paperbacks, 1968. 191 p.

> # 331. Szporluk, R.: "Nationalities and the Russian problem."

### 3. Belorussians

> # 1020. Clemens, W. C.: "The Soviet world faces West."

341. Guthier, Steven L.: "The Belorussians: national identification and assimilation, 1897-1970." *Soviet Studies*, v. 29 # 1 (January, 1977): 37-61; # 2 (April, 1977): 270-283.

342. Lubachko, Ivan S.: *Byelorussia under Soviet rule, 1917-1957*. Lexington: University Press of Kentucky, 1972. 219 p.

Scholarly review of the first forty years of Soviet rule in Belorussia. Concentrates on political history, with the primary theme being the Sovietization of Belorussia under Lenin and Stalin. Of special importance are the chapters relating to the suppression of Belorussian nationalism and the collectivization campaign.

343. Motyl, Alexander J.: *Will the non-Russians rebel?: state, ethnicity, and stability in the USSR*. Ithaca, NY: Cornell University Press, 1987. 188 p.

Investigates the Soviet nationalities problem from the perspective of Soviet internal security policies. Presumes that the USSR as organized before the revolutions of 1989-1991 was a Russian state in which the non-Russian nationalities were largely excluded. Motyl's premise that non-Russians could never rebel against Communist domination has not been borne out: indeed the opposite seems to have been true as the republics played a vital role in the rise of democracy.

> # 332. Szporluk, R.: "West Ukraine and West Bellorussia."

344. Vakar, N. P.: *Belorussia: the making of a nation, a case study.* Cambridge, MA: Harvard University Press, 1956. 297 p.

> # 1917. Zaprudnik, J.: *Belarus.*

### 4. Ukrainians

> # 426. Armstrong, J. A.: *Soviet bureaucratic elite.*

345. Armstrong, John A.: *Ukrainian nationalism* (second edition). New York: Columbia University Press, 1963. 361 p.

Scholarly overview of the efforts of Ukrainian nationalists to forge an independent state. Primarily focused on World War II, although Ukrainian nationalist agitation in the interwar years is also reviewed. Of special import is Armstrong's analysis of the actions of Ukrainian émigrés, leading up to the creation of the Ukrainian Partisan Army (UPA) in 1941. Initially the UPA cooperated with the Nazis against the Soviets. Thereafter, however, the UPA fought both the Soviets and the Germans. This struggle continued until the UPA was finally destroyed in 1950.

> # 1008. Bilinsky, Y.: *The second Soviet republic.*

> # 1900 ---: *Ukraine.*

346. Gitelman, Zvi: "Perceptions of Ukrainians by Soviet Jewish emigrants: some empirical observations." *Soviet Jewish Affairs*, v. 17 # 3 (Winter, 1987): 3-24.

> # 625. Guthier, S. L.: "Popular base of Ukrainian nationalism."

347. Koropeckyj, I. S.: "Soviet Statistics on Ukraine: selective omissions." *Problems of Communism*, v. 37 # 3/4 (May/August, 1988): 95-100.

> # 813. Liber, G.: "Ethnic change in the Ukrainian SSR."

> # 746. Mace, J. E.: "The *Komitety Nezamozhnykh Selyan.*"

> #227. Marples, D. R.: "Chernobyl and Ukraine."

348. Marples, David R.: "The *kulak* in post-war USSR: the West Ukrainian example." *Soviet Studies*, v. 36 # 4 (October, 1984): 560-570.

> # 1886. Paniotto, V.: "The Ukrainian movement for *perestroika*."

349. Sulliwant, Robert S.: *Soviet politics and the Ukraine, 1917-1957*. New York: Columbia University Press, 1962. 438 p.

> # 332. Szporluk, R.: "West Ukraine and West Belorussia."

> # 1155. Tillett, L.: "Ukrainian nationalism & the fall of Shelest."

**5. Jews**

350. Agursky, Mikhail: "Cultural genocide." *Midstream*, v. 33 # 2 (February, 1987): 32-36.

351. Altshuler, M.: *Soviet Jewry since the Second World War: population and social structure*. Westport, CT: Greenwood Press, 1987. 278 p.

Brings together all available data on the demographic structure of Soviet Jewry since 1945. Of special interest is Altshuler's analysis of the data from the census of 1959, 1969, and 1979. Also considers the social conditions of Soviet Jewry, including excurses on such crucial issues as emigration, intermarriage, and geographic distribution.

352. Aronson, Gregor et al (eds.): *Russian Jewry 1917-1967* (translated from Russian by Joel Carmichael). New York: Thomas Yoseloff, 1969. 613 p.

Anthology of studies on the history of Jews in the Soviet Union from the revolutions of 1917 to the fall of Khrushchev. Main focus is on political and social history, with cultural and intellectual given broad treatment.

CONTENTS: G. Aronson: Jewish communal life in 1917-1918 / J. Schechtman: Jewish community life in the Ukraine 1917-1919 / S. Gringauz: The Jewish national autonomy in Lithuania, Latvia, and Estonia / I. Trotzky: Jewish pogroms in the Ukraine and in Byelorussia 1918-1920 / A. Goldstein: The fate of the Jews in German-occupied Soviet Russia / J. Gar: Jews in the Baltic countries under German occupation / S. Gringauz: The death of Jewish Kaunas (Kovno) / G. Aronson: The Jewish question during the Stalin era / G. Swet: Jews in musical life in Soviet Russia; the Jewish theater in Soviet Russia / V. Alexandrova: Jews in Soviet literature / Jewish scientists in Soviet Russia / S. Schwarz: Birobidzhan: an experiment in Jewish colonization / J. Slutzki: The fate of Hebrew in Soviet Russia / J. Schechtman: Soviet Russia, Zionism, and Israel / L. Shapiro: Russian Jewry after Stalin / S. Gepstein: Russian Zionists in the struggle for Palestine / I. Trotzky: New Russian-Jewish immigration in the United States / J. Margolin: Russian-Jewish immigration into Israel / A. Sedych: Russian Jews in émigré literature.

353. Baron, Salo W.: *The Russian Jew under Tsars and Soviets* (second edition). New York: Macmillan Publishing, 1976. 468 p.

Surveying 200 years of Jewish history in Imperial Russia and the Soviet Union, Baron integrates political, social, and intellectual trends chronologically from the 1790s to the 1970s. Survival of Jewry in Russia, despite the antipathy of Tsarist and Communist officials is the book's main focus. Important subthemes are the revival of Russian Jewry since the Holocaust and the continued vitality of Jews as a national minority.

354. Belotserkovsky, Vadim: "What is Russian antisemitism?" *Midstream*, v. 33 # 4 (April, 1987): 6-10.

355. "Birobidzhan: behind the facade." (introduced and annotated by Lukasz Hirszowicz). *Soviet Jewish Affairs*, v. 18 # 1 (Spring, 1988): 71-75.

> # 1019. Checinski, M.: "Soviet-Polish relations and Polish Jews."

356. Cullen, Robert B.: "Soviet Jewry." *Foreign Affairs*, v. 65 # 2

(Winter, 1986/1987): 252-266.

357. Ettinger, Shmuel: "The 'Jewish question' in the USSR." *Soviet Jewish Affairs*, v. 15 # 1 (1985): 11-16.

358. Fain, Benjamin and Mervin Verbit: *Jewishness in the Soviet Union: report of an empirical study*. Jerusalem: The Tarbuth Foundation, 1984. 132 p.

Report and analysis of the first-ever independent public opinion poll done on Soviet Jewry. A broad sample of Soviet Jews, including some *refuseniks*, were polled on three issues: religion, Jewish education, and Jewish-Gentile relations. Reproducing the questionaire in full, Fain and Verbit quantify the reponses and analyze their meaning for the future of Soviet Jewry.

359. Feingold, Henry: "Soviet Jewish survival, American Jewish power." *Midstream*, v. 34 # 2 (February, 1978): 11-22.

360. Freedman, Theodore (ed.): *Antisemitism in the Soviet Union: its roots and consequences*. New York: Freedom Library Press of the Anti-Defamation League of B'nai B'rith, 1984. 664 p. [PB]

Anthology of studies on Russian antisemitism based on dual symposia held in Jerusalem and Paris in April 1978, and March 1979, respectively. Studies a wide range of factors effecting Soviet antisemitism. Central to the analysis are the official roles that antisemitism and anti-Zionism have played in the Soviet Union since the late 1960s. This edition also includes citations from both *samizdat* and official sources.

CONTENTS: S. Ettinger: The historical roots of antisemitism in the USSR / R. Nudelman: Contemporary Soviet antisemitism: form and content / G. Ilin: The character of Soviet antisemitism / Y. Tsigelman: Antisemitisn in Soviet publications / D. Tiktina : The reception of antisemitic propaganda in the USSR / A. Voronel: The reasons for antisemitism in the USSR / E. Sotnikova: The Jewish problem in *Samizdat* and the emigration press / L. Dimerski-Tsigelman: The attitude toward Jews in the USSR / S. Hirsh: State and popular antisemitism in Soviet Lithuania / M.

Azbel: Aspects of antisemitism and the fight against it / L. Dulzin: The status of Jews in Soviet society / C. Abramsky: The Soviet attitude toward Jews: ideology and practice / W. Korey: The Soviet *Protocols of the Elders of Zion* / S. J. Roth: Anti-Zionism and antisemitism in the USSR / U. Terracini: Israel as a factor in Soviet antisemitism / S. Ettinger: Historical and internal political factors in Soviet antisemitism / L. Schwartz: Soviet antisemitism and Jewish scientists / E. Litvinoff: The Slavophile revival and its attitude to Jews / S. Tartakovsky: Antisemitism in daily life / G. Freiman: I am a Jew, it turns out / R. Okuneva: Antisemitic notions: strange analogies / Y. Tsigelman: The universal Jewish conspiracy in Soviet antisemitic propaganda / R. Okuneva: Jews in the Soviet school syllabus / M. Kaganskaya: Intellectual fascism in Soviet establishment culture / J. Vogt: When Nazism became Zionism: an analysis of political cartoons / Excerpts from Soviet publications and *samizdat* / N. Bibichovka: Antisemitic and anti-Israeli publications in the USSR 1960-1981.

361. Friedberg, Maurice: *How things were done in Odessa: cultural and intellectual pursuits in a Soviet city*. Boulder, CO: Westview Press, 1991. 156 p.

Profile of Odessa under Communist rule based on interviews with 100 Soviet-Jewish émigrés from the city. Primary emphasis is on cultural and intellectual life in the 1950s and 1960s. Reviews education, entertainment, and the intrusion of Communist party bureaucracy into all facets of daily life. Provides the reader with an intertesting insight into Soviet daily life on a micro scale.

362. ---: "Jewish ethnicity in the Soviet Union." *Midstream*, v. 18 # 7 (August/September, 1972): 54-62.

363. Gilbert, Martin: *The Jews of hope*. New York: Elisabeth Sifton Books/Viking Press, 1985. 237 p.

Biographical history of Soviet Jewish *refuseniks*, underscoring their courageous struggle to open the gates leading to free emigration. Based primarily on interviews with several *refuseniks*, Gilbert's own reflections on aspects of Russian Jewish history are interspersed throughout.

> # 799. Gilboa, Y. A.: *The black years of Soviet Jewry.*

364. Gitelman, Zvi: *A century of ambivalence: the Jews of Russia and the Soviet Union, 1881 to the present.* New York: Schocken Books in cooperation with YIVO Institute for Jewish research, 1988. 336 p.

Illustrated survey of Russian Jewish history from the pogroms of 1881 to the beginnings of *glasnost*. Concentrates on social history, although political and intellectual trends are not ignored. The chapters unfold chronologically with the last chapter glimpsing at Soviet Jewry in the late 1980s and offering a few observations about developments in the near future.

> # 346. ---: "Perceptions of Ukrainians."

365. ---: "Shaping Jewish identity in the USSR and eastern Europe." *Midstream*, v. 36 # 3 (April, 1990): 16-21.

366. ---: "Soviet political culture: insights from Jewish émigrés." *Soviet Studies*, v. 29 # 4 (October, 1977): 543-564.

367. Harris, David A.: "Crisis in Soviet Jewry." *Midstream*, v. 32 # 3 (March, 1986): 6-8.

Issues facing Soviet Jewry shortly after the rise of Gorbachev and considering the virtual end of emigration at the time.

368. Harris, David and Izrail Rabinovich: *The jokes of oppression: the humor of Soviet Jews.* Northvale, NJ: J. Aronson, 1988. 276 p.

Collection of jokes reflecting the humor Soviet Jews used as a defense mechanism during the darkest years of their oppression. Offers an irreverent but insightful perspective on Soviet Jewry and life in the USSR.

369. Institute of Jewish Affairs: *Soviet antisemitic propaganda: evidence from books, press and radio.* London: The Institute, 1978. 105 p. [PB]

Illustrated examination of Soviet antisemitism. Of special importance are the reproduced cartoons which represent official attitudes toward Jewry, Zionism, and Israel. The compilers allow the sources to speak for themselves, adding only introductory comments that place texts into context. Includes two lists: one of newspapers that have published antisemitic articles and another of antisemitic books published between 1975 and 1978. Continuing concern about neo-Fascist Russian antisemitism, for example connected with the *Pamyat* movement, give this booklet added meaningfulness.

370. Kochan, Lionel (ed.): *The Jews in Soviet Russia since 1917* (third edition). Oxford: Oxford University Press for the Institute of Jewish Affairs, London, 1978. 431 p. [PB]

Anthology of historical studies on Soviet Jewry. The studies are all thematically organized, thus avoiding the pitfall of repetition. Leonard Schapiro's introduction and Shmuel Ettinger's chapter on the revolution also investigate the background of Jewish history in the last years of the Tsarist Empire. Each author approaches the subject from an individual methodological perspective. Reviews both Soviet theory and practice, with approximately equal emphasis. Considered a classic collection, the book is useful for both specialized and general reader.

CONTENTS: S. Ettinger: The Jews in Russia at the outbreak of the revolution / S. Levenberg: Soviet Jewry: some problems and perspectives / J. Miller: Soviet theory on the Jews / C. Abramsky: The Birobidzhan project, 1927-1959 / W. Korey: The legal position of Soviet Jewry: a historical enquiry / J. B. Schechtman: The USSR, Zionism, and Israel / A. Nove and J. A. Newth: The Jewish population: demographic trends and occupational patterns / J. Rothenberg: Jewish religion in the Soviet Union / M. Friedberg: Jewish themes in Soviet Russian literature / Y. A. Gilboa: Hebrew literature in the USSR / C. Shmeruk: Yiddish literature in the USSR / R. Ainsztein: Soviet Jewry in the Second World War / B. D. Weinryb: Antisemitism in Soviet Russia / Z. Katz: After the Six-Day War / P. Lewis: The Jewish question in the open: 1968-71 / L. Hirszowicz: The Soviet-Jewish problem: internal and inter-enational developments, 1972-1976.

371. Korey, William: "The origins and development of Soviet antisemitism: an analysis." *Slavic Review*, v. 31 # 1 (March, 1972): 111-135.

372. ---: *The Soviet cage: antisemitism in Russia*. New York: The Viking Press, 1973. 369 p.

Collection of Korey's essays that review the causes and results of Soviet antisemitism. Although each essay is independent, all are interconnected. Of special interest are the essays charting Soviet distortion of the Holocaust. Korey also discusses various Soviet trials of Jewish dissidents, concluding that a truly free country cannot keep a part of its citizens incarcerated against their will.

373. ---: "Soviet treatment of the Holocaust: history's 'memory hole'." *Midstream*, v. 34 # 8 (November, 1988): 16-22.

374. Kort, Michael: "The Soviet economy and the plight of Soviet Jewry." *Midstream*, v. 30 # 6 (June/July, 1984): 12-15.

> # 552. Navrozov, L.: "Solzhenitsyn's world history."

375. Nedava, Joseph: *Trotsky and the Jews*. Philadelphia: The Jewish Publication Society of America, 1972. 299 p.

Examination of Leon Trotsky's attitude toward Jews, Judaism, and the Jewish question. Nedava studies the subject chronologically, dividing Trotsky's attitude into four different eras: before 1914, when Trotsky advocated assimilation; 1914 to 1926, when Trotsky ignored the problem; 1926 to 1932, when Trotsky began to express doubts about Marxist-Leninist Jewish policy; and from 1932 to 1940, when Nazism forced Trotsky to turn to a more positive attitude toward Jewish national identity. Nedava admits that Trotsky spent most of his life attempting to escape from his own Judaism, but the world-wide rise of antisemitism forced him to reassess his position.

> # 325. Pinkus, B.: "Extra-territorial national minorities."

376. Pinkus, Benjamin: *The Jews of the Soviet Union: the history*

*of a national minority*. New York: Cambridge University Press, 1988. 397 p.

Survey of modern Soviet Jewry. Almost exclusively focused on political history, Pinkus concentrates on national and ethnic issues relating to Soviet Jewry. Each section also includes documents further elucidating his points. Secondary focus is on Jewish cultural history and on the relations between Soviet Jews and their environment. Divided chronologically, the lion's share of the book is devoted to the Stalinist era.

377. Rabkin, Yakov M.: "The Soviet Jewish revival." *Midstream*, v. 28 # 8 (October, 1982): 43-50.

> # 1015. Ro'i, Y.: *Struggle for Soviet Jewish emigration*.

378. Sawyer, Thomas E.: *The Jewish minority in the Soviet Union*. Boulder, CO: Westview Press, 1979. 353 p.

Historical survey of Soviet treatment of Jews in both theory and practice. Primarily focusing on civic status, Sawyer views antisemitism as a subtheme. Most of the book reviews the post-Khrushchev era, although Sawyer includes both Leninist and Stalinist policies. The book culminates in an analysis of the Jewish emigration issue from 1948 to 1978.

379. Schnall, David J.: "Soviet Jewry: malaise within the movement." *Midstream*, v. 26 # 4 (April, 1980): 8-13.

380. Schwarz, Solomon M.: *The Jews in the Soviet Union*. Syracuse, NY: Syracuse University Press, 1951. 380 P.

Political study on the status of Soviet Jewry. Concentrates on the Stalinist era. Schwarz analyses Stalin's policy toward Jews and explains why antisemitism has remained a feature in Russian life. Now superseded by more recent studies, the book is still a classic and remains worth reading.

381. Szajkowski, Zosa: *An illustrated sourcebook of Russian antisemitism 1881-1978*. New York: Ktav Publishing House,

1979/1980. 478 p.

Illustrated collection of ephemera and sources on Russian and Soviet antisemitism. Volume I, *Nineteenth Century*, covers the period from 1881 to 1903; Volume II, *Twentieth Century*, covers 1903 to 1978. Of special interest in Volume II are Chapters 5-8, which respectively deal with the Civil War, emigration, Soviet antisemitism, and the White and Red terror. The wealth of different materials collated by Szajkowski exemplifies the rich source material awaiting intensive historical study.

382. Weinberg, Henry H.: "Soviet Jewry: faith and defiance." *Midstream*, v. 33 # 7 (August/September, 1987): 11-14.

### 6. Muslims

383. Ali, Sheikh R.: "The Muslim minority in the Soviet Union." *Current History*, v. 78 # 456 (April, 1980): 175-177, 186.

384. Behbehani, Hashim S. H.: *The Soviet Union and Arab nationalism, 1917-1966*. London/New York: KPI, 1986. 252 p.

385. Bennigsen, Alexandre: "Mullahs, Mujahidin, and Soviet Muslims." *Problems of Communism*, v. 33 # 6 (November/December, 1984): 28-44.

386. ---: "Soviet Muslims and the world of Islam." *Problems of Communism*, v. 29 # 2 (March/April, 1980): 38-51.

387. --- and Chantal Lamercier-Quelquejoy: *Islam in the Soviet Union*. New York: Praeger, 1967. 272 p.

Investigates the state of national, ethnic, and religious identification among the Soviet Union's large Muslim population. Despite the title, religious issues are given only partial attention: the book's primary focus is the regional nationalism that has grown in the USSR's Muslim republics.

388. --- and S. Enders Wimbush: *Muslims of the Soviet empire: a*

*guide*. Bloomington: Indiana University Press, 1986. 294 p.

History and guide to the Muslim minorities in the USSR. The book is divided into two parts: Part I offers a chronological review of Muslims in the territories that eventually became the USSR, while Part II surveys Muslims geographically. Both sections include extensive citations of statistical material which, in effect, make the book's scope encyclopedic.

389. Crisotomo, Rosemarie: "The Muslims in the Soviet Union." *Current History*, v. 81 # 477 (October, 1982): 327-330, 339-340.

390. Ro'i, Yaacov: "The task of creating the new Soviet man: 'atheistic propaganda' in the Soviet Muslim areas." *Soviet Studies*, v. 36 # 1 (January, 1984): 26-44.

391. Wheeler, Geoffrey: *Racial problems in Soviet Muslim Asia* (second edition). New York: Oxford University Press, 1962. 67 p.

**7. Other Nationalities**

392. Balzer, Marjorie M.: "Ethnicity without power: the Siberian Khanty in Soviet society." *Slavic Review*, v. 42 # 4 (Winter, 1983): 633-648.

393. Bruchis, Michael: "The language policy of the CPSU and the linguistic situation in Soviet Moldavia." *Soviet Studies*, v. 36 # 1 (January, 1984): 108-126.

394. Glaskow, W. G.: *History of the Cossacks*. New York: Robert Speller and Sons, 1972. 163 p.

Sociological history of the Don Cossacks, written by a White Russian émigré officer of Cossack origins. Ends his account with the 1920s and Cossack bolshevization. Glaskow does not deal with Cossack collaboration with the Nazis in World War II, nor with the treatment of Cossacks in the postwar years.

395. Gleason, Gregory: "Fealty and loyalty: informal authority

structures in Soviet Asia." *Soviet Studies*, v. 43 # 4 (1991): 613-628.

> # 312. Heitman, S.: *Third Soviet emigration.*

396. Kirby, E. Stuart: "The Soviet Far east: a broad view." *International Affairs*, v. 47 # 1 (January, 1971): 63-78.

397. Lane, Cristel O.: "Socio-political accomodation and religious decline: the case of the Molokan sect in Soviet society." *Comparative Studies in Society and History*, v. 17 # 2 (April, 1975): 221-237.

> # 742. Lane, D.: "Ethnic stratification in Soviet Kazakhstan."

398. Liely, Helmut: "Shepherds and reindeer Nomads in the Soviet Union." *Soviet Studies*, v. 31 # 3 (July, 1979): 401-416.

399. Livezeanu, Irina: "Urbanization in a low key and linguistic change in Soviet Moldavia." *Soviet Studies*, v. 33 # 3 (July, 1981): 327-351; # 4 (October, 1981): 573-592.

> # 201. Lubin, N.: "Women in Soviet Central Asia."

> # 320. Manning, C. A.: "Soviet Union and the Slavs."

400. Mars, Gerald and Yochanan Altman: "The cultural bases of Soviet Georgia's second economy." *Soviet Studies*, v. 35 # 4 (October, 1983): 546-560.

401. North, Robert N.: "The development of Soviet Asia." *Current History*, v. 77 # 430 (October, 1977): 123-127, 136-138.

> # 266. ---: "Soviet northern development."

402. Parsons, J. W. R.: "National integration in Soviet Georgia." *Soviet Studies*, v. 34 # 4 (October, 1982): 547-569.

> # 325. Pinkus, B.: "Extra-territorial national minorities."

403. Pool, Jonathan: "Developing the Soviet Turkic tongues: the

language of the politics of languge." *Slavic Review*, v. 35 # 3 (September, 1976): 425-442.

404. Rywkin, Michael: "Central Asia and Soviet manpower." *Problems of Communism*, v. 28 # 1 (January/February, 1979): 1-13.

405. Sheehy, Ann: "Some aspects of regional development in Soviet Central Asia." *Slavic Review*, v. 31 # 3 (September, 1972): 555-563.

406. Shorish, M. Mobin: "The pedagogical, linguistic, and logistical problems of teaching Russian to the local Soviet Central Asians." *Slavic Review*, v. 35 # 3 (September, 1976): 443-462.

407. Silver, Brian: "Bilungualism and maintenance of the mother tongue in Soviet Central Asia." *Slavic Review*, v. 35 # 3 (September, 1976): 406-424.

408. Suh, Dae-Sook (ed.): *Koreans in the Soviet Union*. Honolulu: Center for Korean Studies, University of Hawaii, 1987. 138 p.

Examination of the history of ethnic Koreans in the Soviet Union's Pacific maritime provinces. Two of the five articles deal with historical issues, while two others review cultural and ethnic problems. The last article addresses the political attitudes of Soviet Koreans toward the Korean People's Democratic Republic (North Korea).

CONTENTS: T. Hara: The Korean movement in the Russian maritime provine, 1905-1922 / H. Wada: Koreans in the Soviet Far East, 1917-1937 / Y. S. Chey: Soviet Koreans and their culture in the USSR / H. Kimura: Korean minorities in Soviet Central Asia and Kazakhstan / D.S. Suh: Soviet Koreans and North Korea.

409. Taagepera, Rein: "Soviet collectivization of Estonian agriculture: the deportation phase." *Soviet Studies*, v. 32 # 3 (July, 1980): 379-397.

410. Vardys, Stanley: "The problem of nationality: modernization and Baltic nationalism." *Problems of Communism*, v. 24 # 5 (September/ October, 1975): 32-48.

## C. IDEOLOGIES AND INSTITUTIONS

### 1. Overviews

411. Agursky, Mikhail: *The third Rome: National Bolshevism in the USSR*. Boulder, CO: Westview Press, 1987. 426 p.

Investigation of the National Bolshevist concept as it applied to the Soviet Union. Agursky defines national bolshevism as an etatist philosophy whose sole purpose was to legitimize the Soviet state. The core of the book is an analysis of National Bolshevik ideologies that fused xenophobic nationalism with a Marxist-Leninist veneer. Inter alia Agursky deals with the Jewish problem and concludes that antisemitism is merely one facet of National Bolshevist xenophobia. The only lacuna is an analysis of parallel national bolshevik ideologies -- especially as developed in Germany in 1922-1923.

412. Alexandrov, Victor: *The Kremlin, nerve-centre of Russian history*. New York: St. Martin's Press, 1963. 335 p.

413. Anisimov, Oleg: "The Soviet citizen -- a profile." *Russian Review*, v. 10 # 1 (January, 1951): 15-25.

414. Aronsfeld, C. C.: "Soviet propaganda: Hitler and the Zionists." *Midstream*, v. 31 # 9 (November, 1985): 13-16.

Posits that a virtual fountain of venomous Soviet anti-Israel (and anti-Jewish) propaganda, diligently espoused by all branches of government within the USSR, distorts the meaning of the Holocaust by equating Zionism with Nazism.

> # 982. Bolsover, G. H.: "Soviet ideology and propaganda."

415. Brumberg, Abraham (ed.): *In quest of justice: protest and dissent in the Soviet Union today*. New York: Frederick A. Praeger, 1970. 477 p.

Compilation of *samizdat* sources, most of which appeared in

*Problems of Communism* in 1968. The documents may be said to fall into three categories: letters to Soviet leaders protesting bureaucratic caprice, transcripts of trials or police investigations of dissidents, and literature that was distributed covertly. Each of the documents is preceeded by a brief commentary, while explanatory notes add to the usefulness of this dramatic anthology.

416. Clews, John C.: *Communist propaganda techniques*. New York: Praeger, 1964. 326 p.

Surveys the Soviet use of propaganda. Both external and internal propaganda are included. Clews scores the cynicism of Soviet propagandists and explores the use of "front" organizations in furthering Soviet goals. A provocative early analysis that still has much to offer in the way of unusual insights.

417. Evans, Alfred B., Jr.: "The decline of developed socialism? some trends in recent Soviet ideology." *Soviet Studies*, v. 38 # 1 (January, 1986): 1-23.

418. ---: "Developed socialism in Soviet ideology." *Soviet Studies*, v. 29 # 3 (July, 1977): 409-428.

419. Gaucher, Roland (comp.): *Opposition in the USSR, 1917-1967* (translated from Russian by Charles L. Markman). New York: Funk & Wagnalls, 1969. 547 p.

Collects a variety of anti-Soviet sources covering half a century of opposition. Divides the subject by period and by the opponents' political orientation. Some of the sources cited include: Whites, Mensheviks, and Socialist Revolutionaries in the Lenin era; *Kulaks*, Ukrainian nationalists, and religious leaders in the Stalin era; and the general *samizdat* that arose after the Khrushchev era.

420. Heller, Michael: "The lure of 'National Bolshevism'." *Midstream*, v. 30 # 2 (February, 1984): 52-55.

421. Malia, Martin E.: *The Soviet tragedy: a history of socialism in Russia*. New York: The Free Press, 1992. 216 p.

Beginning with the Bolshevik Revolution of October 1917, Malia reviews three major transformations in Soviet communism: war communism, New Economic Program communism, and Stalinism. Less attention is devoted to the post-Stalin years, although Malia does review how *glasnost* would fail to reform the Soviet Union. In essence, he attributes communism's failure to the utopian elements contained in its quest for a perfect society. Malia's conclusion predicts the Soviet Union's eventual collapse, although he could not foresee its dissolution and replacement with the Commonwealth of Independent States.

422. Mamatey, Victor S.: *Soviet Russian imperialism*. Princeton, NJ: Van Nostrand, 1964. 192 p.

Uses the concept of imperialism to analyze Soviet national behavior internally and externally. Internally, Soviet actions have been little more than the Russification policies adopted by the Tsarist regime. These policies have been pursued consistently, to the detriment of minority nations. Similarly, external Soviet policies have been dedicated to increasing the spatial area of the Russian empire, again in continuing Tsarist expansionist policies.

> # 470. Odom, W. E.: "Soviet military: the party connection."

423. Pallot, Judith: "Rural settlement planning in the USSR." *Soviet Studies*, v. 31 # 2 (April, 1979): 214-230.

> #231. Schapiro, L.: "The International Department of the CPSU."

424. Unger, Aryeh L.: "Political participation in the USSR: YCL and CPSU." *Soviet Studies*, v. 33 # 1 (January, 1981): 107-124.

425. White, Stephen: "The effectiveness of political propaganda in the USSR." *Soviet Studies*, v. 32 # 3 (July, 1980): 323-348.

### 2. The Bureaucracy

426. Armstrong, John A.: *The Soviet bureaucratic elite: a case study of the Ukrainian apparatus*. New York: Praeger, 1959. 174 p.

Studies the career patterns of mid-level members of the Communist party apparat in the Ukraine from 1938 to 1957.

> #51 ---: "Tsarist and Soviet elite administrators."

427. Azrael, Jeremy R.: *Managerial power and Soviet politics*. Cambridge, MA: Harvard University Press, 1966. 258 p.

> # 1020. Clemens, W. C.: "The Soviet world faces West."

428. Fairbanks, Charles H., Jr. and Susan A. Thronton: "Soviet decision making and bureaucratic representation: evidence from the Smolensk archive and an American comparison." *Soviet Studies*, v. 42 # 4 (October, 1990): 627-654.

429. Gregory, Paul R.: "Soviet bureau behavior: *Khozyaistvenniki* and *Apparatchiki*." *Soviet Studies*, v. 41 # 4 (October, 1989): 511-525.

430. Hough, Jerry F.: *The Soviet prefects*. Cambridge, MA: Harvard University Press, 1969.

Detailed study of the relationship between local Communist Party organization and national bureaucracy. Thoroughly embraces Soviet economic and political organization, including industrial management.

431. Miller, Robert F.: "The role of the Communist party in Soviet research and development." *Soviet Studies*, v. 37 # 1 (January, 1985): 31-59.

432. Oliver, James H.: "Turnover and family circles in Soviet administration." *Slavic Review*, v. 32 # 3 (September, 1973): 527-545.

Argues that rapid turnover of bureaucratic positions is not designed to prevent creation of networks at lower level.

433. Rigby, T. H.: "Staffing USSR incorporated: the origins of the *nomenklatura* system." *Soviet Studies*, v. 40 # 4 (October, 1988): 523-537.

434. Stuart, Robert C.: "Women in Soviet rural management." *Slavic Review*, v. 38 # 4 (December, 1979): 603-613.

435. Vidmer, Richard F.: "Soviet studies of organization and management: a 'jungle' of competing views." *Slavic Review*, v. 40 # 3 (Fall, 1981): 404-422.

436. Yanev, George: "Bureaucracy as culture: a comment." *Slavic Review*, v. 41 # 1 (Spring, 1982): 104-111.

### 3. The Legal System

437. Berman, Harold J.: *Justice in the USSR: an interpretation of Soviet law* (revised edition) New York: Random House/Vintage Books, 1963. 322 p.

438. Conquest, Robert: *Justice and the legal system in the USSR.* New York: Frederick A. Praeger, 1968. 152 p.

439. Fox, Irving K. (ed.): *Water resources law and policy in the Soviet Union.* Madison: University of Wisconsin Press, 1971. 256 p.

Explores water resource policy in the Soviet Union from a legislative perspective. Based on translated versions of key Russian texts, including the "Principles of Water Law of the USSR and Union Republics" enacted by the Supreme Soviet in 1970.

440. Grzybowski, Kazimierz: *Soviet public international law: doctrines and diplomatic practice.* Durham, NC: Rule of Law Press, 1970. 544 p.

Chronicles the development of Soviet international law theory from 1917 to 1967. Primarily composed of key documents on the subject, the book includes Grzybowski's extensive excurses, footnotes, and bibliographic references. In addition to standard topics, Grzybowski also includes discussions on Soviet theory on the law of sea, air, and space.

441. Hazard, John N., Isaac Shapiro, and Peter B. Maggs (eds.):

*The Soviet legal system: contemporary documentation and historical commentary* (second edition). Dobbs Ferry, NY: Oceana Publications, 1969. 687 p.

Collection of cases from Soviet domestic law, divided into three categories: the state and citizens; Soviet Socialist administration; and legal rights and obligations of citizens. Inter alia a wide range of laws and judicial issues are elucidated. Cases are cited in detail and include a commentary by the authors.

442. --- et al: *The Soviet legal system: the law in the 1980s*. New York: Columbia University Press, 1984. 424 p.

Selected texts in twenty-three chapters elucidating social and legal problems facing the Soviet judiciary during the 1980s and the legislative response to those problems.

> #169. Huskey, E.: "Specialists in the Soviet Communist party."

443. Juviler, Peter H.: *Revolutionary law and order: politics and social change in the USSR*. New York: The Free Press, 1976. 274 p.

History of Soviet law and the Soviet judiciary from 1917 to the 1970s. In order to provide background, Juviler begins his survey with Tsar Alexander IIs reform of the Imperial Law Code in 1864. Juviler reviews the state of human rights in Russia at any given period. Thus, an important subtheme of his book is dissidents' treatment.

444. Lampert, Nick: "Law and order in the USSR: the case of economic and official crime." *Soviet Studies*, v. 36 # 3 (July, 1984): 366-385.

445. Makepeace, R. W.: *Marxist ideology and Soviet criminal law*. Totowa, NJ: Barnes & Noble, 1980. 319 p.

Studies the development of Soviet juridical theory since 1917. Makepeace also compares Soviet legal practice to Marxist theory. Notes that there are wide divergences between the theory of a classless society and the practice in the modern Soviet Union. Of special importance is Makepeace's analysis of the judiciary under Stalin. Not only did the promulgated legislation have no relation to Marxist (or even Marxist-Leninst) ideology, but the "laws" themselves often appeared unrelated to any specific societal ill.

446. Slider, Darrell: "Reforming the workplace: the 1983 Soviet law on labor collectives." *Soviet Studies*, v. 37 # 2 (April, 1985): 173-183.

447. Solomon, Peter H., Jr.: "The case of the vanishing acquittal: informal norms and the practice of Soviet criminal justice." *Soviet Studies*, v. 39 # 4 (October, 1987): 531-555.

448. Van Den Berg, Ger P.: "The Soviet Union and the death penalty." *Soviet Studies*, v. 35 # 2 (April, 1983): 154-174.

449. Zile, Zigurds L. (ed.): *Ideas and forces in Soviet legal history: a reader in the Soviet state and law*. New York: Oxford University Press, 1992. 512 p.

Anthology of translations of over 350 key documents on the Soviet legal system. Illuminates the role that law has played within the Soviet system, especially in the Leninist and Stalinist eras, when the system was presumed to be above the law. Includes both primary and secondary sources, utilizing an exploration of the past as the only means to understand the present.

### 4. The Military

450. Aspaturian, Vernon V.: "The Soviet military-industrial complex: does it exist?" *Journal of International Affairs*, v. 26 # 1 (1972): 1-28.

451. Boyd, Alexander: *The Soviet air force since 1918*. New York: Stein and Day/Publishers, 1977. 260 p.

Comprehensively studying the rise of Soviet air power since 1918. Boyd bases his book on an extensive list of sources which includes dozens of Soviet works not previously available in the United

States. A minor factor in Soviet military planning under Lenin, air power became a crucial feature of Russian military planning under Stalin. Throughout World War II the air arm remained a ground support force. However, afterward the Soviet air force became an independent force tasked with a vital strategic role. Moreover, in the 1950s and 1960s the Soviets achieved several important innovations, among them the introduction of the first swept-wing fighter to enter combat (the MIG-15) and the first Mach-3 jet aircraft (the Ye-266, a precursor of the MIG-25). Although the development of Soviet naval power commanded greater attention, Boyd argues cogently that the Soviet air force is militarily the most important branch of the Soviet armed forces.

452. Burgess, William H. (ed.): *Inside Spetsnaz: Soviet special operations, a critical analysis*. Novato, CA: Presidio Press, 1990. 308 p.

Anthology assessing the real power of Soviet special forces. During the Cold War the very term *Spetsnaz* elicited a nearly hysterical response fron NATO planners and sensationalist journalists. Instead of sensationalism, the authors offer balanced evaluations of current Soviet special force capabilities based on historical precedents (primarily World War II) and contemporary sources.

CONTENTS: W. H. Burgess: Assessing *Spetsnaz* / R. D. Smith: Western misperceptions / J. J. Dziak: Historical precedents / O. A. Lock: The Spanish Civil War / W. H. Burgess: *Spetsnaz* engineers in the Great Patriotic War: an overview / J. F. Gebhardt and W. H. Burgess: The Far North origin of naval *Spetsnaz* / J. F. Gebhardt: The Arctic: Petsamo-Kirkenes, 7 to 30 October 1944 / W. H. Burgess and J. F. Gebhardt: Manchuria, 1945 / K. Amundsen: *Spetsnaz* and Soviet Far North strategy / J. H. Merritt: Prague to Kabul / D. C. Isby: Afghanistan / W. H. Burgess: *Spetsnaz* and the deep operation / J. Shortt: Organization, capabilities, and counter measures.

453. Cooper, Julian: "The military and higher education in the USSR." *Annals*, v. 502 (March, 1989): 108-119.

454. Cooper, Leo: *The political economy of Soviet military power.* Houndmills, UK: Macmillan, 1989. 263 p.

Investigates Russian defense expenditure during the Cold War as viewed by the Soviets. In order to place military expenditure into context, Cooper also analyzes Soviet national security policy and strategic thinking. Chapter One places contemporary Soviet strategy into historical context. Information in the later chapters tends to diffuse and some of the material cited is actually irrelevant to the subject. In contrast, Cooper's discussion of the Gorbachev era is quite useful. Although Cooper offers no predicitons regarding future trends, his suggestion that the way to end the Cold War is to engage the USSR in an interdependent relationship with the rest of the world appears to be correct.

> # 983. Courtney, A.: "The background of Russian sea-power."

> #287. Després, L.& K. Khinchuk: "Soviet agriculture."

455. Gabriel, Richard A.: *The new Red Legions* (2 vols.). Westport, CT: Greenwood Press, 1980. 534 p.

Important sociological investigation into the Red Army, based on interviews with 161 Jewish émigrés. The respondents reflect every region of the USSR and every rank level within the army, but insufficient data compelled Gabriel to leave out the Soviet navy and air force. Based on his reviews -- the complete questionaire and all the responses are reproduced in Volume 2 -- Gabriel calls for a new evaluation of Soviet military capabilities. In particular, he noted the low morale, medicore leadership, and ethnic tensions that hampered the Soviet army in Afghanistan (a subject not directly covered in the book) and which led to the breakup of the united Commonwealth of Independent States army.

456. Glantz, David M.: *The military strategy of the Soviet Union: a history*. London: Frank Cass, 1991. 450 p.

Surveys the means by which the Soviet military has articulated and implemented its strategic and operational plans. Organized chronologically, although mainly emphasizing the years after World War II. Basing his position on then newly-released Soviet documents, Glantz also offers a tentative assessment of that nation's probable future strategy. Although Glantz could not anticipate the collapse of the USSR, some of his predictions regarding the scaling back of Soviet military operations have proven correct.

457. Gorshkov, Sergei G.: *Red star rising at sea* (translated from Russian by Theodore P. Neely). Annapolis, MD: U.S. Naval Institute Press, 1974. 150 p. [PB]

Authoritative review of Soviet naval strategy, written by the commander-in-chief of the Soviet navy. Gorshkov's review is strictly chronological, with a commentary appended by members from the United States navy for each chapter. Admiral Elmo Zumwalt's introduction and conclusion help place the chapters into context. A firm advocate of a blue-water navy, Gorshkov may be considered the father of the contemporary Soviet, Russian, and Republican fleet.

> # 582. Gross, N.: "Youth and the army in the USSR."

458. Hansen, James H.: *Correlation of forces: four decades of Soviet military development*. New York: Praeger, 1987. 236 p.

459. Hasegawa, Tsuyoshi: "Soviets on nuclear-war fighting." *Problems of Communism*, v. 35 # 4 (July/August, 1986): 68-79.

460. Jacobs, Walter D.: "Soviet strategic effectiveness." *Journal of International Affairs*, v. 26 # 1 (1972): 60-72.

461. Jones, David R.: "Russian tradition and Soviet military policy." *Current History*, v. 82 # 484 (May, 1983): 197-200, 230-232.

462. Jones, Ellen: *The Red Army and society: a sociology of the Soviet military*. London: Allen & Unwin, 1985. 280 p.

Sociological study of the Soviet military focusing on manpower and organizational issues. The book is fully documented, including citations from numerous Soviet sources, and its journalistic style is appropriate both for non-experts and scholars.

463. Lee, William T.: "The politico-military-industrial complex of the USSR." *Journal of International Affairs*, v. 26 # 1 (1972): 73-86.

464. Leebaert, Derek (ed.): *Soviet military thinking*. Winchester, MA: Allen & Unwin, 1981. 300 p.

Thorough analysis of Soviet strategical and tactical thinking, written by a panel of experts on the Soviet military. Offers a broad comparative perspective, which places Soviet military thought into the context of the Cold War.

CONTENTS: R. Bathurst: Two languages of war / D. Leebaert: The context of Soviet military thinking / F. W. Ermarth: Contrasts in American and Soviet strategic thought / S. Sienkiewicz: Soviet nuclear doctrine and the prospects for strategic arms control / R. Garthoff: Mutual deterrence, parity and strategic arms limitation in Soviet policy / N. Leites: The Soviet style of war / M. MccGwire: Soviet naval doctrine and strategy / Ch. Jones: Soviet military doctrine and Warsaw Pact exercises / D. Holloway: Doctrine and technology in Soviet armaments.

465. Maddock, Roland T.: *The political economy of Soviet defense spending*. Basingstoke, UK: Macmillan, 1988. 224 p.

Brief investigation of Soviet defense spending. Maddock's first two chapters place Soviet defense expenditure into political and operational context. The remainder of the book offers insight into the impact of defense spending on the Soviet economy. Of special importance is the fact that Maddock's entire study is tentative: since Soviet defense spending is unknown -- in both real and proportional terms -- his entire effort is based on a series of estimates. Nevertheless, Maddock elucidates a significant element in the history of the Communist regime.

466. Mahoney, Shane E.: "Defensive doctrine: the crisis in Soviet military thought." *Slavic Review*, v. 49 # 3 (Fall, 1990): 398-408.

467. MccGwire, Michael: *Military objectives in Soviet foreign policy*. Washington, DC: The Brookings Institution, 1987. 530 p.

Analyzes the development of Soviet military strategy in the postwar era. Also investigates patterns of Soviet military procurement. The breadth of his analysis makes the book compelling and it has become a classic account of Soviet military policy. MccGwire has discovered a consistency in Soviet military thinking about the means to wage war and the goals of such a war. Although framed in purely defensive terms -- as a way to preserve socialism against the encroachment of capitalism -- the Soviets have always emphasized rapid offensive operations. Moreover, despite the buildup of ICBMs, Mccgwire argues that the Soviets consistently pursued a conventional war strategy. This strategy rested on the assumption that the United States would not respond to an exclusively conventional attack with nuclear weapons. It followed, therefore, that the Red Army had to plan for a World War II style *blitzkrieg* that would defeat NATO forces before the United States could deploy its economic might, leaving American leaders with three options: (1) nuclear omnicide, (2) aquiesence in a Soviet dominated Europe, or (3) a protracted conventional campaign that would prove too costly for American public opinion.

468. Moynahan, Brian: *The claws of the bear: a history of the Soviet armed forces from 1917 to the present*. Boston: Houghton Mifflin / London: Hutchinson, 1989. 468 p.

Fast-paced popular history of the world's largest army. Describes the Red Army's origins in the 1917 Revolutions, its evolution under Stalin, and its apotheosis in the Russo-German war. Primary emphasis is on post-World War II, although the Great Patriotic War's many major battles are described in great detail. Relies heavily on published sources. Moynahan posits that the Red Army is the Soviet Union's predominant institution and a force to be reckoned with.

469. Odom, William E.: "The militarization of Soviet society." *Problems of Communism*, v. 25 # 5 (September/October, 1976): 34-51.

470. ---: "The Soviet military: the party connection." *Problems of Communism*, v. 22 # 5 (September/October, 1973): 12-26.

471. Rosefielde, Steven: "Soviet defense spending: the contribution of the new accountancy." *Soviet Studies*, v. 42 # 1 (January, 1990): 59-80.

472. Scott, Harriet F. and William F. Scott: *The armed forces of the USSR*. Boulder, CO: Westview Press, 1979. 439 p.

Authoritative analysis of the strategy and operational doctrine of the Soviet armed forces. After a brief historical survey of the Red Army from 1917 to 1945, the Scotts examine the changes in Soviet military science in the nuclear age. In addition, the Scotts study the capabilities of each branch of the armed forces. A final chapter weighs the military capability of the Soviet forces in a number of potential operational scenarios.

473. Shultz, Richard H. and Roy Godson: *Desinformatsia: active measures in Soviet strategy*. Washington, DC: Pergamon Brassey's, 1984. 210 p.

Focuses on the active measures used by the USSR against the West to further the Soviet political agenda. Shultz and Godson identify two types of active measures: covert support for "neutral" front groups combined with the publication (or release) of disinformation in order to discredit adversaries. The two tactics come together, for example, in some of the movements in NATO states that argued for unilateral disarmament.

474. Spielman, Karl F.: "Defense industrialists in the USSR." *Problems of Communism*, v. 25 # 5 (September/October, 1976): 52-69.

475. Steinberg, Dmitri: "Trends in Soviet military expenditure." *Soviet Studies*, v. 42 # 4 (October, 1990): 675-700.

476. Tyusevich, S. A.: *Soviet armed forces: a history of their organizational development*. Washington, DC: United States Government Printing Office, 1984. 516 p. [PB]

477. Yinon, Oded: "The Soviet doctrine of total war." translated from Hebrew by Gertrude Hirschler. *Midstream*, v. 27 # 10 (December, 1981): 7-11.

### 5. The KGB and Internal Security

478. Andrew, Christopher and Oleg Gordievsky: *KGB: the inside story of its foreign operations from Lenin to Gorbachev*. New York: Harper-Collins Publishers, 1990. 776 p.

The first history of the Soviet secret intelligence agency to use certain archival material made available shortly before the end of the Communist era. Organized as a chronological survey of developments from Lenin's *Cheka* (established 1917) until the mid-1980s, the work significantly includes the memory of Colonel Oleg Gordievsky, the former London station chief of the KGB who also wrote secret internal histories of KGB activities. Providing the most extensive detail to date on KGB active measures in the West, it includes a list of 144 residents (agents) identified by location and period of activity (some going back to World War II). Details on many specific KGB operations are also featured, such as Trotsky's assassination in Mexico City by Stalinist agents on August 21, 1940. Written as both a history and a warning against complacency toward the West, *KGB: the inside story* also details Soviet intelligence failures, resulting in a balanced evaluation of the KGB's activities.

479. Bittman, Ladislav: *The KGB and Soviet disinformation*. McLean, VA: Pergamon/Brassey's, 1985. 227 p.

Exposé of the KGB campaign to sow disinformation and thereby gain the upper hand in relation to the United States. Most of Bittman's examples deal with sub-Saharan Africa and Latin America. Despite the potential pitfalls of seeing a conspiracy at every turn, Bittman is judicious in his evaluations and tries to differentiate between dissent and treason. On the other hand, it is not clear how Bittman would evaluate the events between 1990 and 1992, as they seem to imply that at least some of the claims made by anti-Communist prophets during the early- and mid-1980s were not completely correct in their dire predictions.

480. Deriabin, Peter: *Watchdogs of terror: Russian bodyguards from the Tsars to the Commissars*. New Rochelle, NY: Arlington House, 1972. 448 p.

Places the history of the Russian and Soviet security services. Primarily focused on the role played by these agencies in protecting Russian officials but also notes the differences between the Russian guards and parallel agencies in the West. The appendixes add data to the main text, clarifying which organizations are (or were) responsible for specific activities. Deriabin's book thus provides insight into aspects of secret police history not normally seen by most Westerners.

481. Freemantle, Brian: *KGB*. New York: An Owl Book/Holt, Rinehart and Winston, 1984. 192 p. [PB]

Journalistic history of the KGB from its origins in 1917 (as the *Cheka*). Too brief to be more than an introduction, Freemantle, nevertheless, does manage to include a number of interesting assessments. An appendix deals with the fate of Raoul Wallenberg, the Swedish diplomat who was involved in rescuing Budapest's Jews from the Nazis before he disappeared after being taken into Soviet custody in 1945.

482. Heilbrunn, Otto: *The Soviet secret services*. New York: Praeger Publishers, 1956. 216 p.

483. Hingley, Ronald: *The Russian secret police: Muscovite, imperial Russian and Soviet political security operations*. New York: Simon and Schuster, 1970. 313 p.

Surveys the history of Russian and Soviet security services from 1565 to 1970. More than half the book details the Soviet secret services: *Cheka*, GPU, NKVD, and the KGB founded respectively by Lenin, Stalin, and Khrushchev. The chapters develop chronologically. Subjects such as the Stalinist purges, the Katyn massacre, and the Khrushchev thaw are dealt with inter alia. By viewing police issues over a long span, Hingley is able to provide insights into both the changes and the consistencies in Russian and Soviet history.

> # 2006. Penkovsky, O.: *The Penkovsky papers*.

# 4

# Cultural and Intellectual History

## A. OVERVIEWS

484. Baron, Samuel H.: "Plekhanov, Trotsky, and the development of Soviet historiography." *Soviet Studies*, v. 26 # 3 (July, 1974): 380-395.

> # 134. Belasco, M. J.: *The Soviet Union*.

485. Brown, J. A., Jr.: "Public opinion in the Soviet Union." *Russian Review*, v. 9 # 1 (January, 1950): 37-44.

486. Downing, John: "The intersputnik system and Soviet television." *Soviet Studies*, v. 37 # 4 (October, 1985): 465-483.

487. Enteen, George M.: "Writing party history in the USSR: the case of E. M. Iaroslavskii." *Journal of Contemporary History*, v. 21 # 2 (April, 1986): 321-339.

488. Friedburg, Maurice: "Soviet bibliophiles and their foes: a review article." *Slavic Review*, v. 35 # 4 (December, 1976): 699-714.

489. Grant, Steven A.: "*Obshchina* and *Mir*." *Slavic Review*, v. 35 # 4 (December, 1976): 636-651.

490. Inkeles, Alex and Kent Geiger (eds.): *Soviet society: a book of readings*. Boston: Houghton Mifflin, 1961. 703 p.

> # 462. Jones, E.: *The Red Army and society.*

> # 744. Liber, G.: "Book publishing in the Ukrainian SSR."

491. McCann, James M.: "Beyond the Bug: Soviet Historiography of the Polish-Russian war of 1920." *Soviet Studies*, v. 36 # 4 (October, 1894): 475-493.

492. Mickiewicz, Ellen: *Split signals: television and politics in the Soviet Union*. New York: Oxford University Press, 1988. 304 p.

Considers television's impact on Soviet reform during the Gorbachev era. Primarily based on interviews with Soviet media figures, Mickiewicz also includes an intriguing comparison of Soviet Television during the Chernenko and Gorbachev eras with American news broadcasts during the same years.

> # 748. Miller, M. A.: "Freudian theory under Bolshevik rule."

493. Riordan, James: "Soviet youth: pioneers of change." *Soviet Studies*, v. 40 # 4 (October, 1988): 556-572.

494. ---: *Sport in Soviet society: development of sport and physical education in Russia and the USSR*. New York: Cambridge University Press, 1977. 435 p.

Studies the role of sport in Soviet society. Includes background information on sport in imperial Russia as well. Despite his concentration on physical education in the Soviet school system, Riordan also investigates all other aspects of sports in the USSR.

495. Sinyavsky, Andrei: *Soviet civilization: a cultural history* (translated from Russian by Joanne Turnbull and Nikolai Formozov). New York: Arcade Publishing, 1988, 291 p.

Chronologically organized cultural history of the Soviet Union from Lenin to Gorbachev. The two chapters on Stalin's national-cultural ideology are especially interesting. Written before the transformations that began in 1989, Sinyavsky briefly deals with the impact of *glasnost* and *perestroika* on Soviet culture.

496. Sorlin, Pierre: *The Soviet people and their society: from 1917 to the present* (translated from Russian by Daniel Weissbort). New York: Praeger, 1969. 293 p.

497. Zuzanek, Jiri: "Time-budget trends in the USSR: 1922-1970." *Soviet Studies*, v. 31 # 2 (April, 1979): 188-213.

## B. CULTURAL STUDIES

498. Abramsky, Chimen: "Hebrew incunabula in Leningrad." *Soviet Jewish Affairs*, v. 17 # 1 (Spring, 1987): 53-60.

499. Bachman, John E.: "Recent Soviet historiography of Russian revolutionary populism." *Slavic Review*, v. 29 # 4 (December, 1970): 599-612.

500. Biggart, John: "Bukharin and the origins of the proletarian culture debate." *Soviet Studies*, v. 39 # 2 (April, 1987): 229-246.

501. Booker, Edward E.: "Publishing in the USSR and Yugoslavia." *Annals*, v. 421 (September, 1975): 118-129.

> # 393. Bruchis, M.: "The linguistic situation in Soviet Moldavia."

502. Christian, David: "The supervisory function in Russian and Soviet history." *Slavic Review*, v. 41 # 1 (Spring, 1982): 73-90.

503. Daniels, Robert V.: "Soviet historians prepare for the fiftieth." *Slavic Review*, v. 26 # 1 (March, 1967): 113-118.

504. Deza, Mikhail and Mervyn Matthews: "Soviet theater audiences." *Slavic Review*, v. 34 # 4 (December, 1975): 716-730.

505. Dunlop, John B.: "Soviet cultural politics." *Problems of Communism*, v. 36 # 6 (November/December, 1987): 34-56.

506. Enteen, George M.: "Marxists versus non-Marxists: Soviet historiography in the 1920s." *Slavic Review*, v. 35 # 1 (March, 1976): 91-110.

> # 796. Fitzpatrick, S.: "Culture and politics under Stalin."

507. Fitzpatrick, Sheila: "The emergence of *Glaviskusstvo*: class war on the cultural front, Moscow, 1928-29." *Soviet Studies*, v. 23 # 2 (October, 1971):236-253.

508. Frankel, Jonathan: "Party genealogy and the Soviet historians (1920-1938)." *Slavic Review*, v. 25 # 4 (December, 1966): 563-605.

> # 361. Friedberg, M.: *How things were done in Odessa.*

509. Gaet, Felice D.: "The Soviet film audience: a confidential view." *Problems of Communism*, v. 23 # 1 (January/February, 1974): 56-70.

510. Garrard, John and C. Garrard: "Soviet book hunger." *Problems of Communism*, v. 34 # 5 (September/October, 1985): 72-81.

511. Gorky, Maxim: *Culture and the people*. New York: International Publishers, 1939. 224 p.

Selection of Gorky's essays on social, political, and intellectual problems in the Soviet Union. Most of the essays reflect Gorky's role as a publicist -- and to a degree as a polemicist -- and offer readers another view of the great Soviet literary figure.

512. Guins, George C.: "Soviet culture: old trends and new." *Russian Review*, v. 7 # 1 (Fall, 1947): 24-32.

513. Haney, Jack V.: "The revival of interest in the Russian past in the Soviet Union." *Slavic Review*, v. 32 # 1 (March, 1973): 1-16. Responses with a reply by Haney, pp. 17-44.

514. Heer, Nancy: *Politics and history in the Soviet Union*. Cambridge, MA: Massachusetts Institute of Technology Press, 1971. 319 p.

Analyzes the doctrinal influences of the Communist party on Russian historiography. Chronologically, Heer concentrates on the Khrushchev era from 1956 to 1966 to exemplify the twists and turns in the Party line and their impact on the way history was written in the Soviet Union. Heer notes that in Communist ideology the past is not merely a subject but a portent which can be used to legitimize Party policy.

515. Holmes, Larry E.: "Soviet rewriting of 1917: the case of A. G. Shliapnikov." *Slavic Review*, v. 38 # 2 (June, 1979): 224-242.

516. Kagarlitsky, Boris: *The thinking reed: intellectuals and the Soviet state from 1917 to the present* (translated from Russian by Brian Pearce). London: Verso, 1988. 374 p.

Chronicles the often stormy relationship between the intelligentsia and the Soviet state since the revolution. Kagarlitsky notes that the intellectual climate has changed often over the course of the seventy years reviewed in the book. Since Lenin there have been two eras of intellectual stagnation -- under Stalin and under Brezhnev (1928 to 1953 and 1964 to 1984 respectively) -- and two of intellectual ferment -- during the Khrushchev thaw and since Gorbachev introduced *glasnost* and *perestroika*. One of Kagarlitsky's major subthemes is the importance of *glasnost*: the author himself is an example of the new intellectual freedom he describes, as he was imprisoned in the late 1970s for advancing ideas against the Party line, and an earlier version of the book had to be circulated covertly.

> # 1944. Knight, A.: "Beria and the cult of Stalin."

517. Krupnik, Igor: "Jewish holdings of the Leningrad ethnographic museum." *Soviet Jewish Affairs*." v. 19 # 1 (Spring, 1989): 35-48.

518. Likhachev, Dmitrii S.: *Reflections on Russia*. Boulder, CO: Westview Press, 1991. 150 p.

Collection of Likhachev's essays on historiography and culture under the impact of *glasnost*. Of special importance is the essay on nationalism. Likhachev contrasts patriotism, which he views as a legitimate form of ethnic identification, with xenophobia, which he views as a dangerous form. Important because of Likhachev's position as chairman of the Soviet Cultural Fund, this is the first collection of his writings available to English-language readers.

> # 399. Livezeanu, I. "Linguistic change in Soviet Moldavia."

519. Mazour, Anatole G.: *An outline of modern Russian historiography* (second edition). Princeton, NJ: Van Nostrand, 1958. 200 p.

520. McClelland, James G.: "Utopianism versus revolutionary heroism in Bolshevik policy: the proletarian culture debate." *Slavic Review*, v. 39 # 3 (September, 1980): 403-425.

521. Oinas, Felix J.: "Folklore and politics in the Soviet Union." *Slavic Review*, v. 32 # 1 (March, 1973): 45-58.

522. Remington, Thomas F.: "Politics and professionalism in Soviet journalism." *Slavic Review*, v. 44 # 3 (Fall, 1985): 489-503.

523. Taylor, Richard: "A 'cinema for the millions': Soviet Socialist realism and the problem of film comedy." *Journal of Contemporary History*, v. 18 # 3 (July, 1983): 439-461.

524. Tempest, Richard: "Youth Soviet style." *Problems of Communism*, v. 33 # 3 (May/June, 1984): 60-64.

Studies the culture of contemporary young adults Soviets. Posits that they rely heavily on Western innovations, especially pop-music, disco-dancing, pizza, windsurfing, and yoga.

525. Vucinich, Alexander: *Empire of knowledge: The Academy of Sciences of the USSR (1917-1970)*. Berkeley, CA: University of California Press, 1984. 484 p.

Detailed history of the development of The Soviet Academy of Sciences. Notes that intellectual freedom has not been a hallmark of Soviet history. To the contrary, Soviet scientists have been under continous pressure to conform to an ever-changing Party line. Vucinich concentrates on a number of startling cases, the best-known of which is Trofim Lysenko's dictatorship over the academic study of biology between 1946 and 1953.

## C. LITERATURE

### 1. Analyses of Soviet Literature

526. Alter, Robert: "*Shtetl* and revolution." *Commentary*, v. 59 # 2 (February, 1975): 70-75.

527. Barratt, Andrew and Edith W. Clowes: "Gorky, *glasnost* and *perestroika*: the death of a cultural superhero?" *Soviet Studies*, v. 43 # 6 (1991): 1123-1142.

528. Barzun, Jacques: "Russian politics in the Russian classics." *Commentary*, v. 91 # 5 (May, 1991): 41-47.

529. Dowler, Wayne: "Echoes of *Pochvennichestvo* in Solzhenitsyn's *Ausgust 1914*." *Slavic Review*, v. 34 # 1 (March, 1975): 109-122.

Investigates the ideological background of Solzhenitsyn's literary theory, identifying him with the so-called "Native Soil Movement" of the mid-nineteenth century.

530. Dunham, Vera S.: *In Stalin's time: middleclass values in Soviet fiction*. New York: Cambridge University Press, 1976. 283 p.

Focuses attention on the literature of the Stalinist era. Dunham operates from a revisionist perspective, arguing that Stalinist literature did not adhere to a "Socialist realism," as has been hithertofore assumed. Instead, she defines Russian literature in the Stalinist era as reflecting middle class values: efficiency, honesty, material progress, and, to a degree, greed. The weakness of Dunham's thesis lies in her use of terminology although her implication -- that Stalin represented both a bourgeoise and subsequently fascist forms of communism -- seems compelling.

531. Eberstadt, Nick: "The latest myth about the Soviet Union."

*Commentary*, v. 83 # 5 (May, 1987): 17-27.

532. Emiot, Israel: *The Birobidzhan affair: a Yiddish writer in Siberia* (translated from Yiddish by Max Rosenfeld). Philadelphia: The Jewish Publication Society, 1981. 220 p.

Memoir of the "black years of Soviet Jewry" by a *Yiddish* author who moved to Birobidzhan. Emiot was later arrested and sent to a Siberian *gulag*. Offering a sensitive personal perspective, the book is also a poignant reminder of the individual element to great historical movements.

533. Fanger, Donald: "Solzhenitsyn: art and foreign matter." *Problems of Communism*, v. 21 # 3 (May/June, 1972): 57-63.

534. Frankel: Edith: "The Tvardovsky controversy." *Soviet Studies*, v. 34 # 4 (October, 1982): 601-615.

535. Friedberg, Maurice: "Soviet letters under Brezhnev." *Problems of Communism*, v. 29 # 3 (May/June, 1980): 53-64.

536. Gerschenkorn, Alexander: "Recent Soviet novels: some impressions." *Soviet Studies*, v. 30 # 4 (October, 1978): 443-465.

537. Giblian, George: "The urban theme in recent Soviet Russian prose: notes toward a typology." *Slavic Review*, v. 37 # 1 (March, 1978): 40-50.

538. Goldberg, Anatol: *Ilya Ehrenburg: writing, politics, and the art of survival*. New York: Viking Press, 1984. 312 p.

Judicious biography of the well-known Russian Jewish author and propagandist, Ilya Ehrenburg. Posits that Ehrenburg was a survivor: he did not have too many dogmatic ideological orientations. This hypothesis permits Goldberg to explain the seeming contradictions in Ehrenburg's life: notably Ehrenburg's apologia for Stalin simultaneous with support for the Khrushchev thaw as well as his Jewish publication during World War II and advocacy of radical assimilation thereafter.

539. Jacobson, Dan: "The example of Solzhenitsyn." *Commentary*, v. 47 # 5 (May, 1969): 81-84.

540. Kain, Richard M.: "The plight of intelligentsia in the Soviet novel." *Russian Review*, v. 2 # 1 (Fall, 1942): 70-79.

541. Karpovich, Michael: "Soviet historical novel." *Russian Review*, v. 5 # 2 (Spring, 1946): 53-63.

542. Katayev, Valentin: *The grass of oblivion: a memoir of literary Russia in the early Soviet days* (translated from Russian by Robert Daglish). New York: McGraw, 1969. 222 p.

543. Kern, Gary: "Solzhenitsyn's portrait of Stalin." *Slavic Review*, v. 33 # 1 (March, 1974): 1-22.

544. Kiziria, Dodona: "Four demons of Valentin Kataev." *Slavic Review*, v. 44 # 4 (Winter, 1985): 627-662.

545. Lampert, Nick: "Social criticism in Soviet drama: the plays of Aleksandr Gelman." *Soviet Studies*, v. 39 # 1 (January, 1987): 101-115.

546. Lewis, Philippa: "Peasant nostalgia in contemporary Russian literature." *Soviet Studies*, v. 28 # 4 (October, 1976): 548-569.

> # 1951. Markish, S.: "The example of Isaac Babel."

> # 1952. ---: "A Russian writer's Jewish fate."

547. Marsh, Rosalind J.: "Soviet fiction and the nuclear debate." *Soviet Studies*, v. 38 # 2 (April, 1986): 248-270.

548. Medvedev, Zhores: *Ten years after Ivan Denisovich* (translated from Russian by H. Steinberg). New York: A. Knopf, 1973. 202 p.

Traces the literary politics connected to Alexander Solzhenitsyn's writings. Also examines Soviet intellectuals' perceptions on the issue of freedom of thought versus subservience to Communist party ideology.

> # 611. Miller, J.: *Jews in Soviet culture.*

549. Monas, Sidney: "*Gulag* and points West." *Slavic Review*, v. 40 # 3 (Fall, 1981): 444-456.

Analysis of Solzhenitsyns *Gulag archipelago* (see # 572); rejoinder by John B. Dunlop and reply by Monas, pp. 457-463.

550. Murphy, A. B.: "Academic life in some recent Soviet fiction." *Soviet Studies*, v. 33 # 3 (July, 1981): 421-432.

551. Navrozov, Lev: "Solzhenitsyn's world history: *August 1914* as a new *Protocols of the elders of Zion.*" *Midstream*, v. 31 # 6 (June/July, 1985): 46-53.

Accuses Nobel laureate of antisemitism. Main focus is on the revised edition of Solzhenitsyn's *August 1914*, which blames the Bolshevik *putsch* on the Jews.

552. O'Connor, Katherine T.: "Boris Pasternak's *My sister -- life*: the book behind the verse." *Slavic Review*, v. 37 # 3 (September, 1978): 399-411.

553. Paterson, Nadya: "Science fiction and fantasy: a prelude to the literature of *glasnost.*" *Slavic Review*, v. 48 # 2 (Summer, 1989): 254-268.

554. Podhoretz, Norman: "The terrible question of Aleksandr Solzhenitsyn." *Commentary*, v. 79 # 2 (February, 1975): 17-24.

Defends Solzhenitsyn against charges of overt antisemitism and anti-democratic leanings.

> # 823. Rosefielde, S.: "Solzhenitsyn's *Gulag archipelago.*"

555. Sandomirsky, Vera: "Soviet war poetry." *Russian Review*, v. 4 # 1 (Fall, 1944): 47-66.

556. Sheldon, Richard: "Viktor Shklovsky and the device of ostensible surrender." *Slavic Review*, v. 34 # 1 (March, 1975): 86-108.

Sheldon argues that Shklovsky used a Communist veneer to get his dissident works published.

557. Shneidman, N. N.: "The Russian classical literary heritage and the basic concept of Soviet literary education." *Slavic Review*, v. 31 # 3 (September, 1972): 626-638.

558. ---: "Soviet theory of literature and the struggle around Dostoevsky in recent Soviet scholarship." *Slavic Review*, v. 34 # 3 (September, 1975): 523-538.

559. Swayze, Harold: *Political control of literature in the USSR, 1946-1959*. Cambridge, MA: Harvard University Press, 1962. 301 p.

560. Szmeruk, Chone: "Jewish literature in the Soviet Union during the Holocaust period to 1948: *Yiddish* publications in the USSR (from the late thirties to 1948)." *Yad Vashem Studies*, v. 4 (1960): 99-134.

561. Windle, Kevin: "The theme of fate in Solzhenitsyn's *August 1914*." *Slavic Review*, v. 31 # 2 (June, 1972): 399-411.

562. Zand, Michael: "The literature of the Mountain Jews of the Caucasus." *Soviet Jewish Affairs*, v. 15 3 2 (May, 1985): 3-22.

### 2. Belles Lettres

563. Babel, Isaac: *Benya Krik, the gangster, and other stories* (ed. by Avrahm Yarmolinsky). New York: Schocken Books, 1979. 150 p.

One of the best-known collections of short stories by Soviet Jewish author and victim of Stalinist purges, Isaac Babel. Focuses on the Jewish underworld of Moldavanka, a Jewish *shtetl*-city in Babel's imagination. Intimately laced within the stories is the author's nostalgia for his people and his compassionate hope that Jewry find a secure haven from persecution and antisemitic violence.

564. Fedayev, A.: *The young guard* (translated from Russian by V. Dutt). Moscow: Foreign Language Publishing House, n.d. 716 p.

Propagandistic novel of the experiences of *Komsomol* members, facing the Nazi onslaught at the front, behind enemy lines, and as members of partisan groups in Nazi-occupied Soviet territory during the Great Patriotic War (World War II).

565. Grossman, Vasily: *Life and fate*. New York: Harper & Row, 1985. 880 p.

Historical novel of the Great Patriotic War, concentrating on the epic struggle at Stalingrad from the fall of 1942 to the spring of 1943.

566. Koestler, Arthur: *Darkness at Noon* (translated from German by Daphne Hardy). New York: Macmillan, 1941. 117 p.

Novelized study of the Stalinist purge trials. The main character, Rubashov, is closely modeled on the figure of Nikolai Bukharin, an early Bolshevik revolutionary and a member of the all exclusive Politburo. Koestler offers an important commentary on the totalitarian mind.

567. Kuznetsov, Anatoly: *Babi Yar: a documentary novel* (translated from Russian by Jacob Guralski). New York: Dial Press, 1967. 399 p.

Documentary historical novel of the massacre of Jews at Babi Yar, a ravine on the outskirts of Kiev. In two days (September 29/30, 1941), the Nazis and their Rumanian and Ukrainian collaborators murdered more than 33,000 Jews from Kiev -- men, women, and children, old and young. Thereafter, the Nazis used Babi Yar as an execution site for numerous other Jews, and an estimated 100,000 Gypsies, Communist officials, and resisters. Kuznetsov interweaves fictional elements with documentary evidence and with his own personal observations to create a unique novel of great emotional power. The Dial Press edition also includes part of Yevgeny Yevtushenko's epic poem "Babi Yar."

568. Le Carré, John: *The Russia house*. New York: Alfred A. Knopf, 1989. 353 p.

Political thriller and love story of the relationship between a British publisher and a Russian contact seeking to transmit highly sensitive material to the CIA.

569. Solzhenitsyn, Alexander: *August 1914* (translated from Russian by Michael Glenny). New York: Farrar, Straus and Giroux, 1972. 622 p.

Controversial history of the events leading up to World War I, the Russian revolutions of 1917, and the rise of communism. Solzhenitsyn sees these events as the beginning of a terrifying tragedy for Russia and the Russian people. The controversy derives primarily from material added to the new edition and relates to two issues: Solzhenitsyn's messianic fervor -- which some have described as neo-Stalinist and totalitarian -- and his clear implications that the entire tragedy of Communist rule in the Soviet Union may be traced back to the Jews. For more details on the later controversy see # 551.

570. ---: *The cancer ward* (translated from Russian by Rebecca Frank, Nicholas Bethell and David Burg). New York: Dial Press, 1969. 616 p.

571. ---: *The first circle* (translated from Russian by Thomas P. Whitney). New York: Harper & Row, 1968. 580 p.

Autobiographical novel recounting Solzhenitsyn's incarceration in a Soviet *gulag* in 1949. Also offers a portrait of Stalin's last years and Solzhenitsyn's comments on Russian and Soviet literature.

572. ---: *The gulag archipelago*. New York: Harper & Row, 1975. 660 p.

Fictionalized anthology of stories from the Soviet concentration camp system. Solzhenitsyn also offers a brief history of the *gulag*, which he estimates claimed sixty-five million Russian lives between 1917 and 1959. Solzhenitsyn experienced the *gulag* as a prisoner in the late 1940s and his first hand experience adds color and meaning to every phrase of his prose.

573. ---: *The oak and the calf: sketches of literary life in the Soviet Union* (translated from Russian by Harry Willets). New York: Harper & Row, 1980. 568 p.

Collection of autobiographical sketches and reflections by the Nobel prize lauriate. Includes reflections on his books and on political issues. The latter display Solzhenitsyn's attitude toward Jews, democrats, and other real or imagined enemies of the USSR.

574. ---: *One day in the life of Ivan Denisovich* (translated from Russian by Ralph Parker, Max Hayward and Ronald Hingley; introduced by Marvin L. Kalb; foreword by Alexander Tvardovsky). New York: Dutton, 1963. 106 p.

Classic novel of prisoner life in the Stalinist concentration camps.

575. Theroux, Paul: "A real Russian ikon: a story." *Commentary*, v. 48 # 6 (December, 1969): 69-73.

576. Trifonov, Yury: *Dissapearance*. Ann Arbor, MI: Ardis Books, 1992. 381 p.

Autobiographical novel of Stalin's purges. Focuses on the experience of eleven year-old Igor Bayukov, the son of a middle level *apparatchik*. Trifonov's untimely death in 1981 left the book uncompleted, but the remainder stands as an extraordinary testimony to a trying period of time.

## D. EDUCATION

577. Anderson, Barbara A., Brian D. Silver, and V. A. Velkoff: "Education of the handicapped in the USSR: exploration of the statistical picture." *Soviet Studies*, v. 34 # 3 (July, 1987): 468-487.

578. Anisimov, O.: "The Soviet system of education." *Russian Review*, v. 9 # 2 (April, 1950): 87-97.

> # 592. Biddulph, H. L.: "Religious participation of youth."

579. Brown, Archie: "Political science in the Soviet Union: a new stage of development?" *Soviet Studies*, v. 36 # 3 (July, 1984): 317-344.

> # 453. Cooper, J.: "The military and higher education."

580. Evans, Alfred Jr.: "Trends in Soviet secondary school histories of the USSR." *Soviet Studies*, v. 28 # 2 (April, 1976): 224-243.

581. Gross, Natalie: "Youth and the army in the USSR in the 1980s." *Soviet Studies*, v. 42 # 3 (July, 1990): 481-498.

> # 807. Joravsky, D.: "Stalinist mentality and higher learning."

> # 747. McClelland, J. C.: "Approaches to higher education."

582. Meek, Dorothea L. (ed.): *Soviet youth: some achievements and problems* (translated from Russian by author). London: Routledge & Kegan Paul, 1957. 251 p.

Based on a selection of articles in the Soviet press, with commentaries by Meek.

583. O'Dell, Felicity and David Lane: "Labor socialization and occupational placement in Soviet education." *Soviet Studies*, v. 28 # 3 (July, 1976): 418-429.

584. Ploss, Sidney I.: "Soviet party history: the Stalinist legacy." *Problems of Communism*, v. 21 # 4 (July/August, 1972): 32-41.

585. Riordan, Jim (ed.): *Soviet youth culture*. Basingstoke, UK: Macmillan, 1989. 148 p.

Anthology assessing the state of Soviet youth, principly under the impact of *perestroika*. Except for the first essay, which offers a general review of the subject, the essays are of a thematic nature. As in other countries, Soviet youth seek a community of friends. These communities may be the Communist Party Youth Group, *Komsomol*, rock music societies, or street gangs. All of them provide members with some form of socialization experience.

The same holds true for schools, as Kuebart's essay amply proves. Of special importance, however, is Bridger's essay on rural youth: previously, it was not clear how far into the hinterlands the effects of *perestroika* had penetrated.

CONTENTS: T. Frisby: Soviet youth culture / J. Riordan: The Komsomol / P. Easton: The rock music community / S. Bridger: Rural youth / F. Kuebart: The political socialization of schoolchildren / J. Riordan: Teenage gangs, 'Afgantsy' and neo-Fascist.

586. Shimoniak, Wasyl: *Communist education: its history, philosophy, and politics*. Chicago: Rand McNally, 1970. 506 p.

Broad discussion of the inter-relationship between education and politics in fourteen Communist states. The bulk of attention falls on education in the Soviet Union, since in many ways it is the model for other Communist states. Also investigates the history of education in the Tsarist era as background to the Communist era. Shimoniak concludes by elucidating the impact of education on the individual and society.

587. Shneidman, N. N.: *Literature and ideology in Soviet education*. Lexington, MA: D. C. Heath, 1973. 207 p.

Investigation of Soviet educational theory and practice. Divided into two roughly equal parts: Part I reviews the concepts that bind Soviet education at every level. This part also notes the critical input of party ideology in carrying education from theory into the classroom. Part II further investigates the theme, concentrating on selected curricula and educational materials with the study of Russian literature used as an example.

> # 557. ---: "The Russian classical literary heritage."

588. Shore, Maurice J.: *Soviet education: its psychology and philosophy*. New York: Philosophical Library, 1947. 346 p.

> # 406. Shorish, M. M.: "Problems of teaching Russian."

> # 329. Silver, B. D.: "The status of national minority languages."

> # 1418. Taubman, W.: *The view from Lenin hills*.

589. Theen, Rolf H. W.: "Political science in the USSR." *Problems of Communism*, v. 21 # 3 (May/June, 1972): 64-70.

590. Timasheff, N. S.: "The Soviet school experiment." *Russian Review*, v. 4 # 1 (Spring, 1945): 72-87.

## E. RELIGION IN THE SOVIET UNION

### 1. Christian Denominations

591. Anderson, John: "The Council for Religious Affairs and the shaping of Soviet religious policy." *Soviet Studies*, v. 43 # 4 (1991): 689-710.

592. Biddulph, Howard L.: "Religious participation of youth in the USSR." *Soviet Studies*, v. 31 # 3 (July, 1979): 417-433.

593. Bociurkin, Bohdan R.: "The shaping of Soviet religious policy." *Problems of Communism*, v. 22 # 3 (May/June, 1973): 37-51.

Deals only with Russian Orthodox and Roman Catholic churches.

594. Bourdeaux, Michael: *Patriarch and prophets: persecution of the Russian Orthodox Church today*. New York: Praeger Publishers, 1970. 359 p.

Anthology and analysis of the persecution of the Russian Orthodox Church in the 1960s. The documents are culled from a wide variety of sources, including both the Soviet government and the *samizdat*. Bourdeaux analyzes these documents in order to place Nikita Khrushchev's anti-religion campaign into political and ideological context.

595. ---: *Religious ferment in Russia: Protestant opposition to Soviet*

*religious policy*. New York: St. Martin's Press, 1968. 255 p.

Deals with efforts by the Russian Baptist movement to gain religious freedom during the Khrushchev era. Primarily focused on the "Initiator's Movement," a protest group seeking an end to government interference in the internal affairs of religious minorities.

596. Curtiss, John S.: *The Russian Church and the Soviet state*. Boston: Little, Brown, 1953. 387 p.

597. Fletcher, William C.: *Religion and Soviet foreign policy, 1945-1970*. New York: Oxford University Press, 1973. 179 p.

Evaluates the role that organizations and religious individuals have played in Soviet foreign affairs since World War II. Argues that, despite Soviet anti-religious propaganda, the Church has played a positive role at international conferences and has thus contributed greatly to furthering Soviet goals in the world.

598. ---: *The Russian Orthodox Church underground, 1917-1970*. New York: Oxford University Press, 1971. 314 p.

Studies the response of Russian Orthodox Church figures to Soviet sponsored persecution. The Church leaders could not contemplate a direct confrontation with the authorities, but refused to cease their activities. Instead, they simply went underground, thereby insuring the Church's continuation. Governmental measures to uproot the Church failed -- in fact, persecution reinvigorated it and raised its stature in the eyes of the Russian masses.

599. Katz, Zev: "Sociology of religion in the USSR: a beginning?" *Slavic Review*, v. 30 # 4 (December, 1971): 870-875.

600. Kolarz, Walter: *Religion in the Soviet Union*. New York: St. Martin's Press, 1962. 513 p.

601. Petro, Nicolo N. (ed.): *Christianity and Russian culture in Soviet society*. Boulder, CO: Westview Press, 1990. 244 p.

Examination of religion in the Soviet Union. The book brings Western scholars together with a multi-denominational group of Soviet religious activists. Primarily oriented toward the status of Russian Orthodox Christianity, although non-Orthodox Christian denominations and Judaism are not ignored. The lack of an essay on Islam and Muslim-Christian relations in the contemporary Soviet Union makes this work incomplete.

CONTENTS: P. Walters: Religion in the Soviet Union: survival and revival / Archbishop Makarii: The contemporary status of religion in the USSR / V. Al'brekht: The legal status of religious organizations and the clergy in the USSR / A. Bessmertnyi-Anzimirov: Freedom of religion: moving away from the Stalinist legal code / G. Rahr: Russian Orthodoxy under Gorbachev / D. Durasoff: The Soviet state and Russian Protestants / M. Agursky: Maksim Gorky and the decline of Bolshevik theomachy / L. Brom: Soviet man as believer and atheist: Alexander Zinoviev's spiritual stratum / V. Petrochenkov: Christian patterns in contemporary Soviet Prose / D. Shlapentokh: Christianity in recent Soviet films: the case of Russophile ideology / O. Gruenwald: The icon in Russian art, society and culture / M. Heifetz: The resurgence of Christianity and Russian-Jewish relations / N. N Petro: Challenge of the "Russian idea": rediscovering the legacy of Russian religious philosophy.

602. Pushkarev, Sergei: *Self-government and freedom in Russia*. Boulder, CO: Westview Press, 1988. 158 p.

Two essays that investigate the place of Russian orthodoxy within contemporary Soviet politics. The first essay concentrates on the history of the Russian Orthodox Church, from the adoption of Christianity in 988 to the Bolshevik Revolution. The second essay views the Russian Orthodox Church today, emphasizing recent religious revival in Eastern Europe. Although too brief to give an in-depth analysis, the work does offer an interesting insight into the role of religion in contemporary Russia.

603. ---, Vladimir Rusak, and Gleb Yakunin: *Christianity and government in Russia and the Soviet Union: reflections on the millenium*. Boulder, CO: Westview Press, 1988. 166 p.

Three essays exploring the history of Russian Orthodoxy in modern times. An expert on the history of religion in Russia has written each of the three essays including two Russian Orthodox priests. In addition to historical insights, the authors consider the possible future development of religion in a period of increasing freedom.

CONTENTS: S. Pushkarev: The role of the orthodox church in Russian history / V. Stepanoff: Witness of the destruction of the church / G. Yakunin: Contemporary Orthodox church and the prospects for a religious renaissance in the Soviet Union.

604. Shirley, Eugene B. Jr. and Michael Rowe (eds.): *Candle in the wind: religion in the Soviet Union* (foreword by Richard Schifter). Washington, DC: Ethics and Public Policy Center, 1989. 328 p.

Anthology reviewing the place of religion in Russian history. The first two essays offer a general overview of the history of religion in Russia from medieval times until 1964. The remaining nine articles are thematic and focus on the 1970s and 1980s. Beside the Christian denominations -- which receive the bulk of attention -- Islam, Judaism, and Budhism are also analyzed in penetrating essays written by recognized experts.

CONTENTS: K. H. Schroeder: Religion in Russia: to 1917 / A. Sorokowski: Church and state 1917-1964 / J. Anderson: Legaslitive and administrative control of religious bodies / M. Sapiets: Anti-religious propaganda and education / P. Walters: How religious bodies respond to state control / M. Rowe: Religious persecution and discrimination / H. Bräker: Buddhism / M. Broxup: Islam / J. Goodman: Judaism / J. Ellis: The religious renaissance: myth of reality? / P. Ramet: Gorbachev's reforms and religion.

605. Timasheff, N. S.: "The Church in the Soviet Union, 1917-1941." *Russian Review*, v. 1 # 1 (November, 1941): 20-30.

606. Waddams, H. M.: "Communism and the churches." *International Affairs*, v. 25 # 3 (July, 1949): 295-306.

607. Walters, Philip: "Soviet policy on religion." *Soviet Jewish Affairs*, v. 15 # 1 (1985): 72-78.

## 2. Judaism

608. Khazanov, Anatoly: "Igor Krupnik's survey of Jewish studies in the USSR: a comment." *Soviet Jewish Affairs*, v. 17 # 3 (Winter, 1987): 51-54.

609. Krupnik, Igor: "The contribution of the younger generation of Soviet scholars to Jewish studies in the USSR." *Soviet Jewish Affairs*, v. 17 # 2 (Summer/Fall, 1987): 35-48.

610. Lvov, Arkady: "Jewish education in Russia: then and now." (translated from Russian by Matthew Callaway). *Midstream*, v. 27 # 1 (January, 1981): 31-33.

611. Miller, Jack (ed.): *Jews in Soviet culture*. New Brunswick, NJ: Transaction Books, for the Institute of Jewish Affairs, London, 1984. 331 p.

Anthology comprising first-hand studies detailing the contribution of Jews to Soviet culture. The work does not specifically refer to the inner culture of Soviet Jews, although that is an implicit subtheme. The essays on Isaac Babel and Ilya Ehrenburg offer interesting insights into two significant Soviet Jewish writers: Babel, who was influenced by his Jewishness; and Ehrenburg, who was not so influenced.

CONTENTS: S. Ettinger: The position of Jews in Soviet Culture: a historical survey / I. Golomstock: Jews in Soviet art / J. Brown: Jews in Soviet music / B. Munitz: A structural study of Jews in Russian literary criticism / E. Sicher: The Jewishness of Babel / A. Goldberg: Ilya Ehrenburg / I. A. Rubin: The Jewish contribution to the development of oriental studies in the USSR / Y. Yakhut: Jews in Soviet philosophy.

612. Rothenberg, Joshua: *The Jewish religion in the Soviet Union*. New York: Ktav Publishing House and the Philip W. Lown Graduate Center for Contemporary Jewish Studies, Brandeis University, 1971. 242 p.

Milestone study on the treatment of Judaism in the USSR since

Stalin. Rothenberg notes that Jews continue to suffer religious difficulties in the Soviet Union, despite the ostensibly secular (and anti-religious) orientation of the state. These difficulties exist beside political problems suffered by Jews -- such as their forced assimilation, and the traditional antisemitism that pervaded some strata of the political elite after Stalin's death.

613. Schulman, Elias: *A history of Jewish education in the Soviet Union*. New York: Ktav Publishing House and The Institute for East European Jewish Studies, Brandeis University, 1971. 184 p.

Surveys the *Yiddish* language school system that briefly existed in the Soviet Union. Between 1917 and 1930 some 160,000 Jewish children received an education in *Yiddish* schools run by the *Yevsektsias*. This education was Jewish in form but Marxist-Leninist in content and was designed to increase Jewish assimilation into the surrounding environment.

**F. SCIENCE AND MEDICINE**

> # 782. Bailes, K. E.: "Soviet science in the Stalin period."

614. Bell, John D.: "Giving birth to the new Soviet man: politics and obstetrics in the USSR." *Slavic Review*, v. 40 # 1 (Spring, 1981): 1-16.

> # 250. Conyngham, W. J.: "Technology and decision making."

615. Counts, George S. and Nucia Lodge: *The country of the blind: the Soviet system of mind control*. Boston: Houghton Mifflin, 1949. 378 p.

Investigates the abuse of psychology and psichiatry in the USSR.

616. Field, Mark G.: *Doctor and patient in Soviet Russia* (foreword by Paul D. White). Cambridge, MA: Harvard University Press, 1957. 266 p.

617. Harvey, Mose L. et al: *Science and technology as an instrument*

*of Soviet policy* (foreword by Foy D. Kohler). Coral Gables, FL: The Center for Advanced International Studies, University of Miami, 1972. 219 p.

Investigates the international ramifications of Soviet policies on scientific research.

> # 1026. Healey, D.: "*Sputnik* and Western defense."

618. Ispa, Jean: "Soviet and American childbearing experiences and attitudes: a comparison." *Slavic Review*, v. 42 # 1 (Spring, 1983): 1-13.

> # 808. Josephson, P. R.: "Stalinist politics of science."

619. Kneen, Peter: "Soviet science under Gorbachev." *Soviet Studies*, v. 41 # 1 (January, 1989): 67-87.

620. Lewis, R. A.: "Innovation in the USSR: the case of synthetic rubber." *Slavic Review*, v. 38 # 1 (March, 1979): 48-59.

621. Parrott, Bruce: "Technology and the Soviet system." *Current History*, v. 82 # 486 (October, 1983): 326-329, 339.

622. Podolski, Edward: "Some achievements of Soviet medical research." *Russian Review*, v. 6 # 1 (Fall, 1946): 77-83.

623. Solomon, Susan G.: "David and Goliath in Soviet public health." *Soviet Studies*, v. 41 # 2 (April, 1989): 254-275.

624. Taylor, Jeanne P.: "Soviet science and technology." *Current History*, v. 75 # 440 (October, 1978): 104-108, 131-135.

# 5

# The Origins of the Soviet State

## A. THE REVOLUTIONS OF 1917

> # 1919. Abraham, R.: *Alexander Kerensky.*

625. Ascher, Abraham: "The Kornilov affair." *Russian Review*, v. 12 # 4 (October, 1953): 235-252.

626. Avrich, Paul (ed.): *The Anarchists in the Russian Revolution.* Ithaca, NY: Cornell University Press, 1973. 179 p.

Collection of primary sources on the role played by Russian Anarchists in the Russian revolutions of 1917. Most of the selections are from the Anarchist press; a few date to the early 1920s. A careful reading of the documents leads to a clear conclusion regarding the failure of Anarchists to substantially effect the ideological makeup of post-revolutionary Russia.

627. Burbank, Jane: *Intelligentsia and revolution: Russian views of bolshevism, 1917-1922.* New York: Oxford University Press, 1986. 340 p.

Studies the response of Russian intellectuals to bolshevism. All of the surveyed intellectuals -- both Socialists and non-Socialist democrats -- opposed bolshevism, but they agreed on little else.

Burbank offers an important comparative perspective of the non-Communist opposition in Russia during Lenin's early years.

628. Carr, E. H.: *The Bolshevik revolution 1917-1923* (3 volumes). London/New York: Macmillan Publishing, 1950-1953. 1,444 p.

Broad but detailed history of the Soviet Union, part of a series of fourteen volumes covering the period from 1917 to the Spanish Civil War that began in 1936. Focuses on political history, but also deals with Lenin's economic and social policy. Leninist practice is compared to Marxist theory, in light of Lenin's interpretive deviations. Also included are an incisive analysis of the New Economic Policy (NEP) and an explanation of the police system established by Lenin. Volume 3 concentrates on foreign policy, including the Treaty of Versailles and the founding of the Comintern.

> # 717. Channon, J.: "Tsarist landowners after the revolution."

> # 1932. Cohen, S. F.: *Bukharin and the Bolshevik Revolution.*

629. Collins, D. N.: "A note on the numerical strength of the Russian Red Guard in October 1917." *Soviet Studies*, v. 24 # 4 (October, 1972): 270-280.

630. Daniels, Robert V.: *Red October: the Bolshevik revolution of 1917*. New York: Charles Scribner's Sons, 1967. 269 p.

Comprehensive analysis of the Bolshevik *putsch*. Organized around one central question: was the *putsch* a carefully planned and well executed masterstroke or not? Daniels argues that it was not -- Lenin lost hope of an insurrection after the failure to topple the provisional government in July 1917. Instead, the *putsch* was a spontaneous outburst by lower-level Bolshevik leaders, which Lenin then guided to victory. Based on a somewhat revisionist outlook that has not been fully accepted by other scholars, Daniels' book is, nevertheless, intriguing and offers a perspective on a fluid and dynamic period of Russian history.

631. Ferro, Marc: "The Russian soldier in 1917: undisciplined, patriotic, and revolutionary." *Slavic Review*, v. 30 # 3 (September,

1971): 483-512.

632. Gill, G. J.: "The failure of rural policy in Russia, February-October 1917." *Slavic Review*, v. 37 # 2 (June, 1978): 241-258.

633. ---: "The mainsprings of peasant action in 1917." *Soviet Studies*, v. 30 # 1 (January, 1978): 63-86.

634. ---: *Peasants and government in the Russian revolution*. New York: Barnes & Noble, 1979. 233 p.

Chronicles the relationship between the provisional government and the peasants in 1917. The latter articulated a clear demand for action from the Kerensky government: specifically demanding the fair re-distribution of land seized from wealthy *kulaks*. Kerensky responded by rejecting this demand until stability had been reestablished. When peasant disturbances were put down forcefully they became alienated from the provisional government. Lenin promised to redistribute land and the peasants thus came to support the Bolsheviks.

635. Guthier, Steven L.: "The popular base of Ukrainian nationalism in 1917." *Slavic Review*, v. 38 # 1 (March,1979): 30-47.

636. Haimson, Leopold H. (ed.): *The Mensheviks: from the Revolution of 1917 to the Second World War* (translated from Russian by G. Vaicar). Chicago: University of Chicago Press, 1974. 476 p.

Collection of eyewitness testimonies on the history of the Mensheviks from the revolution of February 1917 to the end of the 1930s. The testimonies offer an important insight into Menshevik ideology as well as the history of the Menshevik party, its persecution by Lenin, and the emigration of Menshevik leaders. Extensive notes explain terms and identify figures mentioned in the text. The book is especially useful for students of Soviet political history.

637. Hasegawa, Tsuyoshi: "The Bolsheviks and the formation of the Petrograd Soviet in the February Revolution." *Soviet Studies*, v. 29 # 1 (January, 1977): 86-107.

638. ---: "The formation of the militia in the February Revolution: an aspect of the origins of dual power." *Slavic Review*, v. 32 # 2 (June, 1973): 303-322.

639. Hedlin, Myron W.: "Zinoviev's revolutionary tactics in 1917." *Slavic Review*, v. 34 # 1 (March, 1975); 19-43.

640. Jones, David R.: "The officers and the October Revolution." *Soviet Studies*, v. 28 # 2 (April, 1976): 207-223.

> # 112. Kochan, L.: *Russia in revolution*.

641. Koenker, Diane: "The evolution of party consciousness in 1917: the case of the Moscow workers." *Soviet Studies*, v. 30 # 1 (January, 1978): 38-62.

642. Leonhard, Wolfgang: "The Bolshevik revolution turns 70." *Foreign Affairs*, v. 66 # 2 (Winter, 1987/1988): 388-409.

643. Lincoln, W. Bruce: *Passage through armageddon: the Russians in war and revolution, 1914-1918*. New York: Simon and Schuster, 1986. 640 p.

Mixes social, political, and military history to present a picture of Russia in World War I and the Civil War. Assesses the failure of the provisional government in 1917, but notes that ultimately Lenin's skill as a revolutionist cannot be overlooked. Of special significance is how Lincoln attempts to integrate the Russian populace's perspective into the overall story of a most sad era in Russian history.

644. Longley, D. A.: "The divisions of the Bolshevik party in March 1917." *Soviet Studies*, v. 23 # 4 (April, 1972): 61-76.

645. Lossky, N. O.: "Reflections on the origins and meaning of the Russian revolution." *Russian Review*, v. 10 # 4 (October, 1951): 293-300.

646. McNeal, R. H.: *The Russian revolution: why did the Bolsheviks win?* New York: Holt, Rinehart and Winston, 1960. 62 p. [PB]

Student's anthology of previously published selections on the Russian revolution. Part of a series entitled *Problems in World Civilizations*, the anthology is oriented toward senior high school students or college undergraduates. The seven selections represent all -- or almost all -- of the major actors in the Bolshevik *putsch*. The documents are divided into four sections: two selections by Bolshevik leaders (Stalin and Trotsky), two selections from non-Bolshevik Socialists (N. N. Sukhanov and V. M. Chernov), a poignant piece by Alexander Kerensky, and two selections from counter-revolutionary sources (P. N. Miliukov and General A. I. Denikin). A brief bibliography and chronology round out this useful teaching tool.

647. Melançon, Michael: "Who wrote what and when?: proclamations of the February Revolution in Petrograd, 23 February-1 March 1917." *Soviet Studies*, v. 40 # 3 (July, 1988): 479-500.

Response by D. A. Longley in v. 41 # 4 (October, 1989): 625-645.

648. Melgunov, S. P.: *The Bolshevik seizure of power*. (translated from Russian by James S. Beaver; edited by Boris S. Pushkarev). Santa Barbara, CA: ABC-Clio, 1972. 260 p.

Investigates the Bolshevik *putsch* of October-November 1917. Melgunov, an ardent anti-Communist, used every available source for this work. His thesis is that Lenin was working *de facto* if not *de jure* as a German agent. Furthermore, the Bolsheviks were able to seize power because their opponents, who were preoccupied with World War I, could not devote their full attention to protecting the provisional government.

649. Moorehead, Alan: *The Russian Revolution*. New York: Harper & Row, 1958. 303 p. [PB]

Popular history of the revolutions of 1917. Moorehead equally stresses both the March and October Revolutions, although his theme is the method by which Lenin and the Communist party undermined the provisional government. Ends with the signing of the Treaty of Brest-Litovsk -- by which Lenin withdrew Russia from World War I -- and the beginning of the Russian Civil War.

650. Nelson, Harold W.: *Leon Trotsky and the art of insurrection, 1905-1917*. London: Frank Cass, 1988. 158 p.

651. Page, Stanley W.: "The role of the Proletariat in March 1917: contradictions within the official Bolshevik version." *Russian Review*, v. 9 # 2 (April, 1950): 146-149.

652. Pipes, Richard: *The Russian Revolution*. New York: Alfred A. Knopf, 1990. 944 p.

Intensive history of the Bolshevik *coup*, the culmination of Pipes' lifelong study of Soviet history. By far the most comprehensive work on the subject, *The Russian Revolution* is based on an extensive list of sources, including many only recently made available. Pipes begins with the St. Petersburg student disorders of 1899, but concentrates on the period between 1917 and 1918. A major subtheme of Pipes' book is the outset of the Red Terror: Lenin, claims Pipes, literally began the terror campaign that culminated in the murder of millions during the collectivization drives (1929-1932) and the so-called terror famine (1932-1934). Pipes promises a second volume to complete the history of the Soviet Union until Lenin's death in 1924.

653. --- (ed.): *Revolutionary Russia*. Cambridge, MA: Harvard University Press, 1968. 365 p.

Anthology containing twenty-four papers read at a symposium held at Harvard University in 1967 and offering historical reflections on the Russian Revolutions. The essays summarize the state of knowledge with regard to this crucial turning point in Russian history. Pointing to avenues for further research, this anthology is important for students and scholars alike.

CONTENTS: G. F. Kennan: The breakdown of the Tsarist autocracy / R. Pipes: The origins of bolshevism: the intellectual evolution of young Lenin / G. Katkov: German political intervention in Russia during World War I / L. Schapiro: The political thought of the first provisional government / O. Anweiler: The political ideology of the leaders of the Petrograd Soviet in the

Spring of 1917 / M. Ferro: The aspirations of Russian society / D. Geyer: The Bolshevik insurrection in Petrograd / J. Keep: October in the provinces / J. Erickson: The origins of Red Army / J. M. Meijer: Town and country in the Civil War / E. H. Carr: A historical turning point: Marx, Lenin, Stalin / M. Rubel: The relationship of bolshevism to Marxism / A. B. Ulam: The uses of revolution.

654. Rabinowitch, Alexander: *The Bolsheviks come to power: the revolutions of 1917 in Petrograd*. New York: W. W. Norton, 1976. 393 p.

Detailed study of the Bolshevik *putsch* in Petrograd (Leningrad). Reviews the period from the abortive Bolshevik revolution in July 1917 through gerneral Lavr Kornilov's attempted counter-revolution in August and culminates in the final collapse of the provisional government in October. Rabinowitch highly criticizes the Kerensky government's policies, but his in-depth analysis of Lenin's tactics offers an important contribution to understanding the Communist party's ultimate victory.

655. ---: *Prelude to revolution: the Petrograd Bolsheviks and the July 1917 uprising*. Bloomington: Indiana University Press, 1968. 229 p.

Investigates the abortive Bolshevik *putsch* of July 1917. At the same time that Lenin and the Bolshevik Central Committee were calling for moderation, members of the Petrograd soviet were secretly plotting with the party military organization to topple the provisional government. The government easily silenced the resulting series of disturbances on July 3-4, 1917. The Bolsheviks managed to avoid complete destruction and as the provisional government continued to waffle on internal policy, they were then able to seize power.

656. Raleigh, Donald J.: *Revolution on the Volga: 1917 in Saratov*. Ithaca, NY: Cornell University Press, 1986. 373 p.

Carefully reconstructs the course of the revolutions in a provincial city. Raleigh eschews a purely political approach, using social history methods instead. The book includes a full analysis of both the February and October revolutions. As a result of the new insights he provides, Raleigh concludes that the Bolshevik victory was a genuine social upheaval, not just a revolution imposed from above by professional rabble rousers.

657. Reed, John: *Ten days that shook the world* (foreword by V. I. Lenin; edited with introduction and notes by Bertram D. Wolfe). New York: Vintage Books/Random House, 1960. 439 p. [PB]

Reprint of a popular, but propagandistic, history of the Bolshevik *putsch* by an American journalist who witnessed the events as they transpired. Reed, one of the founders of the CPUSA, is the only American buried in the Kremlin wall. Despite the propaganda, Reed provides an interesting insight into the mindset of the Communist party leadership at the time of the revolution. This edition includes a new introduction by Bertram Wolfe that places Reed's ideology into context.

658. Rosenberg, William G.: *Liberals in the Russian revolution: the Constitutional Democratic party, 1917-1921.* Princeton, NJ: Princeton University Press, 1974. 534 p.

History of revolutionary Russia as viewed by the *Kadet* party founded by Pavel N. Miliukov. The *Kadets* -- their name stood for Constitutional Democrats -- sought the creation of a liberal, democratic state on the Anglo-American model. Although divided internally, the *Kadets* represented one of the two or three important parties in the anti-Tsarist, anti-Bolshevik provisional parliament. Rosenberg distinguishes two periods in Party's history and divides the book accordingly. Part I details Party activity during the and after the March Revolution. The *Kadets* acted as a loyal opposition to the policies espoused by the provisional government of Alexander Kerensky (who was a Socialist Revolutionary). Part II details how the Party was smashed by Lenin -- because it participated in the anti-Bolshvik front in 1917 and 1918. Despite persecution, *Kadet* ideas have recently returned to prominence in the Russian democratic revolution of 1991-1992. Rosenberg's study is well crafted and is based on a careful analysis of all pertinent documents on the history and ideology of the *Kadets*.

659. ---: "Russian labor and Bolshevik power after October." *Slavic*

*Review*, v. 44 # 2 (Summer, 1985): 213-238. Comments with a reply by Rosenberg, pp. 239-256.

> # 122. Salisbury, H. E.: *Black night, white snow*.

660. Saul, Norman E.: "Lenin's decision to seize power: the influence of events in Finland." *Soviet Studies*, v. 24 # 4 (April, 1973): 491-505.

661. Schapiro, Leonard: *The Russian Revolutions of 1917: the origins of modern communism*. New York: Basic Books, 1984. 239 p.

Comprehensive historical overview of the revolutions, written by one of the deans of American Sovietology. Special emphasis is given to the means Lenin used to seize power from the provisional government. Although brief, Schapiro's chapter on the Civil War is masterful and helps place the ultimate Bolshevik victory into context. The story continues until Lenin's death and provides an assessment of the revolution in an epilogue. A useful appendix briefly reviews the ideological positions of the different Russian parties.

662. Shukman, Harold: *Lenin and the Russian Revolution*. New York: G. P. Putnam's Sons, 1967. 224 p.

Narrative of the last two decades of Imperial Russia, culminating with a telescoped account of the Revolutions of 1917. Shukman's most complete sections deal with the atmosphere on the eve of the revolution; his condemnation of Tsarist abuses is concise, clear, and full of moral fervor.

663. Snow, Russell E.: "The Russian Revolution of 1917-1918 in Transbaikalia." *Soviet Studies*, v. 23 # 2 (October, 1971): 201-215.

664. Stone, Helena M.: "Another look at the Sisson forgeries and their background." *Soviet Studies*, v. 37 # 1 (January, 1985): 90-102.

Investigates the authenticity of documents purporting to prove German complicity in the Bolshevik *coup*.

> # 381. Szajkowski, Z.: *Russian antisemitism.*

665. Trotsky, Leon: *The history of the Russian Revolution* (translated from Russian by Max Eastman). New York: Simon, 1936. 504 p.

> # 703. Ulam, A. B.: *The Bolsheviks.*

> # 152. ---: *Russia's failed revolutions.*

666. Wade, Rex A.: *Red guards and workers' militias in the Russian Revolution.* Stanford, CA: Stanford University Press, 1984. 391 p.

Traces the evolution of the workers' militia that eventually became the Red Guard. Primarily focused on Petrograd, Wade also considers conditions in Moscow and the provincial cities as well. Wade traces the militia's development from a defensive force that arose in the aftermath of the February 1917 Revolution, to the alliance with the Bolsheviks and the October 1917 Revolution. Thereafter, the Red Guards were absorbed into the Red Army.

667. White, James D.: "The February Revolution and the Bolshevik Vyborg district committee." *Soviet Studies*, v. 41 # 4 (October, 1989): 602-624.

668. ---: "The Sormovo-Nikolaev *Zemlyachestvo* in the February Revolution." *Soviet Studies*, v. 31 # 4 (October, 1979): 475-504.

669. Williams, Albert R.: *Journey into revolution: Petrograd, 1917-1918.* Chicago: Quadrangle Books, 1969. 364 p.

Pro-Bolshevik journalistic account of the Communist seizure of power and the opening stages of the Civil War. Williams was influenced by John Reed's *Ten days that shook the world* (see # 657), but offers a more sophisticated analysis of the revolutions and Lenin's role in them.

> # 186. Wolfe, B. D.: *Revolution and reality.*

## B. "WAR COMMUNISM"

### 1. The Civil War

670. Arslanian, Artin H. and R. L. Nicols: "Nationalism and the Russian Civil War: the case of volunteer army-Armenian relations, 1918-1920." *Soviet Studies*, v. 31 # 4 (October, 1979): 559-573.

> # 628. Carr, E. H.: *The Bolshevik Revolution 1917-1923*.

671. Figes, Orlando: *Peasant Russia, Civil War: the Volga countryside in revolution (1917-1921)*. New York: Oxford University Press, 1991. 432 p. [PB]

Pioneering study of the Russian Civil War in the Volga region. Figes was the first Western scholar permitted to use the Soviet archives for research on a twentieth century topic.

672. Jones, Stepen: "The establishment of Soviet power in Transcaucasia: the case of Georgia, 1921-1928." *Soviet Studies*, v. 40 # 4 (October, 1988): 616-639.

673. Kenez, Peter: *Civil War in South Russia, 1918: the first year of the volunteer army*. Berkeley: University of California Press, 1971. 351 p.

Monograph studying the history of the White volunteer army in the Ukraine during the Russian Civil War. Kenez notes that the Whites failed for two primary reasons: their lack of a clear program and their Russian nationalism. The former robbed the Whites of mass support; the latter robbed them of Ukrainian support. Under the circumstances, the anti-Bolshevik forces were divided and then overwhelmed.

674. ---: *Civil War in South Russia, 1919-1920: the defeat of the Whites*. Berkeley: University of California Press, 1977. 396 p.

Important history of the Civil War that seeks to explain the White Army's defeat. Sequel to *Civil War in South Russia, 1918* (see #

673). Primarily focused on the White's political failures, although Kenez offers a detailed social analysis of the White volunteer army as well. Of special interest is Kenez's wholesale condemnation of the White leaders: they are described, in turn, as corrupt, vain, and sadistic. They were also antisemitic, and Kenez is careful to integrate the history of White pogroms (and other antisemitic outrages) into his account.

675. ---: "The ideology of the White movement." *Soviet Studies*, v. 32 # 1 (January, 1980): 58-83.

676. Mawdsley, Evan: *The Russian Civil War*. London: Allen and Unwin, 1987. 351 p.

Chronological history of the Russian Civil War, from the Bolshevik *putsch* of October 1917 to final victory in November 1920. Mawdsley's theme is an often asked question: did the Reds win the war or did the Whites lose it? Despite his excellent synthesis of available primary and secondary sources, Mawdsley hedges on his answer to that question: he notes that, in essence, the answer to both questions is "yes."

> # 491. McCann, J. M.: "Beyond the Bug."

677. Nove, Alec: "The Red Army in the Civil War: a note on a new source." *Soviet Studies*, v. 31 # 3 (July, 1979): 443-444.

678. Olcott, Martha B.: "The Basmachi or Freemen's revolt in Turkestan 1918-1924." *Soviet Studies*, v. 33 # 3 (July, 1981): 352-369.

679. Poliakov, Yuri A.: *The Civil War in Russia: its causes and significance*. Moscow: Novosti Press Agency Publishing House, 1981. 114 p.

> # 753. Ritter, W. S.: "The liquidation of anti-Soviet resistance."

680. Summers, Anthony and Tom Mangold: *The file on the Tsar: the fate of the Romanovs -- dramatic new evidence*. London: Victor Gollancz, 1976. 416 p.

Investigates the fate of the Imperial family and especially the claim that not all of them were executed by Bolshevik guards on July 17, 1918.

**2. The Allied Intervention**

681. Bradley, John: *Allied intervention in Russia (1917-1920)*. New York: Basic Books, 1968. 251 p.

Documents the diplomatic and military elements that led to the Allied decision to intervene in the Russian Civil War. Based on American, British, and French archival material, Bradley has discovered that the Allies did not pursue an exclusively anti-Bolshevik policy. Indeed, he argues, had Lenin been willing to remain in World War I the Allies would not have attempted to overthrow the new regime.

682. Carley, Michael J.: "Allied intervention and the Russian Civil War, 1917-1922." *International History Review*, v. 11 # 4 (November, 1989): 689-700.

683. Durham, Martin: "British revolutionaries and the suppression of the left in Lenin's Russia, 1918-1924." *Journal of Contemporary History*, v. 20 # 2 (April, 1985): 203-219.

684. Eudin, Xenia J.: "The German occupation of the Ukraine in 1918." *Russian Review*, v. 1 # 1 (November, 1941): 90-105.

685. Keenan, George F.: *The decision to intervene: the prelude to Allied intervention in the Bolshevik revolution*. Princeton, NJ: Princeton University Press, 1958. 528 p.

Careful investigation of the Allied intervention in the Russian Civil War (1918-1919). Primarily views the issue from U.S. President Woodrow Wilson's perspective. Denies that Wilson acted out of intense anti-Bolshevik feeling. Drawing upon State Department papers, Keenan argues that Wilson may have been misled regarding the Bolshevik threat to Allied war materials as well as regarding the fate of a Czech military contingent in Russia. These two elements -- not a vain effort to force Lenin to remain in the war -- were Wilson's justifications for intervention.

686. Ogden, Dennis: "Britain and Soviet Georgia." *Journal of Contemporary History*, v. 23 # 2 (April, 1988): 245-258.

687. White, John A.: *The Siberian intervention*. Westport, CT: Greenwood Press, 1969. 471 p.

Definitive study of the Anglo-American-Japanese intervention in the Asian theatre of operations during the Russian Civil War. White briefly reviews the other theatres of operation as well. Comprehensively examines the political and military aspects in this controversial issue. White's objectivity is a model for the scholarly study of Soviet history.

### 3. The Origins of Communist Autarchy

688. Avrich, Paul: *Kronstadt 1921*. Princeton, NJ: Princeton University Press, 1970. 271 p.

Investigates the truth behind the most important anti-Bolshevik uprising in Soviet history until 1989. While Soviet historians have condemned the Kronstadt mutineers as White counter-revolutionaries, Avrich has discovered that they really were populists seeking to force Lenin to live up to the democratic promises he had made in 1917 and 1918. According to Avrich, all parties participated in the mutiny, although Anarchists predominated in the leadership. Avrich's incisive analysis helps explain how Lenin ultimately seized a monopoly of power for his Bolshevik party.

689. Blank, Stephen: "Soviet nationality policy and Soviet foreign policy: the Polish case 1917-1921." *International History Review*, v. 7 # 1 (February, 1985): 103-128.

690. Brovkin, Vladimir: "Workers' unrest and the Bolshevik response in 1919." *Slavic Review*, v. 49 # 3 (Fall, 1990): 350-373.

691. Buchanan, H. R.: "Lenin and Bukharin on the transition from

capitalism to socialism: the Meshchersky controversy, 1918." *Soviet Studies*, v. 28 # 1 (Janaury, 1976): 66-82.

692. Day, Richard B.: "Preobrazhensky and the theory of the transition period." *Soviet Studies*, v. 27 # 2 (April, 1975): 196-219.

693. Duval, Charles: "Yakov M. Sverdlov and the All-Russian Central Executive Committe of Soviets (VTsIK): a study in Bolshevik consolidation of power October, 1917-July 1918." *Soviet Studies*, v. 31 # 1 (January, 1979); 3-22.

694. Lyandres, Semion: "The 1918 attempt on the life of Lenin: a new look at the evidence." *Slavic Review*, v. 48 # 3 (Fall, 1989): 432-448.

695. Pipes, Richard: *The formation of the Soviet Union: communism and nationalism, 1917-1923*. New York: Atheneum, 1968. 365 p.

Investigates the means by which Lenin forged the Soviet Union. Pipes specifically concentrates on the conquest of Georgia, thereby documenting the creation of a new autocracy almost as corrupt as that of the Tsarist administration.

696. Rabinowitch, Alexander: "The evolution of local Soviets in Petrograd, November 1917-June 1918: the case of the first city district Soviet." *Slavic Review*, v. 46 # 1 (Spring, 1987): 20-37.

697. Radkey, Oliver H.: *The Sickle under the hammer: the Russian Socialist Revolutionaries in the early months of Soviet rule*. New York: Columbia University Press, 1963. 525 p.

698. Remington, T.: "Institution building in Bolshevik Russia: the case of state *kontrol*." *Slavic Review*, v. 41 #1 (Spring, 1982): 91-103.

On the early Bolshviks' attempt to establish control structures in all facets of Russian society.

699. Roberts, Paul C.: "War communism: a re-examination." *Slavic Review*, v. 29 # 2 (June, 1970); 238-261.

> # 653. Rosenberg, W. G.: *Liberals in the Russian revolution.*

700. Sakwa, Richard: "The commune state in Moscow in 1918." *Slavic Review*, v. 46 # 3/4 (Fall/Winter, 1987): 429-449.

701. Schapiro, Leonard: *The origin of the Communist autocracy: political opposition in the Soviet state, first phase, 1917-1922.* London: G. Bell for the London School of Economics and Political Science, University of London, 1955. 397 p.

702. Stites, Richard: *Revolutionary dreams: utopian vision and experimental life in the Russian revolution.* New York: Oxford University Press, 1988. 344 p.

Dissects the ideas about proper social organization prevalent among a vide selection of the intelligentsia during and after the Bolshevik *coup*. Among others that Stites reviews are science fiction writers, students, and even Bolshevik leaders. All sketched visions that Stites defines as utopian, since all assumed the possibility that national action could create a perfect future.

703. Ulam, Adam B.: *The Bolsheviks: the intellectual and political history of the triumph of communism in Russia.* New York: Collier Books, 1968. 598 p. [PB]

Political and intellectual history of bolshevism from 1900, when the party was organized, to Lenin's death in 1924. Interweaves Lenin's biography with a detailed examination of the party he created. After surveying the ideological currents in the Party, Ulam includes a thorough study of the march of events that led to the *putsch* in October 1917. Of special importance is Ulam's argument that Lenin created the conditions used by Stalin to impose a totalitarian order on an already authoritarian government.

704. White, Stephen: "Communism and the East: the Baku Congress, 1920." *Slavic Review*, v. 33 # 3 (September, 1974): 492-514.

### 4. The Economy

705. Bunyan, James: *The origin of forced labor in the Soviet state 1917-1921: documents and materials.* Baltimore, MD: The John Hopkins University Press, 1968. 276 p.

Documents the introduction of forced labor into what was supposed to be the workers' paradise of the Soviet Union. Focuses on the means by which Lenin militarized labor, thus undermining the utopian elements in Communist ideology. Interweaves original documents with historical narrative and also cites key statistics on the subject. Bunyan ends with the year 1921, when "War Communism" had run its course and the most offensive elements of Leninist policy were abolished.

706. Chase, William: "Volunteerism, mobilization and coersion: *Subbotniki,* 1919-1921." *Soviet Studies,* v. 41 # 1 (January, 1989): 111-128.

The militarization of Soviet labor under "War Communism."

707. Husband, William B.: *Revolution in the factory: the birth of the Soviet textile industry, 1917-1920.* New York: Oxford University Press, 1990. 237 p.

Offers a new perspective on Soviet industrial procedures before the New Economic Policy was instituted. Also investigates the extent of support for the Bolsheviks among textile workers.

708. Lih, Lars T.: *The Bolshevik sowing committee of 1920: apotheosis of war communism?* Pittsburgh, PA: University of Pittsburgh Center for Russian and East European Studies, 1990. 50 p.

709. ---: "Bolshevik *Razverstka* and War Communism." *Slavic Review,* v. 45 # 4 (Winter, 1986): 673-688.

710. Oppenheim, Samuel A.: "The Supreme Economic Council 1917-1921." *Soviet Studies,* v. 25 # 1 (July, 1973): 3-27.

## C. LENINIST RUSSIA: DOMESTIC POLICY

> # 285. Atkinson, D.: *The end of the Russian land commune.*

711. Ball, Alan: "Lenin and the question of private trade in Soviet Russia." *Slavic Review*, v. 43 # 3 (Fall, 1984): 399-412.

712. ---: "NEP's second wind: 'the new trade practice'." *Soviet Studies*, v. 37 # 3 (July, 1985): 371-385.

713. Baykov, Alexander: *The development of the Soviet economic system*. Cambridge: Cambridge University Press, 1970. 514 p.

Assessment of the first three years of Lenin's rule in the Soviet Union. Concentrates on the economic policies espoused during the period of "War Communism" and shortly thereafter. Baykov ends with the transition to the New Economic Program (NEP). Also assesses the changes in the economy that Stalin instituted from 1928 to 1939.

714. Broido, Vera: *Lenin and the Mensheviks: the persecution of Socialists under bolshevism*. Boulder, CO: Westview Press, 1987. 216 p.

Integrating the personalities, ideologies, and social context of the Menshevik wing of the All Russian Social Democratic Party, Broido systematically investigates the Party's persecution and eventual destruction. The Mensheviks supported the position that Russian socialism had to develop in a strict sequence, with the Party acting as a cadre while waiting for conditions to ripen into revolution. In contrast, Lenin and the Bolsheviks argued that the Party could foster a revolutionary atmosphere in order to skip stages toward the final Communist party victory. This antagonism led to Lenin's decision to crush the Mensheviks after the Bolshevik takeover. Broido's work raises many points related to contemporary issues. In particular, readers may see the parallels and contrasts between Lenin's Communist revolution and the democratic revolution of 1990. The text implies that under conditions of a Menshevik victory -- unlikely, but hardly impossible -- the Soviet Union would have been vastly different from the state built by Lenin and Stalin.

715. Brooks, Jeffrey: "Public and private values in the Soviet press, 1921-1928." *Slavic Review*, v. 48 # 1 (Spring, 1989): 16-35.

716. Brower, Daniel R.: "The Smolensk scandal and the end of NEP." *Slavic Review*, v. 45 # 4 (Winter, 1986): 689-706.

717. Channon, John: "Tsarist landowners after the revolution: former *Pomeshchiki* in rural Russia during NEP." *Soviet Studies*, v. 39 # 4 (October, 1987): 575-598.

In the aftermath of the Revolution the Communist regime ordered the collectivization of all privately owned land. Channon deals with the Soviet decree ordering expulsion of former *Pomeshchiki* who, after the revolution, continued to reside on land that had belonged to them. This decree took effect on January 1, 1926.

718. Chase, William: *Workers, society, and the Soviet state: labor and life in Moscow, 1918-1929*. Champaign: University of Illinois Press, 1987. 344 p.

Social history of Leninist Russia, exploring the relationship between the workers and the state. According to Chase the Russian working class cannot be viewed as a monolithic entity. Workers were divided by amount of skill possessed, age, and degree of urbanization. Nevertheless, the workers remanied a unified force supporting the Bolsheviks. In the late 1920s Chase notes a clear leftist trend among these proletarians: they were radicalized by the New Economic Plan (NEP) and became the staunchest supporters of Stalin's Five Year Plans. Chase tentatively proposes that Stalin's "revolution from above" must be seen as a "revolution from above and below." Chase's conclusions are intriguing and deserve further investigation as basic archival data becomes more available.

719. Dale, Paddy: "The instability of the infant vanguard: worker party members 1928-1932." *Soviet Studies*, v. 35 # 4 (October, 1983): 504-524.

720. Daniels, Robert V.: *The conscience of the revolution: Communist opposition in Soviet Russia*. Boulder, CO: Westview Press, 1988. 524 p.

Investigates the movements opposing Leninism within the Communist Party Soviet Union (CPSU) from the revolution to 1928. Posits a distinction between the leftist opposition, which sought a more rapid bolshevization, and the rightist opposition, which was more moderate in its positions. Daniels views opposition from the perspective of the crises that racked the Soviet Union in its earliest days: the withdrawl from World War I and "war communism"; the economic crisis of 1921 and the New Economic Policy; and the controversy over the party's development after the rebound of the mid-1920s. Daniels explains the factors causing the opposition to ultimately fail and thus offers insights into contemporary efforts to reform Soviet communism.

721. Davis, Christopher: "Economic problems of the Soviet health service: 1917-1930." *Soviet Studies*, v. 35 # 3 (July, 1983): 343-361.

722. Day, Richard B.: *Leon Trotsky and the politics of economic isolation*. New York: Cambridge University Press, 1973. 221 p.

Assesses the theory of permanent revolution as advocated by Leon Trotsky. In this theory, world revolution was suspended until such a time as Russia had overcome its backwardness. Day also investigates how Trotsky's enemies -- especially Stalin -- used his theory, which they saw as defeatist, against him. Posits that Trotsky mistakenly made economic isolation a central part of his ideology as a defensive measure.

723. Dohan, Michael R.: "The economic origins of Soviet autarky 1927/28-1934." *Slavic Review*, v. 35 # 4 (December, 1976): 603-635.

> # 683. Durham, M.: "Suppression of the left in Lenin's Russia."

724. Edmondson, Charles M.: "An inquiry into the termination of Soviet famine relief programs and the renewal of grain export, 1922-1923." *Soviet Studies*, v. 33 # 3 (July, 1981); 370-385.

725. ---: "The politics of hunger: the Soviet response to famine, 1921." *Soviet Studies*, v. 29 # 4 (October, 1977): 506-518.

726. Felshtinsky, Yuri: "The legal foundations of the immigration

and emigration policy of the USSR (1917-1927)." *Soviet Studies*, v. 34 # 3 (July, 1982): 327-348.

727. Figes, Orlando: "The village and *Volost* Soviet elections of 1919." *Soviet Studies*, v. 40 # 1 (January, 1988): 21-45.

728. Fitzpatrick, Sheila: "The Bolsheviks' dilemma: class, culture and politics in early Soviet years." *Slavic Review*, v. 47 # 4 (Winter, 1988): 614-619.

729. ---: *The Commissariat of Enlightenment: Soviet organization of education and the arts under Lunacharsky, October 1917-1921.* New York: Cambridge University Press, 1970. 380 p.

Thorough study of the reorganization of Soviet education in the early years after the Bolshevik's seized power. Fitzpatrick details the relationship between the Communist party, the Commissariat of Enlightenment, and the intelligentsia during a crucial period of Russian history.

730. ---: *Education and social mobility in the Soviet Union, 1921-1934*. New York: Cambridge University Press, 1979. 335 p.

Studies the educational policy adopted by the Soviet Union from the period of the New Economic Policy to the end of Stalin's first Five-Year plan. Also elucidates the educational goals of the Bolshevik party and its internal opposition movements. A 1924 purge of students and faculty assured the complete bolshevization of universities while the 1929 reorganization of the entire educational system removed any traces of dissent or free thinking. Fitzpatrick notes that Soviet education did succeed in one sphere -- it allowed all students attain their highest levels regardless of class origins -- but did so at the loss of academic freedom.

731. ---: "*Ordzhonikidze*'s takeover of *Vesenkha*: a case study in Soviet bureaucratic politics." *Soviet Studies*, v. 37 # 2 (April, 1985): 153-172.

732. ---: "The 'soft' line on culture and its enemies: Soviet cultural policy 1922-1927." *Slavic Review*, v. 33 # 2 (June, 1974): 267-287.

733. Gerson, Leonard: *The secret police in Lenin's Russia.* Philadelphia: Temple University Press, 1976. 347 p.

History of *Cheka*, the Soviet Union's first secret police. Using both a thematic and chronological organization, Gerson evaluates Lenin's use of limited -- as opposed to Stalin's unlimited -- terror to attain Communist party goals. Since the *Cheka* had no check on its powers of investigation and punishment except the Politburo, readers can only agree that Lenin inexorably paved the path for Stalin's creation of a totalitarian state in the USSR.

734. Gitelman, Zvi: *Jewish nationality and Soviet politics: the Jewish section of the CPSU, 1917-1930.* Princeton, NJ: Princeton University Press, 1972. 573 p.

Intensive study of the *Yevsektsias*, the Jewish sections of the Communist party created by Lenin. Also explains the background of Tsarist Jewry policy as well as Communist theory on Jewish nationalism. Views the *Yevsektsias* as essentially following the Leninist model: national in form but Socialist in content. Thus, the *Yevsektsias* were, objectively, an agent for assimilation, denationalization, and Bolshevization of Soviet Jewry. However, subjective factors also turned the *Yevsektsias* into a form of neo-*kehilla* with Soviet Jews viewing the *Yevsekts* as "their" representatives before the government. The *Yevsektsias* were disbanded in the Stalinist era, and replaced by an even more strict policy of assimilation and Bolshevization.

735. Gooderham, Peter: "The *Komsomol* and worker youth: the inculcation of 'Communist values' in Leningrad during NEP." *Soviet Studies*, v. 34 # 4 (October, 1982): 506-528.

> # 626. Haimson, L. H.: *The Mensheviks.*

736. Hatch, John B.: "The 'Lenin levy' and the social origins of Stalinism: workers and the Communist party in Moscow, 1921-1928." *Slavic Review*, v. 48 # 4 (Winter, 1989): 558-577.

737. ---: "Working-class politics in Moscow during the early NEP: Mensheviks and workers' organizations, 1921-1922." *Soviet Studies*,

v. 39 # 4 (October, 1987): 556-574.

738. Holmes, Larry: "Soviet schools: policy pursues practice, 1921-1928." *Slavic Review*, v. 48 # 2 (Summer, 1989): 234-253.

739. Hughes, James: "The Irkutsk affair." *Soviet Studies*, v. 41 # 2 (April, 1989): 228-253.

740. Kreindler, Isabelle: "A neglected source of Lenin's nationality policy." *Slavic Review*, v. 36 # 1 (March, 1977): 86-100.

741. Kuromiya, Hiroaki: "The crisis of proletarian identity in the Soviet factory, 1928-1929." *Slavic Review*, v. 44 # 2 (Summer, 1985): 280-297.

742. Lane, David: "Ethnic and class stratification in Soviet Kazakhstan." *Comparative Studies in Society and History*, v. 17 # 2 (April, 1975): 165-189.

743. Leggett, George: *The Cheka: Lenin's political police*. New York: Oxford University Press, 1981. 514 p.

Thorough investigation of the first Soviet secret police force, the *Cheka*. Lenin tasked *Cheka* with a number of missions, of which the political mission was most important. Thus, *Cheka* was first and foremost an instrument of Bolshevik terror. *Cheka*'s leader, Feliks Dzerzhinsky, organized the agency as judge, jury, and executioner. Additionally, Leggett reviews *Cheka*'s external role as an espionage and counter-intelligence agency. Using much new material -- including some originating with Soviet sources -- the book fills an important gap in Western knowledge of the early Soviet police state.

744. Liber, George: "Language, literacy, and book publishing in the Ukrainian SSR, 1923-1928." *Slavic Review*, v. 41 # 4 (Winter, 1982): 673-685.

745. Lumer, Hyman (ed.): *Lenin on the Jewish question*. New York: International Publishers, 1974. 155 p. [PB]

Collection of twenty-nine of Lenin's articles and other writings that either directly or indirectly deal with Jews. Arranged chronologically, the articles cover the period from 1903 to 1918. Explanatory notes are found at the end of the book. This material suggests the trend upon which Lenin acted regarding Jews: condemnation of antisemitism coupled with the rejection of any form of Jewish nationalism, even the Socialist nationalism of the *Bund*. Although Lumer accepts Lenin's conclusions uncritically, readers are free to draw their own conclusions regarding the appropriateness of Lenin's policy. As a result, the collection is important for both scholars and general readers.

746. Mace, James E.: "The *Komitety Nezamozhnykh Selyan* and the structure of Soviet rule in the Ukrainian countryside, 1920-1933." *Soviet Studies*, v. 35 # 4 (October, 1983): 487-503.

747. McClelland, James C.: "Bolshevik approaches to higher education, 1917-1921." *Slavic Review*, v. 30 # 4 (December, 1971): 818-831.

748. Miller, Martin A.: "Freudian theory under Bolshevik rule: the theoretical controversy during the 1920s." *Slavic Review*, v. 44 # 4 (Winter, 1985): 625-646.

749. Miller, Robert F.: "Soviet agricultural policy in the twenties: the failure of cooperation." *Soviet Studies*, v. 27 # 2 (April, 1975): 220-244.

750. Narkiewicz, Olga A.: *The making of the Soviet state apparatus*. Manchester, UK: Manchester University Press, 1970. 238 p.

Explores the origins of the Communist party apparat, with the aid of documents from the Smolensk archives. Concludes that the New Economic Policy was only partially successful. Urban employment combined with administrative inefficiency made Stalin's collectivization campaign inevitable. Narkiewicz's work serves as a useful explanation for the bridge between Leninism and Stalinism.

751. Peris, Daniel: "The 1929 Congress of the Godless." *Soviet Studies*, v. 43 # 4 (1991): 711-732.

752. Pethybridge, R. W.: "Railways and press communications in Soviet Russia in the early NEP period." *Soviet Studies*, v. 38 # 2 (April, 1986): 194-206.

753. Ritter, William S.: "The final phase in the liquidation of anti-Soviet resistance in Tadzhikistan: Ibrahim Bek and the Basmachi, 1924-1931." *Soviet Studies*, v. 37 # 4 (October, 1985): 484-493.

754. Rosefielde, Steven: "An assessment of the sources and uses of *gulag* forced labor 1929-1956." *Soviet Studies*, v. 33 # 1 (January, 1981): 51-87.

755. Schechtman, Joseph B.: *Zionism and Zionists in Soviet Russia: greatness and drama*. New York: Zionist Organization of America, 1966. 94 p.

Surveys Soviet treatment of Zionists from 1917 to the 1960s. Despite the status of the Zionist movement within the Jewish community, the Bolsheviks opposed manifestations of Jewish nationality -- which Lenin defined as an artificial nationalism deriving from capitalist contradictions. In that context, the Jewish Bolsheviks, the members of the *Yevsektsias*, were the most adament opponents of Zionist activities. Despite persecution, and the cruel accusation concocted by Communist propagandists in the 1960s that Zionists had collaborated with the Nazis, the Zionist movement continued to operate in the underground and reemerged with great fervor in the late 1960s.

756. Scherr, Barry: "Notes on literary life in Petrograd, 1918-1922: a tale of three houses." *Slavic Review*, v. 36 # 2 (June, 1977): 256-267.

757. Schultz, Kurt S.: "Building the 'Soviet Detroit': the construction of the Nizhnii-Novgorod automobile factory, 1927-1932." *Slavic Review*, v. 49 # 2 (Summer, 1990): 200-212.

> # 125. Shanin T.: "The rural history of Russia 1905-1930."

758. Shelley, Louise: "Soviet criminology: its birth and demise, 1917-1936." *Slavic Review*, v. 38 # 4 (December, 1979): 614-628.

759. Solnick, Steven L.: "Revolution, reform and the Soviet telephone system, 1917-1927." *Soviet Studies*, v. 43 # 1 (1991): 157-176.

760. Solomon, Peter H.: "Local political power and Soviet criminal justice, 1922-1941." *Soviet Studies*, v. 37 # 3 (July, 1985): 305-329.

Studies political intervention in the Soviet criminal justice system during the Leninist era.

761. ---: "Soviet penal policy, 1917-1934: a reinterpretation." *Slavic Review*, v. 39 # 2 (June, 1980): 195-217.

> # 605. Timasheff, N. S.: "The church in the Soviet Union."

762. Viola, Lynne: "Notes on the background of Soviet collectivization: metal worker brigades in the countryside, Autumn 1929." *Soviet Studies*, v. 36 # 2 (April, 1984): 205-222.

763. Wheatcroft, Stephen G.: "On assessing the size of forced concentration camp labor in the Soviet Union, 1929-1956." *Soviet Studies*, v. 33 # 2 (April, 1981): 265-295.

764. White, James D.: "Early Soviet historical interpretations of the Russian Revolution 1918-1924." *Soviet Studies*, v. 37 # 3 (July, 1985): 330-352.

On the politicization of historiography under Lenin.

## D. LENINIST RUSSIA IN GLOBAL CONTEXT

765. Carr, Edward H.: *German-Soviet relations between the two wars 1919-1939*. Baltimore, MD: The John Hopkins University Press, 1951. 146 p.

The book is based on a series of lectures on diplomatic history given by the distinguished historian/author in 1951 at the Walter Hines Page school of international relations.

766. Chamberlin, William H.: "Russia and Europe, 1918-1944."

*Russian Review*, v. 4 # 1 (Fall, 1944): 3-9.

767. Crowe, Sibyl: "The Zinoviev letter: a reappraisal." *Journal of Contemporary History*, v. 10 # 3 (July, 1975): 407-432.

Reviews Comintern efforts in 1924 to stir up a prolatarian revolt in England.

768. Day, Richard B.: *The "crisis" and the "crash": Soviet studies of the West (1917-1939)*. New York: Schocken Books, 1981. 300 p.

Interesting investigation of how Soviet political scientists and ideologues explained conditions in the West from the Revolutions of 1917 to the outbreak of World War II in 1939. Day notes that Communists operated with a series of *a priori* assumptions inherited from Marx, regarding the historical inevitability of a global revolution to overturn Capitalism. However, reality was far different from Marx's prediction, causing Marxist-Leninist thinkers to attempt to explain the apparent contradiction. During the 1920s the Communists found an obvious, but ultimately incorrect, explanation: they assumed that each economic crisis -- the "Great Inflation" in Germany (1923-1924), for example -- would be the final one before the revolution would fulfill Marx's prophecy. The stock market crash of October 1929 offered a similar opportunity, especially since it led to the rise of Nazism in Germany. Marxist theorists could then interpret fascism as the final form of capitalism in its last gasp.

769. Debo, Richard K.: "Litvinov and Kamenev -- ambassadors extraordinary: the problem of Soviet representation abroad." *Slavic Review*, v. 34 # 3 (September, 1975): 463-482.

770. ---: "The Monuilskii mission: an early Soviet effort to negotiate with France, August 1918-April 1919." *International History Review*, v. 8 # 2 (May, 1986): 214-235.

771. Fischer, Louis: *Russia's road from peace to war: Soviet foreign relations, 1917-1941*. New York: Harper & Row, 1969. 499 p.

Attempts to interpret Soviet behavior in international affairs during the Leninist and Stalinist eras. Notes that Soviet foreign policy was a mixture of ideological and pragmatic elements: the exact mixture depending on the period and country in question.

772. ---: *The Soviets in world affairs: a history of relations between the Soviet Union and the rest of the world, 1917-1929*. New York: Vintage Books/Random House, 1960. 656 p. [PB]

Classic investigation of Leninist foreign policy, primarily viewed from the Anglo-French perspective. Encompases two eras, that of "war communism" from 1917 to 1921 and the period of peace and economic recovery between 1921 and 1929. The second period is identical to the period of Lenin's NEP. Fischer views the second period as particularly significant because it was a time of lost opportunities shortly before the 1929 stock market crash, the worldwide economic depression, and the rise of Nazism. Based on sources that only just became available in the 1950s and on interviews with key members of the Soviet foreign ministry, Fischer's work is a model of historical investigation.

773. Glenny, M. V.: "The Anglo-Soviet trade agreement, March 1921." *Journal of Contemporary History*, v. 51 # 2 (April, 1970): 63-82.

774. Gorodetsky, Gabriel: *The precarious truce: Anglo-Soviet relations 1924-1927*. Cambridge: Cambridge University Press, 1977. 289 p.

Studies the tenuous relations between Britain and the Soviet Union after the death of Lenin but before the rise of Stalin. This period coincided with the first Labour government in London and the creation of the Anglo-Russian Joint Advisory Council (AR-JAC). Given the unavailability of Soviet documents, Gorodetsky views the subject from an almost exclusively British perspective. AR-JAC survived the Labour government's fall in 1925, but increasing Soviet paranoia regarding an iminent war threat caused it to collapse in 1927.

775. Himmer, Robert: "Soviet policy toward Germany during the Russo-Polish War, 1920." *Slavic Review*, v. 35 # 4 (December,

1976): 665-682.

776. Horvath, Janos: "Economic aid flow from the USSR: a recount of the first fifteen years." *Slavic Review*, v. 29 # 4 (December, 1970): 613-632.

777. Hudson, George E.: "Soviet naval doctrine under Lenin and Stalin." *Soviet Studies*, v. 28 # 1 (January, 1976):

778. Krammer, Arnold: "Russian counterfeit dollars: a case of early Soviet espionage." *Slavic Review*, v. 30 # 4 (December, 1971): 762-773.

779. Lazitch, Branko and Milorad M. Drachkovitch: *Lenin and the Comintern*. Stanford, CA: Hoover Institution Press, 1972. 683 p.

Describes Lenin's relations with the *Comintern*, primarily focused on covert operations in Europe. Reveals considerable data on Communist subversive activities in France, Germany, and Italy. The authors reveal an interesting tidbit: Lenin's emisaries, sent to advise regional Communist partys on how to arrange their activities, were actually sent to monitor deviations from party discipline and to ensure strict adherence to the party line.

780. Low, Alfred D.: "The Soviet Union, the Austrian Communist party, and the *Anschluss* question, 1918-1938." *Slavic Review*, v. 39 # 1 (March, 1980): 1-26.

781. Manne, Robert: "The Foreign Office and the failure of the Anglo-Soviet rapproachment." *Journal of Contemporary History*, v. 16 # 4 (October, 1981): 725-755.

Delves into the background of the attempt to create a united front against the Nazis in the 1930s.

# 6

# Stalinist Russia

## A. DOMESTIC POLICY

782. Bailes, Kendall E.: "Soviet science in the Stalin period: the case of V. I. Vernadskii and his school, 1928-1945." *Slavic Review*, v. 45 # 1 (Spring, 1986): 20-37.

783. ---: "Stalin and the making of a new elite: a comment." *Slavic Review*, v. 39 # 2 (June, 1980): 286-289.

Response to Sheila Fitzpatrick (see # 797); a reply by Fitzpatrick is on pp. 290-291.

> # 716. Brower, D. R.: "The Smolensk scandal."

784. Campbell, Robert: "What makes a five-year plan feasible." *Slavic Review*, v. 32 # 2 (June, 1973): 258-263.

Reply to Holland Hunter's "The overambitious five-year plan." (see # 804).

785. Carr, Edward H.: *Socialism in one country* (3 vols, bound as 4). New York: Macmillan Publishing, 1958-1964. 2,773 p.

Volumes 5-8 of Carr's 14 volume *History of Soviet Russia*. Deals with the reorganization of the regime after Lenin's death. Volume One covers social and economic developments, primarily the end of the New Economic Policy. Volume Two deals with local and national politics, concentrating on Stalin's rise to power. Volume Three's two parts cover foreign relations and *Comintern* policy. Notes that despite their lofty rhetoric the Communists actually adopted a pragmatic approach to problem-solving: they appeared to lack an overall strategy and often over-reacted to minor setbacks.

786. Chamberlin, W. H.: "Russia today and tomorrow." *International Affairs*, v. 14 # 2 (March/April, 1935): 217-230.

787. Cohen, Stephen F.: "Stalin's revolution reconsidered." *Slavic Review*, v. 32 # 2 (June, 1973): 264-270.

Reply to article by Holland Hunter, see # 804.

788. Dallin, David Y. and Boris I. Nikolaevsky: *Forced labor in Soviet Russia*. New Haven, CT: Yale University Press, 1947.

789. Daniels, Robert V.: "The Soviet succession: Lenin and Stalin." *Russian Review*, v. 12 # 3 (July, 1953): 153-172.

790. Davies, R.: "The Socialist market: a debate in Soviet industry, 1932-1933." *Slavic Review*, v. 43 # 2 (Summer, 1984): 201-223.

791. --- and S. G. Wheatcroft: "Further thoughts on the first Soviet five-year plan." *Slavic Review*, v. 34 # 4 (December, 1975): 790-802.

> # 721. Davis, C.: "Problems of the Soviet health service."

> # 723. Dohan, M. R.: "The economic origins of Soviet autarky."

> # 530. Dunham, V. S.: *In Stalin's time*.

> # 532. Emiot, I.: *The Birobidzhan affair*.

792. Evans, Janet: "The Communist Party of the Soviet Union and the women's question: the case of the 1936 decree 'In Defense

of Mother and Child'." *Journal of Contemporary History*, v. 16 # 4 (October, 1981): 757-775.

793. Fainsod, Merle: *Smolensk under Soviet rule*. Cambridge, MA: Harvard University Press, 1958. 484 p.

Classic reconstruction of Soviet rule in a single city, based on documents captured by the Nazis when they occupied Smolensk in July 1941. The documents were later seized by American troops in Germany and transferred to the Hoover Institute of War and Peace Studies at Stanford University. Fainsod was among the first to realize that the documents offer an unprecedented insider's view of Soviet politics.

794. Fisher, Ralph T., Jr.: *Pattern for Soviet youth: a study of the Congress of the Komsomol, 1918-1954*. New York: Columbia University Press, 1959. 452 p.

795. Fitzpatrick, Sheila: "Cultural revolution in Russia, 1928-1932." *Journal of Contemporary History*, v. 9 # 1 (January, 1974): 33-52.

796. ---: "Culture and politics under Stalin: a reappraisal." *Slavic Review*, v. 35 # 2 (June, 1976): 211-231.

> # 730. ---: *Education and social mobility*.

797. ---: "Stalin and the making of a new elite, 1928-1939." *Slavic Review*, v. 38 # 3 (September, 1979): 377-402.

798. --- and Lynne Viola (eds.): *A researcher's guide to sources on Soviet social history in the 1930s*. Armonk, NY: M. E. Sharpe Publishers, 1990. 296 p.

Anthology of bibliographic essays on Soviet social history in the 1930s. Most of the essays date to a 1982 conference of the American Association for the Advancement of Slavic Studies. The essays are all thematic with each author offering a guide to published and archival sources in Russia that are available to researchers. Since they do not review the specific issues involved but only the research techniques useful in studying Soviet history, the essays will most likely score only a scholarly audience.

CONTENTS: L. Viola: Introductory notes for researchers / S. Fitzpatrick: Sources on the social history of the 1930s: overview and critique / P. K. Grimsted: Archival resources from the 1920s and 1930s: Soviet archival developments and reference aids for the social historian / L. Viola: Archival research in the USSR: a practical guide for historians / J. A. Getty: Guide to the Smolensk archive / A. Bezborodov: Annual reports of industrial enterprises in Soviet archives as a historical source for the 1930s / L. Vida: Guide to document series on collectivization / L. H. Siegelbaum: Guide to document series on industrialization / P. H. Solomon, Jr.: Laws and administrative acts: sources and finding aids / S. G. Wheatcroft: Statistical sources for the study of Soviet social history in the prewar period / S. Fitzpatrick: Newspapers and journals / P. H. Solomon, Jr.: Legal journals and Soviet social history / J. A. Getty: Soviet city directories / V. Z. Drobizhev, E. J. Pivovar, and A. K. Sokolov: *Perestroika* and the study of sources on Soviet social history / H. Kuromiya: Soviet memoirs as a historical source / ---: Guide to émigré and dissident memoir literature / M. Von Hagen: A note on military sources.

799. Gilboa, Yehoshua A.: *The black years of Soviet Jewry*. Boston: Little, Brown, 1971. 418 p.

Reviews the fate of Soviet Jewry during the Stalinist era, concentrating on the years from 1939 to 1953. Gilboa carefully documents the systematic destruction of Jewish culture, the lack of a Soviet response to the Holocaust, and Stalin's increasing antisemitism. Gilboa notes that Stalin's death prevented another tragedy for Soviet Jewry that began with the so-called Doctors' Plot and was to signal the complete deportation of Soviet Jewry to the interior of the country. Thus, this work offers an important analysis of the rise of semi-official antisemitism in the Soviet Union.

> # 734. Gitleman, Z.: *Jewish nationality and Soviet politics*.

800. Greenberg, Linda L.: "Policy-making in the USSR Academy of Sciences." *Journal of Contemporary History*, v. 8 # 4 (October, 1973): 67-80.

801. Gregory, Paul R.: "The Stalinist command economy." *Annals*, v. 507 (January, 1990): 18-25.

802. Harris, Jonathan: "The origins of the conflict between Malenkov and Zhdanov: 1939-1941." *Slavic Review*, v. 35 # 2 (June, 1976): 287-303.

> # 736. Hatch, J. B.: "The social origins of Stalinism."

803. Hazard, John N.: "The federal organization of the USSR." *Russian Review*, v. 3 # 2 (Spring, 1944): 21-29.

804. Hunter, Holland: "The overambitious first five-year plan." *Slavic Review*, v. 32 # 2 (June, 1973): 237-257.

805. ---: "Soviet agriculture with and without collectivization, 1928-1940." *Slavic Review*, v. 47 # 2 (Summer, 1988): 203-216.

806. Inkeles, Alex and Raymond Bauer: *The Soviet citizen*. Cambridge, MA: Harvard University Press, 1959. 533 p.

Based on interviews with Russian refugees, Inkeles and Bauer examine daily life in the Soviet Union during the 1930s and early 1940s.

807. Joravsky, David: "The Stalinist mentality and the higher learning." *Slavic Review*, v. 42 # 4 (Winter, 1983): 575-600.

808. Josephson, Paul R.: "Physics, Stalinist politics of science and cultural revolution." *Soviet Studies*, v. 40 # 2 (April, 1982): 245-265.

809. Khachaturov, T. S.: "Organization and development of railway transport in the USSR." *International Affairs*, v. 21 # 2 (April, 1945): 220-235.

810. Kuromiya, Hiroaki: "*Edionachalie* and the Soviet industrial manager, 1928-1937." *Soviet Studies*, v. 36 # 2 (April, 1984): 185-204.

The institutionalization of single-person management in all plants.

811. Lewin, Moshe: "The disappearence of planning in the plan." *Slavic Review*, v. 32 # 2 (June, 1973): 271-287.

812. ---: *The making of the Soviet system: essays in the social history of interwar Russia*. New York: Pantheon Books, 1985. 355 p. [PB]

Pioneering study on the social history of the Stalin era. Organized as a series of independent essays on three themes: Russian rural society in transition from tsarism to communism, collectivization, and the economic and social impact of Bolshevik rule in the USSR. Lewin operates with a somewhat revisionist perspective: in particular he denies that the Soviet Union has ever had a totalitarian government. Lewin distinguishes between authoritarian governments and totalitarian ones and identifies two forms of authoritarian systems, claiming that the Soviet Union has experienced both: personal authoritarianism under Stalin and bureaucratic authoritarianism under Stalin's successors.

813. Liber, George: "Urban growth and ethnic change in the Ukrainian SSR, 1923-1933." *Soviet Studies*, v. 41 # 4 (October, 1989): 574-591.

814. Mehnert, Klaus: *Stalin versus Marx: the Stalinist historical doctrine*. London: George Allen and Unwin, 1952. 128 p.

Argues that by restoring Russian nationalism to a place of prominence in Communist ideology, Stalin essentially undid Marx. Viewing the new Stalinist nationalism from the perspective of Russian historiography, Mehnert posits that the origins of the reorientation are to be found in the early 1930s. The Great Patriotic War saw the most extensive use of nationalist symbols by Stalin and the Soviet regime.

815. Merridale, Catherine: "The reluctant opposition: the right 'deviation' in Moscow, 1928." *Soviet Studies*, v. 41 # 3 (July, 1989): 382-400.

816. Morrison, David J.: "The Soviet peasantry's real expenditure in socialized trade, 1928-1934." *Soviet Studies*, v. 41 # 2 (April, 1989): 175-193.

817. Morrison, H.: "Impressions of the situation in Soviet Russia." *International Affairs*, v. 13 # 1 (January/February, 1934): 62-78.

818. Nordahl, Richard: "Stalinist ideology: the case of the Stalinist interpretation of monopoly capitalist politics." *Soviet Studies*, v. 26 # 2 (April, 1974): 239-259.

819. Nove, Alec: "A note on Trotsky and the 'left opposition,' 1929-1931." *Soviet Studies*, v. 29 # 4 (October, 1977): 576-589.

820. Odom, William E.: *The Soviet volunteers: modernization and bureaucracy in a public mass organization*. Princeton, NJ: Princeton University Press, 1973. 360 p.

Studies the history of Russia's largest all-volunteer organization, *Osoaviakhim* (the Society of Friends of Defense and Aviation-Chemical Construction). Founded in 1927 *Osoaviakhim* served as a civil defense agency for most of the 1930s. Odom concentrates on the tensions between "volunteerism" and bureaucracy in a totalitarian state. By the mid 1930s *Osoaviakhim* had developed into a widely ramified para-military organization with 13 million members. At that point *Osoaviakhim* became a bureaucratic battle-field between the military and Communist party leadership.

821. Rassweiler, Anne D.: "Soviet labor policy and the first five-year plan: the Dneprostroi experience." *Slavic Review*, v. 42 # 2 (Summer, 1983): 230-246.

822. Rigby, T. H.: "Early provincial cliques and the rise of Stalin." *Soviet Studies*, v. 33 # 1 January, 1981): 3-28.

823. Rosefielde, Steven: "The first 'great leap forward' reconsidered: lessons of Solzhenitsyn's *Gulag archipelago*." *Slavic Review*, v. 39 # 4 (December, 1980): 569-587. Comments with a reply, pp. 588-615.

824. Salter, John: "N. I. Bukharin and the market question." *History of Political Economy*, v. 22 # 1 (Spring, 1990): 65-79.

> # 755. Schechtman, J. B.: *Zionism and Zionists in Soviet Russia*.

> # 758. Shelley, L.: "Soviet criminology."

825. Smolka, H. P.: "Soviet development in the Arctic." *International Affairs*, v. 16 # 4 (July/August, 1937): 564-578.

> # 605. Timasheff, N. S.: "The church in the Soviet Union."

826. Tucker, Robert C.: "The rise of Stalin's personality cult." *American Historical Review*, v. 84 # 2 (April, 1979): 347-366.

827. Viola, Lynne: "The campaign to eliminate the *kulak* as a class, Winter 1929-1930: a reevaluation of the legislation." *Slavic Review*, v. 45 # 3 (Fall, 1986): 503-524.

828. Wolfe, Bertram D.: *Communist totalitarianism: keys to the Soviet system*. Boulder, CO: Westview Press, 1985. 328 p. [PB]

Collection of essays that survey twenty years of Soviet history, coinciding generally with the Stalinist era. Attempts to view the Soviet system as a series of "keys," crucial concepts or policies that explain Communist totalitarianism. Wolfe concentrates on the durable components in Soviet politics, while offering general observations on totalitarianism. Each of the keys is subdivided into chapters that cover a specific subsidiary topic. Wolfe's observation that communism could not be reformed has generally been proved correct.

829. Zaletski, Eugene: *Stalinist planning for economic growth, 1933-1952*. Chapel Hill: University of North Carolina Press, 1980. 788 p.

Detailed study of Stalinist economic policy. Zaleski has accumulated every bit of relevant statistical information, which allows him to evaluate the success of the Stalinist command economy and to place economic activities into the context of Stalin's quest for power.

### B. FOREIGN POLICY TO 1939

830. Carr, E. H.: *Twilight of the Comintern, 1930-1935*. New York: Pantheon Books, 1982. 461 p.

History of Soviet relations with Communist parties throughout the world. The basis for such relations was the *Comintern*, that is the Communist (Third) International. Primarily concentrates on the Soviet response to the rise of Hitler in the years before Stalin accepted the idea of the popular front. In light of this chronological context, the book concentrates on the Communist failure to halt German fascism, and posits that the cause of failure was the divisive battle Communists waged in a vain attempt to seize control of Social Democratic parties in the West. In addition to Moscow's perspective, Carr surveys the major European Communist parties as well as those of China and Japan. Adding further insight to Carr's evaluation is his copious citation of alternate Communist sources, such as Trotsky's articles in the Russian-language *Byulleten Opposzitsii* (published in France). Carr's last book, *Twilight of the Comintern* was planned and executed as an adendum to his 14 volume *History of Soviet Russia*. The only lacuna in this otherwise comprehensive work is that Carr hardly mentions either Jews or Nazi antisemitism. However, the lack is not a reflection on Carr; rather it reflects contemporary Communist policy that did not pay sufficient attention to the ideological elements of Nazi racism.

831. Cattell, David T.: *Soviet diplomacy and the Spanish Civil War.* Berkeley: University of California Press, 1957. 204 p. [PB]

Investigates from the Soviet perspective the international climate on the eve of World War II. Weighs the different interpretations of Soviet and British foreign policy to explain Stalin's actions. Cattell places Soviet inervention into the context of Western appeasement: Stalin intervened because the Allies would not. The Spanish experience taught the Soviets and the Western Allies two different lessons: Stalin concluded from the Civil War that both Britain and France were unreliable. Eventually he signed the non-agression pact with Germany. The British concluded that the Soviets were irrelevant to an anti-Nazi alliance. Since the British also overrated the Poles considerably, the stage was set for the disasters in August and September 1939.

832. Clarke, J. Calvitt: *Russia and Italy against Hitler: the Bolshevik-Fascist rapprochement of the 1930s.* Westport, CT: Greenwood Press, 1991. 240 p.

Studies the paradoxical warming of relations between Stalinist Russia and Fascist Italy in the early 1930s. Fearful of Nazi intentions and Anglo-French appeasement, Stalin sought a reliable ally to check Hitler. Since Italy was simultaneously pursuing a rapproachment with England and France -- represented by the so-called Stresa Front -- a unified anti-Nazi front could have been established. These two parallel anti-Nazi fronts prevented an earlier *Anschluss*. After 1935, however, both alliances collapsed; primarily as a result of the Italian invasion of Ethiopia and Mussolini's rapproachment with Hitler. Still, Clarke's work points to the diplomatic possibilities that may have prevented the outbreak of World War II.

833. Coox, Alvin D.: "The Lake Khasan affair of 1938: overview and lessons." *Soviet Studies*, v. 25 # 1 (July, 1973): 51-65.

834. Dallin, Alexander: Personality, nationalism, and commitment." *Slavic Review*, v. 36 # 4 (December, 1977): 596-598.

835. Dallin, David J.: *Soviet Russia and the Far East*. New Haven, CT: Yale University Press, 1948. 398 p.

> # 768. Day, R. B.: *The crisis and the crash*.

> # 771. Fischer, L.: *Russia's road from peace to war*.

836. Ganjoo, Satish: *Soviet-Afghan relations*. Delhi, India: Akashdeep Publishing House, 1990. 155 p.

837. Garver, John W.: *Chinese-Soviet relations, 1937-1945*. New York: Oxford University Press, 1988. 301 p.

Focuses on the three way relations between Stalin, the Chinese Communists led by Mao Zedong, and Chiang Kai-Shek's *Koumintang* regime during World War II. Garver views this as a crucial era which ultimately influenced the final Communist victory in the Chinese Civil War (1947-1949). However, Garver is careful to point out that during the war Stalin supported both Mao and Chiang -- seeing a vigorous China as a vital bullwark against Japanese expansion. Placing Russian and Chinese policies in context, Garver has made an important contribution towards understanding the diplomatic history of World War II and the Cold War.

838. Gillette, Philip S.: "Motivational-ideational analysis of Stalin's foreign policy." *Slavic Review*, v. 36 # 4 (December, 1977): 592-595.

> # 777. Hudson, G. E.: "Soviet naval doctrine."

839. Jukes, G.: "The Red Army and the Munich Crisis." *Journal of Contemporary History*, v. 26 # 2 (April, 1991): 195-214.

840. Kennan, George F.: "Some thoughts on Stalin's foreign policy." *Slavic Review*, v. 36 # 4 (December, 1977): 590-591.

> # 1365. Kovalio, J.: "Stalinist foreign policy in the early 1930s."

841. Large, J. A.: "The origins of Soviet collective security policy, 1930-1932." *Soviet Studies*, v. 30 # 2 (April, 1978): 212-236.

842. Lobanov-Rostovsky, A.: "Russia and Germany: an historical survey of Russo-German relations." *Russian Review*, v. 2 # 2 (Spring, 1943): 27-44.

> # 780. Low, A. D.: "Soviet Union and the *Anschluss* question."

843. Oudendyk, W. J.: "Soviet policy in the Far East." *International Affairs*, v. 15 # 6 (November/December, 1936): 824-845.

844. Reese, Roger: "A note on the consequence of the expansion of the Red Army on the eve of World War II." *Soviet Studies*, v. 41 # 1 (January, 1989): 135-140.

845. Schulman, Marshall D.: *Stalin's foreign policy reappraised*. Cambridge, MA: Harvard University Press, 1963. 320 p.

846. Tucker, Robert C.: "The emergence of Stalin's foreign policy." *Slavic Review*, v. 36 # 4 (December, 1977): 563-589.

847. ---: "On matters evidential: a reply." *Slavic Review*, v. 36 # 4 (December, 1977): 604-607.

> # 884. Uldricks, T. J.: "The impact of the great purges."

848. Uldricks, Teddy J.: "Stalin and Nazi Germany." *Slavic Review*, v. 36 # 4 (December, 1977): 599-603.

849. Vakar, Nicholai P.: "Russia and the Baltic states." *Russian Review*, v. 3 # 1 (Fall, 1943): 45-54.

## C. THE TERROR

850. Antonov-Ovseyenko, A. V.: *The time of Stalin: portrait of tyranny*. New York: Harper & Row, 1981. 374 p.

Memoir-history of the Stalinist terror. Antonov-Ovseyenko integrates his own personal story of imprisonment and torture within the broader history of the *gulags* and terror. He also discusses the fate of Stalinism as a means of government in the USSR after Stalin's death: Khrushchev sought to undo Stalin's capricious abuses while Brezhnev reintroduced a degree of Stalinism into the Soviet system.

> # 70. Arendt, H.: *The origins of totalitarianism*.

851. Arnot, R. Page: "The Soviet trial." *Labour Monthly*, v. 20 # 5 (May, 1938): 298-306.

852. Brook-Shepherd, Gordon: *The storm petrels: the flight of the first Soviet defectors*. New York: Ballantine Books, 1982. 243 p. [PB]

Biographical history of the six earliest defectors from Stalinist Russia. Views them as the heralds of the Cold War, even though most defected in the 1930s and 1940s. Each of the six fled for a different reason: Grigory Agabekov, for example, defected because he fell in love with a Russian émigré living in Belgium. Walter Krivitsky, on the other hand, fled because he was a Jew who, having taken part in the Stalinist purges, was about to be purged himself. Offers an interesting insight into the inner politics of the Soviet Union during a critical period of history.

> # 1930. Butson, T. G.: *The Tsar's lieutenant.*

853. Carmichael, Joel: *Stalin's masterpiece: the show trials and purges of the thirties -- the consolidation of the Bolshevik dictatorship.* New York: St. Martin's Press, 1976. 238 p.

854. Conquest, Robert: "Excess deaths and camp numbers: some comments." *Soviet Studies*, v. 43 # 5 (1991): 949-952.

855. ---: "Forced labor statistics: some comments." *Soviet Studies*, v. 34 # 3 (July, 1982): 434-439.

856. ---: *The great terror: Stalin's purge of the thirties.* New York: Oxford University Press, 1990. 584 p.

Intensive history of Stalin's crimes originally published by Macmillan in 1968. The Oxford edition is updated to include materials that were made available after 1985. Conquest untangles the web of misinformation that surrounded the purges. Of special importance is his explanation of the causes for the purge, and specifically Stalin's motivations. Widely considered the authoritative work, this is a book that ought to be read by everyone seeking to understand Stalinist totalitarianism.

857. ---: *The harvest of sorrow: Soviet collectivization and the terror-famine.* New York: Oxford University Press, 1987. 412 p.

Intensive and erudite study into the Ukrainian terror famine in 1932 and 1933. Links the famine with Stalin's attempt to force collectivization on the *kulaks*, a process that began in 1929 but completed as a result of the famine. Conquest argues that the use of food as a weapon in Stalin's ideological war was tantamount to genocide.

858. ---: *Inside Stalin's secret police: NKVD politics, 1936-1939.* London: Macmillan, 1985. 222 p.

Charts internal developments in the Soviet secret police during the purge era. Although the text is of great interest, the nineteen appendixes which cover half the book are its crucial elements.

Included in these appendixes are: a list of NKVD personnel, police representatives at the Seventeenth Communist Party Congress, NKVD officials involved in the 1940 Katyn massacres, and details regarding the fate of the NKVD officers after the purges.

859. ---: *Stalin and the Kirov murder*. New York: Oxford University Press, 1989. 192 p.

Investigation into Stalin's role in the assassination of Sergei Kirov, then a key member of the CPSU Central Committee. By eliminating the second most powerful member of the Soviet political apparatus, and Stalin's heir apparent, the assassins directly led to the Stalinist terror of the 1930s. Based on extensive documentation, including 200 volumes of testimony collected during the Khrushchev thaw which were not published until the 1980s. Conquest establishes Stalin's role in the murder and clearly shows how he used it as a pretext for his extensive purges.

860. ---: "What is terror?" *Slavic Review*, v. 45 # 2 (Summer, 1986): 235-237.

861. Davies, R. W.: "The Syrtsov-Lominadze affair." *Soviet Studies*, v. 33 # 1 (January, 1981): 29-50.

Refers to the events that transpired after the defeat of the Communist "right" opposition leaders -- Nikolai N. Bukharin, Aleksei Rykov, and Mikhail Tomsky -- in November 1929. On December 1, 1938 two further members of the *Politburo*, Sergei Syrstov and Besso Lominadze, were expelled on Stalin's orders, under suspicion of sympathy with Stalin's opponents.

862. Dyadkin, Iosif G.: *Unnatural deaths in the USSR, 1928-1954* (translated from Russian by Tania Dereguine). New Brunswick, NJ: Transaction Books, 1983. 63 p.

Intensive investigation into Soviet depopulation policies. Dyadkin carefully reconstructs the rise and fall of the Soviet population, concluding that some seventy-eight million Russian souls were lost during the Stalin era: due to the terror famine, the purges, World War II, and the postwar punishment of nationalities considered collectively guilty of collaboration with the Nazis.

863. Ellman, Michael: "A note on the number of 1933 famine victims." *Soviet Studies*, v. 43 # 2 (1991): 375-380.

864. Getty, J. Arch: "Party and purge in Smolensk: 1933-1937." *Slavic Review*, v. 42 # 1 (Spring, 1983): 60-79.

865. Greenbaum, Avraham: "A note on the tradition of the twenty-four Soviet martyrs." *Soviet Jewish Affairs*, v. 17 # 1 (Spring, 1987): 49-52.

> # 566. Koestler, A.: *Darkness at noon*.

866. Kotkov, George: *The trial of Bukharin*. New York: Stein and Day, 1969. 255 p.

867. Karklins, Rasma: "The organization of power in Soviet labor camps." *Soviet Studies*, v. 41 # 2 (April, 1989): 276-297.

> # 1945. Laqueur, W.: *Stalin*.

868. Leites, Nathan and E. Bermant: *Ritual of liquidation: the case of the Moscow trials*. Glencoe, IL: The Free Press, 1954. 515 p.

869. Levytsky, Boris (comp.): *The Stalinist terror in the thirties*. Stanford, CA: Hoover Institution Press, 1974. 525 p.

Includes biographical entries on 234 victims of the Stalinist terror and their rehabilitation in the Khrushchev era.

870. Mace, James E.: "Famine and nationalism in Soviet Ukraine." *Problems of Communism*, v. 33 # 3 (May/June, 1984): 37-50.

Details the Stalinist 1932-1933 terror-famine policy that eliminated hundreds of thousands of *kulak*'s in large areas of the Ukraine.

871. McGlothlen, Ronald: "Plotter's masterpiece." *Military History*, v. 7 # 1 (August, 1990): 10-12, 20, 59-60.

Argues that *Sicherheitsdienst* chief Reinhard Heydrich forged documents about an impending military *coup* by Red Army leaders and then leaked them to Stalin, setting off the massive military purge.

872. McNeal, Robert H.: "The decisions of the CPSU and the great purge." *Soviet Studies*, v. 23 # 2 (October, 1971): 177-185.

873. ---: "Demonology: the orthodox Communist image of Trotskyism." *International Journal*, v. 32 # 1 (Winter, 1976/1977): 20-40.

> # 1954. Medvedev, R.: *All Stalin's men.*

874. Medvedev, Roy A.: *Let history judge: origins and consequences of Stalinism* (translated from Russian by Colleen Taylor). New York: Alfred A. Knopf, 1971. 566 p.

History of the Stalinist terror as viewed by Russia's first public dissident author. Concentrates on the purge trials held between 1937 and 1939. Integrates documents that were previously unknown in the West. Medvedev is thus able to add important details to the broadly known story on Soviet totalitarianism in the 1930s and 1940s.

875. Nove, Alec: "How many victims in the 1930s." *Soviet Studies*, v. 42 # 2 (April, 1990): 369-374; # 4 (October, 1990): 811-814.

> # 754. Rosefielde, S.: "Sources and uses of *gulag* forced labor."

876. Rosefielde, Steven: "Excess collectivization deaths 1929-1933: new demographic evidence." *Slavic Review*, v. 43 # 1 Spring, 1984): 83-88.

877. ---: "Incriminating evidence: excess deaths and forced labor under Stalin -- a final reply to critics." *Soviet Studies*, v. 39 # 2 (April, 1987): 292-313.

878. Seth, Ronald: *The executioners: the story of Smersh*. New York: Hawthorn Books, 1968. 199 p.

Investigation of the Soviet secret police, primarily focusing on the counterintelligence agency *Smersh* that was founded just before World War II. Seth, a member of the British Special Operations Executive during the war, has used his contacts to piece together what would otherwise be a shadowy story.

879. Shulman, Marshall: "A national response to the Soviet challenge." *International Affairs*, v. 61 # 3 (Summer, 1985): 375-383.

880. Solomon, Peter H., Jr.: "Soviet criminal justice and the great terror." *Slavic Review*, v. 46 # 3/4 (Fall/Winter, 1987): 391-413.

> # 571. Solzhenitsyn, A.: *The first circle.*

> # 572. ---: *The gulag archipelago.*

881. Thurston, Robert W.: "Fear and belief in the USSR's 'Great Terror': response to arrest, 1935-1939." *Slavic Review*, v. 45 # 2 (Summer, 1986): 213-234.

882. ---: "The Soviet family during the Great Terror, 1935-1941." *Soviet Studies*, v. 43 # 3 (1991): 553-574.

> # 576. Trifonov, Y.: *Dissapearance.*

883. Tucker, Robert C. and Stephen F. Cohen (eds.): *The great purge trial.* New York: Grosset & Dunlop, 1965. 725 p.

Reexamination of the Nikolai Bukharin trial of 1938, the last of the major purge trials. The text is divided into three parts: the introductory material placing Bukharin and the so-called Right opposition into context; the transcript of the trial, fully annotated by Tucker and Cohen, and the interpretative sections explaining the motivations of the principal figures involved.

884. Uldricks, Teddy J.: "The impact of the great purges on the People's Commissariat of Foreign Affairs." *Slavic Review*, v. 36 # 2 (June, 1977): 187-204.

> # 827. Viola, L.: "Campaign to eliminate the *kulak* as a class."

> # 763. Wheatcroft, S. G.: "Forced concentration camp labor."

885. Wheatcroft, S. G.: "More light on the scale of repression and excess mortality in the Soviet Union in the 1930s." *Soviet Studies*, v. 42 # 2 (April, 1990): 355-368.

> # 1986. Wittlin, T.: *Commissar.*

# 7

# The Great Patriotic War, 1939–1945

## A. SOVIET DIPLOMACY

886. Ainsztein, Reuben: "Stalin and June 22, 1941: some new Soviet views." *International Affairs*, v. 42 # 4 (October, 1966): 662-672.

887. Altshuler, Mordechai: "The Jewish Anti-Fascist Committee in the USSR in light of new documentation." *Studies in Contemporary Jewry*, v. 1 (1984): 253-291.

888. Beitzell, Robert: *The uneasy alliance: America, Britain, and Russia, 1941-1943*. New York: Alfred A. Knopf, 1972. 404 p.

Carefully documented study of Russian relations with Great Britain and the United States in the first three years of the Grand Alliance. Primarily concentrates on the differing aims of the three main war leaders -- Winston S. Churchill, Franklin D. Roosevelt, and Josef Stalin.

889. Beloff, Max: "Some aspects of Anglo-Soviet relations." *International Affairs*, v. 21 # 2 (April, 1945): 168-179.

890. Brown, Anthony C. and Charles B. MacDonald: *On a field of red: the Communist International and the coming of World War II*. New York: G. P. Putnam's Sons, 1981. 718 p.

Broad study of the secret politics of international relations on the eve of World War II. Views the subject from the perspective of *Comintern* and other illegal Soviet activity but also includes much extraneous material, for example, the flirtation with Nazism by the Duke and Duchess of Windsor. Thus, although not definitive, the work remains important and contributes greatly to the understanding of the origins and course of World War II.

> # 766. Chamberlin, W. H.: "Russia and Europe."

891. Cienciala, Anna M.: "The activities of Polish Communists as a source for Stalin's policy towards Poland in the Second World War." *International History Review*, v. 7 # 1 (February, 1985): 129-145.

> # 837. Garver, J. W.: *Chinese-Soviet relations*.

892. Herman, John: "Soviet peace efforts on the eve of World War II: a review of the Soviet documents." *Journal of Contemporary History*, v. 15 # 3 (July, 1980): 577-602.

893. Kettenacker, Lothar: "The Anglo-Soviet alliance and the problem of Germany, 1941-1945." *Journal of Contemporary History*, v. 17 # 3 (July, 1983): 435-458.

894. Knight, Jonathan: "Russia's search for peace: the London Council of Foreign Ministers, 1945." *Journal of Contemporary History*, v. 13 # 1 (January, 1978): 137-163.

895. Koch, H. W.: " The spectre of a seperate peace in the east: Russo-German peace-feelers, 1942-1944." *Journal of Contemporary History*, v. 10 # 3 (July, 1975): 531-549.

896. Krosbey, Peter H.: *Finland, Germany, and the Soviet Union, 1940-1941: the Petsamo dispute*. Madison: University of Wisconsin Press, 1968. 276 p.

Investigates Russo-German relations before the opening of Operation *Barbarossa*. In 1940 and 1941 Germany and Russia were linked by a non-agression treaty that, in essence, divided eastern

Europe into independent spheres of influence. This arrangement came into conflict over the status of Finland, and specifically expressed itself in Stalin's demand for the Petsamo region. Nazi Germany, already in the process of reevaluating its relationship with the USSR, officially undertook the role of honest broker. Krosbey has attempted to place the entire episode into its diplomatic context and has illuminated a lesser known aspect of World War II diplomacy.

897. Leonhard, Wolfgang: *Betrayal: the Hitler-Stalin pact of 1939.* New York: St. Martin's Press, 1989. 224 p.

Historical investigation of the Nazi-Soviet pact of August 1939. Written from a mildly revisionist perspective, Leonhard views the pact as a betrayal of all ideals that communism supposedly stood for then. Of special interest is how Leonhard links the events of August to September 1939 -- and their implications to the changes taking place in the Soviet Union in 1989.

898. Levin, Dov: "The Jews and the socio-economic Sovietization of Lithuania, 1940-41." *Soviet Jewish Affairs*, v. 17 # 2 (Summer/ Fall, 1987): 17-30; # 3 (Winter, 1987): 25-38.

> # 780. Low, A. D.: "Soviet Union and the *Anschluss* question."

> # 1366. Mayers, D.: "Soviet war aims and the Grand Alliance."

899. Millar, James R.: "Financing the Soviet effort in World War II." *Soviet Studies*, v. 32 # 1 (January, 1980): 106-123.

900. Mitrany, David: "The USSR and south-eastern Europe: permanent factors." *International Affairs*, v. 20 # 3 (July, 1944): 347-356.

901. Munting, Roger: "Lend-lease and the Soviet war effort." *Journal of Contemporary History*, v. 19 # 3 (July, 1984): 495-510.

Argues that historians must revise their evaluation of the impact Lend-lease had on keeping the Red Army fighting in World War II, especially concerning deliveries of food, medicine, and clothing.

902. Nadeau, Remi: *Stalin, Churchill, and Roosevelt divide Europe*. Westport, CT: Greenwood Press, 1990. 272 p.

Studies the Allies' three-way division of Europe. Nadeau has moved beyond the standard approach to note that the Anglo-American Allies did nothing to restrain Stalin's occupation of Eastern Europe. Despite Nadeau's mildly revisionist orientation, he does offer a number of novel insights. His assertion that the post-war division of Europe upset the balance of power between East and West cannot be sustained. Indeed, a contrary thesis -- that the balance of power was restored rather than upset -- could easily be developed.

903. Nazaroff, Alexander: "The Soviet oil industry." *Russian Review*, v. 1 # 1 (November, 1941): 81-89.

904. Pares, Bernard: *Russia and the peace*. New York: Macmillan Publishing, 1944. 293 p.

Investigation of Soviet war aims after the Nazi invasion, as stated by a British historian and expert on Eastern European affairs. Inter alia includes excurses into Russian history. Pares is sympathetic to the Russians and describes the means needed by the Western Allies to "win the peace" after the war against Nazism.

905. Raack, R. C.: "Stalin's plans for World War II." *Journal of Contemporary History*, v. 26 # 2 (April, 1991): 215-227.

906. Rieber, Alfred J.: *Stalin and the French Communist party, 1941-1947*. New York: Columbia University Press, 1962. 395 p.

Studies Stalin's wartime policy toward communism in Western Europe. The French Communist party was among the most active during the war, and gained considerable respect for its contribution to the *maquis*. Yet, Rieber notes, the French Communists failed to capture control of the French government and were unable to advance the Soviet interests in Western Europe. The reason for this failure was the uncritical support that French Communists gave to Stalin's ever twisting ideological policies. Based on numerous sources, Rieber has crafted an important contribution to the internal history of world communism at the beginning of the Cold War.

907. Roberts, Geoffrey: *The unholy alliance: Stalin's pact with Hitler.* Bloomington: Indiana University Press, 1989. 296 p.

New investigation of the Nazi-Soviet pact of August 1939, based on some materials not previously available to scholars. Argues that the traditional picture of the pact must be revised. Far from representing a change in orientation toward collective security and the Western Allies *per se*, Roberts argues that the pact represented Russia's despairing of an alliance with the British and French. Roberts thus lays the blame on both the Allies and the Russians for the failure of collective security: the former for their sloth in offering real guarantees to Stalin and the latter for their intense paranoia.

908. Rotundo, Louis: "Stalin and the outbreak of war in 1941." *Journal of Contemporary History*, v. 24 # 2 (April, 1989): 277-299.

909. Sevostyanov, Pavel: *Before the Nazi invasion: Soviet diplomacy in September 1939-June 1941*. Moscow: Progress Publishers, 1984. 304 p.

One-sided and polemical account of Soviet diplomacy between 1939 and 1941, which is fairly typical of Soviet historical orientations of the pre-*glasnost* era. Sevostyanov fails, for example, to mention elements of the Nazi-Soviet pact such as the secret annex regarding the division of Poland. He also disregards Soviet aggression against neutral Finland in November 1939. On the other hand, Sevostyanov's chapters on the Balkans and the Middle East are of interest, since they elucidate litlle-known aspects of interwar Soviet diplomacy. The most basic misconception found in the book is that it posits that the Soviet Union was at the center of international concerns during the 1930s. Such a position skewers the historical record in essence by projecting realities of the Cold War Era to the years before the Nazi invasion of the USSR on June 22, 1941.

910. Tombs, Isabelle: "Erlich and Alter, 'the Sacco and Vanzetti of

the USSR': an apisode in the wartime history of international socialism." *Journal of Contemporary History*, v. 23 # 4 (October, 1988): 531-549.

Draws a parallel between the execution of two leaders of the Polish-Jewish *Bund* at Stalin's behest with the celebrated Sacco and Vanzetti case.

911. Tsakaloyannis, Panos: "The Moscow Puzzle." *Journal of Contemporary History*, v. 21 # 1 (January, 1986): 37-55.

On the reputed agreement between Stalin and Churchill concerning the postwar division of Eastern Europe.

**B. THE EASTERN FRONT**

> # 1921. Andreyev, C.: *Vlasov*.

> # 752. Burgess, W. H.: *Inside Spetsnaz*.

912. Chameberlin , William H.: "The Soviet-German war: results and prospects." *Russian Review*, v. 1 # 2 (April, 1942): 3-9.

913. Dallin, David J.: "Inside the Red Army." *Russian Review*, v. 3 # 1 (Fall, 1943): 23-30.

914. Dobb, M. H.: *Soviet economy and the war*. London: Routledge, 1941. 88p.

915. Duffy, Christopher: *Red storm on the Reich*. New York: Atheneum / Maxwell Macmillan International, 1991. 403 p.

Reviews the final Red Army drive from Warsaw to Berlin that, together with the Anglo-American drive from the west, culminated in the end of World War II. Duffy provides a meticulous reconstruction of the operation -- on the tactical, strategic and grand strategic levels -- as seen from both the Soviet and Nazi perspective. Despite fanatical German resistance -- the Nazis feared and expected Soviet revenge *en masse* for *Wehrmacht* and

SS atrocities -- the operation that began in mid-January 1945 crushed the *Reich* in just three and a half months: all resistance in Berlin ending on May 1, 1945. The meeting with Anglo-American forces occurred on May 5, and on May 8 the Nazis unconditionally surrendered.

916. Erickson, J.: "The Soviet response to surprise attack: three directives, 22 June 1941." *Soviet Studies*, v. 23 # 4 (April, 1972): 519-553.

> # 564. Fedayev, A.: *The young guard*.

917. Förster, Jürgen: "The *Wehrmacht* and the war of extermination against the Soviet Union." *Yad Vashem Studies*, v. 14 (1981): 7-34.

918. Galagher, Matthew P.: *The Soviet history of World War II: myths, memories, and realities*. New York: Frederick A. Praeger, Publisher, 1963. 205 p. [PB]

Studies the political use of history in the Soviet Union by examining Soviet accounts of World War II. Galagher identifies four areas that have seen Soviet distortions: the initial period of the war -- which Soviet historians have largely ignored; the question of giving credit for victory -- including the evaluation of lend lease; the role played by the Western Allies; and the meaning of the Pacific war. Galagher could have added that the Soviets also distorted the Holocaust: refusing even to identify the Nazis' victims as Jews.

919. Glantz, David M.: *From the Don to the Dnepr: Soviet offensive operations, December 1942-August 1943*. London: Frank Cass, 1991. 450 p.

Micro study of Red Army operations after Stalingrad but before the battle of Kursk, primarily focused on operational and organizational aspects of the Don and Dnepr River Offensives. Since these operations were only partly successful, Glantz views them as part of a maturing force that had plunged rapidly and fully into mechanized warfare.

920. ---: *Soviet military intelligence in war.* London: Frank Cass, 1990. 440 p.

Reviews the history of the GRU (Soviet military intelligence) during World War II and assesses its successes and failures. Although Soviet military intelligence failed continually in the early months of operation *Barbarossa*, intelligence gathering and deception techniques improved, leading to tactical success after the battle of Kursk in 1943.

> # 565. Grossman, V.: *Lifa and fate.*

921. Keyssar, Helene and Vladimir Pozner: *Remembering war: a United States-Soviet dialogue.* New York: Oxford University Press, 1990. 254 p.

Journalistic retrospective of a time before the Cold War when the United States and the Soviet Union were allies: World War II. In addition to the authors' perspective, each chapter integrates twenty-five oral histories. Altogether the book is a reminder that despite crucial differences, Russians and Americans are also linked by a common past experience.

922. Kumanyev, Georgiy: "Some issues in Soviet historiography concerning World War II." *Yad Vashem Studies*, v. 21 (1991): 251-262.

923. Lieberman, Sanford R.: "The evacuation of industry in the Soviet Union during World War II." *Soviet Studies*, v. 35 # 1 (January, 1983): 90-102.

924. Myles, Bruce: *Night witches, the untold story of Soviet women in combat.* Movato, CA: Presidio Press, 1981. 278 p.

Primarily focuses on women combat pilots in the Red Air Force during World War II.

925. Nekrich, Aleksander M.: *"June 22, 1941" -- Soviet historians and the German invasion* (translated from Russian by Vladimir Petrov). Columbia: University of South Carolina Press, 1968. 322 p.

926. Newland, Samuel J.: *Cossacks in the German army 1941-1945.* London: Frank Cass, 1991. 210 p.

Study of Cossack military collaboration with the Nazis during World War II. Of the nearly one million Russians who joined the *Wehrmacht* between 1942 and 1945, only the Cossacks were granted recognition as an independent military force. Eventually, the Cossack units were united into the XV Cossack Cavalry Corps. Primarily focused on the military aspects of Cossack collaboration, Newland also explains the background of Cossack opposition to Stalin and to communism. Details the postwar repatriation of the Cossacks by the United States and Great Britain in 1947.

927. Paul, Allen: *Katyn: the untold story of Stalin's Polish massacre.* New York: Charles Scribner's Sons, 1991. 390 p.

History of the Stalinist massacre of Polish military officers and political leaders. After the Soviets occupied eastern Poland under the terms of the notorious Ribbentrop-Molotov agreement, a total of one million Poles were deported to Siberia. Among the deportees were virtually the entire leadership class, as well as numerous clergymen and teachers. In a related operation, some 15,400 military personnel were executed at three sites in the Katyn forest (near Smolensk). Among the victims were many Jews, including Rabbi Baruch Steinberg, the chief Jewish chaplain of the Polish Armed Forces. In April 1943 the Nazis discovered the site and used it for propaganda purposes in a vain effort to break the allaince between Russia and the Western powers. Paul has made use of materials in Poland, Germany, and Russia that only became available in the Gorbachev years.

928. Piekalkiewicz, Janusz: *Operation "Citadel" Kursk and Orel: the greatest tank battle of the Second World War* (translated from German by Michaela Nierhaus). Novato, CA: Presidio Press, 1987. 288 p.

Documentary history of the decisive clash that turned the tide of World War II on the Eastern Front. Piekalkiewicz cites material from both published and unpublished sources, interweaving his own evaluations and adding details not in the sources. About half the documents originate from Nazi sources; the remainder come from Soviet and Western sources. Of special interest is Piekalkiewicz's claim that British code breakers warned the Red Army of *Wehrmacht* plans in advance on the orders of Prime Minister Winston Churchill.

> # 844. Reese, R.: "The Red Army on the eve of World War II."

929. Seaton, Albert: *The Russo-German war, 1941-1945*. Novato, CA: Presidio Press, 1990 628 p.

Offers a comprehensive overview of the Eastern Front in World War II from 1941 to 1945. In addition to purely military matters, Seaton reviews economic, political, and diplomatic aspects of the war. The only lacuna is a treatment of German occupation policies, the extermination of approximately 1,500,000 Jews, and the battle of the Soviet partisans against the Nazi invaders.

930. Sella, Amnon: "Khalkin-Gol: the forgotten war." *Journal of Contemporary History*, v. 18 # 4 (October, 1983): 651-687.

Reviews the Russo-Japanese clashes in Manchuria in 1939.

931. ---: "Red Army doctrine and training on the eve of the Second World War." *Soviet Studies*, v. 27 # 2 (April, 1975): 245-264.

932. Spring, D. W.: "The Soviet decision for war against Finland, 30 November 1939." *Soviet Studies*, v. 38 # 2 (April, 1986): 207-226.

933. Stalin, Joseph: *The Great Patriotic War of the Soviet Union*. New York: International Publishers, 1945. 167 p.

Collection of Stalin's wartime speeches, from June 1941 to May 1945. Stalin's continuing references to Russian nationalist and religious symbols is of special interest.

934. Stephan, John J.: *The Russian Fascists: tragedy and farce in exile, 1925-1945*. New York: Harper & Row, 1978. 450 p.

Charts the growth of Fascist ideology among Russian émigrés in

France, America, and the Far East. Sees their actions as equal parts tragedy -- because of the fate of the émigrés that made them receptive to fascism -- and farce, because of the Fascists' frequent lapse into unreality. Although carefully documented, the study is not complete, since the history of Russian collaboration with the Nazi invaders during World War II has not been forthrightly studied in the Soviet Union. Despite the lacuna, Stephan's work is an interesting and thought provoking study of Fascist ideology.

935. Stephan, Robert: "Smersh: Soviet military counter-intelligence during the Second World War." *Journal of Contemporary History*, v. 22 # 4 (October, 1987): 585-613.

936. Vihavainen, Timo: "The Soviet decision for war against Finland, November 1939: a comment." *Soviet Studies*, v. 39 # 2 (April, 1987): 314-317.

937. Werth, Alexander: *Russia at war: 1941-1945*. New York: E. P. Dutton, 1964. 1,100 p.

Detailed study on the experience of the Soviet Union in what has come to be known as the Great Patriotic War. Reviews the history of the War chronologically from 1939. Werth does not avoid the unpleasant aspects of Russian participation in World War II: the 1939 Nazi-Soviet pact and the Katyn massacres. On the other hand, Werth expresses considerable admiration for the courage of the Russian people. Werth spent the entire period of the war in Russia as a correspondent for the *London Times*. He thus witnessed the initial disasters and the unprecedented stand of the Red Army, leading to ultimate victory. Werth supplements his own reports with materials originating with Russian and German sources. These sources make Werth's account authoritative if not definitive.

938. Whaley, Barton: *Codeword Barbarossa*. Cambridge, MA: The MIT Press, 1974. 377 p. [PB]

Incisive day-by-day study of the events leading up to the Nazi attack on the Soviet Union on June 22, 1941. Whaley concentrates on the question: why were Soviet troops caught unprepared for the onslaught? This leads him to an assessment of the different intelligence data available to Soviet leaders before the attack. Among other sources, the Soviets could rely on a group of spies in Western Europe (including some in Germany), yet, they ignored all sources because Stalin staunchly refused to believe the reports. Until the last minute he believed that reports of an imminent German attack were a British plot. Written with a specific historical concept in mind, Whaley's book has many applications in the study of intelligence and of intelligence failures.

## C. THE HOLOCAUST IN SOVIET TERRITORY

> # 1005. Altman, I.: "Toward the history of the *Black Book.*"

> # 887. Altshuler, M.: "The Jewish Anti-Fascist Committee."

939. Arad, Yitzhak: "Alfred Rosenberg and the 'Final Solution' in the occupied Soviet territories." *Yad Vashem Studies*, v. 13 (1979): 263-286.

940. ---: "Concentration of refugees in Vilna on the eve of the Holocaust." *Yad Vashem Studies*, v. 9 (1973): 201-214.

941. ---: "The 'Final Solution' in Lithuania in the light of German documentation." *Yad Vashem Studies*, v. 11 (1976): 234-272.

942. ---: "The Holocaust of Soviet Jewry in the occupied territories of the Soviet Union." *Yad Vashem Studies*, v. 21 (1991): 1-47.

943. ---, Shmuel Krakowski, and Shmuel Spector (eds.): *The Einsatzgruppen reports: selections from the dispatches of the Nazi Death Squads' campaign against the Jews July 1941-January 1943* (translated from German by Stella Schossberger). New York: Holocaust Library, 1989. 378 p. [PB]

Anthology of selected reports from the Nazi mobile killing squads (*Einsatzgruppen*) that operated in Eastern Poland and the Soviet Union. The *Einsatzgruppen* were tasked by the SS with killing Russian Jews and eliminating all groups listed in the so-called *Kommisarsbefehl*: all Communist party officials, all resisters, and "all life unworthy of being lived." In the course of their first sweep the *Einsatzgruppen* murdered more than one million Jews and thousands of others in an unprecedented cycle of murder and destruction. The texts included in this volume offer an inside view of this operation.

> # 414. Aronsfeld, C. C.: "Soviet propaganda."

> # 971. Bar-On, Z.: "The Jews in the Soviet partisan movement."

944. Bauer, Yehuda: "Rescue operations through Vilna." *Yad Vashem Studies*, v. 9 (1973): 215-223.

945. Büchler, Yehoshua: "*Kommandostab Reichsführer-SS*: Himmler's personal murder brigades in 1941." *Holocaust and Genocide Studies*, v. 1 # 1 (1986): 11-25.

946. Cholavsky, Shalom: "The German Jews in the Minsk ghetto." *Yad Vashem Studies*, v. 17 (1986): 219-245.

> # 972. ---: *Soldiers from the ghetto.*

947. Edelheit, Abraham J.: "The Soviet Union, the Jews, and the Holocaust." *Holocaust Studies Annual*, v. 4 (1990): 113-134.

Reviews the question of wartime rescue and postwar Soviet distortions of Holocaust history.

948. Ehrenburg, Ilya and Vasily Grossman: *The black book* (translated from Russian by John Glad and James S. Levine). New York: Holocaust Library, 1981. 595 p. [PB]

Comprehensive documentary history of the Holocaust in the Soviet Union. The original text was prepared by the Jewish Anti-Fascist Committee between 1943 and 1946. The work was intended to be part of a multiple volume set documenting the suffering and heroism of Soviet Jewry during the Great Patriotic War. The book was suppressed by the KGB in 1948 for ideological reasons. In 1965 a copy was smuggled out through Poland to Israel and published by *Yad Vashem* in 1980. The present edition is an English translation of that most important documentary work.

949. "Extermination of two Ukrainian Jewish communities: testimony of a German army officer." *Yad Vashem Studies*, v. 3 (1959): 303-320.

> # 917. Förster, J.: "The war of extermination."

950. Gutman, Yisrael and Gideon Greif (eds): *The historiography of the Holocaust period*. Jerusalem: Yad Vashem, 1988.

Proceedings of the fifth *Yad Vashem* historical conference, held in Jerusalem in March 1983. Covering a wide range of topics, each essay investigates the ways that Holocaust history has been written by Jewish and non-Jewish historians. The essays offer important insights on both methodological and factual issues. The five essays that deal with the treatment of the Holocaust in Soviet historiography: primarily with Soviet efforts to distort the Holocaust by robbing Jewish victims of their identity and by accusing Zionists of collaboration with the Nazis.

CONTENTS (articles relevant to the Soviet Union only): Y. Arad: The Holocaust in Soviet historiography / M. Altschuler: Jewish warfare and the participation of Jews in combat in the Soviet Union as reflected in Soviet and western historiography / D. Levin: The Soviet communist motif and its effects on the subject of the Holocaust in the Baltic émigré historiography / S. Spector: The attitude of the Ukrainian diaspora to the Holocaust of Ukrainian Jewry / S. Cholawski: The Holocaust and the armed struggle in Belorussia as reflected in Soviet literature and works by émigrés in the west.

951. Hillgruber, Andreas: "War in the East and the extermination of the Jews." *Yad Vashem Studies*, v. 18 (1987): 103-132.

> # 975. Kahanowitz, M.: "Jewish partisan movement."

> # 372. Korey, W.: *The Soviet cage*.

> # 373. ---: "Soviet treatment of the Holocaust."

952. Korzen, Meir: "Problems arising out of research into the history of the Jewish refugees in the USSR during the Second World War." *Yad Vashem Studies*, v. 3 (1959): 119-140.

> # 567. Kuznetsov, A.: *Babi Yar*.

953. Levin, Dov: "Estonian Jews in the USSR (1941-1945)." *Yad Vashem Studies*, v. 11 (1976): 273-297.

> # 977. ---: *Fighting back*.

> # 898. ---: "Socio-economic Sovietization of Lithuania."

954. ---: "July 1944: the crucial month for the remnants of Lithuanian Jewry." *Yad Vashem Studies*, v. 16 (1984): 333-361.

955. ---: "Lithuanian Jewish refugees in the Soviet Union during World War II, 1941-45." *Studies in Contemporary Jewry*, v. 4 (1988): 185-209.

956. Litani, Dora: "The destruction of the Jews of Odessa in the light of Rumanian documents." *Yad Vashem Studies*, v. 6 (1967): 135-154.

957. Lozowick, Yaacov: "*Rollbahn Mord*: the early activities of *Einsatzgruppe* C." *Holocaust and Genocide Studies*, v. 2 # 2 (1987): 221-241.

958. Pinchuk, Ben-Cion: "Soviet media on the fate of Jews in Nazi-occupied territory (1939-1941)" *Yad Vashem Studies*, v. 11 (1976): 221-233.

959. ---: "Was there a Soviet policy for evacuating the Jews? The case of the annexed territories." *Slavic Review*, v. 39 # 1 (March, 1980): 44-55.

960. Schneider, Gertrude: *Journey into terror: the story of the Riga ghetto*. New York: Ark House, 1979. 229 p.

Personalized history of the ghetto in Riga, Latvia, by one of its survivors, including citations from a diary the author kept while incarcerated there. Focuses primarily on the German Jews who were deported to Riga and perished there.

961. --- (ed.): *The unfinished road: Jewish survivors of Latvia look back*. New York: Praeger Publishers, 1991. 232 p.

Compendium of fifteen eyewitness testimonies of the Nazi extermination of Latvian Jewry. The entire gamut of Holocaust experiences of Latvian Jewry is included: concentration camps, ghettos, deportation, resistance, and escape attempts. Of special interest are the recollections of German and Austrian Jews who were deported to Latvia in 1942-1943, very few of whom survived. All of the testimonies offer a perspective on the courage and endurance of the Jewish victims of Nazi barbarity.

CONTENTS: G. Schneider: The unfinished road / B. Minkowicz: Arrest and expulsion to Siberia / J. Robinson: Julia's story / T. U. Schloss: A farm called Jungernhof / A. Levin: The Jewish SS officer / I. Berner: The death sentence / I. Kleiman: And the Lord spoke on my behalf / N. Ungar: Last Jewish knight of Vienna / S. Springfield: A life saved by a beating / Y. Basner: Tough luck / G. R. Klebanow: The children in camp Kaiserwald / A. Shpungin: The terrors of Dundaga / R. Wassermann: And I almost did not make it / E. S. Schwab: A daughter remembers.

962. Shapiro, Gershon (comp.): *Under fire: the stories of Jewish heroes of the Soviet Union* (translated from Russian by Rose Lavoott; source material edited by Chaya Lifchitz). Jerusalem: Yad Vashem, 1988. 645 p.

Biographical directory of Soviet Jews who served with distinction in the Red Army during World War II and who won the Hero of the Soviet Union award. Each of the heroes' story is told in detail to chronicle Jewish heroism and put paid to the theory of Jewish cowardice in the face of Nazi oppression.

963. Smolar, Hersh: *The Minsk ghetto: Soviet-Jewish partisans against the Nazis* (translated from *Yiddish* by Max Rosenfeld). New York: Holocaust Library, 1989. 175 p. [PB]

Memoir-history of the Jewish partisan movement in Minsk. Elucidates both the Nazi extermination program and Jewish responses to persecution. Smolar also places Jewish resistance into its Soviet context, since Jews *per se* were not permitted to organize independent partisan units (their units had to join general ones). Smolar is brutally blunt about the Russian populace's attitude (including many partisans) toward Jews: at best apathy; at worst antisemitism.

964. Spector, Shmuel: "The Jews of Volhynia and their reaction to extermination." *Yad Vashem Studies*, v. 15 (1983): 159-186.

> # 560. Szmeruk, C.: "Jewish literature in the Soviet Union."

965. "Testimony of Herman F. Graebe, given in Israel." *Yad Vashem Studies*, v. 6 (1967): 283-313.

Complete transcript of tape-recorded testimony by Mr. Graebe at *Yad Vashem* in Fall 1965. The testimony, given in German, was translated into Hebrew and English by *Yad Vashem*'s Department for the Collection of Evidence. A German civil engineer employed by the Nazis in occupied Soviet territories, Graebe accidentally witnessed the destruction of the Jewish community of Rovno and the extermination of thousands of Jews of the Rovno *Oblast.*

966. Tory, Avraham: *Surviving the Holocaust: the Kovno ghetto diary* (edited and introduced by Martin Gilbert; textual and historical notes by Dina Porat; translated from Hebrew by J. Michalowicz). Cambridge, MA: Harvard University Press, 1990. 554 p.

Diary offering a vivid perspective on the destruction of the Jews of Kovno, Lithuania. Tory, as a member of the Kovno *Judenrat*, was in a position which allowed him the opportunity to collect copies of all pertinent documents; these documents are extensively cited throughout. Offers an insightful perspective an almost every issue raised in Holocaust historiography.

**D. THE PARTISAN WAR**

967. Armstrong, John (ed.): *The Soviet partisans in World War II* (foreword by Philip E. Mosley). Madison: University of Wisconsin Press, 1964. 792 p.

968. Asprey, Robert B.: *War in the shadows: the guerrilla in history* (2 vols.). Garden City, NY: Doubleday, 1975. 1,475 p.

Broad history of guerrilla warfare, concentrating on the Viet Nam War. Asprey also discusses the theory of guerrilla warfare -- especially as developed by Chinese Communist leader Mao Zedong. Chapter 22 and 23 deal with the Russian Revolution and the Civil War, while chapters 33 through 37 detail the partisans' struggle on the Eastern Front in World War II.

969. Baritz, J. J.: "The phantom war." *History of World War II*, # 49 (1973): 1365-1372.

970. ---: "The war of the rails." *History of World War II*, # 103 (1974): 2858-2865.

971. Bar-On, Zvi: "The Jews in the Soviet partisan movement." *Yad Vashem Studies*, v. 4 (1960): 167-190.

972. Cholawski, Shalom: *Soldiers from the ghetto*. San Diego, CA: A. S. Barnes, 1980. 182 p.

Memoir-history of the Jewish partisans in Nesvizh, Belorussia. Cholawski describes his efforts to help organize a Jewish underground in Nesvizh, which ultimately led to the first of the ghetto uprisings in Nazi-occupied Eastern Europe.

973. Cooper, Matthew: *The Nazi war against Soviet partisans 1941-1944*. New York: Stein & Day, Publishers, 1979. 217 p.

History of the irregular war on the Eastern Front. Views the issue from three perspectives: that of the partisans, that of the Germans, and that of Russian collaborators with the *Wehrmacht*. The partisan war is viewed from both the military and political perspectives, and he elucidates the parties' successes and failures. Eleven appendixes cite the key German documents on the treatment of civilians and partisans -- dubbed bandits -- in the occupied Eastern territories.

974. Ignatov, P. Z.: *Partisans of the Kuban* (translated from Russian by J. Fineberg). London: Hutchinson, 1945. 212 p.

Diary dealing with the activities of the Ignatov brothers' partisan unit operating in the German rear.

975. Kahanowitz, Moshe: "Why no separate Jewish partisan movement was established during World War II." *Yad Vashem Studies*, v. 1 (1957): 153-167.

976. Kovpak, S. A.: *Our partisan course* (translated from Russian by Ernst and Mira Lesser). London: Hutchinson, 1947. 120 p.

Personal narrative by Soviet Major-General S. A. Kovpak, who commanded large partisan units behind German army lines during the Great Patriotic War.

977. Levin, Dov: *Fighting back: Lithuanian Jewry's armed resistance to the Nazis, 1941-1945* (translated from Hebrew by Moshe Kohn and Dina Cohen; foreword by Yehuda Bauer). New York: Holmes & Meier, 1985. 298 p.

Comprehensive investigation into the attempts of Lithuanian Jewry to resist the Nazis. Also details the extent of Lithuanian-Jewish relations. Levin divides Jewish resistance in Lithuania into three parts: Jewish partisans; ghetto and camp revolts; and Jewish participation in the Lithuanian division of the Red Army. The book also includes a brief, but interesting, sketch of prewar Lithuanian Jewry.

978. Miksche, F. O.: *Secret forces: the technique of underground movements*. London: Faber and Faber, n.d. 181 p.

Handbook of guerrilla warfare, based on the Soviet and East European experience in World War II. Chapter I places the book into context by studying the impact of Marxism on modern warfare.

979. Mountfield, David: *The partisans: secret armies of World War II*. London: Hamlyn, 1979. 192 p.

Geographically organized history of underground warfare in World War II. Mountfield reviews the Soviet partisans' experiences on pp. 171-190.

980. Simonov, Konstantin et al: *Behind the front lines*. London: Hutchinson, 1945. 160 p.

Anthology describing the operations of Soviet partisans during the Great Patriotic War. Primary focus is on Belorussia, the Ukraine, and the Baltic republics. Simonov includes a broad overview on partisan operational tactics within the context of Red Army theories on guerrilla warfare. Provides important insights into the struggle against Nazi invaders.

981. Snow, "Guerrilla tactics in Soviet defense." *American Review of the Soviet Union*, v. 4 # 4 (October/November, 1941): 3-10.

# 8

# The Era of the Cold War

## A. STALIN'S FINAL YEARS

### 1. Overviews

982. Bolsover, G. H.: "Soviet ideology and propaganda." *International Affairs*, v. 24 # 2 (April, 1948): 170-180.

983. Courtney, Anthony: "The background of Russian sea-power." *International Affairs*, v. 30 # 1 (January, 1954): 13-23.

> # 862. Dyadkin, I. G.: *Unnatural deaths in the USSR*.

984. Guins, George C.: "The Academy of Sciences of the USSR." *Russian Review*, v. 12 # 4 (October, 1953): 269-278.

985. Hahn, Werner G.: *Postwar Soviet politics: the fall of Zhdanov and the defeat of moderation, 1945-1953*. Ithaca, NY: Cornell University Press, 1982. 243 p.

Investigates the politics of ideology and science in the last years of Stalin's rule. Andrei Zhdanov, Stalin's deputy from 1946 to 1948, was sacked that year because of his "independent" theories. Hahn notes that Zhdanov's fall was also political, since he had advocated a friendly course toward Yugoslavia as well as peaceful coexistence with the United States. Both of these positions were in opposition to Stalin's views and ultimately signaled Zhdanov's fall from power.

986. Saunders, George (ed.): *Samizdat: voices of the Soviet opposition*. New York: Monad Press, 1974. 464 p.

Anthology of sources displaying the development of Soviet opposition movements. Begins with the opponents of Stalin's regime who survived the Terror, almost all of them in *gulags*, and continues with the opposition that arose during the Khrushchev thaw. After Khrushchev was removed from office in 1964, this democratic opposition developed into the *samizdat* that continued to advocate reform until it finally participated in the democratic reforms of 1989-1991.

987. Schwartz, Harry: *The red phoenix: Russia since World War II*. New York: Frederick A. Praeger, Publisher, 1961. 427 p. [PB]

Journalistic history of the Soviet Union after World War II. Presents a vivid picture of Russia's devastation in 1945. Thereafter, Schwartz reviews developments over the following fifteen years. The chapters are arranged thematically. Although social and intellectual issues are covered, the bulk of the book reviews political and diplomatic developments during Stalin's last years and Khrushchev's abortive thaw.

988. Ulam, Adam B.: *The Communists: the story of power and lost illusions, 1948-1991*. New York: Scribner's, 1992. 528 p.

Important history of the Cold War, written by one of America's foremost Sovietologists. Of special importance is Ulam's re-evaluation of Stalin: Ulam has come to the conclusion that Stalin saw communism as a means to increase his own personal power. In addition, the author evaluates the role of communism in both its rise and fall, as well as its part in the Cold War. Individual chapters consider Nikita S. Khrushchev's aborted reform, the Brezhnev era of détente, and the East European revolutions of 1989.

989. Urban, George: *Stalinism*. New York: St. Martin's Press, 1982. 400 p.

990. Wheeler, G. E.: "Soviet policy in Central Asia." *International Affairs*, v. 31 # 3 (July, 1955): 317-326.

**2. Domestic Policy**

991. Alexandrov, B.: "The Soviet currency reform." *Russian Review*, v. 8 # 1 (January, 1949): 56-61.

992. Berman, Harold J.: "The restoration of law in Soviet Russia." *Russian Review*, v. 6 # 1 (Fall, 1946): 3-10.

993. Brumberg, Abraham: "The Soviet campaign against 'survivals of capitalism'." *Russian Review*, v. 12 # 2 (April, 1953): 65-78.

994. Colton, Timothy J.: "The Zhukov affair reconsidered." *Soviet Studies*, v. 29 # 2 (April, 1977): 185-213.

995. Crowfoot, John and Mark Harrison: "The USSR Council of Ministers under late Stalinism 1944-1954: its production branch composition and the requirements of national economy and policy." *Soviet Studies*, v. 42 # 1 (January, 1990): 39-58.

996. Feshbach, Murray: "The age structure of Soviet population: preliminary analysis of unpublished data." *Soviet Economy*, v. 1 # 2 (April/June, 1985): 177-193.

997. Frankel, Edith R.: "Literary policy in Stalin's last year." *Soviet Studies*, v. 28 # 3 (July, 1976): 391-405.

998. Girnius, Kestutis K.: "The collectivization of Lithuanian agriculture, 1944-1950." *Soviet Studies*, v. 40 # 3 (July, 1988): 460-478.

999. Harrison, Mark: "Macroeconomic efficiency of capital formation in Soviet industry under late Stalinism, 1945-1955." *Soviet Studies*, v. 39 # 2 (April, 1987): 269-280.

1000. Jasny, Naum: "Soviet agriculture and the fourth Five-Year plan." *Russian Review*, v. 8 # 2 (April, 1949): 135-141.

1001. ---: "Soviet grain crops and their distribution." *International Affairs*, v. 28 # 4 (October, 1952): 452-459.

1002. Karasev, Ivan V.: "The reconstruction of agriculture in Pskow *Oblast*, 1945-1953." *Soviet Studies*, v. 43 # 2 (1991): 301-310.

> # 348. Marples, D. R.: "The *kulak* in post-was USSR."

1003. Nicolaevsky, Boris I.: "The new Soviet campaign against the peasants." *Russian Review*, v. 10 # 2 (April, 1951): 81-98.

> # 754. Rosefielde, S.: "Uses of *gulag* forced labor."

1004. Schwarz, Solomon M.: "Economic reconstruction in the Soviet Union." *Russian Review*, v. 4 # 2 (Spring, 1945): 49-61.

> # 409. Taagepera, R.: "Collectivization of Estonian agriculture."

### 3. Minorities Policy

1005. Altman, Ilya: "Toward the history of the *Black Book*." *Yad Vashem Studies*, v. 21 (1991): 221-249.

> # 351. Altshuler, M.: *Soviet Jewry since the Second World War.*

1006. Berard-Zarzycka, Ewa: "Ilya Ehrenburg in Stalin's postwar Russia." *Soviet Jewish Affairs*, v. 17 # 1 (Spring, 1987): 31-48.

1007. Bethell, Nicholas: *The last secret: the delivery to Stalin of over two million Russians by Britain and the United States.* New York: Basic Books, 1974. 224 p.

Chronicles the forcible repatriation of almost two million Russians by the Allied Military Government in Germany and Italy after World War II. Large numbers of repatriatees were prisoners of war and concentration camp inmates considered "tainted" by the NKVD because of their contact with the West. Bethell views the repatriation episode as an early part of the Cold War. He particularly emphasizes Stalin's insistence that all Russians be repatriated, by force if necessary. Indeed, at the Yalta Conference Stalin hinted that liberated Allied POW's would not be returned if the Russians were not returned. In his moral fervor Bethell fails to mention that a large proportion of the repatriated Soviet nationals were Nazi collaborators. Despite the massive repatriation, hundreds of thousands of Ukrainian, Latvian, Lithuanian, and Estonian Nazi collaborators entered Western countries in the late 1940s and 1950s.

1008. Bilinsky, Yaroslav: *The second Soviet republic: The Ukraine after World War II*. New Brunswick, NJ: Rutgers University Press, 1964. 539 p.

Political analysis of Ukrainian development after World War II. Includes social, economic, and demographic data as well, thus placing political results into context. Offers a detailed examination of Ukrainian nationalism after the war.

1009. Brackman, Roman: "Stalin's failed massacre." *Midstream*, v. 33 # 10 (December, 1987): 16-20.

> # 947. Edelheit, A. J.: "The Soviet Union and the Holocuast."

> # 799. Gilboa, Y. A.: *The Black years of Soviet Jewry*.

1010. Goldberg, B. Z.: *The Jewish problem in the Soviet Union: analysis and solution*. New York: Crown Publishers, 1961. 374 p.

Journalistic account of the fate of Soviet Jewry during the Stalin years. Written in the form of an account of three trips to Russia -- in 1934, 1946, and 1959. Inter alia, Goldberg traces social and cultural developments within Soviet Jewry. His primary focus is the continuation of a Jewish problem in the Soviet Union even after the rise of communism. One of the most poignant sections of the book describes the execution of Soviet Jewish intellectuals at Stalin's orders. Goldberg was one of the first to realize that this campaign was part of a larger Stalinist plan to decimate Soviet Jewry.

> # 2003. Markish, E.: *The long return*.

1111. Nekrich, Aleksandr M.: *The punished peoples: the deportation and fate of Soviet minorities at the end of the Second World War* (translated from Russian by George Saunders). New York: W. W. Norton, 1978. 238 p.

Based on previously unavailable documentation, Nekrich's monograph provides case studies of Soviet nationalities policy in the aftermath of World War II. The national groups included in his study were all accused of collaborating with the Nazis (in most cases true) and were punished by being uprooted and relocated within the Soviet Union. The book leaves some questions unanswered -- for example, why were the Volga Germans not treated the same way as other national groups accused of collaboration. This, however, is likely due to a lack of documentation rather than improper methodology. Overall, *The punished peoples* is an important study on the ideology and politics of national minorities in Stalinist Russia.

1012. Pinkus, Benjamin: *The Soviet government and the Jews, 1948-1967: a documented study*. London: Cambridge University Press, 1984. 612 p.

Fact filled volume covering the fate of Jewry in the Soviet Union during Stalin's final years through Khrushchev's abortive thaw. The sections of the book combine analysis with documentation, as the author adeptly places complex issues in their proper context. Pinkus notes a positive correlation between the level of antisemitism in Russia and Soviet policy toward Israel during three crucial periods: Stalin's last years (1948-1953), the Khrushchev thaw (1953-1956), and the period of Khrushchev's withdrawl from liberalization (1959-1963). A companion volume covering the years after the Six-day War has been promised, but has not yet appeared.

1013. Rapoport, Louis: *Stalin's war against the Jews: the doctors' plot and the Soviet solution*. New York: The Free Press, 1990. 318 p.

Journalistic account of Stalin's attempt to purge Soviet Jewry during his last years of life. Begins with the startling revelation that the Kremlin's Jewish doctors were arrested for plotting to poison top Soviet leaders. Rapoport places the doctors' plot into the context of Stalin's antisemitism and the Holocaust. Stalin planned to use the plot -- which in fact he and Lavrentyi Beria, the NKVD chief, concocted -- as the first step in a purge that would culminate in the deportation of all Soviet Jews to Siberia. A chilling and sobering account of Stalin's antisemitism and the insecurity of all national minorities in the USSR.

1014. Rapoport, Yakov: *The doctors' plot of 1953*. Cambridge, MA: Harvard University Press, 1991. 280 p.

Personal history of the 1953 Doctors' Plot. Rapoport, one of nine doctors falsely accused of plotting to kill Stalin, admitted nothing, and utterly refused to testify against the others. Stalin's death prevented the plot's pursuit, thereby halting Stalin's further intentions to systematically purge Soviet Jewry.

1015. Ro'i, Y.: *The struggle for Soviet Jewish emigration, 1948-1967*. New York: Cambridge University Press, 1990. 512 p.

Examines Soviet Jewry's struggle for emigration from the establishment of the State of Israel (May 14, 1948) to the Six-day War (June 5, 1967). In addition to published documents, Ro'i integrates a large number of interviews with Soviet *olim*. Inter alia Ro'i also investigates Russian Jewish identity including the impact of the Holocaust, and popular antisemitism in Russia.

> # 560. Szmeruk, C.: "Jewish literature in the Soviet Union."

1016. Tolstoy, Nikolai: *Stalin's secret war*. New York: Holt, Rinehart, and Winston, 1982. 463 p.

Exposé of Stalin's post World War II purges among the Russian people. Tolstoy contends that some ten million Russians were eliminated either because they collaborated with the Nazis, or because of their alleged counterrevolutionary intentions. Also details the Doctor's Plot and its implications for Soviet Jewry. Tolstoy has produced a work infused with a sense of morality, but with the careful eye of critical schoiarship.

## 4. The Cold War

1017. Buhite, Russel D.: *Soviet-American relations in Asia, 1945-1954*. Norman: University of Oklahoma Press, 1981. 254 p.

Studies the origins of the Cold War in Asia. Centers on two issues: the Chinese Civil War and the Korean War. In both cases Buhite emphasizes the essentially reactive nature of American policy and its responses to Communist attacks.

1018. Bruegel, Bedrich: "Methods of Soviet domination in the satellite states." *International Affairs*, v. 27 # 1 (January, 1951): 32-37.

1019. Checinski, Michael: "Soviet-Polish relations and the Polish Jews." *Midstream*, v. 26 # 5 (May, 1980): 9-15.

1020. Clemens, Walter C., Jr.: "The Soviet world faces West: 1945-1970." *International Affairs*, v. 46 # 3 (July, 1970): 475-489.

Examines Soviet-Western relations in the aftermath of the Potsdam Conference (July 17, 1945).

1021. Colville, John: "How the West lost the peace in 1945." *Commentary*, v. 80 # 3 (September, 1985): 41-47.

1022. Crankshaw, Edward: "Russia in Europe: the conflict of values." *International Affairs*, v. 22 # 4 (October, 1946): 501-510.

1023. ---: "The USSR revisited." *International Affairs*, v. 23 # 4 (October, 1947): 492-499.

1024. Djilas, H. E. Milovan: "Yugoslav-Soviet relations." *International Affairs*, v. 27 # 2 (April, 1951): 167-175.

1025. Healey, Denis: "The Cominform and world communism." *International Affairs*, v. 24 # 3 (July, 1948): 339-349.

1026. ---: "The *Sputnik* and Western defence." *International Affairs*, v. 34 # 2 (April, 1958): 145-156.

1027. Herz, Martin F.: *The beginnings of the Cold War*. Bloomington: Indiana University Press, 1966. 214 p.

Objective study of the origins of the Cold war, based on documents available in the West. Blames both the United States and the Soviet Union for the increasing tension, though ultimately Herz concludes that Russian expansionism was the primary cause for international conflict.

> # 224. Killen, L. R.: *The Soviet Union and the United States.*

> # 894. Knight, J.: "Russia's search for peace."

1028. Külz, H. R.: "The Soviet zone of Germany: a study of developments and policies." *International Affairs*, v. 27 # 2 (April, 1951): 156-166.

> # 1367. Merrick, R.: "British Foreign Office and the Cold War."

> # 902. Nadeau, R.: *Stalin, Churchill, and Roosevelt divide Europe.*

1029. Nogee, Joseph and Robert H. Donaldson: *Soviet foreign policy since World War II*. Elmsford, NY: Pergamon Press, 1981. 319 p.

Textbook written for use in college courses on Soviet history of the Cold War. Written in strict chronological order, Nogee and Donaldson attempt to place Soviet foreign affairs into context. In addition, they focus some attention on the theoretical foundations of Soviet foreign policy. Their annotated bibliography will be especially useful to students and researchers interested in more details on the themes discussed in the book.

> # 1370. Paterson, T. G.: *Soviet-American confrontation.*

> # 906. Rieber, A. J.: *Stalin and the French Communist party.*

1030. Schmid, Alex P. with Ellen Berends: *Soviet military intervention since 1945*. New Brunswick, NJ: Transaction Books, 1985. 223 P.

Investigates the postwar use of the Red Army to further Communist goals beyond the borders of the Soviet Union. Schmid's broad study is supplemented by Berend's ten case studies of direct Soviet military intervention. Schmid carefully distinguishes two types of Soviet interventions: those occuring within the Soviet bloc and those external to the Soviet bloc. This division is somewhat undone by the case studies, since Greece (where the Soviets did not directly intervene), Iran, and Austria (where they did) were not in the Soviet bloc (or any other bloc, for that matter) at the time of Red Army intervention (case studies 6, 7, and 9); yet all of them are considered "interbloc interventions." The fact that the authors find only one extra-bloc intervention -- in Afghanistan -- displays the extent of caution the Soviets maintained regarding adventurism abroad.

1031. Thomas, Hugh: *Armed truce: the beginnings of the Cold War, 1945-1946.* London: Hamish Hamilton, 1986. 667 p.

Describes the international situation at the beginning of the Cold War. Reviews the subject both geographically and thematically. Each of the areas of conflict between the United States and the Soviet Union are descibed in light of local conditions.

1032. Vloyantes, J. P.: *Silk glove hegemony: Finnish-Soviet relations, 1944-1974.* Kent, OH: Kent State University Press, 1975. 208 p.

Chronological study of thirty years of relations between Finland and the USSR. Offers interesting insights into the relations between a small nation and a superpower neighbor, especially in times of crisis. The book thus fills an important role in explaining the history of the Cold War in the Nordic circle.

1033. Winterton, Paul: "The aims of the USSR in Europe." *International Affairs*, v. 22 # 1 (January, 1946): 14-27.

### 5. Relations with China and the Third World

1034. Atkinson, George W.: "The Sino-Soviet treaty of friendship and alliance." *International Affairs*, v. 23 # 3 (July, 1947): 357-366.

1035. Beloff, Max: "Soviet policy in China." *International Affairs*, v. 27 # 3 (July, 1951): 285-296.

1036. Efrat, Moshe: "The economics of Soviet arms transfers to the Third World -- a case study: Egypt." *Soviet Studies*, v. 35 # 4 (October, 1983): 437-456.

> # 837. Garver, J. W.: *Chinese-Soviet relations*.

1037. Golan, Galia: *Soviet politics in the Middle East: from World War II to Gorbachev*. New York Cambridge University Press, 1990. 344 p. [PB]

Broad chronological study of Soviet Middle East policy from World War II to 1989. Organized as a series of case studies, Golan notes that despite shifts in emphasis the Soviets have consistently sought to defend their interests. In addition to the Arab-Israeli conflict, Golan includes the Persian Gulf and Yemen in her survey. She concludes with an interesting but tentative review of Mikhails S. Gorbachev's "new thinking" on the Middle East.

1038. Rezun, Miron: *The Soviet Union and Iran*. Boulder, CO: Westview Press, 1988. 425 p.

Investigation of Soviet-Iranian relations since World War II, with special attention given to diplomatic history as viewed from the Soviet Union. Also notes developments in Iranian attitudes toward the USSR, a subject little known in the West.

1039. Ro'i, Yaacov: *Soviet decision making in practice: the USSR and Israel, 1947-1954*. New Brunswick, NJ: Transaction Books, 1980. 540 p.

Studies and carefully documents the turns in Soviet policy regarding Israel between 1947 and 1954. Begins with Stalin's major *volte face*: abandoning traditional Communist anti-Zionism and supporting the creation of a Jewish state at the United Nations in November 1947. Thereafter Stalin maintained a low key relationship with Israel that worsened as the Jewish problem increased in importance within the Soviet Union. Ro'i has done a good job of integrating the two issues of Soviet Jewry and Soviet relations with Israel and points out a few new interpretations.

1040. --- (comp): *From encroachment to involvement: a documented study of Soviet policy in the Middle East, 1945-1973.* New Brunswick, NJ: Transaction Books, 1974. 616 p.

Documentary history that portrays the key developments in Soviet Middle East policy after World War II. Although a traditional goal of Russian foreign policy had been to establish a permanent presence in the Mediterranean, that was only accomplished in the 1950s. Ro'i has selected a wide variety of documents displaying the twists and turns in Soviet policy: the bulk of his material originates with Soviet sources. Brief introductions and annotations place each document into context and the entire anthology is supplemented with an extensive bibliography.

## B. THE ABORTED KHRUSHCHEV THAW

### 1. Russia After Stalin

> # 1988. Agursky, M.: "God is dead!"

1041. Baras, Victor: "Beria's fall and Ulbricht's survival." *Soviet Studies*, v. 27 # 3 (July, 1975): 381-395.

1042. Bialer, Severyn: "Succession and turnover of Soviet elites." *Journal of International Affairs*, v. 32 # 2 (Fall/Winter, 1978): 181-200.

1043. Crankshaw, Edward: *Russia without Stalin: the emerging pattern*. New York: Viking Press, 1956. 264 p.

1044. Deutscher, Isaac: "The Nineteenth Congress of the Communist Party of the Soviet Union." *International Affairs*, v. 29 # 2 (April, 1953): 149-155.

> # 1449. Hough, J. F.: *Soviet leadership in transition.*

1045. Leonhard, Wolfgang: *The Kremlin since Stalin* (translated from German by Elizabeth Wiskemann and Marian Jackson). New York: Oxford University Press, 1962. 403 p.

1046. Linden, Carl A.: *Khrushchev and Soviet leadership, 1957-1964*. Baltimore, MD: The Johns Hopkins University Press, 1966. 271 p.

Investigates and interprets Khrushchev's rise and fall. Notes that Khrushchev failed to consolidate his power: he faced threats from Communist party conservatives and from reform-minded anti-party groups. Linden notes that Khrushchev sought to reform communism, but was unable to budge the Party *apparat*. When foreign policy disasters resulted -- primarily the embarassing withdrawal during the Cuban Missile Crisis -- Khrushchev was toppled by the conservatives.

1047. Moses, Joel C.: "Regionalism in Soviet politics: continuity as a source of change, 1953-1982." *Soviet Studies*, v. 37 # 2 (April, 1985): 184-211.

1048. Rigby, T. H.: "The Soviet Politburo: a comparative profile 1951-1971." *Soviet Studies*, v. 24 # 1 (July, 1972): 3-23.

1049. Rothberg, Abraham: *The heirs of Stalin: dissidence and the Soviet regime, 1953-1970*. Ithaca, NY: Cornell University Press, 1972. 450 p.

First scholarly study of Soviet dissidents. Rothberg dates the modern dissident movement to the years of the thaw under Khrushchev, although he notes that at no time did even the most liberal Communist leader speak of complete de-Stalinization. Dissent rose with the return to Stalinism after Khrushchev's removal in 1964. Even though Rothberg wrote before the real expansion of dissident movement in the 1970s and 1980s, the book provides the vital background information needed to understand the tide unleashed beginning in 1989.

> # 987. Schwartz, H.: *The red phoenix*.

1050. Skurski, Roger: "The factor proportions problem in Soviet internal trade." *Soviet Studies*, v. 23 # 3 (January, 1972): 450-464.

1051. Swearer, Howard R. and Myron Rush: *The politics of succession in the USSR: materials on Khrushchev's rise to leadership.* Boston: Little, Brown and Company. 1964. 324 p.

1052. Wolfe, Bertram D.: *Khrushchev and Stalin's ghost*. New York: Frederick A. Praeger, 1957. 322 p.

Text with background and analysis of Communist party chairman Nikita Khrushchev's secret report to the Twentieth Congress CPSU on the night of February 24-25, 1956.

**2. The "Thaw"**

1053. Alekseeva, Liudmila: *Soviet dissent: contemporary movements for national, religious, and human rights* (translated from Russian by Carol Pearce and John Glad). Middletown, CT: Wesleyan University Press, 1985. 521 p.

Comprehensive history of the dissident movement in the Soviet Union from 1960 to 1983. Primarily focused on the human rights groups that sprang up after the Khrushchev thaw. Also includes nationalist movements and groups working for religious freedom within the Soviet Union. A separate chapter is dedicated to the dissidents -- primarily Jews and ethnic Germans -- who have made emigration the crux of their struggle.

1054. Avidar, Yosef: *The Party and the army in the Soviet Union.* Philadelphia: Penn State University Press, 1985. 348 p.

Studies military-civil relations during the Khrushchev years, based on interviews with high ranking Red Army officers. Concentrates on the doctrinal developments that derived from the introduction of thermo-nuclear weapons and the subsequent clashes between different branches of the Soviet armed forces.

1055. Ayalti, Chanan: "Moscow's Jews." *Commentary*, v. 34 # 6 (December, 1962): 519-525.

Records his visit to the Soviet Union and his many conversations with Moscow Jews.

> # 1929. Burlatsky, F.: *Khrushchev and the first Russian spring.*

1056. Churchward, L. G.: *The Soviet intelligentsia: an essay on the social structure and roles of the Soviet intellectuals during the 1960s.* Boston: Routledge and Kegan Paul, 1973. 204 p.

Concisely investigates the role played by intellectuals in the Khrushchev and Brezhnev eras. Defines the terminology broadly, including all persons with a higher education. This forces Churchward to admit that the Soviet intelligentsia is not homogenous and represents a range of opinions on social and political issues. Of special importance is his analysis of the then-emerging democratic movement. Given the newness of the democrats' approach, Churchward could not have anticipated that ultimately they would inherit the mantle of rule in the subsequent Commonwealth of Independent States.

1057. Cohen, Stephen F.: "The friends and foes of change: reformism and conservatism in the Soviet Union." *Slavic Review*, v. 38 # 2 (June, 1979): 187-202.

1058. Fainsod, Merle: "Censorship in the USSR: a documented record." *Problems of Communism*, v. 5 # 2 (March/April, 1956): 12-19.

1059. Filtzer, Donald A.: "The Soviet wage reform of 1956-1962." *Soviet Studies*, v. 41 # 1 (January, 1989): 88-110.

1060. Grossman, Joan D.: "Khrushchev's anti-religious policy and the campaign of 1954." *Soviet Studies*, v. 24 # 3 (January, 1973): 374-386.

1061. Hollander, Gayle D.: *Soviet political indoctrination developments in mass media and propaganda since Stalin*. New York: F. A. Praeger, 1972. 244 p.

Scholarly study of the mass media in the Soviet Union. In addition to press sources, Hollander reviews film, radio, and oral propaganda. Hollander also uses a remarkable amount of statistical material collected and published by the Soviets themselves. Thanks to this data she is able to make important generalizations on the impact of propaganda on public opinion and thus offers insights that have broad, comparative implications.

1062. Jasny, Naum: "Improving Soviet planning: thirty-five years of mediocrity." *International Affairs*, v. 37 # 4 (October, 1961): 465-476.

1063. ---: "More Soviet grain statistics." *International Affairs*, v. 32 # 4 (October, 1956): 464-466.

1064. Katkoff, Vladimir: *The Soviet economy 1945-1965*. Westport, CT: Greenwood Press, 1973. 559 p.

1065. Kolarz, W. J.: "Government and people in the Soviet Union today." *International Affairs*, v. 31 # 4 (October, 1955): 435-446.

> # 1015. Ro'i, Y.: *Struggle for Soviet Jewish emigration*.

1066. "Russian art and antisemitism: two documents." *Commentary*, v. 36 # 6 (December, 1963): 433-437.

The article is based on two documents translated into English: Yevtushenko versus Khrushchev, and a speech by Mikhail Romm.

> # 1012. Pinkus, B.: *The Soviet government and the Jews*.

1067. Sayer, Judah (pseud.): "Rabbinical responsa in the USSR." *Commentary*, v. 34 # 1 (July, 1962): 64-69.

1068. Sharlet, Robert: "Dissent and repression in the Soviet Union and Eastern Europe: changing patterns since Khrushchev." *International Journal*, v. 33 # 4 (Fall, 1978): 763-795.

1069. Shlapentokh, Vladimir: "The *Stakhanovite* movement: changing perceptions over fifty years." *Journal of Contemporary History*, v. 23 # 2 (April, 1988): 259-276.

1070. Simon, Gerhard: *Nationalism and policy toward the nationalities in the Soviet Union: from totalitarian dictatorship to post-Stalinist society*. Boulder, CO: Westview Press, 1991. 467 p.

Examines the treatment of national minorities in the Soviet Union from 1920 to the post-Stalinist era. Also views the subject from the national minorities' perspective. An important subtheme is the detotalitarianization of the Soviet Union after Stalin's death. A chapter detailing the rebirth of nationalism in the Soviet Union rounds out this interesting investigation.

1071. Slusser, Robert M.: *The Berlin crisis of 1961: Soviet-American relations and the struggle for power in the Kremlin, June-November 1961*. Baltimore, MD: The John Hopkins University Press, 1973. 509 p.

Micro study of the power struggle in the Kremlin that forms the background to the 1961 Berlin Wall crisis. The lion's share of attention is devoted to a careful analysis of the minutes of the Twenty-Second Communist Party Congress. Slusser does an admirable job of clarifying the Byzantine turns in Soviet power politics. He views this period as a decisive turning point in the Kremlin's history, noting correctly that merely two years after the Congress Nikita Khrushchev was deposed.

1072. Spechler, Dina R.: *Permitted dissent in the USSR: Novy Mir and the Soviet regime*. New York: Praeger Scientific, 1982. 293 p.

Studies the Khrushchev thaw from the perspective of permitted dissent. Concentrates on the journal *Novy Mir*, which became the key exponent for the intelligentsia's liberal ideas. Despite considerable opposition within the Communist party, *Novy Mir* was initially permitted to publish: at times its publication of controversial works, heavily "edited" of course, was even encouraged by the regime. However, *Novy Mir* came under increasing pressure after the rise of Brezhnev's neo-Stalinist regime and was closed down in 1970.

1073. Zaleski, Eugene: *Planning reforms in the Soviet Union, 1962-1966*. Chapel Hill: North Carolina University Press, 1967. 203 p.

### 3. The Cold War and "Peaceful Coexistence"

1074. Aspaturian, Vernon: "Moscow's options in a changing world." *Problems of Communism*, v. 21 # 4 (July/August, 1972): 1-20.

1075. Blight, James G. and David A. Welch: *On the brink: Americans and Soviets reexamine the Cuban missile crisis* (foreword by McGeorge Bundy). New York: Hill and Wang, 1989. 400 p.

Collection that offers a stimulating and important insight, based on the transcript of an unprecedented meeting between American and Soviet political leaders active during the Cuban missile crisis. This was the first time that Soviets and Americans came together face to face to reconsider the events of October 1962 -- events that nearly escalated from Cold War to all-out nuclear war.

1076. Fletcher, William C.: "Religious dissent in the USSR in the 1960s." *Slavic Review*, v. 30 # 2 (June, 1971): 298-316.

1077. Garthoff, Raymond L.: "Cuban missile crisis: the Soviet story." *Foreign Policy*, # 72 (Fall, 1988): 61-80.

1078. Gibney, Frank: *The Khrushchev pattern: coexistence and its workings through international communism*. New York: Duell, 1960. 280 p.

1079. Horelick, Arnold L. and Myron Rush: *Strategic power and Soviet foreign policy*. Chicago: The University of Chicago Press, 1966. 225 p.

Charts the political use of military power in Khrushchev's Soviet Union. Primary focus is on the development and depolyment of ICBMs. Horelick and Rush examine the so-called missile gap of 1957-1961, demolishing it as a myth. Contrary to some opinions, they conclude that the myth was not created by the U.S. military-industrial complex, but was part of a Soviet scheme to convince the West that more ICBMs had been deployed than was actually the case.

1080. Lockwood, Jonathan S.: *The Soviet view of U.S. strategic doctrine*. New Brunswick, NJ: Transaction Books, 1983. 175 p.

Summarizes and analyzes the key Soviet documents on U.S. strategic policy between 1954 and 1980. Lockwood's most important contribution is to show how the Soviets modeled their own strategic doctrine on their interpretation of U.S. strategic doctrine. Soviet doctrine in turn colored the Union's assessment of American strategy leading to a never-ending set of twists and turns that bore no relation to the strategic reality.

### 4. Soviet Foreign Policy

1081. Armstrong, John A.: "The domestic roots of Soviet foreign policy." *International Affairs*, v. 41 # 1 (January, 1965): 37-47.

1082. Baras, Victor: "Stalin's German policy after Stalin." *Slavic Review*, v. 37 # 2 (June, 1978): 259-267.

Analyzes Soviet position on German reunification in light of Stalin's policy toward Germany.

1083. Barnos, Willian J.: "Moscow and South Asia." *Problems of Communism*, v. 21 # 3 (May/June, 1972): 12-31.

> # 1037. Golan, G.: *Soviet politics in the Middle East*.

1084. Mehnert, Klaus: "Soviet-Chinese relations." *International Affairs*, v. 35 # 4 (October, 1959): 417-426.

1085. Ramet, Pedro: *The Soviet-Syrian relationship since 1955: a troubled alliance*. Boulder, CO: Westview Press, 1990. 290 p.

Study of relations between the Soviet Union and Syria. Since 1973 Syria has been the Soviet Union's main ally in the Middle East. Mutual relations, however, go as far back as the Khrushchev era and parallel the United States-Israeli alliance that developed after the Six-day War in 1967. Ramet places both Soviet and Syrian foreign policy in context by offering considerable insight into both Middle Eastern politics and the Cold War.

> # 1040. Ro'i, Y.: *From encroachment to involvement.*

1086. Seton-Watson, Hugh: "Soviet foreign policy on the eve of the summit." *International Affairs*, v. 36 # 3 (July, 1960): 287-298.

1087. Varas, Augusto: "Ideology and politics in Latin American-Soviet relations." *Problems of Communism*, v. 33 # 1 (January/February, 1984): 35-47.

Reviews Soviet ideological and economic trends in Latin America over the past two decades.

1088. Walters, Robert S.: "Soviet economic aid to Cuba: 1959-1964." *International Affairs*, v. 42 # 1 (January, 1966): 74-86.

1089. Wheeler, G. E.: "Russia and the Middle East." *International Affairs*, v. 35 # 3 (July, 1959): 295-304.

1090. Zimmerman, William: *Soviet perspectives on international relations, 1956-1967.* Princeton, NJ: Princeton University Press, 1969. 336 p.

Methodological investigation of Soviet political scientists' view of the United States in the Khrushchev and Brezhnev eras. Zimmerman focuses on three issues that have animated much of the Soviet writing on American history and politics: continuity and change, spontenaity versus preplanning, and the relevance of Marxist-Leninist theory for explaining the American experience. The latter was of special importance to Soviet political scientists, since Marx himself admitted in some of his later writings that American capitalism could be an exception to his theories.

### 5. The Hungarian Revolution

1091. Berecz, Janos: *1956 counter-revolution in Hungary: words and weapons* (translated from Hungarian by Istvan Butykay; revised by Charles Coutts). Budapest: Akademiai Kiado, 1986. 223 p.

Apologetic book attempting to prove that the Hungarian uprising was plotted by Western intelligence agencies, thereby justifying Soviet counter-measures.

1092. Gati, Charles: "Imré Nagy and Moscow, 1953-1956." *Problems of Communism*, v. 35 # 2 (May/June, 1986): 32-49.

1093. Hungarian Freedom Fighters Federation: *Captive Hungary, an unsolved problem of Soviet aggresion*. New York: The Federation, 1960. 69 p.

1094. Lias, Godfrey: "Satellite states in the post-Stalin era." *International Affairs*, v. 30 # 1 (January, 1954): 40-49.

### 6. Evaluations

1095. Breslauer, George W.: "Khrushchev reconsidered." *Problems of Communism*, v. 25 # 5 (September/October, 1976): 18-33.

1096. Brinkley, George A.: "Khurshchev remembered: on the theory of Soviet statehood." *Soviet Studies*, v. 24 # 3 (January, 1973): 387-401.

1097. Brumberg, Abraham (ed): *Russia under Khrushchev: an anthology from Problems of Communism*. London: Methuen, 1962. 660 p.

Selection of articles from *Problems of Communism* surveying developments in the USSR from Stalin's death in 1954 to 1962. Provides both the ideological setting for Khrushchev's thaw and insight into the problems the Soviet Union faced at the time. The anthology offers a unique perspective on Russian affairs. Eleven of the essays seek to answer the question "whither Russia?" These offer ideas that have an up-to-date outlook, especially in light of developments since 1989.

CONTENTS: R. N. C. Hunt: The importance of doctrine / S. L. Sharp: National interest: key to Soviet politics / R. Lowenthal: The logic of one-party rule / L. Labedz: Ideology: the fourth stage / J. Degras: Anatomy of tyranny: Khrushchev's attack on Stalin / R.

Lowenthal: The permament revolution is on again / M. Fainsod: What happened to "collective leadership"? / R. Lowenthal: The nature of Khrushchev's power / M. Fainsod: The Twenty-second Party Congress / J. Berliner: *Blat* is higher than Stalin / L. M. Herman: Taxes and the Soviet citizen / A. Nove: Soviet industrial reorganization / G. Grossman: Communism in a hurry: the "time factor" in Soviet economics / R. A. Feldmesser: Equality and inequality under Khrushchev / S. Bialer: "But some are more equal than others" / P. Barton: Current status of the Soviet worker / A. Kahan: The peasant, the Party, and the system / A. Inkeles: Soviet nationality policy in perspective / E. Goldhagen: Communism and antisemitism / H. Willets: The "literary opposition" / V. Erlich: Soviet literary criticism: past and present / M. Hayward: The struggle goes on / G. Gibian: Recent Soviet literature / L. Lipson: Socialist legality: the road up hill / A. Dallin: Recent Soviet historiography / J. Rühle: The Soviet theater / S. Hook: The import of ideological diversity / R. Aron: Soviet society in transition / A. Nove: Social welfare in the USSR / S. Schwarz: Why the changes? / B. Wolfe: Facts and polemics / B. de Jouvenel: The logic of economics / P. Wiles: The consumer and the system / R. Lowenthal: Ideology, power, and welfare / E. Goldhagen: The glorious future: realities and chimeras / H. Ritvo: Totalitarianism without coersion?

1098. Gass, Oscar: "Russia: Khrushchev and after." *Commentary*, v. 36 # 5 (November, 1963): 353-363.

1099. ---: "Soviet economic developments: Khrushchev and after." *Commentary*, v. 37 # 2 (February, 1964): 54-68.

1100. Leonhard, Wolfgang: "Return to Stalinism in the USSR?" *International Affairs*, v. 33 # 3 (July, 1957): 280-288.

1101. McCauley, Martin (ed.): *Khrushchev and Khrushchevism*. Bloomington: Indiana University Press, 1987. 243 p.

Anthology of essays on the Khrushchev era, based on a symposium held at the University of London in March 1985. The papers are thematically organized, with almost equal division between essays on internal and external policy. McCauley's introduction places

Khrushchev's years in power into historical context and the appended bibliography offers sources for further research.

CONTENTS: M. McCauley: Khrushchev as leader / G. Gill: Khrushchev and systemic development / R. J. Hill: State and ideology / A. Nove: Industry / M. J. Berry: Science, technology and innovation / G. A. E. Smith: Agriculture / D. Filtzer: Labor / A. McAuley: Social policy / M. Shafir: Eastern Europe / H. Hanak: Foreign policy / C. Bluth: Defense and security / F. K. Roberts: Encounters with Khrushchev.

1102. Tompson, William J.: "The fall of Nikita Khrushchev." *Soviet Studies*, v. 43 # 6 (1991): 1101-1122.

## C. THE BREZHNEV REACTION

### 1. Ideological and Domestic Developments

1103. Agursky, Mikhail: "Russian neo-Nazism: a growing threat." *Midstream*, v. 22 # 2 (February, 1976): 35-42.

1104. Avis, George: "Preparatory divisions in Soviet higher education establishments 1969-1979: ten years of radical experiment." *Soviet Studies*, v. 35 # 1 (January, 1983): 14-35.

1105. Blackwell, Robert E.: "Cadres policy in the Brezhnev era." *Problems of Communism*, v. 28 # 2 (March/April, 1979): 29-42.

1106. Breslauer, George W.: "Political succession and the Soviet policy agenda." *Problems of Communism*, v. 29 # 3 (May/June, 1980): 34-52.

1107. Clemens, Walter C., Jr.: "The Sino-Soviet dispute: dogma and dialectics on disarmament." *International Affairs*, v. 41 # 2 (April, 1965): 204-222.

1108. Connor, W. D.: "Generations and politics in the USSR." *Problems of Communism*, v. 24 # 5 (September/October, 1975): 20-31.

1109. Conquest, Robert: *Russia after Khrushchev*. New York: Frederick A. Praeger, 1965. 267 p.

> # 250. Conyngham, W. J.: "Technology and decision making."

1110. Dienes, Leslie: "Soviet energy resources and prospects." *Current History*, v. 71 # 420 (October, 1976): 114-118, 129-132; v. 74 # 435 (March, 1978): 117-120, 131-135.

1111. Dovring, Folke: "Soviet agriculture in 1980." *Current History*, v. 79 # 459 (October, 1980): 88-91, 105-106.

> # 1937. Ebon, M.: *Malenkov, Stalin's successor.*

1112. Ehlers, Robert and Richard Bessel (eds): *Current Soviet policies: the documentary record of the Twenty-Third Congress of the Communist Party of the Soviet Union*. Columbus, OH: Current Digest of the Soviet Press, 1973. 175 p. [PB]

1113. Ellman, Michael: "A note on the distribution of earnings in the USSR under Brezhnev." *Slavic Review*, v. 39 # 4 (December, 1980): 669-671.

> # 308. Feshbach, M.: "Between the lines of the 1979 census."

> # 535. Friedberg, M.: "Soviet letters under Brezhnev."

1114. Gilison, Jerome M.: "Khrushchev, Brezhnev, and constitutional reform." *Problems of Communism*, v. 21 # 5 (September/October, 1972): 69-78.

1115. Ginsburgs, George: "The Soviet Union and the biosphere." *International Journal*, v. 28 # 1 (Winter, 1972/1973): 50-68.

1116. Goldman, Marshall I. : "Soviet trade policy." *Current History*, v. 79 # 459 (October, 1980): 84-87, 102-103.

1117. Grossman, Gregory: "An economy at middle age." *Problems of Communism*, v. 25 # 2 (March/April, 1976): 18-33.

1118. Hahn, Werner G.: *The politics of Soviet agriculture, 1960-1970.* Baltimore, MD: The John Hopkins University Press, 1972. 311 p.

Interesting investigation of Soviet agricultural policy in the 1960s. The book's interest derives more from methodological considerations than from topicality: Hahn has crafted a model of academic Kremlinology, with all the strengths and weaknesses of such a work. Thus, for example, Hahn seeks to assess power relationships based on the photographic lineups of Soviet leaders at Moscow May Day parades. Unlike other similar works Hahn seeks to broaden the range of his sources. For that reason alone, the book offers a model of proper political research.

> # 513. Haney, J. V.: "The revival of interest in the Russian past."

1119. Hanson, Philip: "Success indicators revisited: the July 1979 Soviet decree on planning and management." *Soviet Studies*, v. 35 # 1 (January, 1983): 1-13.

1120. Herspring, Dale R.: *The Soviet high command, 1967-1989: personalities and politics*. Princeton, NJ: Princeton University Press, 1990. 322 p.

1121. Hill, Ian H.: "The end of the Russian peasantry? the social structure and culture of the contemporary Soviet agricultural population." *Soviet Studies*, v. 27 # 1 (January, 1975): 109-127.

> # 1061. Hollander, G. D.: *Soviet political indoctrination.*

1122. Hollander, Paul: "Soviet society today." *Current History*, v. 71 # 420 (October, 1976): 123-126, 137-138.

1123. Hough, Jerry F.: "The generation gap and the Brezhnev succession." *Problems of Communism*, v. 28 # 4 (July/August, 1979): 1-16.

1124. ---: "The man and the system." *Problems of Communism*, v. 25 # 2 (March/April, 1976): 1-17.

1125. ---: "The Soviet system: petrification or pluralism?" *Problems of Communism*, v. 21 # 2 (March/April, 1972): 25-45.

1126. Johnson, D. Gale: "Soviet agriculture and United States-Soviet relations." *Current History*, v. 73 # 430 (October, 1977): 118-122, 133-134.

1127. ---: "The Soviet grain shortage: a case of rising expectations." *Current History*, v. 68 # 406 (June, 1975): 245-248.

1128. Judson, Mitchell R.: "Continuity and change in Soviet ideology." *Current History*, v. 69 # 409 (October, 1975): 137-141, 147.

1129. Karcz, Jerzy F.: "Some major persisting problems in Soviet agriculture." *Slavic Review*, v. 29 # 3 (September, 1970): 417-426.

1130. Katsenelinboigen, A.: "Coloured markets in the Soviet Union." *Soviet Studies*, v. 29 # 1 (January, 1977): 62-85.

1131. Katz, Abraham: *The politics of economic reform in the Soviet Union*. New York: Praeger, 1972. 242 p.

Investigates the attempted economic reform movement of 1965 associated with Soviet Premier Andrei Kosygin. Assesses both the political and economic considerations behind Kosygin's plan, which coincided with the eighth Five-Year Plan. The proposed reforms implied a general de-Stalinization of the Soviet Union while retaining central control over the economy. To a great extent this plan -- never fully developed -- was a precedent for the reforms proposed by Mikhail S. Gorbachev.

1132. Klepikova, Elena and Vladimir Solovyov: "The secret Russian party." *Midstream*, v. 26 # 8 (October, 1980): 12-19.

Posits existence of a secret Russian nationalist entity supported by the KGB and preparing for an eventual *coup d'etat*. Much of the factual basis of the article has since been disputed and dismissed.

1133. Laqueur, Walter: "Russia beyond Brezhnev." *Commentary*, v. 64 # 2 (August, 1977): 39-44.

1134. Little, D. Richard: "Soviet parliamentary committees after Khrushchev: obstacles and opportunities." *Soviet Studies*, v. 23 # 4 (April, 1972): 41-60.

1135. McAuley, Mary: "The hunting of the hierarchy: RSFSR *Obkom* first secretaries and the Central Committee." *Soviet Studies*, v. 26 # 4 (October, 1974): 473-501.

1136. Mickiewicz, Ellen: "The modernization of Party propaganda in the USSR." *Slavic Review*, v. 30 # 2 (June, 1971): 257-276.

1137. Millar, James R.: "The little deal: Brezhnev's contribution to acquisitive socialism." *Slavic Review*, v. 44 # 4 (Winter, 1985): 694-706.

1138. Minagawa, Shugo: "The functions of the Supreme Soviet organs, and problems of their institutional development." *Soviet Studies*, v. 27 # 1 (January, 1975): 46-70.

> # 1047. Moses, J. C.: "Regionalism in Soviet politics."

> # 1956. Murphy, P. J.: *Brezhnev*.

1139. Nove, Alec: "Is there a ruling class in the USSR?" *Soviet Studies*, v. 27 # 4 (October, 1975): 615-638.

1140. ---: "Soviet agriculture under Brezhnev." *Slavic Review*, v. 29 # 3 (September, 1970): 379-410.

1141. Osofsky, Stephen: *Soviet agricultural policy: toward the abolition of collective farms*. New York: Praeger, 1974. 300 p.

Investigates the abortive effort at agricultural reform undertaken by Leonid Brezhnev's regime in the USSR. More broadly, Osofsky reviews and explains the utter failure of Soviet agriculture -- as exemplified by the 1972 U.S.-USSR grain deal.

1142. Powell, David E.: "Labor turnover in the Soviet Union." *Slavic Review*, v. 36 # 2 (June, 1977): 268-285.

1143. Pryde, Philip R.: "Nuclear energy in the Soviet Union." *Current History*, v. 77 # 450 (October, 1979): 115-118, 135.

1144. Rigby, T. H.: "Soviet Communist party membership under Brezhnev." *Soviet Studies*, v. 28 # 3 (July, 1976): 317-337.

1145. ---: "The Soviet regional leadership: the Brezhnev generation." *Slavic Review*, v. 37 # 1 (March, 1978): 1-24.

1146. Riordan, James: "Soviet sport and Soviet foreign policy." *Soviet Studies*, v. 26 # 3 (July, 1974): 322-341.

1147. Rosefilede, Steven: "The changing pattern of Soviet trade." *Current History*, v. 69 # 409 (October, 1975): 133-136, 147-148.

> # 1049. Rothberg, A.: *The heirs of Stalin.*

1148. Rutland, Peter: "The Shchekino method and the struggle to raise labor productivity in Soviet industry." *Soviet Studies*, v. 36 # 3 (July, 1984): 345-365.

Deals with the efforts of the Brezhnev-Kosygin government to reform the Soviet economy through incentives for efficiency.

1149. Shapiro, Jane P.: "The Soviet consumer in the Brezhnev era." *Current History*, v. 75 # 440 (October, 1978): 100-103, 128-131.

1150. ---: "The Soviet leadership enters the 1980s." *Current History*, v. 79 # 459 (October, 1980): 92-95, 106.

1151. Smirnov, L. N. (ed.): *Legislative acts of the USSR, 1977-1979.* Moscow: Progress Publishers, 1983. 381 p.

Compilation of key Soviet social and civil legislation during the Brezhnev years.

1152. Smith, Hedrick: *The Russians*. New York: Quadrangle Books, 1976. 527 p.

Journalistic investigation into daily life in the Soviet Union by a former *New York Times* Moscow correspondent. Smith divides his account into three sections: "The People," "The System," and "Issues." Each section is further subdivided into thematic chapters covering such issues as corruption in Soviet life, the status of women, patriotism, and culture. In his final chapter Smith enquires into the so-called convergence theory. Rejecting convergence with the U.S. on a political level, Smith still notes a significant convergence of the contemporary Soviet system with the Tsarist regime at its height.

1153. Stuart, Robert C.: "The Soviet economy." *Current History*, v. 71 # 420 (October, 1976): 109-113, 132-133; v. 75 # 440 (October, 1978): 109-112, 126.

1154. ---: "The Soviet economy: problems and prospects in the 1970s." *Current History*, v. 69 # 409 (October, 1975): 129-132, 145.

1155. Tillett, Lowell: "Ukrainian nationalism and the fall of Shelest." *Slavic Review*, v. 34 # 4 (December, 1975): 752-768.

1156. Treml, Vladimir G.: "Alcohol in the USSR: a fiscal dilemma." *Soviet Studies*, v. 27 # 2 (April, 1975): 161-177.

1157. Tucker, Robert C.: "Swollen state, spent society: Stalin's legacy to Brezhnev's Russia." *Foreign Affairs*, v. 60 # 2 (Winter, 1981/1982): 414-435.

> # 1982. Wesson, R. G.: "Brezhnev's year."

1158. Wesson, Robert G.: "The Twenty-Fifth Soviet Communist Party Congress." *Current History*, v. 71 # 420 (October, 1976): 119-122, 129.

1159. Willerton, John P., Jr.: "Patronage networks and coalition building in the Brezhnev era." *Soviet Studies*, v. 39 # 2 (April, 1987): 175-204.

## 2. Relations with the Western Alliance

1160. Azrael, Jeremy R.: "Soviet-American relations: notes on détente." *Current History*, v. 75 # 440 (October, 1978): 117-119, 125.

1161. Brown, Seyom: "An end to grand strategy." *Foreign Policy*, # 32 (Fall, 1978): 22-46.

1162. ---: "A cooling off period for U.S.-Soviet relations." *Foreign Policy*, # 28 (Fall, 1977): 3-21.

1163. Buchanan, Thompson R.: "The real Russia." *Foreign Policy*, # 47 (Summer, 1982): 26-45.

1164. Bykov, Vladimir L.: "The USSR and security in Europe: a Soviet view." *Annals*, v. 414 (July, 1974): 96-104.

1165. Caldwell, Laurence T.: "The fate of strategic arms limitation and Soviet-American relations." *International Journal*, v. 36 # 3 (Summer, 1981): 608-634.

1166. ---: "SALT II and the strategic relationship." *Current History*, v. 77 # 450 (October, 1979): 101-105, 136-138.

1167. Campbell, John C.: "Soviet-American relations: détente and dispute." *Current History*, v. 69 # 409 (October, 1975): 113-116, 146-147, 149-150.

1168. ---: "The Soviet Union and the United States in the Middle East." *Annals*, v. 401 (May, 1972): 126-135.

1169. Coffey, J. I.: "Soviet ABM policy: the implications for the West." *International Affairs*, v. 45 # 2 (April, 1969): 205-222.

1170. Douglass, Joseph D.: *Soviet military strategy in Europe*. Elmsford, NY: Pergamon Press, 1980. 238 p.

Chronicles and assesses the growth of Soviet conventional and tactical nuclear forces in Central Europe (especially Czechoslovakia and East Germany) during the 1970s. Notes that the same decade produced major cutbacks in NATO deployments; especially in terms of dismantling most of NATO's tactical nuclear weapons. The result of these developments, according to Douglass, was a growing imbalance in "theatre" forces and a consequent increase in the possibility of war.

1171. Edmonds, Martin and John Skitt: "Current Soviet maritime strategy and NATO." *International Affairs* , v. 45 # 1 (January, 1969): 28-43.

1172. Erickson, John: "Soviet military capabilities." *Current History*, v. 71 # 420 (October, 1976): 97-100, 128, 135-136.

1173. ---: "Soviet military policy in the 1980s." *Current History*, v. 75 # 440 (October, 1978): 97-99, 135-138.

1174. Garthoff, Raymond: *Détente and confrontation: American-Soviet relations from Nixon to Reagan*. Washington, DC: The Brookings Institute, 1985. 1,147 p.

Meticulous detailing of Soviet-American relations between 1969 and 1984. Notes the warming of U.S.-USSR relations that culminated in the summits of 1972 and 1973 and the signing of the SALT agreement. Thereafter, Garthoff notes, relations soured again between the *Yom Kippur* War and the Soviet invasion of Afghanistan in 1979. Also investigates the possibilities of a new era of détente, although Garthoff could not predict the end of the Cold War.

1175. ---: "SALT and the Soviet military." *Problems of Communism*, v. 24 # 1 (January/February, 1975): 21-37.

1176. Gelman, Harry: *The Brezhnev Politburo and the decline of détente*. Ithaca, NY: Cornell University Press, 1984. 268 p.

Relates Soviet foreign policy to internal pressures in the USSR in the late 1970s and early 1980s. Argues that Soviet adventurism abroad during this period was conditioned not by an ideological desire to spread communism, but by political and economic needs. Yet, despite the swings in Soviet foreign policy -- from Cold War to détente and back again -- Gelman also sees some continuity in Soviet foreign policy: he describes it as a competitive urge combined with ideological elements to create a desire to spread communism.

1177. Gibert, Stephen P.: *Soviet images of America.* New York: Crane, Russak & Company, 1977. 168 p.

Studies the Cold War from the Soviet perspective. It is based on a close analysis of articles in almost two dozen journals and thirty-four monographs written in the Soviet Union which deal with Soviet American relations. Gibert and his research team end the account on a pessimistic note since the surveyed materials advocate world revolution and an ultimate confrontation with the United States.

> # 1037. Golan, G.: *Soviet politics in the Middle East.*

> # 216. Goren, R.: *The Soviet Union and Terrorism.*

1178. Graham, Loren R.: "Aspects of sharing science and technology." *Annals*, v. 414 (July, 1974): 84-95.

On scientific and technological exchanges between the United States and the Soviet Union.

1179. Gromyko, Anatoly A.: "The future of the Soviet-American diplomacy." *Annals*, v. 414 (July, 1974): 27-40.

1180. Hewett, E. A.: "Most-favored nation treatment in trade under central planning." *Slavic Review*, v. 37 # 1 (March, 1978): 25-39.

1181. Huntington, Samuel P.: "Trade, technology, and leverage: economic diplomacy." *Foreign Policy*, # 32 (Fall, 1978): 63-80.

1182. Hutchings, R.: "Soviet defence spending and Soviet external relations." *International Affairs*, v. 47 # 3 (July, 1971): 518-531.

1183. Hyland, William G.: "Clash with the Soviet Union." *Foreign Policy*, # 49 (Winter, 1982/1983): 3-19.

1184. ---: "The Soviet Union and the United States." *Current History*, v. 80 # 468 (October, 1981): 309-312, 343-346.

1185. ---: "U.S.-Soviet relations: the long road back." *Foreign Affairs*, v. 60 # 3 (1982): 525-550.

1186. Ivanov, Ivan D.: "Soviet-American economic cooperation: recent development, prospects and problems." *Annals*, v. 414 (July, 1974): 18-26.

1187. Jacobsen, Carl G.: "The changing American-Soviet power balance." *Current History*, v. 79 # 459 (October, 1980): 65-69, 102.

1188. ---: "The Soviet military reappraised." *Current History*, v. 80 # 468 (October, 1981): 305-308, 336-338.

1189. ---: "Soviet strategic capabilities: the superpower balance." *Current History*, v. 73 # 430 (October, 1977): 97-99, 134-136.

1190. Kaiser, Robert G.: "U.S.-Soviet relations: goodby to dètente." *Foreign Affairs*, v. 59 # 3 (1981): 500-521.

1191. Kaser, Michael: "Soviet trade turns to Europe." *Foreign Policy*, # 19 (Summer, 1975): 123-135.

1192. ---: Soviet views of the Western economic crisis." *International Journal*, v. 29 # 4 (Fall, 1974): 636-645.

1193. Kassof, Allen H.: "The exchange of people and ideas." *Annals*, v. 414 (July, 1974): 73-83.

1194. Lambeth, Benjamin S.: "The evolving Soviet strategic threat." *Current History*, v. 69 # 409 (October, 1975): 121-125.

1195. Legvold, Robert: "The problem of European security." *Problems of Communism*, v. 23 # 1 (January/February, 1974): 13-33.

1196. Leonhard, Wolfgang: "The domestic policies of the New Soviet foreign policy." *Foreign Affairs*, v. 52 # 1 (October, 1973): 59-74.

> # 1080. Lockwood, J. S.: *The Soviet view of U.S. strategic doctrine.*

1197. Mackintosh, Malcolm: "The Soviet military: influence on foreign policy." *Problems of Communism*, v. 22 # 5 (September/October, 1973): 1-12.

1198. Maynes, Charles W.: "Old errors in the new Cold War." *Foreign Policy*, # 46 (Spring, 1982): 86-104.

1199. Mshvenieradze, Vladimir: *Anti-communism: who benefits by it?* Moscow: Novosti Press Agency Publishing House, n.d. 131 p.

Propagandistic review of anti-communism, which the author identifies as a form of neo-imperialism. Given the Russian people's rejection of communism it appears beneficial to turn Mshvenieradze's questions regarding "real" and "sham" freedom around and enquire as to who really profitted from communism.

1200. Ovinnikov, Richard S.: "The USSR position on disarmament in the United Nations." *Annals*, v. 414 (July, 1974): 51-63.

1201. Payne, Samuel B., Jr.: "The Soviet debate on startegic arms limitations: 1969-1972." *Soviet Studies*, v. 27 # 1 (January, 1975): 27-45.

1202. Pipes, Richard: "Why the Soviet Union thinks it could fight and win a nuclear war." *Commentary*, v. 64 # 1 (July, 1977): 21-34.

Examines Soviet military doctrine on nuclear weapons.

1203. Popov, V. I., I. D. Ovsyany, and V. P. Nikhamin (eds.): *A study of Soviet foreign policy*. Moscow: Progress Publishers, 1975. 379 p.

Overview of Soviet foreign policy in the 1970s as seen by the Communist party. Reviews the subject geographically, with each chapter covering one region or type of country: Communist, Third World, and Capitalist. The first chapter offers a general review of how the Communist party claimed foreign policy was made in the USSR. As the chapters amply demonstrate, theory and reality were not always in accord.

1204. Potter, William C.: "The Soviet Union and nuclear proliferation." *Slavic Review*, v. 44 # 3 (Fall, 1985): 468-488.

> # 1085. Ramet, P.: *The Soviet-Syrian relationship since 1955*.

> # 1040. Ro'i, Y.: *From encroachment to involvement*.

1205. Rubinstein, Alvin Z.: "Soviet-American relations." *Current History*, v. 71 # 420 (October, 1976): 101-104, 136-137.

1206. ---: "Soviet policy in Europe." *Current History*, v. 73 # 430 (October, 1977): 105-108, 132.

1207. Schwartz, Harry: "The Moscow-Peking-Washington triangle." *Annals*, v. 414 (July, 1974): 41-50.

1208. Shulman, Marshall D.: "Recent Soviet foreign policy: some patterns in retrospect." *Journal of International Affairs*, v. 22 # 1 (1968): 26-27.

On the Twenty-second Communist Congress (1961).

1209. Sivachev, Nikolai V. and Nikolai N. Yakovlev: *Russia and the United States* (translated from Russian by Olga A. Titelbaum). Chicago: University of Chicago Press, 1979. 301 p.

Review of U.S.-USSR relations as seen from the Soviet perspective. Chapters are organized chronologically. Obviously tendentious, the book is still interesting for its statement of the Communist party line of the late 1970s.

1210. Smith, Gerard C.: "SALT after Vladivostok." *Journal of International Affairs*, v. 29 # 1 (Spring, 1975): 7-18.

1211. Sonnenfeldt, Helmut: "Russia, America and détente." *Foreign Affairs*, v. 56 # 2 (January, 1978): 275-294.

1212. Starr, Richard F.: *USSR: foreign policy after détente*. Stanford,

CA: Hoover Institution Press, 1985. 300 p.

Monograph exploring Soviet foreign policy since the mid-1970s. Divided into three equal parts: Part I, "Foundations," covers Soviet decision making on foreign affairs; Part II, "Instrumentalities," focuses on the institutions involved in implementing foreign policy decisions; and Part III, "Regional Policies," surveys Soviet relations with Eastern and Western Europe, the Third World, China, and the United States.

> # 1514. Steele, J.: *Soviet power.*

1213. Talbott, Strobe: "U.S.-Soviet relations: from bad to worse." *Foreign Affairs*, v. 58 # 3 (1979): 515-539.

1214. Timmermann, Heinz: "The CPSU and the Western Communist parties in the 1980s." *International Journal*, v. 37 # 2 (Spring, 1982): 241-262.

1215. Ulam, Adam B.: *Dangerous relations: the Soviet Union in world politics, 1970-1982.* New York: Oxford University Press, 1982. 325 p.

Concentrates on the place of the Soviet Union in international relations in the 1970s. Ulam sees the Soviets as adopting an essentially defensive posture: hoping to maintain its sphere of influence and even extend it wherever Western weakness permits. Ulam was one of the first to note the impact of Chinese power on Soviet calculations regarding the risks of foreign adventures.

1216. ---: "Détente under Soviet eyes." *Foreign Policy*, # 24 (Fall, 1976): 145-159.

1217. ---: "Moscow plays the balance." *Foreign Policy*, # 8 (Fall, 1972): 86-91.

1218. ---: "The USSR and Europe: the destiny of Eastern Europe." *Problems of Communism*, v. 23 # 1 (January/February, 1974): 1-12.

> # 1032. Vloyantes, J. P.: *Silk glove hegemony.*

1219. Wessell, Nils H.: "Changing Soviet-American relations." *Current History*, v. 77 # 450 (October, 1979): 97-100, 132.

1220. Yergin, Daniel: "Politics and Soviet-American trade: the three questions.". *Foreign Affairs*, v. 55 # 3 (April, 1977): 517-538.

### 3. Soviet Foreign Policy in an Era of Détente

1221. Aspaturian, Vernon V.: "Soviet global power and the correlation of forces." *Problems of Communism*, v. 29 # 3 (May/June, 1980): 1-18.

1222. Bissell, Richard: "Soviet policies in Africa." *Current History*, v. 77 # 450 (October, 1979): 124-127, 135-136.

1223. Campbell, John C.: "Soviet policy in Africa and the Middle East." *Current History*, v. 73 # 430 (October, 1977): 100-104, 131-132.

> # 1168. ---: "Soviet Union and United States in the Middle East."

1224. Coker, Christopher: "Adventurism and pragmatism: the Soviet Union, Comecon, and relations with African states." *International Affairs*, v. 57 # 4 (Fall, 1981): 618-633.

1225. Cutler, Robert M.: "Domestic and foreign influences on policy making: the Soviet Union in the 1974 Cyprus conflict." *Soviet Studies*, v. 37 # 1 (January, 1985): 60-89.

1226. Dawisha, Karen: "Soviet decision-making in the Middle East: the 1973 October War and the 1980 Gulf War." *International Affairs*, v. 57 # 1 (Winter, 1980/1981): 43-59.

1227. Dimant-Kass, Ilana: "The Soviet military and Soviet policy in the Middle East 1970-1973." *Soviet Studies*, v. 26 # 4 (October, 1974): 502-521.

1228. Donaldson, Robert H.: "The Soviet Union in South Asia: a friend to rely on?" *Journal of International Affairs*, v. 34 # 2 (Fall/Winter, 1980/1981): 235-258.

1229. Fukuyama, Francis: "A new Soviet strategy." *Commentary*, v. 68 # 4 (October, 1979): 52-58.

1230. Gerschenkorn, Alexander: "Soviet policies versus international cartels: four historical case studies." *Slavic Review*, v. 33 # 1 (March, 1974): 69-90.

1231. Girling, J. L. S.: "Russia and Indochina in international perspective." *International Affairs*, v. 49 # 4 (October, 1973): 608-616.

1232. Golan, Galia: *Yom Kippur and after: the Soviet Union and the Middle East crisis*. New York: Cambridge University Press, 1977. 350 p.

Investigates Soviet Middle East policy from 1972 to 1974, based on a careful study of Russia's press sources. Notes the paradoxical effect of détente on the USSR's foreign policy: although détente implied a decrease in conflict with the West, the Soviet leadership also tried to extend its interests. As a result, the Soviets acted to restrain the Arabs but did so only after the tide of war had clearly turned in Israel's favor.

1233. Gordon, Murray: "Soviet setback in East Africa." *Midstream*, v. 23 # 10 (December, 1977): 6-14.

1234. Hough, Jerry F.: "The world as viewed from Moscow." *International Journal*, v. 37 # 2 (Spring, 1982): 183-197.

1235. Karsh, Efraim: *The cautious bear: Soviet military engagement in the Middle East wars in the post-1967 era*. Boulder, CO: Westview Press, 1985. 97 p.

Brief investigation of Soviet military policy in the Middle East since 1967. Argues that the Soviets have pursued a consistent strategic policy regarding the Middle East. Part and parcel of Soviet policy has been an attempt to gain a strategic advantage without an overt commitment of Soviet forces.

1236. Kempton, Daniel R.: *Soviet strategy toward southern Africa: the national liberation movement connection*. New York: Praeger, 1989. 261 p.

Focuses on Soviet support for the anti-colonial struggle in Angola, Zimbabwe, and Namibia.

1237. Khalizad, Zalmay: "Moscow's double-track policy -- Islamic Iran: Soviet dilemma." *Problems of Communism*, v. 33 # 1 (January/February, 1984): 1-20.

1238. Kimche, Jon: "Brezhnev's Geneva priority." *Midstream*, v. 20 # 2 (February, 1974): 14-22.

1239. ---: "Soviet aims in the Middle East." *Midstream*, v. 13 # 7 (August/September, 1967): 55-59.

1240. ---: "Soviet oil diplomacy before and after the October War." *Midstream*, v. 20 # 10 (December, 1974): 5-12.

1241. Klinghoffer, Arthur J. and Michael Radu: *The Soviet Union in black Africa*. New York: Holmes & Meier, 1989. 140 p.

Systematic study of Soviet foreign policy in sub-Saharan Africa. Begins with the high water mark of the mid-1970s, when the Soviet Union was chief patron of Marxist-Leninist movements of national liberation. Thereafter, Klinghoffer and Radu analyze the circumstances that led to a retrenchment of Soviet aid -- and consequently influence -- to its African client states. Ideological and strategic considerations are integrated throughout and recent changes in Soviet domestic policy are shown to have an important impact on African policy.

1242. McConnell, James M. and Bradford Dismukes: "Soviet diplomacy of force in the Third World." *Problems of Communism*, v. 28 # 1 (January/February, 1979): 14-27.

1243. Papp, Daniel S.: "National liberation during détente: the

Soviet outlook." *International Journal*, v. 32 # 1 (Winter, 1976/1977): 82-99.

> # 1203. Popov, V. I. et al: *A study in Soviet foreign policy.*

1244. Primakov, Evgeni M.: "The USSR and the developing countries." *Journal of International Affairs*, v. 34 # 2 (Fall/Winter, 1980/1981): 269-281.

1245. Quandt, William B.: "Soviet policy in the October Middle East War." *International Affairs*, v. 53 # 3 (July, 1977): 377-389; # 4 (October, 1977): 587-603.

1246. Ramet, Pedro: "The Soviet-Syrian relationship." *Problems of Communism*, v. 35 # 5 (September/October, 1986): 35-46.

> # 93. *Right-wing revisionism today.*

1247. Robinson, Thomas W.: "Soviet policy in East Asia." *Problems of Communism*, v. 22 # 6 (November/December, 1973): 32-50.

1248. Romaniecki, Leon: "The Soviet Union and international terrorism." *Soviet Studies*, v. 26 # 3 (July, 1974): 417-440.

1249. Rubinstein, Alvin Z.: "Moscow and Cairo: currents of influence." *Problems of Communism*, v. 23 # 4 (July/August, 1974): 17-28.

1250. ---: "The Soviet presence in the Arab world." *Current History*, v. 80 # 468 (October, 1981): 313-316, 338-339.

1251. ---: "The Soviet Union and Iran under Khomeini." *International Affairs*, v. 57 # 4 (Fall, 1981): 599-617.

Concludes that Soviet influence on Khomeini's policies was, at best, minimal.

1252. ---: "The Soviet Union in the Middle East." *Current History*, v. 77 # 450 (October, 1979): 106-109, 132-133.

1253. Saeki, Kiichi: "Toward Japanese cooperation in Siberian development." *Problems of Communism*, v. 21 # 3 (May/June, 1972): 1-11.

1254. Saivetz, Carol R. and Sylvia Woodby: *Soviet-Third World relations*. Boulder, CO: Westview Press, 1985. 254 p.

Presents an overview of Soviet foreign policy in relation to the developing world. The authors contend that the Soviet Union did not have a unified grand strategy relating to the Third World; indeed, the Soviets at times worked under constraints of contradictory policies. Saivetz and Woodby also concentrate on the paradox between Soviet foreign policy success in the Third World and the inner decline of Marxist-Leninist ideology during the Brezhnev era.

1255. Sen Gupta, Bhabani: "Moscow and Bangladesh." *Problems of Communism*, v. 24 # 2 (March/April, 1975): 56-68.

1256. Smolansky, O. M.: "Moscow and the Arab-Israeli sector." *Current History*, v. 71 # 420 (October, 1976): 105-108, 133-135.

1257. ---: "Soviet policy in the Middle East." *Current History*, v. 69 # 409 (October, 1975): 117-120, 148.

1258. ---: "Soviet policy in the Middle East and Africa." *Current History*, v. 75 # 440 (October, 1978): 113-116, 127-128.

1259. Spiegel, Steven L., Mark A. Heller and Jacob Goldberg (eds.): *The Soviet-American competition in the Middle East*. Lexington, MA: Lexington Books, 1988. 392 p.

Collection of twenty-one essays examining the Cold War in the Middle East from historical, diplomatic, and political perspectives. Primarily emphasizes the American and Soviet views, with less attention given to the local powers. Special attention is given to key topics such as arms transfer policy, terrorism, oil, and the possibility of Middle East peace.

CONTENTS: S. L. Spiegel: Soviet-American competition in the

Middle East: a profile / R. E. Harkavy and S. G. Neuman: U.S. arms transfer and arms control policies: the Middle East / A. S. Becker: A note on Soviet arms transfers to the Middle East / A. Platt: American arms transfers and other suppliers / G. M. Steinberg: The impact of new technology on the Arab-Israel military balance / S. Feldman: Superpower nonproliferation policies: the case of the Middle East / D. Gold: Toward the Carter doctrine: the evolution of American power projection policies in the Middle East, 1947-1980 / S. Lakoff: The Reagan doctrine and the U.S. policy in the Middle East / E. Karsh: Peacetime presence and wartime engagement: the Soviet case / F. Fukuyama: Soviet military power in the Middle East; or, whatever became of power projection? / B. M. Jenkins: The American response to state-sponsored terrorism / A. Merari: Soviet attitudes toward Middle Eastern terrorism / E. Kanovsky: U.S. economic interests in the Middle East / G. Ofer and J. Pelzman: Soviet economic interests in the Middle East / B. Rubin: The Soviet and U.S. record on Arab-Israeli wars / S. W. Lewis: Soviet and American attitudes toward the Arab-Israel peace process / M. A. Heller: Soviet and American attitudes toward the Iran-Iraq war / J. Goldberg: Consequences of superpower competiton in the Middle East for local conflicts / I. Rabinovich and A. Susser: Mutual encroachment: the United States and the Soviet Union in Syria and Jordan / B. W. Jentleson: The Lebanon War and the Soviet-American competition: scope and limits of superpower influence / A. Ben-Zvi: The management of superpower conflict in the Middle East / A. Yariv: Soviet-American competition in the Middle East.

1260. Valenta, Jiri: "Soviet-Cuban intervention in the Horn of Africa: impact and lessons." *Journal of International Affairs*, v. 34 # 2 (Fall/Winter, 1980/1981): 353-367.

1261. Valkenier, Elizabeth K.: "Great power economic competition in Africa: Soviet progress and problems." *Journal of International Affairs*, v. 34 # 2 (Fall/Winter, 1980/1981): 259-268.

1262. ---: "The USSR, the Third World, and the global economy." *Problems of Communism*, v. 28 # 4 (July/August, 1979): 17-33.

1263. Volsky, George: "The Soviet-Cuban connection." *Current*

*History*, v. 80 # 468 (October, 1981): 325-328, 335, 346.

1264. Watt, D. C.: "The Persian Gulf -- Cradle of conflict?" *Problems of Communism*, v. 21 # 3 (May/ June, 1972): 32-40.

#### 4. Tensions in the Communist Bloc

1265. Bromke, Adam: "Czechoslovakia 1968 -- Poland 1978: a dilemma for Moscow." *International Journal*, v. 33 # 4 (Fall, 1978): 740-762.

1266. Campbell, John C.: "Soviet strategy in the Balkans." *Problems of Communism*, v. 23 # 4 (July/August, 1974): 1-16.

1267. Chapman, Colin: *August 21st: the rape of Czechoslovakia*. London: Cassell, 1968. 124 p.

On-the-spot journalistic account of the Soviet invasion of Czechoslovakia in August 1968. Includes background information on the Sovietization of Czechoslovakia in 1948, Anton Dubcek's reform movement, and the Soviet invasion. Eyewitness reports from Prague by Murray Sayle are extensively quoted.

1268. Davy, Richard: "Soviet foreign policy and the invasion of Czechoslovakia." *International Journal*, v. 33 # 4 (Fall, 1978): 796-803.

> # 1076. Fletcher, W. C.: "Religious dissent in the USSR."

1269. Gati, Charles: "The forgotten region." *Foreign Policy*, # 19 (Summer, 1975): 135-145.

> # 363. Gilbert, M.: *The Jews of hope*.

1270. Gittings, John: "Cooperation and conflict in Sino-Soviet relations." *International Affairs*, v. 40 # 1 (January, 1964): 60-75.

1271. Hinton, Harold C.: "Moscow and Peking since Mao." *Current*

*History*, v. 75 # 440 (October, 1978): 120-122, 126-127.

1272. Jacobsen, C. G.: "Sino-Soviet crisis in perspective." *Current History*, v. 77 # 450 (October, 1979): 110-114, 133-135.

1273. Kanet, Roger E. and Donna Bahry: "Soviet policy in East Europe." *Current History*, v. 69 # 409 (October, 1975): 126-128.

1274. Laqueur, Walter: "Pity the poor Russians?" *Commentary*, v. 71 #2 (February, 1981): 32-41.

Deals with the Soviet armed intervention in Czechoslovakia.

1275. Levine, Steven I.: "Some thoughts on Sino-Soviet relations in the 1980s." *International Journal*, v. 34 # 4 (Fall, 1979): 649-667.

1276. ---: "The unending Sino-Soviet conflict." *Current History*, v. 79 # 459 (October, 1980): 70-74, 104.

> # 1948. "USSR v. A. Shcharansky."

1277. Littell, Robert (ed.): *The Czech black book* (prepared and translated from Czech by the Institute of History of the Czechoslovak Academy of Sciences). New York: Frederick A. Praeger, 1969. 303 p.

1278. Löwenthal, Richard: "The limits of intra-bloc pluralism: the changing threshhold of Soviet intervention." *International Journal*, v. 37 # 2 (Spring, 1982): 263-284.

1279. ---: "Soviet counterimperialism." *Problems of Communism*, v. 25 # 6 (November/December, 1976): 52-63.

1280. Maxwell, Neville: "Why the Russians lifted the blockade at Bear Island." *Foreign Affairs*, v. 57 # 1 (Fall, 1978): 138-145.

1281. Menon, Rajan: "China and the Soviet Union in Asia." *Current History*, v. 80 # 468 (October, 1981): 329-333, 340-342.

1282. Meissner, Boris: *The Brezhnev doctrine*. Kansas City, MO:

Park College, Governmental Research Bureau, 1970. 80 p.

Explores the so-called Brezhnev doctrine, which said that all means available would be used to retain Communist party power in Soviet satellites. The Brezhnev doctrine was applied in Czechoslovakia in August 1968.

1283. Michael, Franz: "China and the Soviet Union: waiting for Mao to die?" *Current History*, v. 68 # 408 (September, 1975): 65-67, 104.

1284. Odom, William E.: "Who controls whom in Moscow." *Foreign Policy*, # 19 (Summer, 1975): 109-123.

1285. Ploss, Sidney I.: "Signs of struggle." *Problems of Communism*, v. 31 # 5 (September/October, 1982): 41-52.

Deals with the Kremlin infighting in the immediate post-Brezhnev period.

1286. Polaris, Jean: "The Sino-Soviet dispute: its economic impact on China." *International Affairs*, v. 40 # 4 (October, 1964): 647-658.

> # 377. Rabkin, Y. M.: "The Soviet Jewish revival."

1287. Racz, Barnabas: "Political changes in Hungary after the Soviet invasion of Czechoslovakia." *Slavic Review*, v. 29 # 4 (December, 1970): 633-650.

1288. Robinson, Thomas W.: "Chinese-Soviet relations in the context of Asian and international politics." *International Journal*, v. 34 # 4 (Fall, 1979): 624-648.

> # 379. Schnall, D. J.: "Soviet Jewry."

1289. Staar, Richard F.: "Soviet policies in East Europe." *Current History*, v. 77 # 450 (October, 1979): 119-123, 136; v. 80 # 468 (October, 1981): 317-320, 342-343.

1290. ---: "Soviet policy in East Europe." *Current History*, v. 79 #

459 (October, 1980): 75-79, 104-105.

1291. ---: "Soviet relations with East Europe." *Current History*, v. 74 # 436 (April, 1978): 145-149, 184-185.

> # 381. Szajkowski, Z.: *Russian antisemitism*.

1292. Terry, Sarah M. (ed.): *Soviet policy in Eastern Europe*. New Haven, CT: Yale University Press, 1984. 400 p.

Anthology surveying the trend in relations between the Soviet Union and its East European satellite states during the early 1980s. The essays may be divided into two groups: those organized geographically and those organized thematically. The tensions inherent in almost every Soviet dominated state in Eastern Europe form the background to almost all the essays, including Garthoff's study of Soviet-American relations. Written just before Yuri Andropov's death, the book provides important background to understanding the revolutions of 1989.

CONTENTS: J. C. Campbell: Soviet policy in Eastern Europe: an overview / A. E. Stent: Soviet policy toward the German Democratic Republic / A. Korbonski: Soviet policy toward Poland / J. Valenta: Soviet policy toward Hungary and Czechoslovakia / W. Zimmerman: Soviet relations with Yugoslavia and Rumania / A. Marer: The political economy of Soviet relations with Eastern Europe / J. P. Hardt: Soviet energy policy in Eastern Europe / S. M. Terry: Theories of Socialist development in Soviet-East European relations / A. R. Johnson: The Warsaw Pact: Soviet military policy in Eastern Europe / P. Hassner: Soviet policy in Western Europe: the East European factor / R. L. Garthoff: Eastern Europe in the context of U.S.-Soviet relations / S. M. Terry: Soviet policy in Eastern Europe: the challenge of the 1980s.

1293. Wilson, Dick: "Sino-Soviet rivalry in Southeast Asia." *Problems of Communism*, v. 23 # 5 (September/October, 1974): 39-51.

1294. Windsor, Philip and Adam Roberts: *Czechoslovakia, 1968: reform, repression and resistance*. London: Chatto & Windus for the

Institute for Strategic Studies, 1969. 199 p.

1295. Zagoria, Donald S.: "The Soviet quandry in Asia." *Foreign Affairs*, v. 56 # 2 (January, 1978): 306-323.

1296. Zauberman, Alfred: "Soviet and Chinese strategy for economic growth." *International Affairs*, v. 38 # 3 (July, 1962): 339-352.

Comparative study on economic and social problems.

### 5. Dissidents and Human Rights

1297. Adams, Jan S.: "Institutional change in the 1970s: the case of the USSR People's Control Committee." *Slavic Review*, v. 37 # 3 (September, 1978): 457-472.

Reviews the *Komitet narodnogo kontrolia* (KNK), the Party Central Control Commission and Workers' and Peasants' Inspectorate, first created by Lenin in 1923 and reorganized by Chairman Nikita S. Khrushchev in November 1962.

1298. Amalrik, Andrei: *Will the Soviet Union survive until 1984?* New York: Harper & Row, 1970. 93 p.

Brief but important essay by a well-known member of the *samizdat*. Amalrik rejects both convergence theory and assumptions of eventual Soviet liberalization. Instead, he examines the parallels between Brezhnev's USSR and Nicholas II's Russia, predicting that the former, like the latter, would collapse leading to the breakup of the new Russian empire. Reading Amalrik after the democratic revolutions between 1989 and 1991 reveals some important insights. Almost all of Amalrik's predictions came true. Indeed, the only prediction proved incorrect was his assumption that the collapse would be the result of a war with China. Instead, the series of peaceful revolutions in the Warsaw Pact and the failed *coup* of August 1991 led to the collapse of a system no longer able to maintain either popular loyalty or mass fear.

1299. Barghoorn, Frederick: *Détente and the democratic movement in the USSR*. New York: The Free Press, 1976. 229 p.

Scholarly investigation of the impact of détente and international diplomacy on the treatment of dissidents in the USSR. Baghoorn argues that despite détente the Cold War has continued; this is especially true of the war of ideas represented by propaganda. Thus, Barghoorn explains the ironic fact that although détente represented a lessening of East-West tensions the Soviets did not ease the plight of dissidents at the time. Pessimistic overall, Barghoorn nevertheless describes the courage of those working for democracy in a neo-Stalinist environment.

1300. Bartol, Kathryn M.: "Soviet computer centers: network or tangle?" *Soviet Studies*, v. 23 # 4 (April, 1972): 608-618.

1301. Brumberg, Abraham: "Dissent in Russia." *Foreign Affairs*, v. 52 # 4 (July, 1974): 781-798.

1302. Brym, Robert J.: "The changing rate of Jewish emigration from the USSR: some lessons from the 1970s." *Soviet Jewish Affairs*, v. 15 # 2 (May, 1985): 23-35.

1303. Chalidze, Valery: "How important is Soviet dissent?" *Commentary*, v. 63 # 6 (June, 1977): 57-62.

Investigates the size and influence of the *samizdat*.

1304. ---: *To defend these rights: human rights in the Soviet Union* (translated from Russian by Guy Daniels). New York: Random House, 1974. 340 p.

Insider's account of the struggle of Russian dissidents to liberalize the Soviet Union. Distinguishes the differences between disparate streams of dissidents: from those who merely want to remove Stalinist distortions, to those who are, in effect, neo-Fascists. Chalidze, a Social Democrat, argues for the gradual replacement of communism with a more open form of social democracy on the West European model. Scoffed at by many experts in the 1970s because he argued for an incremental and willful change, Chalidze's scenario has actually proven itself quite close to reality.

When the democratic revolution did occur, it was swift, non-violent and led -- contrary to the expected -- to capitalism.

1305. Dreyer, Jacob J.: "Dissent in the USSR and the Jewish question." *Midstream*, v. 17 # 3 (March, 1971): 7-20.

1306. Friedberg, Maurice: "From Moscow to Jerusalem -- and points West." *Commentary*, v. 65 # 5 (May, 1978): 63-67.

Personal story describing the difficulties experienced by Soviet Jews seeking to emigrate.

1307. ---: "Soviet Jewry today." *Commentary*, v. 48 # 2 (August, 1969): 45-47.

1308. ---: "The state of Soviet Jewry." *Commentary*, v. 39 # 1 (January, 1965): 38-43.

Gauges the opinions of Soviet leaders regarding Russian Jewry: Leonid Brezhnev, Aleksei Kosygin, Nikolai Podgorny, Anastas Mikoyan, and Mikhail Suslov, are cited among others.

1309. Gitelman, Zvi: "Moscow and the Soviet Jews: a parting of the ways." *Problems of Communism*, v. 29 # 1 (January/February, 1980): 18-34.

1310. Glazer, Nathan et al: *Soviet Jewry: 1969*. New York: Academic Committee on Soviet Jewry, 1970. 95 p.

Brief collection of papers from the Second Conference on Soviet Jewry, held in Washington, DC in 1969. The five major essays review the state of Soviet Jewry, Soviet antisemitism, and Jewish national consciousness in the Soviet Union. Eleven texts from the Jewish *samizdat* are also included.

1311. Goldberg, B. Z.: "Some Soviet policies: fact and fiction." *Midstream*, v. 13 # 6 (June/July, 1967): 39-45.

1312. Harasowska, Marta and Orest Olhovych (eds.): *The international Sakharov hearing*. Baltimore, MD: Smoloskyp Publishers,

1977. 335 p. [PB]

Collection of articles that were derived from the first International Sakharov Hearing on Human Rights Abuses in the Soviet Union that was held in Copenhagen, Denmark in October 1975. The essays, written in the form of testimony, cover a wide range of abuses: the hounding of dissidents, refusal to give exit visas to those wishing to emigrate, and the persecution of religion. Chapter 3 is entirely devoted to the abuse of psychiatry in the USSR. As a conclusion, the editors reproduce the findings of the panel of "judges" who found the Soviet Union guilty of numerous abuses. This edition includes an appendix offering brief biographical data about 111 of the most prominent dissidents.

1313. Hayward, Max (ed.): *On trial: the Soviet State versus Abram Tertz and Nikolai Arzhak.* New York: Harper & Row, 1966. 183 p.

Transcript of the February 10-14, 1966 trial of Andrei Siniovsky and Yuli Daniel, two Soviet citizens active in publishing and distributing *samizdat* literature. In 1965 Siniovsky and Daniel covertly published a book -- under the pseudonyms of Tertz and Arzhak -- critical of the regime's human rights record. They were later arrested by the KGB and charged with defaming the Soviet Union. Upon conviction the two were sentenced to hard labor in a *gulag*.

1314. Heller, Mikhail: "Antisemitism in Soviet mythology." (translated from Russian by Sheila Gutter) *Midstream*, v. 26 # 1 (January, 1980): 8-12.

1315. Hirszowicz, Lukasz: "Anti-Jewish discrimination in education and employment." *Soviet Jewish Affairs*, v. 15 # 1 (1985): 25-30.

1316. Hopkins, Mark: *Russia's underground press: the Chronicle of Current Events* (foreword by Andrei Sakharov). New York: Praeger Publishers, 1983. 201 p.

Chronicles the heroic story of the underground journalists who have reported on the Russian human rights record in the *samizdat* (the secret publication and distribution of banned literature). Although the bibliography lists more than a dozen books consulted, the key documentation is from personal interviews with the editors and reporters of *The Chronicle of Current Events*. The chapter on KGB efforts to disrupt publication of the *Chronicle* proves how potent the *samizdat* press really was. An appendix reproduces a full table of contents for all regular issues of the *Chronicle*.

1317. Korey, William: "The future of Soviet Jewry: emigration and assimilation." *Foreign Affairs*, v. 58 # 1 (Fall, 1979): 67-81.

1318. ---: "Sakharov and the Soviet Jewish national movement." *Midstream*, v. 13 # 6 (June/July, 1967): 35-46.

1319. ---: "Updating *The Protocols of the Elders of Zion*." *Midstream*, v. 22 # 5 (May, 1976): 5-17.

1320. Medvedev, Zhores A.: *The Medvedev papers: "fruitful meetings between scientists of the world" and "secrecy of correspondce is guaranteed by law."* (translated from Russian by Vera Rich). New York: St. Martin's Press, 1971. 471 p.

Two *samizdat* papers translated and reprinted for American audiences. As punishment for his publications, Medvedev was incarcerated in a psychiatric hospital in 1970 and 1971. These two papers deal with the Communist party efforts to undermine the USSR Academy of Sciences by politicizing membership and postal censorship by the KGB.

1321. Navrozov, Lev: "On Soviet dissidence: an interior view." *Commentary*, v. 56 # 5 (November, 1973): 31-36.

1322. Oleszczuk, Thomas: "An analysis of bias in *samizdat* sources: a Lithuanian case study." *Soviet Studies*, v. 37 # 1 (January, 1985): 131-137.

1323. Reddaway, Peter (ed.): *Uncensored Russia: protest and dissent in the Soviet Union -- the unofficial Moscow journal "A Chronicle of Current Events."* New York: American Heritage Press, 1972. 499 p.

Translation of the first eleven issues of *Chronicle of Current Events*, a *samizdat* publication that appeared between April 1968 and December 1969. Reddaway has rearranged the *Chronicle*'s articles into thematic order.

1324. Reich, Walter: "Soviet psychiatry on trial." *Commentary*, v. 65 # 1 (January, 1978): 40-48.

1325. Rubin, Ronald I. (ed.): *The unredeemed: antisemitism in the Soviet Union*. Chicago: Quadrangle Books, 1968. 317 p.

Reader on Soviet antisemitism, based on sources that were published previously, but which are collected together for the first time. A brief introduction offers the historical context of Soviet Jewry from Stalin's time through the abortive Khrushchev thaw. An interesting appendix details Jewish institutions active during the mid-1960s, but is now hopelessly out of date. Twenty years ago the public opening of a *yeshiva* and other Jewish cultural and educational institutions in Moscow was unthinkable, while the mass emigration to Israel was barely a dream in the minds of a small number of visionaries.

1326. Russell, Bertrand and Aron Vergelis: "Soviet antisemitism: an exchange." *Commentary*, v. 39 # 1 (January, 1965): 35-37.

Exchange of opinion on Soviet antisemitism between British philosopher Bertrand Russell and Aron Vergelis, editor of the *Yiddish*-language Soviet magazine, *Sovietish Heimland*. Vergelis, in the exchange of letters, asked Russell to intercede with Soviet authorities that they not suppress Jewish culture.

1327. Sakharov, Andrei D.: *Progress, coexistance and intellectual freedom*. New York: W. W. Norton, 1968. 158 p.

Offers a selection of Sakharov's thoughts on the democratization of the USSR and Soviet-American relations. Sakharov, the father of the Soviet H-bomb, had second thoughts about his country's policies and became one of the main advocates of democracy, economic reform, and intellectual freedom.

1328. ---: *Sakharov speaks*. New York: A. A. Knopf, 1974. 245 p.

Collection of Sakharov's writings on human rights and public affairs. Father of the Soviet H-bomb and one of the leaders of the human rights movement in the USSR, Sakharov covers a wide range of internal and external topics: the treatment of non-Russian nationalities in the USSR, Jewish emigration, freedom of thought, and relations with the United States. Until his death in 1990, Sakharov was one of the keenest defenders of freedom in the Soviet Union.

1329. Scherer, John L.: "A Note on Soviet Jewish emigration, 1971-84." *Soviet Jewish Affairs*, v. 15 # 2 (May, 1985): 37-44.

1330. Schroetter, Leonard: *The last exodus*. New York: Universe Books, 1974. 432 p.

Broad-based survey on the efforts to gain free emigration for those Soviet Jews who desired to leave. Views the issue from both the Soviet Jewish perspective and from the point of view of Jews outside Russia who actively campaigned for free emigration. The chapters on Russian Jewry also offer a brief look into Soviet Jewish history and chronicle the rebirth of (underground) Jewish culture that went hand in hand with the will to emigrate.

1331. Shaffer, Harry G.: *The Soviet treatment of Jews*. New York: Praeger Publishers, 1974. 232 p.

Analyzes the treatment of Jews during the Brezhnev years. Special emphasis is on the rise of Soviet antisemitism (in the guise of anti-Zionism) and the struggle for free emigration. Inter alia Shaffer also traces the development of Soviet Jewry's self identity through two generations of officially sanctioned assimilation.

1332. Sharlet, Robert: "Dissent and repression in the Soviet Union." *Current History*, v. 73 # 430 (October, 1977): 112-117, 130.

1333. ---: "Growing Soviet dissidence." *Current History*, v. 79 # 459 (October, 1980): 96-100.

1334. Shneiderman, S. L.: "The ghost of *Emes* walks in *Pravda*." *Midstream*, v. 22 # 10 (December, 1976): 51-56.

1335. Smolar, Boris: *Soviet Jewry today and tomorrow*. New York/London: Collier-Macmillan, 1971. 228 p.

Journalistic account of the state of Soviet Jewry, primarily concentrating on the period from 1967 to 1970. Smolar offers perceptive comments on conditions in Russia, as well as insights into Russian Jewish history. Based primarily on interviews, the book tends to be anecdotal rather that analytical and thus may contain useful insights for scholars and general readers alike.

1336. Taagepera, Rein: "The 1970 Soviet census: fusion or crystallization of nationalities?" *Soviet Studies*, v. 23 # 2 (October, 1971): 216-221.

> # 152. Ulam, A. B.: *Russia's failed revolutions*.

1337. Wiesel, Elie: *The Jews of silence: a personal report on Soviet Jewry*. New York: Schocken Books/Pantheon, 1966. 160 p. [PB]

Classic account of Soviet Jewry by the 1986 Nobel Peace Prize laureate and noted Holocaust author, based on Wiesel's 1965 visit to Moscow. *The Jews of silence* did much to bring the tragic plight of Soviet Jewry to the attention of the West. Subsequent trips only confirmed Wiesel's fears that silence was the improper response to evil. The new edition contains two additional chapters in which Wiesel notes the almost miraculous Soviet transformation since 1985: while mass emigration was once only a dream it has now become a reality. The expanded edition also includes an epilogue by Martin Gilbert who previously chronicled the suffering and heroism of Soviet Jewish *refuseniks*.

1338. ---: "Will Soviet Jewry survive?" *Commentary*, v. 43 # 2 (February, 1967): 47-52.

1339. Wistrich, Robert S.: "From Lenin to today's black hundreds." *Midstream*, v. 34 # 3 (March, 1978): 4-12.

1340. Zaslavsky, Victor and Robert J. Brym: *Soviet Jewish emigration and Soviet nationality policy*. London: Macmillan, 1983. 185 p.

Intensive study on the emigration of over 250,000 Jews in the period between 1970 and 1983 based on both published sources and interviews with 155 Soviet Jewish emigrants. Includes an interesting presentation of Marxist-Leninist theory on national minorities. Despite the small sample of interviews Zaslavsky and Brym have succeded in understanding the psyche of Soviet Jewish émigrés.

### 6. The Invasion of Afghanistan

1341. Dawisha, Karen: "Moscow's moves in the direction of the Gulf: so near and yet so far." *Journal of International Affairs*, v. 34 # 2 (Fall/Winter, 1980/1981): 219-233.

1342. Freedman, Robert O.: "Soviet policy towards the Middle East since the invasion of Afghanistan." *Journal of International Affairs*, v. 34 # 2 (Fall/Winter, 1980/1981): 283-310.

1343. Khalilzad, Zalmay: "Soviet-occupied Afghanistan." *Problems of Communism*, v. 21 # 6 (November/December, 1980): 23-40.

1344. Kamrany, Nake M.: "Afghanistan under Soviet occupation." *Current History*, v. 81 # 475 (May, 1982): 219, 230-232.

1345. Lenczowski, George: "The Soviet Union and the Persian Gulf: an encircling strategy." *International Journal*, v. 37 # 2 (Spring, 1982): 307-327.

1346. Price, David L.: "Moscow and the Persian Gulf." *Problems of Communism*, v. 28 # 2 (March/April, 1979): 1-13.

1347. Rubinstein, Alvin Z.: "Soviet imperialism in Afghanistan." *Current History*, v. 79 # 459 (October, 1980); 80-83, 103-104.

1348. ---: "The Soviet Union and Afghanistan." *Current History*, v. 82 # 486 (October, 1983): 318-321, 337-338.

1349. Shlapentokh, Vladimir E.: "Moscow's war propaganda and Soviet public opinion." *Problems of Communism*, v. 33 # 5

(September/October, 1984): 88-94.

1350. Smolansky, O. M.: "Soviet policy in Iran and Afghanistan." *Current History*, v. 80 # 468 (October, 1981): 321-324, 339.

1351. Urban, Mark: *War in Afghanistan* (second edition). New York: St. Martin's Press, 1990. 330 p.

Military history of the Soviet-Afghanistan War, concentrating on the operations and tactical history of the war. Urban concludes this important but tentative account with the Soviet withdrawal from Afghanistan in 1989.

# 9

# Western Perceptions of the Soviet Union

## A. EARLY YEARS

1352. Chamberlin, William H.: "The Russian Revolution 1917-1942." *Russian Review*, v. 2 # 1 (Fall, 1942): 3-9.

1353. Davis, Donald E. and Eugene P. Trani: "The American YMCA and the Russian Revolution." *Slavic Review*, v. 33 # 3 (September, 1974): 469-491.

1354. Gillette, Philip S.: "Armand Hammer, Lenin, and the first American concession in Soviet Russia." *Slavic Review*, v. 40 # 3 (Fall, 1981): 356-365.

1355. Hagglund, Roger: "The Russian émigré debate of 1928 on criticism." *Slavic Review*, v. 32 # 3 (September, 1973): 515-526.

1356. Just, Mary: *Rome and Russia: a tragedy of errors*. Westminster, UK: Newman, 1954. 223 p.

1357. Pipes, Richard: *Russia observed: collected essays on Russian and Soviet history*. Boulder, CO: Westview Press, 1989. 240 p.

Collection of Pipes' essays on Russian and Soviet history. Covering medieval and modern eras, these essays review both the continuities and the changes in Russian history. Pipes' primary theme is nationalism and the ways that Russian and Soviet governments have dealt with national minorities. Among them, one essay reviews the Tsarist treatment of Jews, while another deals with Muslims in Soviet Central Asia. These essays suggest a broad comparative history, while the last investigates the varied proposals for solving the nationalities problem.

1358. Raeff, Marc: *Russia abroad: a cultural history of the Russian emigration, 1919-1939*. New York: Oxford University Press, 1990. 256 p.

Cultural history of the Russian émigrés who fled communism after Lenin's takeover. Although representing widely disparate groups, the émigrés had two characteristics in common: they were all anti-Communist and sought to re-create a Russian cultural milieu in exile, the latter of which was successful during the interwar period. Flourishing exile communities were established in Paris, Berlin, and Prague, among other cities.

**B. REACTIONS TO THE STALIN ERA**

1359. Campbell, John R.: *Soviet policy and its critics*. London: Victor Gollancz, 1939. 381 p.

1360. Chamberlain, William H.: "Soviet communism: the transient and the permanent." *Russian Review*, v. 10 # 3 (July, 1951): 169-175.

1361. Crankshaw, Edward: "Russia in Europe: the conflict of values." *International Affairs*, v. 22 # 4 (October, 1946): 501-510.

1362. ---: "The USSR revisited." *International Affairs*, v. 23 # 4 (October, 1947): 492-499.

1363. Herndon, James S. and Joseph O. Baylen: "Col. Philip R. Faymonville and the Red Army, 1934-1943." *Slavic Review*, v. 34 # 3 (September, 1975): 483-505.

Faymonville was first American military atachê in Moscow and one of the founders of the U.S.-Soviet alliance in World War II.

1364. Hook, Sidney: "Memories of the Moscow trials." *Commentary*, v. 77 # 3 (March, 1984): 57-63.

1365. Kovalio, Jacob: "Japan's perception of Stalinist foreign policy in the early 1930s." *Journal of Contemporary History*, v. 19 # 2 (April, 1984): 315-335.

1366. Mayers, David: "Soviet war aims and the grand alliance, George Kennan's views, 1944-1946." *Journal of Contemporary History*, v. 21 # 1 (January, 1986): 57-79.

1367. Merrick, Ray: "The Russia Committee of the British Foreign Office and the Cold War, 1946-1947." *Journal of Contemporary History*, v. 20 # 3 (July, 1985): 453-468.

1368. Nove, Alec: *Economic rationality and Soviet politics, or was Stalin really necessary?* New York: F. A. Praeger, 1964. 316 p.

1369. Passfield, D.: "Soviet communism: its present position and prospects." *International Affairs*, v. 15 # 3 (May/June, 1936): 395-413.

1370. Paterson, Thomas G.: *Soviet-American confrontation: postwar reconstruction and the origins of the Cold War*. Baltimore, MD: Johns Hopkins University Press, 1973. 287 p.

Mildly revisionist history of the Cold War, as seen from the American perspective. Posits that the U.S. attempted to use a carrot and stick approach to moderate Soviet ambitions. Paterson argues that American efforts at economic coercion were counter productive. In placing the lion's share of responsibility for the conflict on the United States, Paterson fails to properly assess Russian actions and intentions.

1371. Taylor, S. J.: *Stalin's apologist Walter Duranty: the New York Times's man in Moscow*. New York: Oxford University Press, 1990. 432 p.

Intellectual and political biography of Walter Duranty, the head of the *New York Times* Moscow bureau during Stalin's reign. Duranty had made his mark by predicting Stalin's rise to power. Thereafter, however, Duranty increasingly came to be an apologist for him. During Stalin's Reign of Terror in the 1930s, Duranty consistently under reported Stalin's crimes. For example, he did not report the Ukrainian terror famine until the facts could no longer be denied. Even then, he played it down. Similarly, Duranty reported the purge trials as valid courts of justice, rather than the show trials they really were.

1372. Werth, Alexander: "The outlook in the USSR." *International Affairs*, v. 22 # 1 (January, 1946): 28-40.

**C. SINCE 1954**

1373. Brzezinski, Zbigniew: *Game plan: a geostrategic framework for the conduct of the U.S.-Soviet conflict*. New York: Atlantic Monthly Press, 1986. 288 p.

Proposes a new grand strategy for the United States with the goal of bringing the Cold War to an end. Lays out the historical context of both the Cold War and United States strategic options, concluding that the latter no longer provide an adequate response to U.S. strategic needs. Thereafter Brzezinski sketches the parameters for a proposed strategy, with special emphasis given to the use of propaganda as a means to wean the Eastern European countries away from communism. It is interesting to note that some of Brzezinski's proposals -- though not consciously pursued -- became the cornerstones of the eventual fall of the Soviet Union. Both propaganda and economic battle strategies, were won by a Western world that had obviously outpaced the Communist bloc nations in every sphere except military output.

> # 135. ---: *The grand failure*.

1374. Caldwell, Lawrence T.: "Washington and Moscow: a tale of two summits." *Current History*, v. 87 # 531 (October, 1988): 305-308, 337-338.

1375. Conquest, Robert: "A new Russia? a new world?" *Foreign Affairs*, v. 53 # 3 (April, 1975): 482-497.

1376. Crozier, Brian: "Getting Gorbachev wrong." *Midstream*, v. 37 # 2 (February/March, 1991): 17-19.

Polemic against Western aid to maintain Communist Party power.

1377. Cullen, Robert (ed.): *The post-containment handbook: key issues in U.S.-Soviet economic relations*. Boulder, CO: Westview Press, 1990. 227 p.

Source book on issues in economic relations between the Soviet Union and the United States. Essays by experts in international banking help place the text into context and project possible future trends in superpower relations.

CONTENTS: S. Dryden: Banking and credit / J. M. Montgomery: The cumbersome apparatus / M. Mastanduno: What is COCOM, and how does it work / R. Cullen: Détente and trade / H. C. Blaney: Economic cooperation and the Helsinki process / J. Kloepfer: Controlling information / S. Carey: Up from autarky / K. L. Tritle: Soviet foreign economic relations, 1970-1995.

1378. Dallin, Alexander: "Bias and blunders in American studies on the USSR." *Slavic Review*, v. 32 # 3 (September, 1975): 560-576. Rejoinder by John A Armstrong, pp. 577-587.

> # 359. Feingold, H.: "Soviet Jewish survival."

1379. Fisher, Harold H.: *The Communist revolution: an outline of strategy and tactics*. Stanford, CA: Stanford University Press, 1955. 89 p.

1380. Ford, Robert A.: "The Soviet Union: the next decade." *Foreign Affairs*, v. 62 # 5 (Summer, 1984): 1132-1144.

1381. Gelman, Harry: "Rise and fall of détente." *Problems of Communism*, v. 34 # 2 (March/April, 1985): 51-72.

Soviet-American dètente in early 1970s.

1382. Gervasi, Tom: *The myth of Soviet military supremacy*. New York: Harper & Row, Publishers, 1986. 416 p.

Journalistic investigation into the military aspects of the Cold War. Asserts that NATO's traditional perceptions of Soviet military supremacy are a myth. As a result of his investigation, Gervasi argues that statements regarding Soviet military superiority -- both nuclear and conventional -- are largely untrue. Gervasi also extensively compares Allied and Soviet weapons, including their use in the Arab-Israeli wars. Gervasi's thesis is, at times, weakened by polemical lapses that, for example, have him exclude the Ukraine, Belorussia, and the Baltic Republics from Europe.

1383. Gottstein, Klaus (ed.): *Western perceptions of Soviet goals: is trust possible?* Boulder, CO: Westview Press, 1990. 445 p.

Investigation into Soviet goals as viewed by analysts in the United States, Canada, and Western Europe. Inter alia the authors trace the information -- and misinformation -- that made international cooperation difficult for the period of the Cold War. Recommending ways to increase mutual trust, the authors also offer insights into Russian goals. Potential means for overcoming mistrust are discussed in order to permit the creation of a world order based on cooperation rather than conflict.

CONTENTS: K. Gottstein: Mutual perceptions of long-range political goals as an obstacle to trust creation / E. Schneider: *Perestroika* or ideology? / K. Birnbaum: Long-term policy perceptions as threat perceptions: extent and limit of their policy salience / G. Niedhart: A Cold War view of the USSR: Konrad Adenauer's perception of Soviet politics / R. Hermann: Coping with the prospect of endless conflict: dilemmas of U.S. policies and the salience of long-term objectives / P. Windsor: The nature and patterns of Western thought about the East-West conflict / D. Munton: Threat perceptions and shifts of public attitudes, 1960s-1980s / M. Richter: Meaning and perception patterns: a preliminary logico-semantic analysis / R. Rogers: Fear of the Soviet Union: individual and cultural reflections / E. Schulz: The "new political thinking" on

Soviet foreign relations / W. Heisenberg: Confidence building measures and Western perceptions of Soviet long-range goals / H. Tolhoek: The world on the road to the year 2000: comparison of trends in Western and Soviet society in the coming fifteen years / ---: Theory of the "pugwash process" or: possibilities and impossibilities of overcoming ideological differences / L. Sigal: Contrasting U.S. perceptions of the military balance in Europe and the management of long-term competition with the Soviet Union / B. L. Smith: The strategic dimensions of Soviet economic reform / M. Späth: Long-term goals in Soviet science and technology policy: confrontation or cooperation with the West? / F. Kuebart: Ideology and public opinion: the role of Soviet education / J. Dean: Expansionism and secretive decision-making: two key problems of the Soviet system / R. Garthoff: Soviet new thinking on the world and foreign policy / N. Nowikow: Developments in Soviet political thinking in foreign policy.

1384. Hanson, Phillip: "Western technology in the Soviet economy." *Problems of Communism*, v. 27 # 6 (November/December, 1978): 20-30.

1385. Himmelfarb, Milton: "Soviet Jews; American orthodoxy." *Commentary*, v. 33 # 1 (January, 1962): 65-68.

1386. Hoffmann, Stanley: "Muscle and Brains." *Foreign Policy*, # 37 (Winter, 1979/1980): 3-27.

1387. Jacobsen, Carl G.: "Soviet-American policy: new strategic uncertainties." *Current History*, v. 81 # 477 (October, 1982): 305-308, 336-339.

1388. Jasny, Naum: "Some thoughts of Soviet statistics: an evaluation." *International Affairs*, v. 35 # 1 (January, 1959): 53-60.

1389. Keeble, Curtis: "The roots of Soviet foreign policy." *International Affairs*, v. 60 # 4 (Fall, 1984): 561-578.

1390. Kessler, Ronald: *Moscow station: how the KGB penetrated the American embassy*. New York: Scribner's, 1989. 352 p.

Journalistic exposé of the means the KGB used to penetrate the U.S. embassy in Moscow. Kessler argues that the security situation in the embassy was so poor, that the embassy was virtually useless as a tool of American foreign policy. Kessler attributes the problem to official neglect and inefficiency, from the U.S. ambassador downward. As an example, Kessler cites the case of USMC guards who were "turned" by KGB women who traded sex for secrets. The book is an interesting case study in the espionage war that characterized the Cold War, although some of Kessler's factual points may be blown out of proportion.

1391. Kimche, Jon: "Are the Russians strong -- or stumbling?" *Midstream*, v. 27 # 2 (February, 1981): 3-6.

Studies the decline of Soviet oil revenues.

1392. Laqueur, Walter: "What we know about the Soviet Union." *Commentary*, v. 75 # 2 (February, 1983): 13-21.

1393. Lebow, Richard N.: "Malign analysts or evil empire? Western images of Soviet nuclear strategy." *International Journal*, v. 44 # 1 (Winter, 1988/1989): 1-40.

1394. Legvold, Robert: "Containment without confrontation." *Foreign Policy*, # 40 (Fall, 1980): 74-98.

1395. Levine, Herbert S.: "An American view off economic relations with the USSR." *Annals*, v. 414 (July, 1974): 1-17.

1396. Lichtheim, George: "The Cold War in perspective." *Commentary*, v. 37 # 6 (June, 1964): 21-26.

1397. Lukacs, John: "The Soviet state at 65." *Foreign Affairs* v. 65 # 1 (Fall, 1986): 21-36.

1398. Luttwak, Edward N.: "Delusions of Soviet weakness." *Commentary*, v. 79 # 1 (January, 1985): 32-38.

1399. ---: *The grand strategy of the Soviet Union*. New York: St. Martin's Press, 1983. 242 p.

Polemic seeking to alert American readers to the continuing threat of Soviet aggression. Luttwak attempts to do so by examining the Red Army's strategic doctrine in the late 1970s and early 1980s. His study has led him to the conclusion that a Sino-Soviet war might be imminent, precisely because of economic and ideological stagnation. In order to avert world catastrophe, the author argues that NATO must be prepared to defend its interests -- and the interests of world peace -- through a policy of military strength combined with skillful diplomacy. Given the reversal of positions in the last decade, it appears clear that Luttwak was not correct in his assessment of the situation. Yet, his argumentation and especially his careful use of available documentation make the book a model of military and political analysis.

1400. Navrozov, Lev: "The Kremlin and the Western politico-cultural establishment." *Midstream*, v. 36 # 8 (December, 1990): 20-25.

Polemic against trusting Gorbachev and Russians.

1401. Oberg, James E.: *Uncovering Soviet disasters: exploring the limits of glasnost*. New York: Random House, 1988. 318 p.

Journalistic investigation of one aspect of *glasnost*: the new Russian openess about both major and minor disasters that Soviet authorities never reported, or did not report in a timely fashion. Heading Oberg's list of disasters is the Chernobyl nuclear power plant disaster on April 26, 1986 which the Soviets initially attempted to deny altogether. Despite the lack of scholarly dispassion and the absence of reference notes (in the traditional sense of the term), Oberg has still collected important data on a combination of military, industrial, and scientific disasters. His list of disasters, contained in Appendix 2, begins in 1935 and ends in 1987. These, however, are only the known disasters; many others have been hidden in the Soviet memory hole so well, that they are entirely unknown. One word of caution seems appropriate: despite all the disasters, the Soviets scored some notable scientific break-throughs. Therefore, an unmitigated collection of failures is no more accurate than a propagandistic catalogue of achievements. Where Oberg succeeds best is in explaining the means by which

Soviet authorities controlled the flow of information and used "truth" for partisan purposes.

1402. Pipes, Richard: "How to cope with the Soviet threat: a long-term strategy for the West." *Commentary*, v. 78 # 2 (August, 1984): 13-30.

1403. ---: *Survival is not enough: Soviet realities and America's future.* New York: Simon and Schuster, 1984. 302 p.

Investigates the Cold War from the United States' perspective. Pipes' divides his book into five chapters, each dedicated to a different aspect of the problem. He argues that so long as the Communist party remains the sole party in power in the USSR, both political collapse and imperialism will continue. Thus, Pipes predicts that the Soviet Union will always remain a military threat as long as the Soviet system remains unchanged. Writing just before the rise of Mikhail S. Gorbachev, Pipes could not predict the course of reform that *glasnost* and *perestroika* wrought. Pipes called for the U.S. to institute a systematic grand strategy to counter the Soviet Union's great plan. In the end it appears that Pipes' strategy was unnecessary, though his prediction that peace with the Soviet Union would only be attainable if the Soviet Union made peace with its own people was proven correct.

1404. Podhoretz, Norman: "Making the world safe for communism." *Commentary*, v. 61 # 4 (April, 1976): 31-41.

Condemns isolationist tendencies of American liberals.

1405. Pond, Elizabeth: *From the Yaroslavsky Station: Russia perceived.* New York: Universe Books, 1981. 296 p.

Pond, an American journalist, bases this travelogue on an extensive trip she took to the Russian hinterland and the USSR's Asian republics. The author chronicles her trip, while interspersing it with personal and historical information in her reflections on Soviet politics and society.

1406. Puddington, Arch: "The new Soviet apologists." *Commentary*,

v. 76 # 5 (November, 1983): 25-31.

1407. Sainer, Arthur: "An open letter to Nathan Sharansky." *Midstream*, v. 33 # 2 (February, 1987): 38-40.

1408. Schlesinger, James: "The eagle and the bear: ruminations on forty years of superpower relations." *Foreign Affairs*, v. 63 # 5 (Summer, 1985): 937-961.

1409. Sharansky, Natan: "As I see Gorbachev." *Commentary*, v. 85 # 3 (March, 1988): 29-34.

1410. Shlapentokh, Vladimir: "The changeable Soviet image of America." *Annals*, v. 497 (May, 1988): 157-171.

1411. Shulman, Marshall I.: "Arms control and disarmament: a view from the USA." *Annals*, v. 414 (July, 1974): 64-72.

1412. Simes, Dimitri K.: "The anti-Soviet brigade." *Foreign Policy*, # 37 (Winter, 1979/1980): 28-42.

1413. ---: "Detenté, Russian-style." *Foreign Policy*, # 32 (Fall, 1978): 47-62.

1414. Storella, Mark C.: *Poisoning arms control: the Soviet Union and chemical/biological weapons*. Cambridge, MA: Institute for Foreign Policy Analysis, 1984. 100 p.

Addresses the evidence of possible Soviet violation of treaties banning the storage, production, and use of chemical and biological weapons. Also examines the threat to international stability posed by such weapons and recommends means to avert future violations of international arms control agreements.

1415. Story, Christopher: "When strong look weak: Soviet reforms." *Midstream*, v. 37 # 7 (October, 1991): 2-8.

Argues that Soviet reforms are a sham and that the events of the last two years are merely disinformation.

1416. Strode, Rebecca V. and Colin S. Gray: "The imperial dimension of Soviet military power." *Problems of Communism*, v. 30 # 6 (November/December, 1981): 1-15.

1417. Stuart, Robert C.: "United States-Soviet trade." *Current History*, v. 76 # 447 (May/June, 1979): 206-208, 229.

1418. Taubman, William: *The view from Lenin hills*. New York: Coward-McCann, 1967. 249 p.

Taubman, an American exchange student at Moscow University, takes a close look at the new generation of Soviet youth. Conveys personalized information of student life in Moscow in the mid-1960s.

1419. Trevelyan, Humphrey: "Reflections on Soviet and Western policy." *International Affairs*, v. 52 # 4 (October, 1976): 527-534.

1420. Ulam, Adam B.: "How to restrain the Soviets." *Commentary*, v. 70 # 6 (December, 1980): 38-41.

1421. Weiss, Avraham: "Public protest and Soviet Jewry." *Midstream*, v. 33 # 2 (February, 1987): 25-28.

1422. Wilson, Duncan: "Anglo-Soviet relations: the effect of ideas on reality." *International Affairs*, v. 50 # 3 (July, 1974): 380-393.

1423. X (pseud.): "The sources of Soviet conduct." *Foreign Affairs*, v. 65 # 4 (Spring, 1987): 852-868.

1424. Zelnick, C. Robert: "The foundering Soviets." *Foreign Policy*, # 57 (Winter, 1984/1985): 92-107.

1425. Zimmerman, William: "Rethinking Soviet policy: changing American perspectives." *International Journal*, v. 35 # 3 (Summer, 1980): 548-562.

1426. ---: "What do scholars know about Soviet foreign policy?" *International Journal*, v. 37 # 2 (Spring, 1982): 198-219.

# 10

# The Soviet Union in Crisis

## A. THE YEARS OF THE "GERONTOCRACY"

### 1. Domestic Policy

1427. Adam, Jan: "The present Soviet incentive system." *Soviet Studies*, v. 32 # 3 (July, 1980): 349-365.

1428. Adomeit, Hannes: "Capitalist Contradictions and Soviet policy." *Problems of Communism*, v. 33 # 3 (May/June, 1984): 1-18.

1429. Altshuler, Mordechai: "Who are the *refuseniks*?: a statistical and demographic analysis." *Soviet Jewish Affairs*, v. 18 # 1 (Spring, 1988): 3-15.

1430. Beissinger, Mark R.: "The age of the Soviet oligarchs." *Current History*, v. 83 # 495 (October, 1984): 305-308, 339-342.

1431. Bergson, Abram: "Soviet economic slowdown and the 1981-85 plan." *Problems of Communism*, v. 30 # 3 (May/June, 1981): 24-36.

On the eleventh Five-Year plan for the Soviet economy.

1432. Birman, Igor: "The financial crisis in the USSR." *Soviet*

*Studies*, v. 32 # 1 (January, 1980): 84-105.

1433. Bornstein, Morris: "Improving the Soviet economic mechanism." *Soviet Studies*, v. 37 # 1 (January, 1985): 1-30.

Surveys the CPSU program to improve the economic mechanism (PIEM) from 1979 to 1984.

1434. Brown, Archie: "Andropov: discipline and reform?" *Problems of Communism*, v. 32 # 1 (January/February, 1983): 18-31.

1435. Butler, William E.: "Soviet policies and legislation." *Soviet Jewish Affairs*, v. 15 # 1 (1985): 155-159.

1436. Dinstein, Yoram: "The international obligations of the USSR in the field of human rights." *Soviet Jewish Affairs*, v. 15 # 1 (1985): 165-170.

1437. Dovring, Folke: "New plans and old results for Soviet agriculture." *Current History*, v. 81 # 477 (October, 1982): 323-326, 341-342.

1438. ---: Soviet agriculture: a state secret." *Current History*, v. 83 # 495 (October, 1984): 323-326, 338-339.

1439. Epstein, Edward J.: "Petropower and Soviet expansionism." *Commentary*, v. 82 # 1 (July, 1986): 23-28.

1440. Feldbrugge, F. J. M.: "Government and shadow economy in the Soviet Union." *Soviet Studies*, v. 36 # 4 (October, 1984): 528-543.

1441. Gitelman, Zvi: "Are nations merging in the USSR?" *Problems of Communism*, v. 32 # 5 (September/October, 1983): 35-47.

1442. Goldman, Marshall I.: "Economic problem in the Soviet Union." *Current History*, v. 82 # 486 (October, 1983): 322-325, 339.

1443. ---: "The Soviet energy pipeline." *Current History*, v. 81 # 477 (October, 1982): 309-312, 339.

1444. Gorlin, Alice C.: "The power of Soviet industrial ministries in the 1980s." *Soviet Studies*, v. 37 # 3 (July, 1985): 353-370.

1445. ---: "Soviet industry and trade." *Current History*, v. 81 # 477 (October, 1982): 318-322, 340-341; v. 83 # 495 (October, 1984): 318-322, 336-338.

1446. Gregory, Paul and Barbara Dietz: "Soviet perceptions of economic conditions during the period of stagnation: evidence from two diverse emigrant surveys." *Soviet Studies*, v. 43 # 3 (1991): 535-552.

1447. Hanson, Philip: "Economic constraints on Soviet policies in the 1980s." *International Affairs*, v. 57 # 1 (Winter, 1980/1981): 21-42.

> # 442. Hazard, J. N.: *The Soviet legal system*.

1448. Hough, Jerry: "Andropov's first year." *Problems of Communism*, v. 32 # 6 (November/December, 1983): 49-64.

1449. ---: *Soviet leadership in transition*. Washington, DC: The Brookings Institution Press, 1980. 175 p.

Brief examination of the changes likely to take place in a post-Brezhnev Soviet Union. Also reviews previous transition periods, primarily the post-Stalin transition to Nikita Khrushchev's rule. Hough concludes that all transitions in Soviet history have been difficult, and predicts that this will become more prevalent in the future as a result of generational differences in the top Communist party leadership. Hough also predicts some fundamental changes in the governance of the USSR, although he could not have anticipated the radical break that occurred after 1989.

1450. ---: "Soviet politics under Andropov." *Current History*, v. 82 # 486 (October, 1983): 330-333, 345-346.

1451. ---: "Soviet succession: issues and personalities." *Problems of Communism*, v. 31 # 5 (September/October, 1982): 20-40.

Reviews foreign policy implications of the Brezhnev succession.

1452. Hyland, William G.: "*Kto Kogo* in the Kremlin." *Problems of Communism*, v. 31 # 1 (January/February, 1982): 17-26.

"Who is who?" power politics inside the Kremlin walls.

1453. Jicinski, B.: "The Politburo's longest campaign." *Midstream*, v. 30 # 7 (August/September, 1984): 7-8.

Investigates the anti-Zionist/anti-Israel campaign waged by the Soviets.

1454. Kitrinos, Robert W.: "International department of the CPSU." *Problems of Communism*, v. 33 # 5 (September/October, 1984): 47-75.

1455. Korey, William: "The Soviet anti-Zionist committee." *Midstream*, v. 31 # 7 (August/September, 1985): 11-17.

1456. Kushnirsky, Fyodor I.: "The limits of Soviet economic reform." *Problems of Communism*, v. 33 # 4 (July/August, 1984): 33-43.

1457. Lapenna, Ivo: "Developments in Soviet domestic legislation." *Soviet Jewish Affairs*, v. 15 # 1 (1985): 160-164.

1458. Litvinov, Pavel (comp.): *The trial of the four: a collection of materials on the case of Galanskov, Ginzburg, Dobrovolsky, and Lashkova, 1967-1968* (translated from Russian by Janis Sapiers et al; edited and annotated by Peter Reddaway). New York: Viking Press, 1972. 434 p.

Transcript and analysis of one of the most crucial human rights trials in the Soviet Union. Following protests after the trial of writers Andrei Siniavsky and Yuli Daniel additional intellectuals were arrested. These, in turn, came to trial in 1968, resulting in conviction of four young intellectuals. Most historians date the Soviet human rights movement to the trial's aftermath. This edition provides the full trial transcript with explanatory notes that clarify the text's lesser known aspects. Leonard Schapiro's foreword adds to the text by placing the trial into historical context.

1459. McCain, Morris A.: "Soviet lawyers in the reform debate: cohesion and efficacy." *Soviet Studies*, v. 34 # 1 (January, 1982): 3-22.

1460. Meissner, Boris: "Transition in the Kremlin." *Problems of Communism*, v. 32 # 1 (January/February, 1983): 8-17.

1461. ---: "The 26th Party Congress and Soviet domestic politics." *Problems of Communism*, v. 30 # 3 (May/June, 1981): 1-23.

1462. Millar, James R.: *Politics, work and daily life in the USSR: a survey of former Soviet citizens*. New York: Cambridge University Press, 1987. 400 p.

Offers the result of a five year sociological study of Soviet Jewish émigrés regarding daily life in the USSR. Designed to illuminate the way that Soviet communism really works. Following up on an earlier study done in the mid-1950s the anthology amply accomplishes its stated goals.

1463. Moses, Joel C.: "Worker self-management and the reformist alternative in Soviet labor policy, 1979-1985." *Soviet Studies*, v. 39 # 2 (April, 1987): 205-228.

1464. Nove, Alec: "The economic problems of Brezhnev's successors." *Journal of International Affairs*, v. 32 # 2 (Fall/Winter, 1978): 201-209.

1465. Odom, William E.: "Choice and change in Soviet politics." *Problems of Communism*, v. 32 # 3 (May/June, 1983): 1-21.

1466. Powell, David E.: "The Soviet labor force." *Current History*, v. 83 # 495 (October, 1984): 327-330, 342-344.

1467. Reddaway, Peter: "Dissent in the USSR." *Problems of Communism*, v. 32 # 6 (November/December, 1983): 1-15.

1468. Rush, M.: "Succeeding Brezhnev." *Problems of Communism*,

v. 32 # 1 (January/February, 1983): 2-7.

1469. Schwarz, Sidney H.: "The messiah and the Kremlin." *Midstream*, v. 30 # 7 (August/september, 1984): 18-20.

1470. Shanor, Donald R.: *Behind the lines: the private war against Soviet censorship*. New York: St. Martin's Press, 1985. 172 p.

Brief investigation of the means used to defeat Soviet imposed censorship of news and information. In addition to *samizdat* literature, Shanor notes the existence of an "underground telegraph" to transmit information. Posits that the revolution in home computers will lead to a virtual end of censorship since control of information flow and storage will be almost impossible.

1471. Simes, D. K.: "National security under Andropov." *Problems of Communism*, v. 32 # 1 (January/February, 1983): 32-39.

> # 446. Slider, D.: "Reforming the workplace."

1472. Sonnenfeldt, Helmut (ed.): *Soviet politics in the 1980s*. Boulder, CO: Westview Press, 1985. 247 p.

Anthology investigating the predicted direction of Soviet politics after Leonid Brezhnev's death and the rise of Konstantin Cherenenko. Most of the articles focus on the need for leadership within the Soviet Union and the Communist party to revive a stagnant economy and solve the Union's numerous social problems. Four of the essays view the issue from a specifically American perspective, viewing the possible options for reform and the potential of a new era of détente.

CONTENTS: T. Gustafson: The Andropov accession / G. W. Lapidus: Soviet politics in the 1980s: strains, dissatisfactions, and diversity / M. Feshbach: Social dynamics in the USSR / V. G. Treml: Alcohol abuse and quality of life in the USSR / D. L. Bond and H. S. Levine: The Soviet domestic economy in the 1980s / G. Schroeder: Prospects for economic reform in the Soviet Union / S. Rosefielde: Soviet arms buildup or U.S. arms decline? Real weapons procurement growth in the Soviet Union and the United

States, 1950-1980 / M. Rush: Impact and implications of Soviet defense spending / R. F. Laird: The impact of the West on the Soviet Union / D. Simes: Can the West affect Soviet Thinking / E. Hewett: Soviet economic relations with the West: U.S. options / S. E. Goodman: Advanced technology: how will the USSR adjust? / W. Leonhard: Soviet foreign policy: interest, motives, and objectives / F. W. Ermarth: The United States and the Soviet strategic challenges: arguments on the structure of our problems / R. Pipes: U.S. policy opportunities / L. Eagleburger: U.S. national interests and the Soviet Union.

1473. Syrkin, Marie: "Soviet Jewish stooges: the anti-Zionist committee." *Midstream*, v. 29 # 7 (August/September, 1983): 50-52.

Details the distorted view of Holocaust history expressed at a news conference by the Soviet Public Anti-Zionist Committee.

1474. Wistrich, Robert: "The anti-Zionist masquerade." *Midstream*, v. 29 # 7 (August/September, 1983): 8-18.

Argues that anti-Zionism is a mask for antisemitism, scoring the political use of both to delegitimize the existence of the State of Israel.

1475. Zlotnik, Marc D.: "Chernenko succeeds." *Problems of Communism*, v. 33 # 2 (March/April, 1984): 17-31.

On the selection of Konstantin Chernenko to succeed Yuri Andropov as general secretary of the CPSU.

### 2. Cracks in the Soviet Bloc

1476. Anderson, Richard D., Jr.: "Soviet decision-making and Poland." *Problems of Communism*, v. 31 # 2 (March/April, 1982): 22-36.

1477. Bialer, Seweryn: "The harsh decade: Soviet policies in the 1980s." *Foreign Affairs*, v. 59 # 5 (Summer, 1981): 999-1020.

1478. ---: *The Soviet paradox: external expansion, internal decline.* New York: Alfred A Knopf, 1986. 480 p.

Important analysis of the paradoxical state of external expansion combined with internal decline in the Soviet Union during the 1970s and early 1980s. Bialer begins by noting that all transitions have been difficult for the Soviets: from Stalin to Khrushchev, Khrushchev to Brezhnev, and then the years of the gerontocracy. According to Bialer, the Communist party and the government bureaucracy both suffer from ossification and paralysis as a result. Accordingly, the Soviets have looked for new challenges -- new conquests -- that would deflect attention away from economic and social collapse in the USSR. Writing just after Gorbachev's rise to power, Bialer could not predict the future course of events. His analysis of the inner collapse of communism and his assertion that Brezhnev's death marked a major turning point for the USSR both proved correct.

1479. Brunsdale, Mitzi M.: "Chronicling Soviet dissidence." *Current History*, v. 81 # 477 (October, 1982): 333-334, 342-343.

1480. Jowitt, Ken: "Soviet neotraditionalism: the political corruption of a Leninist regime." *Soviet Studies*, v.35 # 3 (July, 1983): 275-297.

1481. Lawson, Colin W.: "The Soviet Union and eastern Europe in southern Africa: is there a conflict of interest?" *International Affairs*, v. 59 # 1 (Winter, 1982/1983): 32-40.

1482. Mastney, V. (ed.): *Soviet/East European survey, 1983-1984.* Durham, NC: Duke University Press, 1985. 436 p.

First in a series of research paper collections from the Radio Free Europe/Radio Liberty East European Bureau. About half the chapters deal with the Soviet Union and the remainder with Warsaw Pact nations.

1483. Olcott, Martha B.: "Yuri Andropov and the 'national question'." *Soviet Studies*, v. 37 # 1 (January, 1985): 103-117.

1484. Scanlon, James P.: "Doublethink in the USSR." *Problems of*

*Communism*, v. 34 # 1 (January/February, 1985): 67-72.

1485. Valenta, Jiri: "The explosive Soviet periphery." *Foreign Policy*, # 51 (Summer, 1983): 84-100.

## B. SOVIET FOREIGN POLICY IN FLUX

### 1. The New Cold War

1486. Blacker, Coit D.: "The United States and the Soviet Union." *Current History*, v. 83 # 495 (October, 1984): 309-313, 336.

1487. Caldwell, Laurence T. and G. Willian Benz: "Soviet-American diplomacy at the end of an era." *Current History*, v. 82 # 484 (May, 1983): 205-209, 233-234.

1488. --- and Robert Legvold: "Reagan through Soviet eyes." *Foreign Policy*, # 52 (Fall, 1983): 3-21.

1489. Carmichael, Joel: "The kingdom of God and the KGB." *Midstream*, v. 31 # 5 (May, 1985): 3-9.

Extremely controversial conspiracy theory which claimed that the Vatican was working with the KGB to subvert Western interests in Latin America.

1490. Critchley, W. Harriet: "Polar deployment of Soviet submarines." *International Journal*, v. 39 # 4 (Fall, 1984): 828-865.

1491. Currie, Kenneth: "Soviet general staff's new role." *Problems of Communism*, v. 33 # 2 (March/April, 1984): 32-40.

Posits that the Red Army's general staff has emerged as the dominant voice in Soviet military affairs.

> # 1174. Garthoff, R. L.: *Détente and confrontation*.

1492. Gilberg, Trond et al: "The Soviet Union and northern

Europe." *Problems of Communism*, v. 30 # 2 (March/April, 1981): 1-24.

1493. Hassner, Pierre: "Moscow and the Western alliance." *Problems of Communism*, v. 30 # 3 (May/June, 1981): 37-54.

1494. Hedlin, Myron: "Moscow's line of arms control." *Problems of Communism*, v. 33 # 3 (May/June, 1984): 19-36.

> # 1120. Herspring, D. R.: *Soviet high command*.

1495. Horelick, Arnold: "U.S.-Soviet relations: the return of arms control." *Foreign Affairs*, v. 63 # 3 (1984): 511-534.

1496. Hough, Jerry F.: "Soviet perspectives on European security." *International Journal*, v. 40 # 1 (Winter, 1984/1985): 20-41.

1497. Jacobsen, Carl G.: "East-West relations at the crossroads." *Current History*, v. 82 # 484 (May, 1983): 201-204, 224-227.

1498. Laqueur, Walter: "U.S.-Soviet relations." *Foreign Affairs*, v. 62 # 3 (1983): 561-586.

1499. Malcolm, Neil: *Soviet political scientists and American politics*. New York: St. Martin's Press, 1984. 225 p.

Interesting investigation into the way that Soviet political scientists have viewed the United States in the late twentieth century. Notes that much of the research on American subjects has been undertaken by the Institute for the Study of the United States and Canada, which was established in 1967. Despite official autonomy, the Institute is actually responsible to the International Department of the Communist party and is thus (in effect) part of the Soviet propaganda *apparat*.

1500. Marantz, Paul: "Changing Soviet conceptions of East-West relations." *Current History*, v. 81 # 477 (October, 1982): 331-332, 343-346.

1501. ---: "Soviet-American relations: the uncertain future." *Current*

*History*, v. 82 # 486 (Ocotber, 1983): 305-308, 336-337.

1502. Mastny, Vojtech: "Kremlin politics and the Austrian settlement." *Problems of Communism*, v. 31 # 4 (July/August, 1982): 37-51.

Deals with the signing of the Austrian-Soviet peace treaty that officially ended World War II.

1503. O'Corcora, Michael and Ronald J. Hill: "The Soviet Union in Irish foreign policy." *International Affairs*, v. 58 # 2 (Spring, 1982): 254-270.

1504. Odom, William E.: "Soviet force posture: dilemmas and directions." *Problems of Communism*, v. 34 # 4 (July/August, 1985): 1-14.

1505. Østreng, Willy: "Soviet-Norwegian relations in the Arctic." *International Journal*, v. 39 # 4 (Fall, 1984): 866-887.

1506. Pond, Elizabeth: "Andropov, Kohl, and East-West issues." *Problems of Communism*, v. 32 # 4 (July/August, 1983): 35-45.

1507. Pridham, Kenneth: "The Soviet view of current disagreements between the United States and Western Europe." *International Affairs*, v. 59 # 1 (Winter, 1982/1983): 17-31.

1508. Ra'anan, Uri: "Soviet strategic doctrine and the Soviet-American global contest." *Annals*, v. 457 (September, 1981): 8-17.

1509. Rachwald, Arthur D.: "The Soviet approach to West Europe." *Current History*, v. 82 # 486 (October, 1983): 309-312, 335, 343-345.

1510. Roberts, Cynthia A.: "Soviet military policy in transition." *Current History*, v. 83 # 495 (Ocotber, 1984): 331-334, 345-346.

1511. Simes, Dimitri K.: "Disciplining Soviet power." *Foreign Policy*, # 43 (Summer, 1981): 33-52.

1512. ---: "The new Soviet challenge." *Foreign Policy*, # 55

(Summer, 1984): 113-131.

1513. Sodaro, Michael J.: "Moscow and Mitterrand." *Problems of Communism*, v. 31 # 4 (July/August, 1982): 20-36.

1514. Steele, Jonathan: *Soviet power: the Kremlin's foreign policy: Brezhnev to Andropov*. New York: Simon & Schuster, 1983. 416 p.

Journalistic investigation of Soviet foreign policy in the post-Brezhnev era. Predicts that Yuri Andropov's tenure as Communist party chief would witness a retrenchment of Soviet foreign adventurism due to economic difficulties at home and the continued conservatism of the Communist party leadership.

1515. Stent, Angela: "The USSR and Germany." *Problems of Communism*, v. 30 # 5 (September/October, 1981): 1-24.

1516. Ulam, Adam: "Europe in Soviet eyes." *Problems of Communism*, v. 32 # 3 (May/June, 1983): 22-30.

1517. Vermaat, J. A. Emerson: "The KGB and the West: Eureopean peace movements." *Midstream*, v. 30 # 5 (May, 1984): 7-12.

1518. ---: "Moscow fronts and the European peace movement." *Problems of Communism*, v. 31 # 6 (November/December, 1982): 43-56.

Posits that the Kremlin wages "peace" campaigns in Western Europe, as a ruse to weaken the West's defense system.

1519. Wessell, Nils H.: "Soviet-American arms control negotiations." *Current History*, v. 82 # 484 (May, 1983): 210-214, 228-230.

## 2. Regional Aspects of Soviet Foreign Policy

1520. Brind, Harry: "Soviet policy in the Horn of Africa." *International Affairs*, v. 60 # 1 (Winter, 1983/1984): 75-95.

1521. Campbell, John C.: "Soviet policy in the Middle East." *Current History*, v. 80 # 462 (January, 1981): 1-4, 42-43.

1522. Cassen, Robert (ed.): *Soviet interests in the Third World.* London: Sage Publications, 1985. 329 p.

Collection of sixteen studies from the study group on Soviet affairs of The Royal Institute of International Affairs based in London. Primarily focused on economic aspects of Soviet foreign policy, with special concentration on the limits of Soviet power projection. The essays are arranged by geographic area. Although this results in repetition of some themes, such organization offers an important and incisive comparative study.

CONTENTS: G. Segal: Sino-Soviet relations in the Third World / P. Lyon: The Soviet Union and South Asia in the 1980s / C. Coker: Eastern Europe and the Middle East: the forgotten dimesion of Soviet policy / S. C. Nolutshungu: Soviet-African relations: promise and limitations / R. Luckham: Soviet arms and African militarization / N. Miller and L. Whitehead: The Soviet interest in Latin America: an economic perspective / A. H. Smith: Soviet trade relations with the Third World / S. Deger: Soviet arms sales to developing countries: the economic forces / C. Lawson: The Soviet Union in North-South negotiations: revealing preferences / A. Fforde: Economic aspects of the Soviet-Vietnamese relationship / S. Mehrotra: The political economy of Indo-Soviet relations / F. Halliday: The Soviet Union and South Yemen: relations with a state of Socialist orientation / K. M. Ja'far: The Soviet Union in the Middle East: a case study of Syria / J. Steele: Soviet relations with Angola and Mozambique / A. McAuley: Soviet development policy in central Asia.

1523. Clement, Peter: "Moscow and Southern Africa." *Problems of Communism*, v. 34 # 2 (March/April, 1985): 29-50.

1524. Dibb, Paul: "The Soviet Union as a Pacific power." *International Journal*, v. 38 # 2 (Spring, 1983): 234-250.

1525. Donaldson, Robert H.: "The Soviet Union in the Third World." *Current History*, v. 81 # 477 (October, 1982): 313-317, 339.

1526. Freedman, Robert O.: "Patterns of Soviet policy toward the Middle East." *Annals*, v. 482 (November, 1985): 40-64.

1527. Golan, Galia: "The Soviet Union and the Israeli action in Lebanon." *International Affairs*, v. 59 # 1 (Winter, 1983/1983): 7-16.

Reviews Soviet responses to Israeli Operation Peace for Galilee.

1528. ---: *The Soviet Union and the Palestine Liberation Organization: an uneasy alliance*. New York: Praeger, 1980, 304 p.

1529. Griffith, William E.: "The USSR and Pakistan." *Problems of Communism*, v. 31 # 1 (January/February, 1982): 38-44.

1530. Katz, Mark N.: "Sanaa and the Soviets." *Problems of Communism*, v. 33 # 1 (January/February, 1984): 21-34.

1531. Kimura, Hiroshi: "The Soviet proposal on confidence-building measures and the Japanese response." *Journal of International Affairs*, v. 37 # 1 (Summer, 1983): 81-104.

1532. Leiken, Robert S.: "Fantasies and facts: the Soviet Union and Nicaragua." *Current History*, v. 83 # 495 (October, 1984): 314-317, 344-345.

1533. Menon, Rajan: "The Soviet Union and East Asia." *Current History*, v. 82 # 486 (October, 1983): 313-317, 339-343.

1534. ---: "The Soviet Union, the arms trade, and the Third World." *Soviet Studies*, v. 34 # 3 (July, 1982): 377-396.

1535. Pipes, Richard: "Soviet global strategy." *Commentary*, v. 69 # 4 (April, 1980): 31-39.

> # 1085. Ramet, P.: *The Soviet-Syrian relationship*.

1536. Rothenberg, Morris: "Latin America in Soviet eyes." *Problems of Communism*, v. 32 # 5 (September/October, 1983): 1-18.

1537. Saivetz, Carol R.: *The Soviet Union and the Gulf in the 1980s*.

Boulder, CO: Westview Press, 1989. 139 p.

Places the Soviet Union's relations with the Persian Gulf states into an important chronological context. Beginning with the collapse of the Shah and Soviet invasion of Afghanistan (both in 1979), Saivetz charts the changing international alignments in the Persian Gulf region. Also seeks to place Soviet policy with this region into the broader context of its relations with Third World states. Soviet support for the United Nations' goals during Operation Desert Shield/Desert Storm (1990-1991) may have rendered parts of the book obsolete. Nevertheless, the totality is a useful investigation into Soviet relations with an economically vital and strategic region.

1538. Sella, Amnon: "The fluctuating influence of the USSR in the Middle East." *Soviet Jewish Affairs*, v. 15 # 1 (1985): 135-140.

1539. Spence, J. E.: "Soviet relations with Africa." *Soviet Jewish Affairs*, v. 15 # 1 (1985): 124-128.

1540. Zamostny, Thomas J.: "Moscow and the Third World: recent trends in Soviet thinking." *Soviet Studies*, v. 36 # 2 (April, 1984): 223-225.

## C. THE RISE OF GORBACHEV

1541. Bialer, Seweryn and Joan Afferica: "The genesis of Gorbachev's world." *Foreign Affairs*, v. 64 # 3 (1985): 605-644.

1542. Brown, Archie: "Gorbachev: new man in the Kremlin." *Problems of Communism*, v. 34 # 3 (May/June, 1985): 1-23.

1543. Colton, Timothy J.: "The Soviet Union under Gorbachev." *Current History*, v. 84 # 504 (October, 1985): 305-308, 347.

1544. Gati, Charles: "The Soviet empire: alive but not well." *Problems of Communism*, v. 34 # 2 (March/April, 1985): 73-86.

Soviet leadership crisis on the eve of Mikhail S. Gorbachev's rise to power.

> # 1941. Goldhagen, E.: "Ideological beliefs of Gorbachev."

1545. Gunlicks, Arthur: *The Soviet Union under Gorbachev: assessing the first year*. New York: Praeger, 1987. 163 p.

Anthology of essays based on a symposium held at the University of Richmond (Virginia) in February 1986. Explores not only Gorbachev's policies -- which were fairly conservative in his first year -- but his background as well. Written before Gorbachev's reforms began, the essays provide a look into the social and economic crises which plagued the Soviet Union in the late 1980s and early 1990s and which ultimately led to the collapse of communism.

CONTENTS: A. B. Gunlicks: Gorbachev, the Party, and the Soviet state / H. Sonnenfeldt: Gorbachev's first year: an overview / K. Simis: The Gorbachev generation / D. K. Simes: Soviet foreign policy under Gorbachev: goals and expectations / J. P. Hardt and J. F. Boone: Gorbachev's economic prescriptions: a preliminary analysis / W. D. Connor: Soviet policy under Gorbachev / I. Weil: Soviet culture: new attitudes toward the arts / J. M. Ryle: Gorbachev and the 27th Party Congress of the CPSU.

1546. Gustafson, Thane and Dawn Mann: "Gorbachev's first year: building power and authority." *Problems of Communism*, v. 35 # 2 (May/June, 1986): 1-19.

1547. Hough, Jerry F.: "Gorbachev consolidating power." *Problems of Communism*, v. 36 # 4 (July/August, 1987): 21-43.

1548. ---: "Gorbachev's strategy." *Foreign Affairs*, v. 64 # 1 (Fall, 1985): 33-55.

1549. ---: "The politics of the 19th Party Conference." *Soviet Economy*, v. 4 # 2 (April/June, 1988): 137-143.

1550. Hyland, William G.: "The Gorbachev succession." *Foreign Affairs*, v. 63 # 4 (Spring, 1985): 800-809.

1551. Larrabee, F. Stephen and A. Lynch: "Gorbachev: the road to

Rekyavik." *Foreign Policy*, # 65 (Winter, 1986/1987): 3-28.

1552. Lyne, Roderic: "Making waves: Mr. Gorbachev's public diplomacy, 1985-6." *International Affairs*, v. 63 # 2 (Spring, 1987): 205-224.

1553. Owen, Richard: *Crisis in the Kremlin: Soviet succession and the rise of Gorbachev*. London: Victor Gollancz, 1986. 253 p.

Journalistic account of the succession crisis after the death of Konstantin V. Chernenko. Most of the interest is focused on Mikhail Gorbachev, who was still a virtual unknown at the time the book was written.

1554. Ploss, Sidney I.: "A new Soviet era?" *Foreign Policy*, # 62 (Spring, 1986): 46-60.

1555. Schapiro, Leonard: "The change in the Soviet leadership." *Soviet Jewish Affairs*, v. 15 # 1 (1985): 47-51.

1556. Shlapentokh, Vladimir: "The XXVII Congress -- a case study of the shaping of a new Party ideology." *Soviet Studies*, v. 40 # 1 (January, 1988): 1-20.

1557. Simis, Konstantin: "The Gorbachev generation." *Foreign Policy*, # 59 (Summer, 1985): 3-21.

> # 181. Solovyov, V.: *Behind the high Kremlin walls*.

1558. Svec, Milan: "Removing Gorbachev's end." *Foreign Policy*, # 69 (Winter, 1987/1988): 148-165.

1559. White, Stephen: *Gorbachev in power*. New York: Cambridge University Press, 1990. 268

Analysis of the first five years of *perestroika*, viewing Gorbachev's rule in historical context. White begins with the assumption that Gorbachev initially saw reform as a means to make the Soviet Union more productive. By 1987 it became obvious, however, that economic reform could not procede without fundamental political changes. Under the circumstances White predicted that reform would have to continue, either bearing results or having Gorbachev swept from office. White's prediction was quite accurate, despite the temporary setback for democratization in 1990 and 1991.

1560. Woodby, Sylvia and Alfred B. Evans, Jr. (eds.): *Restructuring Soviet ideology: Gorbachev's new thinking*. Boulder, CO: Westview Press, 1990. 226 p.

Assessment of Gorbachev's ideology by a group of seven Western experts. The authors look at the issue both historically and in terms of contemporary politics. Recognizing that reform was vitally necessary to return the Soviet Union to economic growth and social stability, the authors also question the impact of reform for the Marxist-Leninist state. Indicatively -- and correctly -- the authors have considered the possibility that reform could undermine the legitimacy of the Soviet Union as organized in the 1970s and 1980s. They did not, however, predict the decline of the Soviet Union and its replacement with the Commonwealth of Independent States.

# 11

# The Age of Perestroika

## A. GLASNOST AND PERESTROIKA

### 1. The Ideology of Glasnost

1561. Aron, Leon: "What *glasnost* has destroyed." *Commentary*, v. 88 # 5 (November, 1989): 30-34.

Charts the spiritual turmoil released in the Soviet Union by Mikhail S. Gobachev's reforms.

1562. Battle, John M.: "*Uskorenie*, *glasnost*, and *perestroika*: the pattern of reform under Gorbachev." *Soviet Studies*, v. 40 # 3 (July, 1988): 367-384.

1563. Bialer, Seweryn: "The domestic and international sources of Gorbachev's reforms." *Journal of International Affairs*, v. 42 # 2 (Spring, 1989): 283-297.

1564. ---: "Gorbachev's move." *Foreign Policy*, # 68 (Fall, 1987): 59-87.

1565. Breslauer, George W.: "Linking Gorbachev's domestic and foreign policies." *Journal of International Affairs*, v. 42 # 2 (Spring, 1989): 467-482.

1566. Brown, Archie: "Change in the Soviet Union." *Foreign Affairs*, v. 64 # 5 (Summer, 1986): 1048-1065.

1567. Bukovsky, Vladimir: "Will Gorbachev reform the Soviet Union." *Commentary*, v. 82 # 3 (September, 1986): 19-24.

1568. --- and J. Richard Walsh (eds.): *Glasnost, perestroika, and the Socialist community*. Westport, CT; Praeger, 1990. 176 p.

Anthology offering a preliminary assessment of Gorbachev's impact on the Communist world. The essays may be seen as an early reflection of the radical changes that *glasnost* and *perestroika* wrought. This is especially true for Mason's essay on Poland and Czechoslovakia, but holds true for the other essays as well. It might be noted that not all the essays are unequivocal in their evaluation of the new policies: Stephen Blank particularly questions whether Gorbachev's changes are sincere or are a mirage. Providing an interesting insight into the broader implications of Gorbachev's reforms, the essays also offer background information on the East European revolutions of 1989.

CONTENTS: D. S. Mason: Poland and Czechoslovakia: test cases for *perestroika* / J. R. Walsh: Developing socialism in the Soviet Union and China / D. S. Papp: The impact of "restructuring" and "new thinking" on Soviet-Vietnamese relations / S. Blank: *Glasnost* and Afghanistan: the mirage in the desert / R. U. T. Kim: Gorbachev and the Korean issue / C. Bukovski: Assessing the impact of *glasnnost* and *perestroika*.

1569. Chalidze, Valery: "*Perestroika*, socialism and the constituition." *Annals*, v. 506 (November, 1989): 98-108.

1570. Colton, Timothy J.: *The Dilemma of reform in the Soviet Union*. New York: Council of Relations, 1986. 274 p.

1571. Daniels, Robert V.: *Is Russia reformable?: change and resistance from Stalin to Gorbachev*. Boulder, CO: Westview Press, 1988. 176 p.

Methodologically significant work seeking to answer the question of whether or not the Communist party could reform itself. Daniels began by exploring the bases of the modern Soviet state, especially Stalin's totalitarianism and then analyzing the growing chasm between the Communist party and the Russian intelligentsia. Emphasizes the barriers to internal reform, primarily those inherited as part of the myths of the revolution. One interesting aspect of Daniels' analysis is his observation of generational distinctions within the party, especially in the post-Brezhnev era. Considers reform possible -- since the leadership that matured in the 1930s and 1940s has disappeared -- but unable to predict the eventual irrelevance of the Communist party.

1572. Desai, Padma: *Perestroika in perspective: the design and dilemmas of Soviet reform*. Princeton, NJ: Princeton University Press, 1989. 138 p.

Portrays the political, cultural, and economic elements of *perestroika*, although the political and cultural elements are buried under the weight of Desai's extensive economic analysis. She correctly concludes that the command economy established by Lenin and refined by Stalin is inherently inefficient and is the prime reason for the continuous shortages that have plagued Soviet consumers and led to a crisis of legitimacy for the Socialist-Communist regime.

1573. Goldman, Marshal I.: "*Perestroika* in the Soviet Union." *Current History*, v. 87 # 531 (October, 1988): 313-316, 340-341.

1574. Gooding, John: "The XXVIII Congress of the CPSU in perspective." *Soviet Studies*, v. 43 # 2 (1991): 237-254.

1575. Gorbachev, Mikhail S.: "Document: the revolution and *perestroika*." *Foreign Affairs*, v. 66 # 2 (Winter, 1987/1988): 410-425.

1576. Gross, Natalie: "*Glasnost*: roots and practice." *Problems of Communism*, v. 36 # 6 (November/December, 1987): 69-80.

1577. Hasegawa, Tsuyoshi and A. Pravda (eds.): *Perestroika: Soviet domestic and foreign policies*. Newbury Park, CA: Sage Publications for the Royal Institute of International Affairs, 1990. 288 p.

Links the domestic politics of *glasnost* and *perestroika* to Soviet foreign policy. Primarily focused on Russia, Eastern Europe, and Asia. Also includes an analysis of the economic impact of *perestroika* and the new thinking in the Soviet military. Offers an interesting insight into little considered aspects of Soviet politics in the Gorbachev era.

CONTENTS: A. Pravda: Linkages between Soviet domestic and foreign policy under Gorbachev / T. Hasegawa: *Perestroika* in historical perspective / A. Brown: *Perestroika* and the political system / N. Shimotomai: *Perestroika, glasnost* and society / P. Hanson: Gorbachaev's economic policies after four years / A. Kawato: The Soviet Union: a player in the world economy? / J. Cooper: Soviet reource options: civil and military priorities / N. Koizumi: *Perestroika* in the Soviet military / N. Malcolm: De-Stalinization and Soviet foreign policy: the roots of new thinking / M. Mendras: Soviet foreign policy: in search of critical thinking / Y. Akino: Soviet Asian policy in a new perspective / H. Adomeit: The impact of *perestroika* on Soviet European policy.

1578. Kovrig, Bennett: "Western approaches." *International Journal*, v. 42 # 1 (Winter, 1987/1988): 35-62.

1579. Laqueur, Walter: "*Glasnost* and its limits." *Commentary*, v. 86 # 1 (July, 1988): 13-24.

1580. ---: *The long road to freedom: Russia and glasnost*. New York: Charles Scribner's Sons, 1989. 325 p.

Comprehensive investigation into the causes and meaning of *glasnost*, Gorbachev's term for his effort to reform the Communist regime. Begins with the years of stagnation in the Soviet Union and Gorbachev's rise to power. Thereafter, Laqueur views Russian society through the new prisms that became possible only after 1985. Laqueur notes that Gorbachev's reformist tendency has limits. Given the chronological context, Laqueur proved quite perceptive in noting that reformism was likely to fail in the long-run. Like other Sovietologists, Laqueur appears to have been correct in the conclusion that the only way to reform the system is to replace it.

1581. Lewin, Moshe: "*Perstroika*: a new historical stage." *Journal of International Affairs*, v. 42 # 2 (Spring, 1989): 299-315.

1582. Powell, David E.: "Soviet *glasnost*: definitions and dimensions." *Current History*, v. 87 # 531 (October, 1988): 321-324, 344-345.

1583. Schifter, Richard: "*Glasnost* -- the dawn of freedom?" *Annals*, v. 506 (November, 1989): 85-97.

1584. Tedstrom, John E.: "Analyzing the 'basic provisions'." *Problems of Communism*, v. 36 # 4 (July/August, 1987): 93-98.

1585. Yakovlev, Aleksandr: "Redefining socialism at home and abroad." *Journal of International Affairs*, v. 42 # 2 (Spring, 1989): 333-355.

Interview on reform by Sewryn Bialer.

1586. Zemstov, Ilya and John Farrar: *Gorbachev: the man and the system*. New Brunswick, NJ: Transaction Books, 1989. 462 p.

Chronicles the early period of Gorbachev's presidency. The authors portray Gorbachev's rise to power within the context of a collapsing Soviet system. Recognizing the need for fundamental change, Gorbachev sought to revitalize the USSR by reforming institutional life without discarding those elements of society that continued to operate successfully. This meant that Gorbachev's reforms were incomplete or of a limited duration. The authors have carefully predicted that Gorbachev would continue in his course and that the results of such reforms would be minimal. They did not predict the radical break that would occur in the Soviet Union as a result of the revolutionary changes in Eastern Europe that Gorbachev unleashed.

## 2. Social and Economic Implications

1587. Aganbegyan, Abel: "The economics of *perestroika.*" *International Affairs*, v. 64 # 2 (Spring, 1988): 177-185.

1588. Azrael, Jeremy R.: "Internal trends in Soviet society." *Soviet Jewish Affairs*, v. 15 # 1 (1985): 37-41.

1589. Balzer, Harley D. (ed.): *Five years that shook the world: Gorbachev's unfinished revolution.* Boulder, CO: Westview Press, 1991. 258 p.

Anthology on the first five years of Mikhail S. Gorbachev's presidency in the USSR. Each essay covers a different aspect of the Soviet situation: its crumbling economy, political change, nationalism, health and environmental issues, culture, and foreign relations. Each essay is written by a recognized expert in the field, thus providing an introductory overview to a crucial turning point in Soviet/Russian -- and world -- history.

CONTENTS: Blair D. Ruble: Stepping off the treadmill of failed reforms / G. E. Schroeder: The Soviet economy on a treadmill of *perestroika*: Gorbachev's first five years / M. Feschbach: Social change in the USSR under Gorbachev: population, health, and environmental issues / H. D. Balzer: *Perestroika* as process: lessons from the first five years / J. Woll: *Glasnost*: a kaleidoscope / P. Goble: Imperial endgames, nationality problems, and the Soviet future / H. Goscilo: Alternative prose and *glasnost* literature / A. Stent: The common European home / R. Hube: Gorbachev and U.S.-Soviet relations: the five-year plan no one devised / J. Hough: Rethinking security.

1590. Beissinger, Mark R.: "Political reform and Soviet society." *Current History*, v. 87 # 531 (October, 1988): 317-320, 345.

1591. Bova, Russell: "The role of workplace participation." *Problems of Communism*, v. 36 # 4 (July/August, 1987): 76-86.

1592. ---: "The Soviet military and economic reform." *Soviet Studies*, v. 40 # 3 (July, 1988): 385-405.

1593. Brooks, Karen M.: "Soviet agriculture under *perestroika*." *Current History*, v. 89 # 549 (October, 1990): 329-332, 336-337.

1594. Brovkin, Vladimir: "Revolution from below: informal political associations in Russia 1988-1989." *Soviet Studies*, v. 42 # 2 (April, 1990): 233-258.

1595. Clark, Susan L. (ed.): *Gorbachev's agenda: changes in Soviet domestic and foreign policy*. Boulder, CO: Westview Press, 1989. 422 p.

Assesses the changes wrought by Mikhail S. Gorbachev's rise to power in the Communist party and the Soviet Union. Equal emphasis is placed on domestic and foreign policy. Also contains interesting insight into Gorbachev's opposition -- from the entrenched Communist party *apparatchiks* who oppose reform and from radicals who seek more comprehensive and swifter changes in the Soviet system.

CONTENTS: R. F. Laird: The changing Soviet environment / A. von Borcke: Gorbachev's *perestroika*: can the Soviet system be reformed / E. Teague: *Perestroika*: who stands to gain, who stands to lose? / N. Bregante: Nationalist unrest in the USSR and the challenge to the Gorbachev leadership / H. H. Höhmann: Soviet *perestroika* and systemic change in Eastern Europe: challenges, interdependencies, patterns of response / M. Lavigne: Prospects for Soviet foreign trade reform / H. Vogel: The Gorbachev challenge: to help or not to help? / T. Colton: Gorbachev and the Soviet military / C. Donnelly: Future trends in Soviet military-technical policy / R. Laird: Soviet strategy toward Western Europe: implications for the post-INF environment / R. Allison: Gorbachev's new program for conventional arms control in Europe / H. Coutau-Bégarie: The Soviet naval presence in the Mediterranean / T. Friedgut: Two parallel lines do not intersect: Soviet-Israeli relations, 1988-1989 / G. Segal: Soviet options in the Pacific / S. L. Clark: Japan: Gorbachev's partner in a reluctant détente / K. Maxwell, S. L. Clark and B. A. Jacobs: Soviet relations with Latin America.

1596. Connor, Walter D.: "Social policy under Gorbachev."

*Problems of Communism*, v. 35 # 4 (July/August, 1986): 31-46.

1597. Cooper, Julian M.: "Technology in the Soviet Union." *Current History*, v. 85 # 513 (October, 1986): 317-320, 340-342.

1598. Dovring, Folke: "New directions in Soviet agriculture." *Current History*, v. 86 # 522 (October, 1987): 329-332, 340-341.

1599. Ericson, Richard E.: "Soviet economic reforms: the motivation and content of *perestroika*." *Journal of International Affairs*, v. 42 # 2 (Spring, 1989): 317-331.

1600. Filtzer, Donald A.: "The contradictions of the marketless market: self-financing in the Soviet industrial enterprise, 1986-1990." *Soviet Studies*, v. 43 # 6 (1991): 989-1010.

1601. French, Hilary F.: "Environmental problems and policies in the Soviet Union." *Current History*, v. 90 # 558 (October, 1991): 333-337.

1602. Gagnon, V. P., Jr.: "Gorbachev and the collective contract brigade." *Soviet Studies*, v. 39 # 1 (January, 1987): 1-23.

1603. Goldman, Marshal I.: "Gorbachev and economic reform." *Foreign Affairs*, v. 64 # 1 (Fall, 1985): 56-73.

1604. ---: "Soviet perceptions of Chinese economic reforms and the implications for reform in the USSR." *Journal of International Affairs*, v. 39 # 2 (Winter, 1986): 41-55.

1605. Gorlin, Alice C.: "The Soviet economy." *Current History*, v. 85 # 513 (October, 1986): 325-328, 343-345.

1606. Gregory, Paul R.: "The impact of *perestroika* on the Soviet planned economy: results of a survey of Moscow economic officials." *Soviet Studies*, v. 43 # 5 (1991): 859-874.

1607. ---: *Productivity, slack and time theft in the Soviet economy: evidence from the Soviet Interview Project*. Urbana-Champaign: University of Illinois Press, 1986. 40 p.

1608. Grey, Robert D., Lauri A. Jennisch and Alanna S. Tyler: "Soviet public opinion and the Gorbachev reforms." *Slavic Review*, v. 49 # 2 (Spring, 1990): 261-271.

1609. Gurtov, Mel (ed.): *The transformation of socialism: perestroika and reform in the Soviet Union and China*. Boulder, CO: Westview Press, 1990. 258 p.

Comparative history of reform attempts in the Soviet Union and post-Maoist China. Viewing the transformations in both societies as among the most momentous events in the 1980s and 1990s the authors examine the implications of change for the two Communist superpowers. Historical, social, economic, and political factors are analyzed and all the data are related to the implications of change for international relations.

CONTENTS: M. Gurtov: The transformation of socialism / H. J. Ellison: *Perestroika* and the New Economic Policy (1921-1928): the uses of history / R. H. W. Theen: Party-state relations under Gorbachev: from partocracy to "party" state? / Y. Jiaqi: A comparative study of the features of the Socialist political system and possible reforms / H. Goldblatt: A literature of reform, a reform of literature / G. Houk: Soviet culture and society under Gorbachev / S. Gorbunov: The social consequences of economic restructuring in the USSR / G. Rozman: Shades of excellence: the Communist party and elites in China and the Soviet Union / A. Nagorniy: *Perestroika* in the USSR and reforms in China: contrasts and assessments of their international impact / J. Thornton: The perils of *perestroika* / A. B. Parkanskiy: The international economics of *perestroika*.

1610. Hardt, John P. and Jean F. Boone: "The Soviet Union's trade policy." *Current History*, v. 87 # 531 (October, 1988): 329-332, 341-343.

1611. Hedlund, Stefan: *Private agriculture in the Soviet Union* (introduction by Roy D. Laird). London/New York: Routledge, 1989. 208 p.

Studies the state of Soviet agriculture in the Gorbachev era.

Hedlund's first three chapters establish the parameters for his study, specifically the failure of collective farms to produce enough food for the entire Soviet population. Thereafter he assesses the changes that developed after Gorbachev's rise to power and the limited permission for private farming. Hedlund correctly notes that Gorbachev's early reforms were only partial palliatives and did not solve the basic problem. To do so would require a complete overhaul of the Soviet agricultural system.

1612. Hewett, Ed A.: "Gorbachev's economic strategy: a preliminary assessment." *Soviet Economy*, v. 1 # 4 (October/December, 1985): 285-305.

1613. Hough, Jerry F.: "The politics of successful economic reform." *Soviet Economy*, v. 5 # 1 (January/March, 1989): 3-46.

1614. Johnson, D. Gale: "Agricultural productivity in the Soviet Union." *Current History*, v. 84 # 504 (October, 1985): 321-324, 342.

> # 222. Jones, E.: "Chernobyl and *glasnost*."

1615. Kerblay, Basile: *Gorbachev's Russia* (translated from Russian by Rupert Swyer). New York: Pantheon Books, 1989. 175 p. [PB]

Brief but intense inquiry into the changes that have taken place in the Soviet Union since the rise of Gorbachev. Investigates social, economic, and political trends to summarize the strengths and enemies of reform. Despite the wealth of data, Kerblay has mistakenly assumed the reformers to be an upper strata of intellectuals and democrats: he thus predicted the need for at least two more generations of reform before any fundamental changes could be expected. In fact, reform actually had deep roots among the Russian masses. In reality, communism collapsed in just over two years: from the fall of the Berlin Wall (November 10, 1989) to the raising of the tricolor over the Kremlin on December 20, 1991.

1616. Kontorovich, Vladimir: "Discipline and growth in the Soviet economy." *Problems of Communism*, v. 34 # 6 (November/December, 1985): 18-31.

1617. Kroll, Heidi: "Reform and damages for breach of contract in the Soviet economy." *Soviet Economy*, v. 5 # 3 (July/September, 1989): 276-297.

1618. Kuhnert, Caroline: "More power for the Soviets: *perestroika* and energy." *Soviet Studies*, v. 43 # 3 (1991): 491-506.

1619. Laird, Roy D.: "*Perestroika* and Soviet agriculture." *Problems of Communism*, v. 36 # 6 (November/December, 1987): 81-86.

1620. Laqueur, Walter: "Beyond *glasnost*." *Commentary*, v. 84 # 4 (October, 1987): 63-65.

1621. Litvin, Valentin: "Reforming economic management." *Problems of Communism*, v. 36 # 4 (July/August, 1987): 87-92.

1622. Litwack, John M.: "Discretionary behavior and Soviet economic reform." *Soviet Studies*, v. 43 # 2 (1991): 255-280.

1623. Marples, David R.: "The Chernobyl disaster." *Current History*, v. 86 # 522 (October, 1989): 325-328, 341-343.

1624. Mastny, Vojtech: *Soviet-East European survey, 1986-1987*. Boulder, CO: Westview Press, 1987. 490 p.

Third in a series of Radio Free Europe/Radio Liberty research papers (see # 1482). The book is evenly balanced between material on Russia and material on the Communist bloc. This volume has the beginnings of reform and the incipient democratization movement that originated with Gorbachev's policies of *glasnost* and *perestroika* as its central theme.

1625. ---: *Soviet-East European survey 1987-1988*. Boulder, CO: Westview Press, 1988. 396 p.

Fourth in the series of Radio Free Europe/Radio Liberty research papers (see # 1482). Includes fifty items that trace the development of Gorbachevism and reform in Eastern Europe. The reports provide important insights into the background of the revolutionary events that swept the former Communist bloc countries in 1989 and 1990.

1626. McCauley, Martin (ed.): *The Soviet Union under Gorbachev.* New York: St. Martin's Press, 1987. 247 p.

Anthology of papers delivered at a University of London symposium in March 1986. Primarily focused on the continuities in Soviet politics. All but three of the essays deal with domestic issues: these focus on the problems facing the new Communist party General Secretary and on his probable solutions. The authors could not anticipate the massive changes wrought by Gorbachev's "new thinking" and by the flourishing democratic movements that resulted from *perestroika* and *glasnost.*

CONTENTS: M. McCauley: Gorbachev as leader / R. J. Hill: State and ideology / W. E. Butler: Law and reform / B. Nahaylo: Nationalities / P. Hanson: The economy / K. U. Wädekin: Agriculture / A. H. Smith: Foreign trade / D. Lane: Labor, motivation and productivity / M. Shafir: Eastern Europe / C. Rice: Defense and security / M. Light: Foreign policy.

1627. Moskoff, William (ed.): *Perestroika in the countryside: agricultural reform in the Gorbachev era.* Armonk, NY: M. E. Sharpe, 1990. 135 p.

Studeis Mikhail S. Gorbachev's agricultural policy, with primary focus on efforts to privatize farms and thereby increase production.

CONTENTS: D. A. J. Macey: Gorbachev and Stolypin: Soviet agrarian reform in historical perspective / J. Butterfield: Devolution in decision making and organizational change in Soviet agriculture / E. C. Cook: Reforming Soviet agriculture: problems with farm finances and equity considerations / K. Brooks: Lease contracting in Soviet agriculture in 1989 / D. Van Atta: Full-scale like collectivization, but without collectivization's excesses: the campaign to introduce the family and lease contract in Soviet agriculture / D. G. Johnson: Possible impacts of agricultural trade liberalization on the USSR / M. Marrese: Hungarian agriculture: Lessons for the Soviet Union.

1628. Nove, Alec: "The economic dimensions." *Soviet Jewish Affairs*, v. 15 # 1 (1985): 42-46.

1629. Ofer, Gur: "Budget deficit market disequilibrium and Soviet economic reforms." *Soviet Economy*, v. 5 # 2 (April/June, 1989): 107-161.

1630. Orlov, Yuri: "Before and after *glasnost*." *Commentary*, v. 86 # 4 (October, 1988): 24-34.

1631. Palei, L. V. and K. L. Radzivanovich: "How to carry out economic reform: points of view and reality." *Soviet Studies*, v. 42 # 1 (January, 1990): 25-38.

1632. Pallot, Judith: "Rural depopulation and the restoration of the Russian village under Gorbachev." *Soviet Studies*, v. 42 # 4 (October, 1990): 655-674.

1633. Podell, Janet and Steven Anzovin: *The Soviet Union*. New York: H. W. Wilson Company, 1988. 219 p.

Anthology reprinting fifteen key statements on Gorbachev's Russia. Divided into three sections: Part I reviews the historical and political context of reform, Part II reviews the cultural and intellectual implications of *glasnost*, and Part III reviews the new spirit in Soviet-American relations. The bulk of articles originated in the United States, although two are of Russian origin. Altogether, the collection offers an important insight into developments in the Soviet Union just before the revolutions of 1989 and 1990.

CONTENTS: T. A. Sanction: Can he bring it off? / S. Bialer: Gorbachev's move / D. K. Simes: Gorbachev and a new foreign policy / V. Bukovsky: Will Gorbachev reform the Soviet Union / M. Gorbachev: On Soviet history / K. Vanden Heuvel: Yevtushenko feels a fresh wind blowing / A. Batchan: Mad Russian / B. Keller: Home from Afghanistan / R. G. Suny: The nationality question / M. D. Lemonick: Surging ahead / R. Reagan: The evil empire / M. D. Shulman: Four decades of irrationality: U.S.-Soviet relations / R. Schifter: The Soviet constitution: myth and reality / W. W. Rostow: On ending the Cold War / C. W. Maynes: America's chance.

1634. Potter, William and Lucy Kerner: "The Soviet military's performance at Chernobyl." *Soviet Studies*, v. 43 # 6 (1991): 1027-1048.

1635. Powell, David E.: "The emerging health crisis in the Soviet Union." *Current History*, v. 84 # 504 (October, 1985): 325-328, 339-340.

1636. ---: "The revival of religion." *Current History*, v. 90 # 558 (October, 19919): 328-332.

1637. Riordan, Jim: "Playing to new rules: Soviet sport and *perestroika*." *Soviet Studies*, v. 42 # 1 (January, 1990): 133-146.

> # 585. ---: *Soviet youth culture*.

1638. Ruble, Blair: "The social dimensions of *perestroika*." *Soviet Economy*, v. 3 # 2 (April/June, 1987): 171-183.

1639. Rumer, Boris: "Investment performence in the 12th Five-Year plan." *Soviet Studies*, v. 43 # 3 (1991): 451-472.

1640. ---: "Realities of Gorbachev's economic program." *Problems of Communism*, v. 35 # 2 (May/June, 1986): 20-31.

1641. Scanlan, James P.: "Reforms and civil society in the USSR." *Problems of Communism*, v. 37 # 2 (March/April, 1988): 41-46.

1642. Schroeder, Gertrude E.: "Anatomy of Gorbachev's economic reform." *Soviet Economy*, v. 3 # 3 (July/September, 1987): 219-241.

1643. ---: "Gorbachev 'radically' implementing Brezhnev's reform." *Soviet Economy*, v. 2 # 4 (Ocotber/December, 1986): 289-301.

1644. ---: "The Soviet economy." *Current History*, v. 84 # 504 (October, 1985): 309-312, 340-342.

1645. ---: "The Soviet economy under Gorbachev." *Current History*, v. 86 # 522 (October, 1987): 317-320, 344-346.

1646. Segal, Boris M.: *The drunken society: alcohol abuse and alcoholism in the Soviet Union: a comparative study*. New York: Hippocrene Books, 1990. 618 p.

1647. Shipler, David K.: *Russia: broken idols, solemn dreams* (revised and updated). New York: Penguin Books, 1989. 462 p. [PB]

Journalistic survey of Russian life during the Gorbachev era. Notes that *glasnost* eased Communist party intrusions into daily life considerably although they still remained. Interweaves historical insights into his discussion while also providing interesting thumb-nail sketches of the main players in contemporary Russian politics. An especially interesting chapter details the continuing influence of Western styles and ideas on Russians, both young and old. Inter alia the reader is given insight into the potential problems facing the reform movement.

1648. Slider, Darrell: "Embattled entrepeneurs: Soviet cooperatives in an unreformed society." *Soviet Studies*, v. 43 # 5 (1991): 797-822.

1649. Smith, Hendrick: *The new Russians*. New York: Random House, 1990. 621 p. / New York: Avon Books, 1991. 734 p. [PB]

Journalistic inquiry into Russian daily life in the Gorbachev era. This sequel to Smith's *The Russians* (see # 1152) is primarily focused on *glasnost* and *perestroika*. Smith's first section offers an interesting look into the social, political, and intellectual origins of the reform movement. Thereafter, he charts the impact of reform on all aspects of Russian daily life and on international politics. The Avon Book edition has been updated to include the August 1991 failed *coup*, including the heroic stand at the barricades by Moscow's populace that eventually undid the *coup*. Smith then analyzes the post-*coup* era, which he describes as a second Russian revolution.

1650. Starr, S. Frederick: "Soviet Union: a civil society." *Foreign*

*Policy*, # 70 (Spring, 1988): 26-41.

1651. Sziráczki, György: "Unemployment policy and labor market in transition: from labor shortage to unemployment." *Soviet Studies*, v. 42 # 4 (Octber, 1990): 710-722.

1652. Tedstrom, John E.: (ed.): *Socialism, perestroika, and the dilemmas of Soviet economic reform*. Boulder, CO: Westview Press in cooperation with Radio Free Europe, 1990. 239 p.

Systematic examination of *perestroika*'s impact on the Soviet economy. Builds on earlier studies to explain the inefficiency and waste in the controlled economy, questioning whether reforms will repair the system. The contributors note that in the long-run some substantive ideational changes could lead to fundamental improvements. Predict the rise of a mixed economy moving away from central planning and control.

CONTENTS: R. W. Campbell: How to think about *perestroika* / E. Teague: Redefining socialism in the USSR / M. von Hagen: The NEP, *perestroika*, and the problem of alternatives / P. Hanson: Ownership issues in *perestroika* / V. Sobell: Lessons from Eastern Europe / J. Tedstrom: The reemergence of Soviet cooperatives / K. E. Wädekin: Is there a "privatization" of Soviet agriculture? / H. Heymann, Jr.: *Perestroika* and innovation in Soviet industry / P. Patterson: Prospects for comodity and financial exchanges / M. Alexeev: Retail price reform and the Soviet consumer / A. Trehub: *Perestroika* and social entitlements.

> # 233. Thronton, J.: "Chernobyl and Soviet energy."

1653. Treml, Vladimir G.: "The most recent input-output table: a milestone in Soviet statistics." *Soviet Economy*, v. 5 # 4 (October/December, 1989): 341-359.

1654. Twigg, Judyth: "The anti-expenditure principle: Gosplan's proposals for Soviet economic reform." *Soviet Studies*, v. 43 # 5 (1991): 837-858.

1655. Van Atta, Don: "Theorists of agrarian *perestroika*." *Soviet*

*Economy*, v. 5 # 1 (January/March, 1989): 70-99.

1656. Vodopivec, Milan: "The persistence of job security in reforming Socialist economies." *Soviet Studies*, v. 43 # 6 (1991): 1011-1026.

1657. Wädekin, Karl-Eugen: "The re-emergence of the *kolkhoz* principle." *Soviet Studies*, v. 41 # 1 (January, 1989): 20-38.

1658. Walker, Martin: *The waking giant: the Soviet Union under Gorbachev*. London: M. Joseph, 1986. 282 p.

1659. Winiecki, Jan: "The inevitability of a fall in output in the early stages of transition to the market: theoretical underpinnings." *Soviet Studies*, v. 43 # 4 (1991): 669-676.

### 3. Minorities Policy

1660. Arzt, Donna E.: "The new Soviet emigration law revisited: Implementation and compliance with other laws." *Soviet Jewish Affairs*, v. 18 # 1 (Spring, 1988): 17-28.

1661. Brym, Robert J.: "Soviet Jewish emigration: a statistical test of two theories." *Soviet Jewish Affairs*, v. 18 # 3 (Winter, 1988): 15-23.

1662. Chlenov, Michael A.: "The last journey of Soviet Jewry." *Midstream*, v. 36 # 1 (January, 1990): 3-6.

On massive emigration of Russian Jewry in 1989 and 1990.

1663. ---: "The Soviet Jewish future." *Midstream*, v. 36 # 4 (May, 1990): 3-6.

1664. D'Encausse, Helene C.: "The Islamic minorities." *Soviet Jewish Affairs*, v. 15 # 1 (1985): 88-95.

1665. Dienes, Leslie: "*Perestroika* and the Slavic regions." *Soviet Economy*, v. 5 # 3 (July/September, 1989): 251-275.

1666. Dinstein, Yoram: "Freedom of emigration for Soviet Jews." *Soviet Jewish Affairs*, v. 18 # 3 (Winter, 1988): 3-14.

1667. Feldbrugge, F. J. M.: "The new Soviet law on emigration." *Soviet Jewish Affairs*, v. 17 # 1 (Spring, 1987): 9-24.

1668. Floyd,. David: "*Perestroyka, glasnost* and Soviet Jewry: Gorbachev's address to the January 1987 CPSU plenum." *Soviet Jewish Affairs*, v. 17 # 1 (Spring, 1987): 3-8.

1669. Freedman, Robert O.: "The American Jewish community, Mikhail Gorbachev and Soviet Jewry: what is to be done?" *Soviet Jewish Affairs*, v. 17 # 3 (Winter, 1987): 39-50.

1670. Freiman, Gregory: "The plight of Soviet Jewry." *Soviet Jewish Affairs*, v. 15 # 1 (1985): 96-99.

1671. Friedberg, Maurice: "The euphoria of *glasnost* and Jewish fears." *Midstream*, v. 36 # 3 (April, 1990): 3-8.

1672. Gitelman, Zvi: "The abridgement of the rights of Jews in the fields of nationality, culture and religion." *Soviet Jewish Affairs*, v. 15 # 1 (1985): 79-87.

1673. ---: "Gorbachev's reforms and the future of Soviet Jewry." *Soviet Jewish Affairs*, v. 18 # 2 (Summer/Fall, 1988): 3-15.

1674. "*Glasnost* and the new Russian antisemites." (introduced and annotated by Howard Spier). *Soviet Jewish Affairs*, v. 17 # 2 (Summer/Fall, 1987): 53-68.

> # 367. Harris, D. A.: "Crisis in Soviet Jewry."

1675. Heitman, Sidney: "The third Soviet emigration." *Soviet Jewish Affairs*, v. 18 # 2 (Summer/Fall, 1988): 17-42.

1676. Kagedan, Allan: "Gorbachev and the Jews." *Commentary*, v. 81 # 5 (May, 1986): 47-50.

1677. Kirkwood, Michael: "*Glasnost*, 'the national question' and

Soviet language policy." *Soviet Studies*, v. 43 # 1 (1991): 61-82.

1678. Korey, William: "The current plight of Soviet Jewry." *Midstream*, v. 32 # 9 (November, 1989): 8-11.

Notes the continuities in Gorbachev's early Jewish policy.

1679. Lapidus, Gail W.: "Gorbachev and the national question: restructuring the Soviet federation." *Soviet Economy*, v. 5 # 3 (July/September. 1989): 201-250.

1680. Leibler, Isi J.: "The future of the Soviet Jewry movement." *Midstream*, v. 34 # 2 (February/March, 1988): 6-9.

1681. ---: "Soviet Jewry -- a turning point?" *Midstream*, v. 33 # 2 (February, 1987): 29-32.

1682. Levin, Nora: "Needed: attention to the Soviet Jewish remnant." *Midstream*, v. 34 # 8 (November, 1988): 22-27.

1683. Muller, Jerry Z.: "Communism, antisemitism and the Jews." *Commentary*, v. 86 # 2 (August, 1988): 28-39.

1684. Nezer, Zvi: "The emigration of Soviet Jews." *Soviet Jewish Affairs*, v. 15 # 1 (1985): 17-24.

1685. Olcott, Martha B.: "Gorbachev's national dilemma." *Journal of International Affairs*, v. 42 # 1 (Spring, 1989): 399-421.

1686. "*Pamyat*: an appeal to the Russian people." (introduced and annotated by Howard Spier). *Soviet Jewish Affairs*, v. 18 # 1 (Spring, 1988): 60-71.

1687. "Restructuring Soviet anti-Zionist propaganda." (introduced and annotated by Howard Spier). *Soviet Jewish Affairs*, v. 18 # 3 (Winter, 1988): 46-55.

1688. Weinberg, Henry H.: "Soviet Jewry: new tragic dilemmas." *Midstream*, v. 37 # 7 (October, 1991): 15-17.

**4. Reform and Democracy**

1689. Allison, Graham T., Jr.: "Testing Gorbachev." *Foreign Affairs*, v. 67 # 1 (Fall, 1988): 18-32.

1690. Anderson, John: "Drafting a Soviet law on freedom of conscience." *Soviet Jewish Affairs*, v. 19 # 1 (Spring, 1989): 19-33.

1691. Beissinger, Mark R.: "The new leadership and the Soviet Party Congress." *Current History*, v. 85 # 513 (October, 1986): 309-312, 338-339.

1692. Besançon, Alain: "Gorbachev without illusions." *Commentary*, v. 85 # 4 (April, 1988): 47-57.

1693. Cracraft, James (ed.): *The Soviet Union today: an interpretive guide* (second edition). Chicago: University of Chicago Press, 1988. 382 p.

Anthology providing an overview of Soviet studies. Originally published in 1983, this edition is fully updated to incorporate more recent developments. The essays are grouped into eight thematic sections: "History"; "Politics"; "The Armed Forces"; "The Physical Context"; "The Economy"; "Science and Technology"; "Culture"; and "Society". Of these, "History" is the broadest since it does not even attempt a general survey of Russian or Soviet history. Written after the rise of Mikhail Gorbachev, but before the revolutionary events of 1989-1991, the book is a snapshot of the Soviet Union on the eve of its collapse.

CONTENTS: J. Cracraft: From the Russian past to the Soviet present / N. Tumarkin: Lenin and his cult / S. Cohen: The Stalin question / M. Beissinger: The leadership and the political elite / A. Dallin: Policy-making in foreign affairs / J. E. Carlson: The KGB / J. Rubenstein: Dissent / D. R. Jones: Organization and deployment / M. Tsypkin: The conscripts / E. V. Osgood: Military strategy in the nuclear age / D. Holloway: Arms control / Ch. D. Harris: Basic geography / J. Kramer: Environmental problems / W. C. Brumfield: Architecture and urban planning / J. R. Millar: An overview / M. I. Goldman: The consumer / D. G. Johnson:

Agriculture / P. L. Patterson: Foreign trade / L. R. Graham: Science policy and organization / V. Z. Kresin: Soviet science in practice: an inside view / H. D. Balzer: Education, science, and technology / I. Weil: A survey of the cultural scene / G. Hosking: The politics of literature / I. Christie: The cinema / E. Mickiewicz: The mass media / R. S. Clem: Ethnicity / P. A. Lucey: Religion / M. Fischer: Women / P. B. Maggs: Law / D. E. Powell: A troubled society.

1694. Embree, Gregory J.: "RSFSR election results and roll call votes." *Soviet Studies*, v. 43 # 6 (1991): 1065-1084.

1695. Gleason, Gregory: *Federalism and nationalism: the struggle for republican rights in the USSR*. Boulder, CO: Westview Press, 1990. 170 p.

Provocative investigation into the politics of nationality in the Soviet Union. Gleason argues that the agents for disintegration are inherent within Soviet institutions. On that basis, Gleason has predicted that Mikhail S. Gorbachev's efforts at reform would fail, since federalism is directly opposite the centralized control inherent in Communist party policy. Events in the Soviet Union after the August 1991 *coup* -- and especially the USSR's replacement with the Commonwealth of Independent States -- appear to confirm Gleason's contentions. Thus, the book takes on a new urgency for both scholars and general readers.

1696. Gooding, John: "Gorbachev and democracy." *Soviet Studies*, v. 42 # 2 (April, 1990): 195-232.

1697. Gustafson, Thane and Dawn Mann: "Gorbachev's next gamble." *Problems of Communism*, v. 36 # 4 (July/August, 1987): 1-20.

1698. Hahn, J.: "An experiment in competition: the 1987 elections to the local Soviets." *Slavic Review*, v. 47 # 2 (Fall, 1988): 448-463.

1699. Herspring, Dale R.: "On *perestroyka*: Gorbachev, Yazov, and the military." *Problems of Communism*, v. 36 # 4 (July/August, 1987): 99-107.

1700. Hill, Ronald J.: "The CPSU: from monolith to pluralist?" *Soviet Studies*, v. 43 # 2 (1991): 217-236.

1701. Kiernan, Brendan and Joseph Aistrup: "The 1989 elections to the Congress of People's Deputies in Moscow." *Soviet Studies*, v. 43 # 6 (1991): 1049-1064.

1702. Knight, Amy W.: "The KGB and Soviet reform." *Problems of Communism*, v. 37 # 5 (September/October, 1988): 61-70.

1703. Lampert, Nick: "The *anonimka* under *perestroika*: a note." *Soviet Studies*, v. 41 # 1 (January, 1989): 129-134.

Communist party responses to anonymous members' complaints.

1704. Lih, Lars T.: "Gorbachev and the reform movement." *Current History*, v. 86 # 522 (October, 1987): 309-312, 338.

1705. Mawdsley, Evan: "The 1990 Central Committee of the CPSU in perspective." *Soviet Studies*, v. 43 # 5 (1991): 897-912.

> # 1047. Moses, J. C.: "Regionalism in Soviet politics."

1706. Nove, Alec: "'Radical reform': problems and prospects." *Soviet Studies*, v. 39 # 3 (July, 1989): 452-467.

1707. Odom, William E.: "How far can Soviet reform go?" *Problems of Communism*, v. 36 # 6 (Novemeber/December, 1987): 18-33.

1708. Puddington, Arch: "Life under communism today." *Commentary*, v. 87 # 2 (Fbruary, 1989); 32-38.

1709. Ra'anan, Uri and Charles M. Perry (ed.): *The USSR today and tomorrow: problems and challenges*. Lexington, MA: Lexington Books, 1987. 140 p.

Anthology of studies on contemporary Russia, designed as a student introduction to Soviet studies. The book may be divided into three sections, with the first offering important methodological insights, the second concentrating on Soviet domestic affairs, and the third concentrating on Russia within a global context. Useful for high school and college students, the work could also be profitably read by all those interesting in how information on Russia is obtained and transmitted to the West.

CONTENTS: U. Ra'anan: The USSR: what is ascertainable and how can such knowledge be obtained? / R. Conquest: How to avoid thought on Soviet history / R. Pipes: The USSR or Russia? The historic perspective / D. E. Powell: Soviet society today / I. Lukes: Human nature: the Soviet view / M. I. Goldman: The burden of the Stalinist model: the case of Soviet agriculture, industry, and consumer goods / J. P. Roche: Communist organization, structure, tactics, and front groups / R. H. Shultz: Soviet disinformation and intelligence operations / M. S. Voslensky: Gorbachev, the *nomenklatura*, and the Soviet concept of arms control / J. K. Davis: Soviet strategic-military posture and arms control / A. B. Ulam: U.S.-Soviet relations: current trends.

1710. Rand, Robert: *Comrade lawyer: inside Soviet justice in an era of reform*. Boulder, CO: Westview Press, 1991. 166 p.

Insider's view of the Soviet legal system as it now operates, based on discussions with dozens of Russian lawyers. The background is a Moscow murder trial dating to early 1991. Inter alia provides insight on the Soviet bar, on the criminal justice system in the USSR, and on the changes to both wrought by *glasnost*. Although written in an academic style, anyone interested in the legal practice and judicial procedure could profitably read it.

1711. Revel, Jean-François: "Is Communism reversible." *Commentary*, v. 87 # 1 (January, 1989); 17-24.

1712. Rice, Condoleezza: "Is Gorbachev changing the rules of defense decision-making?" *Journal of International Affairs*, v. 42 # 2 (Spring, 1989): 377-397.

1713. Sedaitis, Judith B. and Jim Butterfield (eds.): *Perestroika from below: social movements in the Soviet Union*. Boulder, CO: Westview Press, 1991. 214 p.

Anthology on grass-roots *perestroika* that notes the growth of a series of non-political social organizations. The groups surveyed include women's organizations, ecological groups, and trade unions. All augur the fundamental transformation of social relationships in the Commonwealth of Independent States, which in turn imply a different form of political relations with a broader base for participation in government.

CONTENTS: J. Sedaitis: The diversity of Soviet workers' movements / R. Bova: Worker activism and the Soviet state / D. Van Atta: Political mobilization in the Soviet countryside / C. Nechemias: The prospects for a Soviet women's movement / L. Essig and T. Mamonova: *Perstroika* for women / C. E. Ziegler: Environmental policy and politics under Gorbachev / D. R. Marples: The greening of Ukraine / J. Butterfield and M. Weigle: Social groups and regime response.

1714. Sharlet, Robert: "Soviet dissent since Brezhnev." *Current History*, v. 85 # 513 (October, 1986): 321-324, 340.

1715. Shlapentokh, Vladimir: *Soviet ideologies in the period of glasnost: responses to Brezhnev's stagnation*. New York: Praeger Publishers, 1988. 211 p.

Investigates the ideological diversity in Gorbachev's Soviet Union. Shlapentokh divides Soviet ideologues into two main fields -- conservatives and liberals -- which are further subdivided. The conservatives, for example, are divided into neo-Stalinists and neo-Fascists, while liberals are divided by the extent of change they seek. Shlapentokh places Gorbachev in the moderate liberal camp and gauges the social and economic impact of his reforms.

1716. Tatu, Michel: "19th CPSU Conference." *Problems of Communism*, v. 37 # 3/4 (May/August, 1988): 1-15.

1717. Unger, Aryeh L.: "The travails of the intra-Party democracy in the Soviet Union: the elections to the 19th Conference of the CPSU." *Soviet Studies*, v. 43 # 2 (1991): 329-354.

1718. Vaxberg, Arkady: "Civil rights in the Soviet Union." *Annals*,

v. 506 (November, 1989): 109-114.

1719. White, Stephen: "Democratization in the USSR." *Soviet Studies*, v. 42 # 1 (January, 1990): 3-24.

1720. ---: "Propagating Communist values in the USSR." *Problems of Communism*, v. 34 # 6 (November/December, 1985): 1-17.

Soviet ideological indoctrination.

### 5. Perestroika and Intellectual Freedom

1721. Cohen, Stephen F. and Katrina Vanden Heuvel: *Voices of glasnost: interviews with Gorbachev's reformers*. New York: W. W. Norton, 1989. 339 p.

Collection of fourteen interviews with leading figures in the Soviet reform movement. Each interview is prefaced by a brief biography. Published after the 1988 Moscow summit but before the August 1991 *coup* and the collapse of the Soviet Union. Primarily shows the diversity of thought among reformers. Cohen's brief introduction places the interviews into a proper historical and political context. Superseded by later events, the interviews still provide a fascinating insight into the attitudes of the key supporters of democratic reform in Russia.

1722. Fairbanks, Charles H., Jr.: "Gorbachev's cultural revolution." *Commentary*, v. 88 # 2 (August, 1989): 23-27.

1723. Heleniak, Tim and Albert Motivans: "A note on *glasnost* and the Soviet statistical system." *Soviet Studies*, v. 43 # 3 (1991): 473-490.

1724. Hirszowicz, Lukasz: "Breaking the mould: the changing face of Jewish culture under Gorbachev." *Soviet Jewish Affairs*, v. 18 # 3 (Winter, 1988): 25-45.

> # 619. Kneen, P.: "Soviet science under Gorbachev."

1725. Kogan, J.: "The plight of Jewish scientists." *Midstream*, v. 33 # 2 (February, 1987): 37-38.

1726. Korotich, Vitalii: "The media under Gorbachev." *Journal of International Affairs*, v. 42 # 2 (Spring, 1989): 357-362.

Based on an interview with the Soviet editor conducted by Anthony Gardner.

1727. Melville, Andrei and Gail W. Lapidus (eds.): *The glasnost papers: voices on reform from Moscow*. Boulder, CO: Westview Press, 1990. 359 p.

Compendium of Russian sources supporting *glasnost*. Introductions to each document and a comprehensive conclusion place the statements into context. Offers important insights into the *weltanschauung* of the USSR's democratic opinion makers.

1728. Nove, Alec: *Glasnost in action: cultural renaissance in Russia*. Boston: Unwin Hyman, 1989. 251 p.

Surveys the impact of *glasnost* on intellectual life in the Soviet Union and finds that Gorbachev's reforms have touched off a veritable intellectual revolution. Nove draws examples from every sphere of intellectual life: films, books, theater, and religious activities. Of special importance, according to Nove, is the spirit of questioning that pervades the Russian intelligentsia -- they now seek, as they never had previously, to investigate the past in an honest and forthright manner. Nove predicts a cultural renaissance in the Soviet Union, noting that the indicators point to a transition away from communism.

1729. Pittman, Riitta H.: "*Perestroika* and Soviet cultural politics: the case of the major literary journals." *Soviet Studies*, v. 42 # 1 (January, 1990): 111-132.

1730. Sherlock, Thomas: "Politics and history under Gorbachev." *Problems of Communism*, v. 37 # 3/4 (May/August, 1988): 16-42.

1731. Surovell, Jeffrey: "Ligachev and Soviet politics." *Soviet Studies*,

v. 43 # 2 (1991): 355-374.

1732. Tarasulo, Isaac J. (ed.): *Gorbachev and glasnost: viewpoints from the Soviet press*. Wilmington, DE: Scholarly Resources, 1989. 363 p. [PB]

Anthology of press sources discussing the implications of *glasnost* and *perestroika*. The thirty-three articles are divided into six sections: "Reinterpretations of History," "Economic Reforms," "Unofficial Groups and Soviet Youth," "National, Religious, and Social Issues," "Foreign and Military Issues," and "Party Struggle and Political Reform." Each section provides a brief introduction on context. In addition, the notes are cross referenced with related documents. Each chapter contains a brief annotated bibliography, and a useful glossary rounds out this fascinating look into the Soviet debate on reform.

## B. THE TWILIGHT OF THE COLD WAR

### 1. Soviet-American Relations

1733. Armacost, Michael: "Implications of Gorbachev for U.S.-Soviet relations." *Journal of International Affairs*, v. 42 # 2 (Spring, 1989): 445-456.

1734. Azrael, Jeremy R. and Stephen Sestanovich: "Superpower balancing acts." *Foreign Affairs*, v. 64 # 3 (1985): 479-498.

1735. Beloff, Max: "1989, a farewell to arms: a rejoinder." *International Affairs*, v. 65 # 3 (Summer, 1989): 415-417.

Another view on Gorbachev's revolution, see # 1743.

1736. Bialer, Seweryn and Michael Mandelbaum (eds.): *Gorbachev's Russia and American foreign policy*. Boulder, CO: Westview Press, 1988. 510 p.

Anthology viewing the reforms wrought by Gorbachev as viewed from the U.S. perspective. Views Gorbachev's reforms in historical context, beginning with the travails of reform in the post-Stalinist era. The majority of the essays, however, concentrate on the policy implications of *glasnost* for the United States.

CONTENTS: S. F. Starr: The changing nature of change in the USSR / S. Fitzpatrick: Sources of change in Soviet history: state, society, and the entrepreneurial tradition / R. Campbell: The Soviet economic model / R. Legvold: War, weapons, and Soviet foreign policy / R. Cullen: Human rights: a thaw imperiled / T. J. Colton: Gorbachev and the politics of system renewal / T. Gustafson: The crisis of the Soviet system of power and Mikhail Gorbachev's political strategy / S. Bialer: Gorbachev's program of change: sources, significance, prospects / J. Gaddis: The evolution of U.S. policy goals toward the USSR in the postwar era / M. Mandelbaum: Western influence on the Soviet Union / J. S. Nye, Jr.: Gorbachev's Russia and U.S. options / W. H. Luers: U.S. policy and Gorbachev's Russia / W. G. Hyland: East-West relations / S. Bialer: The Soviet Union and the West: security and foreign policy.

1737. Blacker, Coit D.: "The new United States-Soviet détente." *Current History* v. 88 # 540 (October, 1989): 321-324, 357-359.

1738. Brement, Marshall: "U.S.-USSR: possibilities in partnership." *Foreign Policy*, # 84 (Fall, 1991): 107-124.

1739. Caldwell, Lawrence T.: "Soviet-American relations: the Cold War ends." *Current History*, v. 89 # 549 (October, 1990): 305-308, 343-346.

1740. ---: "United States-Soviet relations and arms control." *Current History*, v. 86 # 522 (October, 1987): 305-308, 344, 346.

> # 1374. ---: "Washington and Moscow."

1741. Garthoff, Raymond L.: "The Bush administration's policy toward the Soviet Union." *Current History*, v. 90 # 558 (October, 1991): 311-316.

1742. Hough, Jerry F.: "The future of Soviet-American relations." *Current History*, v. 85 # 513 (October, 1986): 305-308, 345-346.

1743. Howard, Michael: "1989: a farewell to arms?" *International Affairs*, v. 65 # 3 (Summer, 1989): 407-413.

One view on the Gorbachev revolution. For Max Beloff's response see # 1735.

1744. Hyland, William G.: "Regan-Gorbachev III." *Foreign Affairs*, v. 66 # 1 (Fall, 1987): 7-21.

1745. Jacobsen, Carl G.: "Soviet-American arms control: hope or hoax?" *Current History*, v. 84 # 504 (October, 1985): 317-320, 342-344.

1746. Kass, Ilana: "The U.S.-Soviet strategic relationship." *Annals*, v. 517 (September, 1991): 25-38.

Posits that the relationship is inverted -- the U.S. is at the apex of world influence, the Soviet Union at its nadir. Kass holds the strong conviction that the superpowers remain equal only in that they can destroy each other (and the rest of the world) in a nuclear holocaust.

1747. Lambeth, Benjamin and Kevin Lewis: "The Kremlin and SDI." *Foreign Affairs*, v. 66 # 4 (Spring, 1988): 755-770.

> # 1551. Larrabee, F. S.: "Gorbachev: the road to Rekyavik."

1748. Luttwak, Edward N.: "Gorbachev's strategy, and ours." *Commentary*, v. 88 # 1 (July, 1989): 29-36.

1749 Perkovich, George: "Counting the costs of the arms race." *Foreign Policy*, # 85 (Winter, 1991/1992): 83-105.

Deals with the Startegic Arms Reduction Treaty (START) talks.

1750. Pipes, Richard: "Soviet relations with the USA." *Soviet Jewish Affairs*, v. 15 # 1 (1985): 107-112.

1751. Rivkin, David B. Jr.: "What does Moscow think?" *Foreign Policy*, # 59 (Summer, 1985); 85-122.

On the American Strategic Defense Initiative.

1752. Udalov, Vadim V.: "The concept of balance of interest and U.S.-Soviet interaction." *Annals*, v. 518 (November, 1991): 165-167.

1753. Whelan, Joseph G.: *The Moscow summit, 1988: Reagan and Gorbachev in negotiation*. Boulder, CO: Westview Press, 1990. 141 p.

Examines the impact of *perestroika* and *glasnost* on Soviet-American relations. This is accomplished by closely analyzing the 1988 Moscow summit. Gives high marks to both President Ronald Reagan and President Mikhail S. Gorbachev for achieving the results they sought through forthright negotiations. Also analyzes the summit's symbolic features and implications for future international diplomacy.

1754. Williams, Phil: "U.S.-Soviet relations: beyond the Cold War?" *International Affairs*, v. 65 # 2 (Spring, 1989): 273-288.

## 2. The End of East-West Tensions

1755. Adomeit, Hannes: "Soviet relations with Western Europe." *Soviet Jewish Affairs*, v. 15 # 1 (1985): 113-120.

1756. Benn, David W.: "*Glasnost*, dialogue and East-West relations." *International Affairs*, v. 65 # 2 (Spring, 1989): 289-303.

1757. Butler, William E.: "International law, foreign policy and the Gorbachev style." *Journal of International Affairs*, v. 42 # 2 (Spring, 1989): 363-375.

1758. Clark, Susan L. (ed.): *Soviet military power in a changing world*. Boulder, CO: Westview Press, 1991. 324 p.

Thematically organized anthology assessing the changes wrought by *glasnost* in the area of Soviet military policy. Considers the issues from both military and cilivian perspectives. Clark reviews such matters as nuclear weapons policy, conversion from military to civilian production, and ethnic tensions in the Soviet military.

CONTENTS: S. L. Clark: Changing Soviet security environment / C. Jones: The post-Soviet military and the future of Europe / C. Bluth: Soviet forces and security issues / S. L. Clark: Soviet nuclear forces and the new European security environment / E. M. Holoboff: The crisis in Soviet military reform / P. Almquist: Soviet military acquisition: from a sellers' market to a buyers? / L. van Metre: Defense conversion: last trump or last rite / D. R. Herspring: The high command and the future of the Soviet military personnel system / S. L. Clark: Ethnic tensions and the Soviet military / S. Blank: Winter storm in the Baltic: the Soviet armed forces and domestic security / R. F. Laird: Rethinking the role of Soviet military power.

1759. Codevilla, Angelo M.: "Is there still a Soviet threat?" *Commentary*, v. 86 # 5 (November, 1988): 23-28.

1760. Ellison, Herbert J.: "United front strategy and Soviet foreign policy." *Problems of Communism*, v. 34 # 5 (September/October, 1985): 45-64.

1761. Gawad, Atef A.: "Moscow's arms-for-oil diplomacy." *Foreign Policy*, # 63 (Summer, 1986): 147-168.

1762. Green, William C. and Theodore Karasik (eds.): *Gorbachev and his generals: the reform of Soviet military doctrine*. Boulder, CO: Westview Press, 1990. 240 p.

Important investigation of Gorbachev's military policy. Charts Gorbachev's efforts to apply both *glasnost* and *perestroika* to the Red Army, while military leaders opposed Gorbachev's proposed ideational reforms. The denouement of military conservatism, as we now know, was the abortive August 1991 *coup*. Ironically, although the *coup* failed to overturn the reform movement, it led to Gorbachev's downfall and the old Soviet Union's disintegration.

CONTENTS: W. F. Scott: Soviet miltary doctrine: continuity and change? / W. C. Green: Assessing Soviet military literature: attempts to broker the Western debate / T. Nichols and T.

Karasik: Civil-military relations under Gorbachev: the struggle over national security / F. Wehling: Old soldiers never die: Marshal Akhromeev's role is Soviet defense decision-making / D. Goure: Soviet doctrine and nuclear forces into the twenty-first century / S. Blank: Soviet military doctrine's requirements for a space TVD / P. Cronin: *Perestroika* and Soviet military personnel / P. J. Dobriansky and D. B. Rivkin, Jr.: Changes in Soviet military thinking: how do they add up and what do they mean for western security? / W. C. Green: Soviet military reference works as a guide in Soviet military doctrine / T. Nichols: The unresolved agenda / G. Burkhart: The Soviet military leadership / R. E. Newnham: Gorbachev and the Soviet military: a chronology.

> # 1577. Hasegawa, T.: *Perestroika.*

1763. Haslam, Jonathan: "The UN and the Soviet Union: new thinking?" *International Affairs*, v. 65 # 4 (Fall, 1989): 677-684.

1764. Hough, Jerry F.: *Russia and the West: Gorbachev and the politics of reform.* (Second edition) New York: Touchstone Books/Simon and Schuster, 1990. 286 p. [PB]

Up-to-date investigation of the impact of *glasnost* on Soviet-American relations. The second edition incorporates and analyzes the East European revolutions of 1989. Hough maintains that Gorbachev has sought to undo the wrongs wrought by Stalinism by breaching the Iron Curtain and reopening friendly relations with the West. although written in haste, Hough was still unable to take the events of the Persian Gulf War and the August 1991 *coup* into account. However, he did anticipate the possibility of U.S.-Soviet cooperation in the Middle East and other Cold War troublespots, such as Southern Africa.

1765. Janes, Robert W.: "The Soviet Union and Nothern Europe: new thinking and old security constraints." *Annals*, v. 512 (November, 1990): 163-172.

Posits that Soviet diplomacy in Northern Europe presents insights into Gorbachev's policy of a common European home.

1766. Jones, David R.: "The two faces of Soviet military power." *Current History*, v. 86 # 522 (October, 1987): 3132-316, 336-337, 344.

1767. Kiser, John W.: "How the arms race really helps Moscow." *Foreign Policy*, # 60 (Fall, 1985); 40-51.

1768. Kramer, Mark: "The role of the CPSU International Department in Soviet foreign relations and national security policy." *Soviet Studies*, v. 42 # 3 (July, 1990): 429-446.

1769. ---: "Soviet foreign policy after the Cold War." *Current History*, v. 90 # 558 (October, 1991): 317-322.

1770. ---: "Soviet military policy." *Current History*, v. 88 # 540 (October, 1989): 337-340, 349-353.

1771. Larrabee, F. Stephen: "Gorbachev and the Soviet military." *Foreign Affairs*, v. 66 # 5 (Summer, 1988): 1002-1026.

1772. Lippmann, Walter: "The Cold War." *Foreign Affairs*, v. 65 # 4 (Spring, 1987): 869-884.

1773. Lynch, Allen: *The Cold War is over -- again*. Boulder, CO: Westview Press, 1992. 216 p.

Revisionist history of the end of the Cold War. Lynch argues that the Cold War did not end with Gorbachev's fall and disintegration of the Soviet Union. Instead, he argues that the Cold War ended in 1975 -- with the signing of the Helsinki accords that *de facto* recognized Soviet domination of Eastern Europe. Events of the late 1980s and early 1990s -- especially the reunification of Germany -- did not end the Cold War, but signaled the overturning of the first post-Cold War new order. Lynch's provocative thesis offers an interesting perspective covering the last twenty years of European history as well as insight into current developments. The author also attempts to predict developments in the near future, although it is impossible to judge his accuracy. Whether or not one accepts his thesis, this is a thought-provoking book that offers an important insight into international relations in the 1990s.

1774. Macdonald, Hugh: *The Soviet challange and the structure of Euopean security*. Brookfield, VT: Gower Publishing, 1990. 317 p.

1775. Mackintosh, Malcolm: The Russian attitude to defence and disarmament." *International Affairs*, v. 61 # 3 (Summer, 1985): 385-394.

1776. Malcolm, Neil: "The 'common European home' and Soviet policy." *International Affairs*, v. 65 # 4 (Fall, 1989): 659-676.

1777. Marantz, Paul: "Soviet 'new thinking' and East-West relations." *Current History*, v. 87 # 531 (October, 1988): 309-312, 345-347.

1778. MccGwire, Michael: *Perestroika and Soviet national security*. Washington, DC: The Brookings Institution, 1991. 481 p. [PB]

Detailed investigation of the changes made in Soviet military thought resulting from *perestroika*. Inter alia, MccGwire details the changing patterns of Soviet national security thought since 1945 and reappraises international relations during the Cold War era. The development of Soviet strategic weapons theory is central to MccGwire's analysis. Ends with the events that transpired between 1989 and 1991 which led to the end of the Cold War. MccGwire concludes by asking what will replace it now that the Soviet Union has ceased to exist.

1779. Miller, John H.: "The geographical disposition of the Soviet armed forces." *Soviet Studies*, v. 40 # 3 (July, 1988): 406-433.

1780. Odom, William E.: "Soviet military doctrine." *Foreign Affairs*, v. 67 # 2 (Winter, 1988/1989): 114-134.

1781. Parrott, Bruce: "Soviet national security under Gorbachev." *Problems of Communism*, v. 37 # 6 (November/December, 1988): 1-36.

1782. Rice, Condoleezza: "The Soviet military under Gorbachev." *Current History*, v. 85 # 513 (October, 1986): 313-316, 342-343.

1783. Rogov, Sergey M.: "Détente is not enough." *Foreign Policy*, # 74 (Spring, 1989): 86-102.

1784. Rostow, Eugene V.: "Why the Soviets want an arms-control agreement, and why they want it now." *Commentary*, v. 83 # 2 (February, 1987): 19-26.

1785. Rostow, W. W.: "On ending the Cold War." *Foreign Affairs*, v. 65 # 4 (Spring, 1987): 831-851.

1786. Rowen, Henry S. and Charles Wolf, Jr. (eds.): *The impoverished superpower: perestroika and the Soviet military burden.* San Frasisco, CA: ICS Press, 1990. 372 p.

CONTENTS: A. Åslund: How small is Soviet national income? / R. E. Ericson: The Soviet statistical debate: Khanin vs. TsSU / D. Derk Swain: The Soviet military sector: how it is defined and measured / N. D. Michaud: The paradox of current Soviet military spending / D. F. Epstein: The economic cost of Soviet security and empire / C. M. Davis: The high-priority military sector in a shortage economy / A. J. Alexander: Soviet weapons acquisition in the era of *perestroika* / S. M. Meyer: Economic constraints in Soviet military decision-making / G. G. Hildebrandt: Models of the military sector in the Soviet economy / V. Kontorovich: The long-run decline in Soviet R&D productivity / B. Z. Rumer: What happened to Soviet investment?

1787. Simes, Dimitri K.: "Gorbachev: a new foreign policy?" *Foreign Affairs*, v. 65 # 3 (1987): 477-500.

1788. Spaulding, Walter: "Shifts in CPSU ID." *Problems of Communism*, v. 35 # 4 (July/August, 1981): 80-86.

On the Communist party International Department.

1789. Stevens, Sayre: "Balistic missile defense in the Soviet Union." *Current History*, v. 84 # 504 (October, 1985): 313-316, 344-347.

1790. Vartanov, Rafael V. and Alexei Roginko: "New dimesions of Soviet Arctic policy: views from the Soviet Union." *Annals*, v. 512

(November, 1990): 69-78.

1791. Wettig, Gerhard: *Changes in Soviet policy towards the West*. Boulder, CO: Westview Press, 1991. 193 p.

Meticulous investigation into Soviet foreign policy in the Gorbachev era. Argues that the rise of the new European Common Market (EC-92) has created a novel situation for the USSR that makes basic changes in the Soviet system necessary. Wettig is the first author to fully gauge the impact of German reunification on the Soviet Union, but his predictions have been overtaken by later events, especially the collapse of the USSR and its replacement by the Commonwealth of Independent States.

1792. Williams, E. S. (ed.): *Soviet air power: prospects for the future: perestroika and the Soviet air forces*. London: Tri-Service Press, 1990. 247 p.

1793. Woodby, Sylvia: *Gorbachev and the decline of ideology in Soviet foreign policy*. Boulder, CO: Westview Press, 1989. 127 p.

Analyzes the decline of ideological factors in Soviet foreign policy in the first years of Gorbachev's presidency. Whereas the USSR was officially committed to a policy of fomenting a global revolution, in reality Soviet foreign policy had always been pragmatic. Woodby argues, however, that Gorbachev even removed the veneer of Marxism-Leninism from Soviet foreign relations, thus creating an unprecedented new situation in international affairs. Although Soviet support for the United Nations' goals in the 1991 Persian Gulf War seems to prove Woodby's thesis, the Union's collapse and the subsequent end of the Cold War have cast into some doubt her assertion that Gorbachev created the new reality: it seems rather that he was swept up in the tide of his own arguments, not all of whose implications Gorbachev himself understood.

1794. Ziebart, Geoffrey: "Soviet naval developments in east Asia." *Journal of International Affairs*, v. 42 # 2 (Summer, 1989): 457-475.

### 3. Perestroika and Reform in Eastern Europe

1795. Assetto, Valerie J.: *The Soviet bloc in the IMF and the IBRD*. Boulder, CO: Westview Press, 1987. 208 p.

1796. Braun, Aurel: "Whither the Warsaw pact in the Gorbachev era?" *International Journal*, v. 42 # 1 (Winter, 1987/1988): 63-105.

1797. --- (ed.): *The Soviet-East European relationship in the Gorbachev era: the prospects for adaptation*. Boulder, CO: Westview Press, 1990. 249 p.

Anthology investigating Soviet relations with Eastern Europe under the impact of *glasnost*. The essays are arranged thematically, rather than geographically. While such an organization makes for the diffusion of specific national issues -- especially in light of the 1989 revolutions in Warsaw Pact countries -- this is the only way to avoid repetitiveness. Primary focus is on political, economic, and security issues.

CONTENTS: K. Dawisha: Soviet political and ideological perceptions and policies toward Eastern Europe under Gorbachev / C. H. McMillan: Soviet efforts to restructure the CMEA: the case of regional energy relations / E. Luttwak: Soviet military concerns and prospects in Eastern Europe / A. Korbonski: East European political and ideological perceptions and concerns / P. Marer: Reforms in the USSR and Eastern Europe: is there a link? / I. Volgyes: The lesser ally view: Eastern Europe and the military relationship with the Soviet Union / M. Kroan: Lands in between: the politics of cultural identity in contemporary Eastern Europe / A. Braun: On reform, perceptions, misperceptions, trends and tendencies.

1798. "East-West relations and Eastern Europe: a Soviet-American dialogue." *Problems of Communism*, v. 37 # 3/4 (May/August, 1988): 55-70.

1799. Gati, Charles: "Gorbachev and Eastern Europe." *Foreign Affairs*, v. 65 # 5 (Summer, 1987): 958-975.

1800. Hauner, Milan: "Soviet Eurasian empire and the Indo-Persian corridor." *Problems of Communism*, v. 36 # 1 (January/February, 1987): 25-35.

> # 225. Kramer, J. M.: "Chernobyl and Eastern Europe."

1801. Kramer, John M.: "Soviet-CEMA ties." *Problems of Communism*, v. 34 # 4 (July/August, 1985): 32-47.

Details the loosening of Soviet-Eastern European economic ties.

1802. Kraus, Michael: "Soviet policy toward east Europe." *Current History*, v. 86 # 523 (Noember, 1987): 353-356, 390-393.

1803. Kusin, Vladimir V.: "Gorbachev and Eastern Europe." *Problems of Communism*, v. 35 # 1 (January/February, 1986): 39-53.

1804. Lynch, Allen: "The changing contours of Soviet-East European relations." *Journal of International Affairs*, v. 42 # 2 (Spring, 1989): 423-434.

1805. Mason, David S.: "*Glasnost, perestroika* and Eastern Europe." *International Affairs*, v. 64 # 3 (Summer, 1988): 431-448.

Questions whether Gorbachev is aiming for reform, revolution, or is all this just a facade?

1806. Navrozov, Lev: "The Kremlin's quest for world rule and ten Western myths." *Midstream*, v. 37 # 4 (May, 1991): 19-23.

Polemical article arguing that the Soviet withdrawal from Eastern Europe is actually a Communist plot to disinform the West.

1807. Ploss, Sidney I.: *Moscow and the Polish crisis: an interpretation of Soviet policies and intentions*. Boulder, CO: Westview Press, 1986. 200 p.

Concentrates on the aftermath of the Polish leadership's imposition of martial law in 1981.

1808. Varga, Ivan: "Opaque *glasnost*? Eastern Europe and Gorbachev's reforms." *International Journal*, v. 42 # 1 (Winter, 1987/1988): 18-34.

**4. The New Spirit of Cooperation**

1809. Adams, Jan S.: "Incremental activism in Soviet Third World Policy: the role of the International Department of the CPSU Central Committee." *Slavic Review*, v. 48 # 4 (Winter, 1989): 614-630.

1810. Albright, David E.: "Soviet economic development and the Third World." *Soviet Studies*, v. 43 # 1 (1991): 27-60.

1811. Anderson, Lisa: "Quahdhafi and the Kremlin." *Problems of Communism*, v. 34 # 5 (September/October, 1985): 29-44.

1812. Banerjee, Jyotirmoy: "Moscow's Indian alliance." *Problems of Communism*, v. 36 # 1 (January/February, 1987): 1-12.

1813. Doran, Charles F.: "Conflict and cooperation: between the Cold War and the Gulf." *Annals*, v. 518 (November, 1991): 153-164.

1814. Duncan, W. Raymond and Carolyn McGiffert Ekedhal: *Moscow and the Third World under Gorbachev*. Boulder, CO: Westview Press, 1990. 248 p.

Explores Gorbachev's new thinking as reflected in Soviet policy toward the Third World. Although relations between the Soviet Union and many Third World countries developed as a result of events preceding Gorbachev, the main theme is how his "new thinking" effected the scope of Soviet foreign policy. Includes five case studies: Afghanistan, the Middle East, the Far East, Sub-Saharan Africa, and Latin America.

1815. Dupree, Louis: "The Soviet Union and Afghanistan in 1987." *Current History*, v. 86 # 522 (October, 1987): 333-335.

1816. Ellison, Herbert J.: "Changing Sino-Soviet relations."

*Problems of Communism*, v. 36 # 3 (May/June, 1987): 17-29.

1817. Freedman, Robert O.: "Relations between the USSR and Israel since the accession of Gorbachev." *Soviet Jewish Affairs*, v. 18 # 2 (Fall, 1988): 43-63.

1818. Fukuyama, Francis: "Gorbachev and the Third World." *Foreign Affairs*, v. 64 # 4 (Spring, 1986): 715-731.

1819. ---: "Patterns of Soviet Third World policy." *Problems of Communism*, v. 36 # 5 (September/October, 1987): 1-13.

1820. Golan, Galia: "Gorbachev's Middle East strategy." *Foreign Affairs*, v. 66 # 1 (fall, 1987): 41-57.

1821. ---: "Moscow and Third World national liberation movements: the Soviet role." *Journal of International Affairs*, v. 40 # 2 (Winter/Spring, 1987): 303-323.

> # 1037. ---: *Soviet politics in the Middle East*.

1822. Horn, Robert C.: "Soviet policy in east Asia." *Current History*, v. 86 # 522 (October, 1987): 321-324, 338-340.

1823. Hsiung, James C.: "Soviet-Chinese dètente." *Current History*, v. 84 # 504 (October, 1985): 329-333.

1824. Irwin, Zachary T.: "The USSR and Israel." *Problems of Communism*, v. 36 # 1 (January/February, 1987): 36-45.

1825. Kamrany, Nake M.: "The continuing war in Afghanistan." *Current History*, v. 85 # 513 (October, 1986): 333-336.

1826. Katz, Mark N.: "The Soviet Union and the Third World." *Current History*, v. 85 # 513 (October, 1986): 329-332, 339-340.

1827. ---: "Soviet policy in the Gulf States." *Current History*, v. 84 # 498 (January, 1985): 25-28.

Soviet efforts to gain influnce in the Arabian peninsula.

1828. ---: "Soviet policy in the Middle East." *Current History*, v. 87 # 526 (February, 1988): 57-60, 83.

1829. Khalizad, Zalmay: "Moscow's Afghan war." *Problems of Communism*, v. 35 # 1 (January/February, 1986): 1-20.

1830. ---: "The Soviet dilemma in Afghanistan." *Current History*, v. 84 # 504 (October, 1985): 334-337.

1831. Kimura, Hiroshi: "Soviet focus on the Pacific." *Problems of Communism*, v. 36 # 3 (May/June, 1987): 1-16.

1832. Kramer, Mark N.: "Soviet arms transfers to the Third World." *Problems of Communism*, v. 36 # 5 (September/October, 1987): 52-68.

1833. Leifer, Michael: "The Soviet Union in Asia." *Soviet Jewish Affairs*, v. 15 # 1 (1985): 121-123.

1834. Levine, Steven I.: "The end of Sino-Soviet estrangement." *Current History*, v. 85 # 512 (September, 1986): 245-248, 279-280.

1835. Menon, Rajan: "Soviet arms to the Third World: characteristics and consequences." *Journal of International Affairs*, v. 40 # 1 (Summer, 1986): 59-76.

1836. Mukerjee, Dilip: "Indo-Soviet economic ties." *Problems of Communism*, v. 36 # 1 (January/February, 1987): 13-24.

1837. Noorzoy, M. Siddieq: "Soviet economic interests in Afghanistan." *Problems of Communism*, v. 36 # 3 (May/June, 1987): 43-54.

1838. Nosenko, Vladimir: "Moscow's Middle East policy during *perestroika*." *Midstream*, v. 38 # 2 (February/March, 1992): 9-11.

1839. Page, Stephen: "Patterns of Soviet activity in Southwest Asia." *International Journal*, v. 41 # 2 (Spring, 1986): 300-323.

1840. Patman, Robert G.: *The Soviet Union in the Horn of Africa:*

*the diplomacy of intervention and disingagement*. New York: Cambridge University Press, 1990. 411 p.

Primarily focused on Soviet involvement in the Ethiopian conflicts of the 1970s and 1980s.

1841. Phillips, James: "Gorbachev's 'new thinking' on the Middle East." *Midstream*, v. 35 # 6 (August/September, 1989): 12-15.

Investigates the possible reorientation of Soviet Middle East policy.

1842. Pollick, David: "Moscow and Aden: coping with a *coup*." *Problems of Communism*, v. 35 # 2 (May/June, 1986): 50-70.

1843. Ramati, Yohanan: "Russia has changed." *Midstream*, v. 38 # 1 (January, 1992): 4-6.

On Commonwealth of Independent States' Middle Eastern policy.

1844. ---: "The Soviet Union and the Gulf crisis." *Midstream*, v. 36 # 9 (January, 1991): 6-8.

New spirit of cooperation with anti-Saddam Hussein coalition: a real change in Soviet policy or disinformation?

1845. Robinson, Thomas W.: "The new ear in Sino-Soviet relations." *Current History*, v. 86 # 521 (September, 1987): 241-244, 303-304.

1846. Rubinstein, Alvin Z.: "Afghanistan at war." *Current History*, v. 85. #509 (March, 1986): 117-120, 128-131.

1847. ---: "Gorbachev's Middle East policy: an interim assessment." *Soviet Jewish Affairs*, v. 17 # 2 (Summer/Fall, 1987): 3-16.

1848. ---: "The Soviet withdrawal from Afghanistan." *Current History*, v. 87 # 531 (October, 1988): 333-336, 339-340.

1849. Saikal, Amin and W. Maley (ed.): *The Soviet withdrawal form Afghanistan*. New York: Cambridge University Press, 1989. 177 p.

Military and political analysis of the Soviet withdrawal from Afghanistan. Based on a symposium held at the Australian National University in Canberra in August 1988. The book explores both the background to and implications of the withdrawal, although the latter gets the lion's share of attention. Jukes' essay is of particlar interest and charts the performance of the Soviet military in operations against the *Mujahideen.* As the first major work on the Afghan War, the book may be superseded in the future, but it will never be surpassed for analytical importance.

CONTENTS: W. Maley: The Geneva accords of April 1988 / A. Saikal: Regional politics of the Afghan crisis / L. Dupree: Post-withdrawal Afghanistan: light at the end of the tunnel / T. H. Rigby: The Afghan conflict and Soviet domestic politics / G. Jukes: The Soviet armed forces and the Afghan war / R. F. Miller: Afghanistan and Soviet alliances / L. Holmes: Afghanistan and Sino-Soviet relations / R. I. Falk: The Afghanistan 'settlement' and the future of world politics / J. L. Richardson: Management of the Afghan crisis.

1850. Saivetz, Carol R.: "Islam and Gorbachev's policy in the Middle East." *Journal of International Affairs*, v. 42 # 2 (Spring, 1989): 435-444.

1851. ---: "'New thinking' and Soviet Third World policy." *Current History*, v. 88 # 540 (October, 1989): 325-328, 354-357.

## C. THE COLLAPSE OF THE SOVIET UNION

### 1. The East European Revolutions

1852. Alksnis, Viktor: "Suffering from self-determination." *Foreign Policy*, # 84 (Fall, 1991): 61-71.

> # 1797. Braun, A.: *Soviet-East European relationship.*

1853. Childs, David: "East Germany: coping with Gorbachev." *Current History*, v. 88 # 541 (November, 1989): 385-388, 400-401.

1854. Gati, Charles: *The bloc that failed: Soviet-East European relations in transition*. Bloomington: Indiana University Press, 1990. 226 p. [PB]

First review of the revolution that has swept Eastern Europe since 1989. As an answer to the question of how the Warsaw Pact collapsed so quickly, Gati offers a review of Soviet-East European relations since Stalin. Special emphasis is placed on the strains that began appearing after Gorbachev's rise in 1985. The majority of the book offers a detailed analysis of the changes that Gorbachev has wrought. Although brief, the book offers numerous interesting insights and is an important introduction to the beginning of a new era in history.

> # 1764. Hough, J. F.: *Russia and the West*.

> # 1773. Lynch, A.: *The Cold War is over - again*.

1855. Mason, David S.: *Revolution in East-Central Europe: the rise and fall of communism and the Cold War*. Boulder, CO: Westview Press, 1992. 224 p.

Scholarly investigation of the rise, decline, and ultimate fall of communism in Eastern Europe. To place the revolutions in context, Mason first explains the Sovietization of the East European states. Since the Communist regimes were imposed by Soviet power, they lacked legitimacy. As a result, opposition movements arose, but were held in check by the threat of -- or actual use of -- violence. Still, the opposition continued to mount until economic collapse brought down the entire system of government in the former Communist states. In his final chapter Mason charts the current march of events and predicts future trends for the fledgling democracies created by the Revolutions of 1989.

1856. McAdams, A. James: "The new logic of Soviet-GDR Relations." *Problems of Communism*, v. 37 # 5 (September/ October, 1988): 47-60.

> # 1806. Navrozov, L.: "The Kremlin's quest for world rule."

1857. Rachwald, Arthur R.: "Soviet-East European relations." *Current History*, v. 88 # 541 (November, 1989): 377-380, 408-409.

1858. Smyser, W. R.: "USSR-Germany: a link restored." *Foreign Policy*, # 84 (Fall, 1991): 125-141.

1859. Taagepera, Rein: "A note on the March 1989 elections in Estonia." *Soviet Studies*, v. 42 # 2 (April, 1990): 329-340.

> # 1791. Wettig, G.: *Changes in Soviet policy towards the West*.

1860. White, Stephan: "Rethinking the CPSU." *Soviet Studies*, v. 43 # 3 (1991): 405-428

Evaluates the likely fate of the Communist party after the transformation of Eastern Europe, but before the August *coup*.

### 2. The Crisis of Glasnost

1861. Aage, Hans: "Popular attitudes and *perestroika*." *Soviet Studies*, v. 43 # 1 (1991): 3-26.

1862. Borovik, Artyom: "Waiting for democracy." *Foreign Policy*, # 84 (Fall, 1991): 51-60.

1863. Brundy, Yitzhak M.: "The heralds of opposition to *perestroika*." *Soviet Economy*, v. 5 # 2 (April/June, 1989): 162-200.

1864. Burg, Steven L.: "The European republics of the Soviet Union." *Current History*, v. 89 # 549 (October, 1990): 321-324, 340-342.

1865. ---: "The Soviet Union's nationalities question." *Current History*, v. 88 # 540 (October, 1989): 341-344, 359-362.

> # 1376. Crozier, B.: "Getting Gorbachev wrong."

1866. Dallin, Alexander and Gail W. Lapidus (eds.): *The Soviet system in crisis: a reader of Western and Soviet views*. Boulder, CO:

Westview Press, 1991. 500p.

Important collection of documents and studies on the collapse of the Soviet Union, assembled literally as the events transpired. The editors plan to write revised and updated editions, which means that the work will become a valuable resource for students, scholars, and policymakers alike. Dallin and Lapidus include a panoply of documents, organized into seven sections: "The Roots of *Perestroika*," "Soviet Political Debates," "The Economy," "Nationalism and the Future of the Federal System," "Foreign Policy and National Security," and "The Future of the System." Among the documents are Gorbachev's important December 7, 1988 speech at the United Nations General Assembly, Boris N. Yeltsin's speech at the Russian parliament of May 22, 1990, and Eduard S. Sheverdnadze's December 22, 1990 speech at the Supreme Soviet. The documents and essays offer readers a deeper understanding of events transforming the Commonwealth of Independent States and offer a glimpse into the future.

1867. Di Leo, Rita: "The Soviet Union 1985-1990: after Communist rule the deluge?" *Soviet Studies*, v. 43 # 3 (1991): 429-450.

1868. Goldman, Marshall I.: "The future of Soviet economic reform." *Current History*, v. 88 # 540 (October, 1989): 329-332, 348-349.

1869. ---: "The Soviet economy and the need for reform." *Annals*, v. 507 (January, 1990): 26-34.

1870. ---: "Soviet energy runs out of gas." *Current History*, v. 89 # 549 (October, 1990): 313-316.

1871. ---: *What went wrong with perestroika*. New York: W. W. Norton, 1991. 258 p.

Broad effort to explain the failure of *perestroika*. Goldman is best at explaining Gorbachev's economic failure as well as sketching the personalities active in the Kremlin since 1985. Less successful is Goldman's effort to explain why *perestroika* failed. As a result, the book is less useful for scholars; it does, however, fill an important role in providing background for lay readers otherwise reliant on press reports.

1872. Grossman, Gregory: "Sub-rosa privatization and marketization in the USSR." *Annals*, v. 507 (January, 1990): 44-52.

1873. Hajda, Lubomyr: "The nationalities problem in the Soviet Union." *Current History*, v. 87 # 531 (October, 1988): 325-328, 347, 352-353.

1874. Hazan, Baruch A.: *Gorbachev and his enemies: the struggle for perestroika*. Boulder, CO: Westview Press, 1990. 320 p.

Investigation into the politics of *perestroika*. Identifies Gorbachev's primary opponents, but concentrates on the conservative Communists. Prominent among the latter include the military, the KGB, and Party *appartchiks* who feared losing their special status. In August 1991 -- just months after Hazan completed his very insightful text -- these groups came together in an abortive *coup* that galvinized Russia's democratic forces. This led to the old Soviet Union's demise and its replacement with the Commonwealth of Independent States.

1875. Hewett, Ed A.: "*Perestroika* and the Congress of People's Deputies." *Soviet Economy*, v. 5 # 1 (January/March, 1989): 47-69.

1876. Hosking, Geoffrey: *The awakening of the Soviet Union*. Cambridge, MA: Harvard University Press, 1990. 208 p.

Details the steady de-totalitarianization of the Soviet Union in the 1980s. Begins with insight into how Russians are now revising the history of the revolutions and moves on from there to the creation of a new "civil society." Among the movements that Hosking cites as especially important are the environmentalists, but he also notes the preciptous rise of hypernationalism, for example in the Azerbaidzahn-Armenian dispute over Nagorno-Karabakh.

1877. Hunter, Shireen T.: "Nationalist movements in Soviet Asia." *Current History*, v. 89 # 549 (October, 1990): 325-328, 337-339.

1878. Kaiser, Robert G.: "The Soviet pretense." *Foreign Affairs*, v. 65 # 2 (Winter, 1986/1987): 236-251.

1879. ---: "The USSR in decline." *Foreign Affairs*, v. 67 # 2 (Winter, 1988/1989): 97-113.

1880. Kux, Stephan: *Soviet federalism: a comparative perspective*. Boulder, CO: Westview Press, 1990. 117 p.

Examines the relationship between the Soviet republics on the eve of their breakup. Analyzes the reasons that federalism has failed to unify the republics, creating the crisis of legitimacy that culminated in the December 1991 replacement of the Soviet Union with the Commonwealth of Independent States. Also addresses economic, social, and diplomatic issues in the relationship of the Soviet central government to the republics. Offers possible scenarios for future developments, though Kux could not ultimately foresee the complete disintegration of central government in the USSR.

1881. Lavigne, Marie: *Financing the transition in the USSR: the Shatalin plan and the Soviet economy*. Boulder, CO: Westview Press, 1991. 35 p.

Study of the proposed 1990 plan to convert the Soviet Union from a controlled to a market economy. The plan was drawn up by a team of economists from Russia and thirteen of the other fourteen republics that made up the Soviet Union, now comprising the Commonwealth of Independent States. Only Georgia -- which decided not to join the Commonwealth -- was not represented. Lavigne asks three questions: is the plan feasible? how much will it cost? and will carrying the plan through require increased Western aid? The book has been overtaken by events following its publication: the centrally controlled economy could not be transformed since it no longer existed. Then too, the key European republics -- Russia, Ukraine, and Belarus -- had begun the difficult road to both democracy and capitalism.

1882. Lih, Lars T.: "Soviet politics: breakdown or renewal?" *Current History*, v. 89 # 549 (October, 1990): 309-312, 339-340.

1883. ---: "The transition era in Soviet politics." *Current History*, v. 88 # 540 (October, 1989): 333-336, 353-354.

1884. McKinney, Judith R.: "Confusion in Soviet economic reform." *Current History*, v. 89 # 549 (October, 1990): 317-320, 342-343.

1885. Mlynar, Zdenek: *Can Gorbachev change the Soviet Union: the international dimensions of political reform*. Boulder, CO: Westview Press, 1990. 184 p.

Perceptive study that investigates *glasnost* and *perestroika*. Mlynar, a classmate of Mikhail Gorbachev's, seeks an answer to a seemingly simple question: can the Soviet Union be reformed, or must it be entirely swept away in order to allow true democracy to develop? Although this question has now been rendered academic, Mlynar offers many important insights into the psyche of the Soviet leaders. He also offers a cogent analysis of the implications of reform for the rest of the world, with or without the disintegration of the Soviet Union.

> # 1955. Morrison, J.: *Boris Yeltsin*.

1886. Paniotto, Vladimir: "The Ukrainian movement for *perestroika Rukh*: a sociological survey." *Soviet Studies*, v. 43 # 1 (1991): 177-182.

1887. Pipes, Richard: "Gorbachev's Russia: breakdown or crack-down?" *Commentary*, v. 89 # 3 (March, 1990): 13-25.

1888. Popkova-Pijasheva, Larissa: "Why is the plan incompatible with the market?" *Annals*, v. 507 (January, 1990): 80-90.

1889. Ra'anan, Uri (ed.): *The Soviet empire: the challenge of national and democratic movements*. Lexington, MA: Lexington Books, 1990. 254 p.

Anthology exploring the impact of reform on the Soviet Union. Primarily focused on the democratic movement in Russia, although attention is also given to the nationalities problem. The first essay sets the tone for the collection, as it asks whether or not the

Communist party can survive reforms. It now appears that the answer must be a conditional no: neither the Communist party nor the Soviet Union appear to have survived the last gasp of conservative opposition to democracy and market economics.

CONTENTS: I. Lukes: Will the CPSU survive Gorbachev's reform? / E. Teague: The emergence of parliamentary opposition in the USSR / A. Knight: The KGB and democratization: a new legal order? / U. Ra'anan: The Russian problem: conceptual and operational aspects / R. Szporluk: National reawakening: the Ukraine and Belorussia / W. Clemens: Baltic communism and nationalism: *Kto Kovo*? / R. F. Baumarin: National movements in the Transcaucasus and Central Asia: Moscow's dilemma / T. Rakowska-Harmstone: The Soviet armed forces: the challenge of reform and the ethnic factor.

1890. Revel, Jean F.: "Hastening the death of communism." *Commentary*, v. 88 # 4 (October, 1989): 19-23.

1891. Schroeder, Getrude D.: "A critical time for *perestroika*." *Current History*, v. 90 # 558 (October, 1991): 323-327.

1892. ---: "Economic reform of socialism: the Soviet record." *Annals*, v. 507 (January, 1990): 35-43.

1893. Sestanovich, Stephen: "Gorbachev's foreign policy: a diplomacy of decline." *Problems of Communism*, v. 37 # 1 (January/February, 1988): 1-15.

1894. Shelton, Judy: *The coming Soviet crash: Gorbachev's desperate pursuit of credit in Western financial markets*. New York: The Free Press, 1989. 246 p.

Examines Soviet efforts to borrow enough money to make *perestroika* successful. Shelton divides her work into three parts: Part I examines the precarious financial situation of the Soviet Union; Part II explains how the Soviet government acquires outside financing; and Part III offers an overview of what Shelton thinks Western policy ought to be. As the financial crisis in post-Soviet Union Russia seems to prove, Shelton's analysis of the importance of financial stability for continued democratization has proven correct.

1895. Timofeyev, Lev (ed.): *The anti-Communist manifesto: whom to help in Russia* (translated from Russian by V. Kisin and O. Glebov). Belvue, WA: Free Enterprise Press, 1991. 96 p.

Brief pamphlet arguing for complete reform of the Soviet Union. The most basic changes called for are the Communist party's elimination, transition to a market economy, and democracy. The pamphlet comprises six statements with a brief foreword by Richard Pipes.

1896. Tolz, Vera (comp.) and Melanie Newton (ed.): *The USSR in 1989: a record of events*. Boulder, CO: Westview Press in cooperation with Radio Liberty, 1990. 800 p.

Day-by-day chronology of a crucial year in Soviet and East European history. Also includes a commentary on the events and the texts of the key diplomatic and political documents of that year.

1897. Wilhelm, John H.: "Crisis and collapse: what are the issues?" *Soviet Studies*, v. 42 # 2 (April, 1990): 317-328.

1898. Whitesell, Robert S.: "Why does the Soviet economy appear to be allocatively efficient?" *Soviet Studies*, v. 42 # 2 (April, 1990): 259-268.

1899. Winiecki, Jon: "Obstacles to economic reform of socialism: a property-rights approach." *Annals*, v. 507 (January, 1990): 65-71.

Tries to answer the question of why economic reforms failed under the Soviet system.

### 3. From the August Coup to the Fall of the USSR

1900. Bilinsky, Yaroslav: *Ukraine: from nationality to nation*. Boulder, CO: Westview Press, 1992. 250 p.

> # 1854. Gati, C.: *The bloc that failed.*

1901. Goble, Paul A.: "Forget the Soviet Union." *Foreign Policy*, # 86 (Spring, 1992): 56-65.

1902. Gorbachev, Mikhail S.: *The August coup: the truth and the lessons*. New York: Harper Collins Publishers, 1991. 127 p.

Brief memoir of the August 1991 *coup* by the last president of the Soviet Union and the father of *glasnost*.

1903. Gordon, Murray: "Communism's collapse: the impact on Jewish communities." *Midstream*, v. 36 # 3 (April, 1990): 9-13.

Discusses Russia, the Baltic Republics, and former Warsaw Pact states.

1904. Hough, Jerry F.: "Assessing the *coup*." *Current History*, v. 90 # 558 (October, 1991): 305-310.

1905. Korotich, Vitaly: "The Ukraine rising." *Foreign Policy*, # 85 (Winter, 1991/1992): 73-82.

1906. Krasnov, Vladislav: *Russia beyond Communism: a chronicle of national rebirth*. Boulder, CO: Westview Press, 1991. 300 p.

Investigation of Russian nationalism and Russian nationalists. Notes that while Gorbachev's reforms have transformed the Soviet Union, the question still remains as to how Russia will proceed in a post-Communist world. Key thinkers reviewed include Alexander Solzhenitsyn, Andrei Sakharov, Alexander Yakovlev, and Dimitrii Lighachev, among others. Krasnov also deals with the sources of Stalinism, the neo-Fascist *Pamyat* movement, Russian and Soviet antisemitism, and his predictions of a new Russia's emergence. The questions about the future posed in Krasnov's last three chapters, and especially his enquiries regarding Boris Yeltsin's political orientation, are of double importance in light of the events that transpired between August and December 1991.

1907. Kull, Steven: *Burying Lenin: the revolution in Soviet ideology and foreign policy*. Boulder, CO: Westview Press, 1992. 224 p.

Seeks to explain the swift changeover in the former Soviet Union. Kull bases himself on incisive interviews with Soviet leaders and published sources. He concludes that the untenable economic situation created by sixty years of Leninism forced a "new thinking" upon the upper echelons of the Soviet leadership. In turn, the "new thinking" resulted in the revolutionary changes that swept Eastern Europe between 1989 and 1991.

> # 1773. Lynch, A.: *The Cold War is over - again.*

1908. Navrozov, Lev: "The more the Kremlin changes . . ." *Midstream*, v. 37 # 8 (November, 1991): 16-20.

1909. Olcott, Martha B.: "The slide into disunion." *Current History*, v. 90 # 558 (October, 1991): 338-344.

1910. Pozner, Vladimir: *Eyewitness: a personal account of the unravelling of the Soviet Union*. New York: Random House, 1992. 240 p.

Personalized account of the failed August 1991 *coup* by a Russian journalist who now lives in the United States. Pozner, a commentator for the Soviet press and spokesman for Mikhail S. Gorbachev, has written his account of the events leading up to the collapse of the USSR. Although the book was produced hastily, Pozner's analysis remains trenchant. He includes data -- on fake military manoeuvers, for example -- that have not been reported in the American press. Interspersed in his tale of the dramatic victory are historical insights explaining the background of *perestroika* and *glasnost*.

1911. Simes, Dimitri K.: "Russia reborn." *Foreign Policy*, # 85 (Winter 1991/1992): 41-62.

1912. Sobchak, Anatoly: *The death and life of perestroika*. New York: the Free Press, 1991. 220 p.

First person narrative by the mayor of Petrograd (formerly

Leningrad) who was also one of the leaders of the Russian reform movement. Although a strong supporter of democratic reforms and opposed to Communist party rule, Sobchak did not see any utility in breaking up the Union. Instead, he advocated creation of a true federal republic, based on a multi-party system that would be responsive to the people's needs.

1913. ---: *For a new Russia: the Mayor of St. Petersburg's own story of the struggle for justice and democracy*. New York: The Free Press, 1991. 191 p.

1914. Solzhenitsyn, Aleksandr: *Rebuilding Russia: reflections and tentative proposals* (translated from Russian and annotated by Alexis Klimoff). New York: Farrar Straus and Giroux, 1991. 119 p.

1915. Sturua, Melor: "The real *coup*." *Foreign Policy* # 85 (Winter 1991/1992): 63-72.

1916. Vernikov, Andrei: "New entrants in Soviet foreign trade: behavior patterns and regulations in the transitional period." *Soviet Studies*, v. 43 # 5 (1991): 823-836.

1917. Zaprudnik, Jan: *Belarus: between East and West*. Boulder, CO: Westview Press, 1992. 224 p.

1918. Zaslavskaya, Tatyana: *The second Socialist revolution: an alternative Soviet strategy* (translated from Russian by Susan M. Davies with Jenny Warren). Bloomington: Indiana University Press, 1991. 241 p.

Proposes an alternate strategy for reforming the Soviet Union. Zaslavskaya, president of the Russian Sociological Association, proposes that a humanized Leninism cannot save the Soviet Union: only a complete reform and the establishment of a social democratic regime on the West European model can do so. Inter alia, she surveys the history of *glasnost* and *perestroika*, thus providing numerous important insights into contemporary Soviet (now Russian) issues.

# 12

# Biographies and Memoirs

## A. BIOGRAPHIES

1919. Abraham, Richard: *Alexander Kerensky: the first love of the revolution*. New York: Columbia University Press, 1987. 503 p.

Biography of the head of the provisional government that ruled Russia from March to November 1917. Half the book deals with the period of the provisional government. Abraham notes, correctly, that the government's collapse was not solely due to its own incompetence; to the contrary, Abraham defends Kerensky's actions because of the humanitarian spirit and desire for true democracy that animated most of his actions. The first work to make full use of Kerensky's personal papers, this is an authoritative but not definitive biography.

1920. Alexander, Edward: "Scharansky's secret." *Commentary*, v. 82 # 4 (October, 1986): 52-56.

1921. Andreyev, Catherine: *Vlasov and the Russian liberation movement: Soviet reality and émigré theories*. New York: Cambridge University Press, 1987. 251 p.

Political biography of Soviet General Andrei A. Vlasov. Captured by the Nazis in the early months of Operation *Barbarosa*, Vlasov eventually formed a collaborationist army of anti-Stalinist Russians under Nazi tutelage. This force, called *Komitet Osvobozhdeniya Narodov Rosii* (KONR, the Russian Liberation Movement), only entered combat in 1945, ironically against both the Red Army and the *Wehrmacht*. Andreyev places Vlasov's ideas into context and offers a vivid explanation of the developments that led to his defection. By means of careful analysis of KONR propaganda, Andreyev is also able to judge the impact of Vlasov's movement on Russian dissidents, both in and out of the Soviet Union, and thereby explain Vlasov's ultimate failure.

1922. Barber, John: "Stalin's letter to the editors of *Proletarskaya Revolutsiya*." *Soviet Studies*, v. 28 # 1 (January, 1976): 21-41.

> # 71. Barfield, R.: "Lenin's utopianism."

> # 1006. Berard-Zarzycka, E.: "Ilya Ehrenburg in Stalin's Russia."

1923. Bergman, Jay: "The political thought of Vera Zasulich." *Slavic Review*, v. 38 # 2 (June, 1979): 243-258.

1924. Biggart, John: "Kirov before the revolution." *Soviet Studies*, v. 23 # 3 (January, 1972): 345-372.

1925. Bilinsky, Yaroslav: "Shcherbytskyi, Ukraine, and Kremlin politics." *Problems of Communism*, v. 32 # 4 (July/August, 1983): 1-20.

1926. Bonner, Elena: *Mothers and daughters*. New York: Alfred A. Knopf, 1992. 349 p.

Chilling memoir of life in the Stalinist Soviet Union by the wife of dissident Andrei Sakharov. Despite the fact that her parents were Party loyalists (her father was a high-ranking official in the Comintern) they were denounced in 1937 as counter-revolutionaries and deported. Viewing the purges through the eyes of a young adult she condemns Stalin's crimes in no uncertain terms.

1927. Breslauer, George W.: "Evaluating Gorbachev as a leader." *Soviet Economy*, v. 5 # 4 (October/December, 1989): 299-340.

> # 691. Buchanan, H. R.: "Lenin and Bukharin."

1928. Bullock, Allen: *Hitler and Stalin: parallel lives*. London: Harper Collins, 1991. 1189 p.

Dual biography of two of the twentieth century's greatest tyrants. Adopts the somewhat dubious approach of alternating chapters on each of his subjects in strictly chronological order. Despite the pitfalls of such a format, Bullock succeeds portraying the two men in their proper historical context.

1929. Burlatsky, Fedor: *Khrushchev and the first Russian spring* (translated from Russian by Daphne Skillen). New York: Charles Scribner's Sons, 1992. 286 p.

Intimate portrait of the Khrushchev thaw, by the Soviet premier's private secretary and speech writer. Begins with the anti-Stalinist secret speech that Khrushchev delivered at the Twentieth Communist Party Congress in 1956. For the next five years Khrushchev steered the Soviet Union into a reformist trend. Burlatsky views the Khrushchev thaw as a precursor to *glasnost*. After 1961, however, Khrushchev moved away from freedom, and in 1964 Khrushchev was himself removed signaling, the return of Stalinism.

1930. Butson, Thomas G.: *The Tsar's lieutenant: the Soviet marshal*. New York: Praeger, 1984. 281 p.

Biography of Soviet Field Marshal Mikhail N. Tukhachevsky. Begins with Tukhachevsky's career in World War I when he returned from imprisonment in Germany. Tukhachevsky, who had joined the Red Army in 1918, began a steady rise to prominence. By the late 1920s he was its most prominent officer, ascending to the position of marshal of the Soviet Union in 1935. Unlike his slow rise to army leadership, Tukhachevsky's fall was rapid and spectacular. Accused in 1937 of collaboration with Nazi Germany in a planned counter-revolution, Tukhachevsky was the first victim of Stalin's military purges.

1931. Carmichael, Joel: *Trotsky: an appreciation of his life*. New

York: St. Martin's Press, 1975. 398 p.

Political biography of Leon Trotsky, one of the fathers of the Soviet Union. Begins with a description of Trotsky as a young adult and procedes through his career as Menshevik activist, his conversion to bolshevism, and his raising of the Red Army in 1918. Carefully and objectively evaluates the good and bad aspects of Trotsky's career from the Revolution until his removal from the Communist party. Thereafter, Carmichael descibes Stalin's slow but steady destruction of Trotsky's supporters and the global effort to kill the arch-devil created by Communist party propaganda.

1932. Cohen, Stephen F.: *Bukharin and the Bolshevik revolution: a political biography, 1888-1938*. New York: Oxford University Press, 1980. 512 p. [PB]

Political biography of one of the best-known "old" Bolsheviks who was tried in a very public show-trial and executed in 1938. Cohen presents Bukharin as a realistic alternative to totalitarianism that brought Russia to the verge of economic ruin, especially since Bukharin never behaved in as ruthless a manner as Stalin. Inter alia, Cohen reviews the history of the CPSU during the 1920s and 1930s. The Oxford edition includes an introduction that places Bukharin's brand of socialism into the context of *perestroika*.

1933. Crankshaw, Edward: *Khrushchev, a career*. New York: Viking Press, 1966. 311 p.

> # 722. Day, R. B.: *Leon Trotsky*.

> # 692. ---: "Preobrazhensky and the theory of transition period."

1934. Deutscher, Isaac: *The prophet armed: Trotsky, 1871-1921*. New York: Oxford University Press, 1954. 540 p.

1934a. ---: *The prophet unarmed, 1921-1929* (volume 2). New York: Oxford University Press, 1959. 400 p.

1934b. ---: *The prophet outcast, 1929-1940* (volume 3). New York: Oxford University Press, 1963. 543 p.

Massive three volume biography on the life and political career of Lev Trotsky (1879-1940).

1935. Djilas, Milovan: *Conversations with Stalin* (translated from Serbo-Croat by Michael B. Petrovich). New York: Harcourt, Brace & World, 1962. 211 p.

Text of conversations with the Soviet leader by a Yugoslav diplomat, who later broke with Tito and became Yugoslavia's most prominent dissident.

1936. Dunn, David: "Maksim Litvinov: commissar of contradictions." *Journal of Contemporary History*, v. 23 # 2 (April, 1988): 221-243.

> # 693. Duval, C.: "Yakov M. Sverdlov."

1937. Ebon, Martin: *Malenkov, Stalin's successor*. New York: McGraw-Hill, 1953. 384 p.

1938. Elwood, Ralph C.: *Roman Malinovsky: a life without cause*. Newtonville, MA: Oriental Research Partners, 1977. 107 p.

Brief but interesting biography of a Bolshevik activist accused of being a Tsarist government agent and executed after the Bolshevik revolution. Sheds some light on the Tsarist *Okhrana* (secret police) and on the early Soviet Union.

1939. ---: "Trotsky's questionaire." *Slavic Review*, v. 29 # 2 (June, 1970): 296-301.

1940. Gilbert, Martin: *Shcharansky: hero of our time*. New York: Viking Press, 1986. 467 p.

First full length biography of the best-known Jewish dissident working for emigration from the Soviet Union. Written in a scholarly format, the book still retains a polemical element: to prove the utter falsehood of accusations of treason that ended in Anatoly (Nathan) Shcharansky's trial and thirteen years of imprisonment. Despite the polemical element, Gilbert helps put

Shcharansky's life into context and it is a fitting tribute to the dissidents who created the democratic movement in the 1980s and early 1990s.

> # 538. Goldberg, A.: *Ilya Ehrenburg.*

1941. Goldhagen, Erich: "The ideological beliefs of Mikhail Gorbachev." *Midstream*, v. 36 # 2 (February/March, 1990): 3-9.

1942. Hayes, Nicholas: "Kazem-Bek and the Young Russians' revolution." *Slavic Review*, v. 39 # 2 (June, 1980): 255-268.

Aleksandr L. Kazem-Bek was the leader of the quasi-Fascist *Mladorossy* party in Germany during the 1920s. He was among the first to identify Stalin's national bolshevism and equated Stalinism with fascism.

1943. Hobson, Christopher Z. and Ronald D. Tabor: *Trotskyism and the dilemma of socialism.* Westport, CT: Greenwood Press, 1988. 551 p.

Detailed investigation of Leon Trotsky's political philosophy, including an extensive critique of some of Trotsky's key ideas. Hobson and Tabor include the history of Trotskyist groups throughout the world in their review, thus permitting them a balanced evaluation of Trotsky's contribution to the history of socialism. In addition, the authors compare Trotsky's critique of the Soviet Union with the historical reality during the 1920s and 1930s. Despite the wealth of material they cover, Hobson and Tabor have managed to avoid the pitfalls of redundancy and thus add an important component to the study of Soviet history.

> # 1124. Hough, J. F.: "The man and the system."

1944. Knight, Amy: "Beria and the cult of Stalin: rewriting Transcaucasian Party history." *Soviet Studies*, v. 43 # 4 (1991): 749-764.

1945. Laqueur, Walter: *Stalin: the glasnost revelations.* New York: Charles Scribner's Sons, 1990. 382 p.

Political biography of Joseph Stalin, based on material published in the Soviet Union since 1987. Stalin's life story is told in a brief chapter. The remainder of the book details specific aspects of his career within the context of Soviet Union's history. Among the topics covered are the collectivization scheme, the purges of the 1930s, the war years, and Stalin's infusion of nationalism into the Soviet system. A concluding chapter summarizes Stalin's importance during the last forty years of Soviet history.

1946. Lee, Eric: "A mole who vaulted to the top." *Military History*, v. 3 # 5 (April, 1987): 8, 66-68.

Investigates Stalin's early career, including accusations that he acted as a double agent for the Tsarist secret police, *Okhrana*.

1947. *Lenin: his life and work*. Moscow: Novosti Press Agency Publishing House, n.d., n.p.

A rare pictorial review.

1948. Levkov, Ilya: "USSR v. A. Shcharansky." *Midstream*, v. 24 # 5 (May, 1978): 24-34.

Documents regarding Shcharansky's trial for treason.

1949. Lichtheim, George: "Reflections on Trotsky." *Commentary*, v. 37 # 1 (January, 1964): 52-60.

1950. Loe, Mary: "Maksim Gorkii and the *Sreda* Circle: 1899-1905." *Slavic Review*, v. 44 # 1 (Spring, 1985): 49-66.

1951. Markish, Simon: "The example of Isaac Babel." *Commentary*, v. 64 # 5 (November, 1977): 36-45.

1952. ---: "A Russian writer's Jewish fate." *Commentary*, v. 81 # 4 (April, 1986): 39-47.

On Vasily Grossman.

1953. McNeal, Robert H.: *Bride of the revolution: Krupskaya and*

*Lenin*. Ann Arbor: University of Michigan Press, 1972. 326 p.

Biographical study of Lenin's wife, Nadezhda Krupskaya. Argues that their courtship and marriage was more a "revolutionary merger" than a love affair, although the two were devoted to one another.

1954. Medvedev, Roy: *All Stalin's men* (translated from Russian by Harold Shukman). Garden City, NY: Anchor Press/Doubleday, 1984. 184 p.

Biographical study of six of Stalin's bloodiest henchmen. Each of the sketches is brief and to the point, with Medvedev showing how each of his subjects behaved during the Terror and thereafter. Ignoring whatever personal feelings they may have had, all six sycophants carried out Stalin's orders without question. This especially held true of Mikhail Suslov, Stalin's chief ideologist: he had to continually justify Stalin's changing policies in light of Marxism-Leninism-Stalinism. Offering a glimpse into Stalin's inner circle, Medvedev provides a keen insight into the totalitarian personality as well.

1955. Morrison, John: *Boris Yeltsin: from Bolshevik to democrat*. New York: Dutton, 1991. 303 p.

1956. Murphy, Paul J.: *Brezhnev: Soviet politician*. Jefferson, NC: McFarland Press, 1981. 373 p.

Journalistic biography of Soviet Communist party leader Leonid Brezhnev. Despite the lack of firm documentation, Murphy carefully pieces together the available evidence to describe Brezhnev's career. Murphy concludes that Brezhnev was a manipulator who sought power, rather than an ideologue seeking to impose a vision on the Communist party.

1957. Navrozov, Lev: "Stalin under Western eyes." *Commentary*, v. 57 # 4 (April, 1974): 66-70.

Review essay on Adam B. Ulam's *Stalin: the man and his era* (see # 1980) and other biographies.

> # 375. Nedava, J.: *Trotsky and the Jews.*

1958. Nove, Alec: "New light on Trotsky's economic views." *Slavic Review*, v. 40 # 1 (Spring, 1981): 84-97.

1959. Oppenheim, Samuel A.: "Between left and right: G. Ia. Sokolnikov and the development of the Soviet state, 1921-1929." *Slavic Review*, v. 48 # 4 (Winter, 1989): 592-613.

Grigory Sokolnikov was first finance minister of the USSR

1960. ---: "The making of a right communist -- A. I. Rykov to 1917." *Slavic Review*, v. 36 # 3 (September, 1977): 420-440.

Biography of Aleksei Ivanovich Rykov, Lenin's interior minister and a supporter of Nikolai Bukharin "right" faction.

1961. Page, W.: "Lenin: prophet of world revolution from the East." *Russian Review*, v. 11 # 2 (April, 1952): 67-77.

1962. Pawel, Ernst: "Karl Radek: a forgotten pillar of bolshevism." *Midstream*, v. 18 # 5 (May, 1972): 33-45.

1963. Phillips, Hugh: "From a Bolshevik to a British subject: the early years of Maksim M. Litvinov." *Slavic Review*, v. 48 # 3 (Fall, 1989): 388-398.

1964. Remington, Thomas F.: "Varga and the foundation of Soviet planning." *Soviet Studies*, v. 34 # 4 (October, 1982): 585-600.

Evgeny Varga served as head of the USSR Academy of Sciences Institute for World Economics until he was purged for anti-Stalinist deviations in 1947.

1965. Rigby, T. H.: "Was Stalin a disloyal patron?" *Soviet Studies*, v. 38 # 3 (July, 1986): 311-324.

1966. Ruble, Blair A.: "Romanov's Leningrad." *Problems of Communism*, v. 32 # 6 (November/December, 1983); 36-48.

Brief biographical sketch of Grigoriy Romanov, the First Secretary of the Leningrad *Oblast* Communist Party Committee from 1970 to the Summer of 1983. Highlights Romanov's new role as Secretary of the CPSU Central Committee in Moscow.

> # 824. Salter, J.: "N. I. Bukharin and the market question."

1967. Schapiro, Leonard: "Was Lenin necessary?" *Commentary*, v. 38 # 6 (December, 1964): 57-60.

1968. --- and Peter Reddaway (eds.): *Lenin: the man, the theorist, the leader -- a reappraisal*. Boulder, CO: Westview Press, 1987. 317 p.

Anthology marking the fiftieth anniversary of the Bolshevik takeover in Russia, reprinted for the seventieth anniversary. The contributors concentrate on Lenin, using him -- as well as their assessment of his personality and his tactics -- as a means to understand the Bolshevik Revolution. The contributions thus synthesize Lenin's biography with an understanding of the revolution placing early Soviet history into an important methodological context.

CONTENTS: L. Schapiro: Lenin after fifty years / V. S. Frank: Lenin and the Russian intelligentsia / P. Reddaway: Literature, the arts, and the personality of Lenin / G. Katkov: Lenin as philosopher / J. C. Rees: Lenin and Marxism / B. R. Bociurkiw: Lenin and religion / J. Keep: Lenin as tactician / J. Erickson: Lenin as Civil War leader / A. Nove: Lenin as economist / H. Willetts: Lenin and the peasants / I. Lapenna: Lenin, law, and legality / M. Holdsworth: Lenin and the nationalities question.

1969. Schechter, Gerrold L. and Peter S. Deriabin: *The spy who saved the world*. New York: Scribner's, 1992. 430 p.

Biography of Colonel Oleg Penkovsky, the highest ranking KGB officer ever to turn double agent for the CIA. Penkovsky offered his service to the Americans in 1961. His information thus came at a crucial time in U.S.-Soviet relations and the authors claim that the American success during the Cuban Missile Crisis may be attributed to Penkovsky. In 1962, however, KGB counter-intelligence exposed Penkowsky and executed him. The authors have made use of considerable new documentation to reconstruct Penkovsky's career and his impact.

> # 756. Scherr, B.: "Notes on literary life in Petrograd."

> # 124. Senese, D.: "S. M. Kravchinski."

1970. Shub, David: *Lenin: a biography*. Harmondsworth, UK: Pelican Books, 1966. 496 p. [PB]

Political biography of the father of the Soviet Union, part of a series on modern political leaders. Views Lenin in the context of both Russian history and Socialist ideology. Shub writes from the perspective of the Mensheviks, although he is not vicious in evaluating Lenin. He does not deny that Lenin created a dictatorship and posits that Lenin set the stage for Stalin's Terror. The last chapter offers an in-depth analysis of Lenin's political testament. An appendix offers citations from Lenin's writings, providing an overview of the political thought that created the Soviet Union.

1971. ---: "New light on Lenin." *Russian Review*, v. 11 # 3 (July, 1952): 131-137.

1972. Sicher, Efraim: "The 'Jewish Cossack': Isaac Babel in the first Red Cavalry." *Studies of Contemporary Jewry*, v. 4 (1988): 113-134.

1973. Souvarine, Boris: *Stalin: a critical survey of bolshevism*. New York: Longmans, Green & Co., 1939. 690 p.

Sympathetic biography of Stalin, written by one of the founders of the Parti Communiste Francaise (the French Communist Party). Also surveys the theory and practice of communism from its Soviet inception in 1917 onward.

1974. Stalin, Josef: "Lenin." *Labour Monthly*, v. 16 # 1 (January, 1934): 25-31.

Text of speech delivered by Stalin at the Military School in the

Kremlin, on January 18, 1924.

1975. Teller, Judd L.: "Portrait of a Soviet Zionist." *Commentary*, v. 54 # 1 (July, 1972): 56-61.

1976. Toynbee, Arnold: "A centenary view of Lenin." *International Affairs*, v. 46 # 3 (July, 1970): 490-500.

1977. Tucker, Robert C.: *Stalin as revolutionary, 1879-1929: a study in history and personality*. New York: W. W. Norton, 1973. 519 p.

Analytical biography of Stalin, covering the period from his birth to his ascendence to power in the Soviet Union. Primarily focused on Stalin's personality and his ideological orientation. Tucker bases himself on a careful analysis of Stalin's writings in addition to the works of those close to Stalin.

1978. ---: *Stalin in power: the revolution from above, 1928-1941*. New York: W. W. Norton, 1990. 707 p.

Biography of Joseph Stalin, following up on some of the ideas in Tucker's *Stalin as revolutionary* (see # 1977). In this volume, Tucker concentrates on Stalin's "revolution from above" as exemplified by the collectivization campaign. Tucker explains Stalin's motivations as primarily personal -- a lust for power and for self-agrandizement that would offer him both fame and glory. Ends with the German invasion of the USSR in June 1941 -- Tucker views Stalin's performance as war leader as nothing less than disastrous. Although based on an extensive bibliography, Tucker has not made as much use as possible of sources published after 1985.

1979. Tumarkin, Nina: *Lenin Lives! the Lenin cult in Soviet Russia*. Cambridge, MA: Harvard University Press, 1983. 315 p.

Compares the realities of Lenin's life and career with the 1960s revival of a personality cult regarding the first Bolshevik leader of the USSR. The original Lenin cult existed from 1924 to 1933; this secular worship resulted in Lenin's mummification but was later eclipsed by the Stalin cult. After Stalin, however, Communist authorities returned Lenin to a near divine status: partly to justify de-Stalinization and partly to give themselves some semblance of legitimacy in popular eyes.

1980. Ulam, Adam B.: *Stalin: the man and his era*. New York: Viking Press, 1973. 760 p.

Classic political biography of Stalin. Attempts to place Stalin into a specific period, thus explaining how he came to power and how he shaped the Soviet Union. Studiously avoids attempts to psychoanalyze Stalin, though Ulam notes the dictator's growing paranoia in the late 1950s. In his chapters on the 1930s and 1940s, Ulam concentrates on foreign policy issues, with less attention focused on the purges and economic affairs. The only lacuna to Ulam's work is that it lacks an analysis of Stalin's ideology.

1981. Von Laue, Theodore H.: "Stalin in focus." *Slavic Review*, v. 42 # 3 (Fall, 1983); 373-389.

1982. Wesson, Robert G.: "Brezhnev's year: politics in the USSR." *Current History*, v. 73 # 430 (October, 1977): 109-111, 132-133.

1983. White, James D.: "Chinese studies of Bukharin." *Soviet Studies*, v. 43 # 4 (1991): 733-748.

1984. Wistrich, Robert S.: "Leon Trotsky's theory of fascism." *Journal of Contemporary History*, v. 11 # 4 (October, 1976): 157-184.

1985. ---: *Trotsky: the fate of a revolutionary*. London: Rowman and Littlefield, 1980. 235 p.

Comprehensive biography capturing the essence of Trotsky's theoretical viewpoints on communism and his political accomplishments for it. Although reduced to an "un-person" in Stalinist Russia, Trotsky played an important role in organizing the Red Army during the Civil War. Thereafter, he became one of Lenin's right hand men. Defeated by Stalin, Trotsky was murdered by NKVD assassins in Mexico in August 1940. Within the biographical framework, Wistrich pays particularly careful attention to Trotsky's ideology. Contrary to the apologist conclusions, Wistrich has discovered many links between Trotsky's ideas and the brutal totalitarianism Stalin created: the militarization of labor, the suppression of dissent, and the theory of "permanent revolution" used to justify a variety of internal and external activities by the Communist party. Since Lenin knew about, and approved, all of Trotsky's actions, it is clear to Wistrich that Stalin's terror developed out of a bolshevik milieu, not in opposition to it.

1986. Wittlin, Thaddeus: *Commissar: the life and death of Lavrenty Pavlovich Beria*. New York: Macmillan Publishing, 1972. 566 p.

Critical biography of Stalin's chief henchman Lavrenty Beria, primarily focusing on the period 1945-1953. Also details Beria's role in the Kirov murder and the great blood purges of the 1930s. Based on extensive citations from the writings of Soviet defectors, the book is somewhat under documented. Wittlin still manages to portray Beria as a monster in all of the implications of that word.

1987. Wolfe, Bertram D.: *Three who made a revolution: a biographical history* (fourth edition). New York: Dial Press, 1948. 661 p.

> # 1586. Zemstov, I.: *Gorbachev: the man and the system*.

## B. MEMOIRS

1988. Agursky, Mikhail: "'God' is dead!" *Midstream*, v. 31 # 1 (January, 1985): 38-41.

Memoir of the events that transpired in Moscow during the weeks preceeding and immediately following Stalin's death.

1989. Akhmedov, Ismail: *In and out of Stalin's GRU: a Tatar's escape from Red Army intelligence*. Frederick, MD: University Publications of America, 1984. 232 p.

Memoir of a Tatar GRU (*Glavnoye Razvedyvatelnoye Upravleniye*, Military Intelligence) agent who defected to the West in 1942. Provides numerous important details regarding the history of Russian military intelligence operations in the late 1930s and early

1940s. This is a story that has not often been told and it offers an important insight into GRU activities.

1990. Akselrod, Yulia: "Why my grandfather Leon Trotsky must be turning in his grave." *Commentary*, v. 87 # 4 (April, 1989): 39-43.

Reflective memoir by Leon Trotsky's granddaughter: her son, a staunch Revionist-Zionist lives in Hebron and is a reserves officer in the Israel Defense Forces.

1991. Amalrik, Andre: *Involuntary journey to Siberia* (translated from Russian by Manya Harari and Max Hayward). New York: Harcourt, Brace, Jovanovich, 1970. 297 p.

Memoir of life in the *gulag* by one of the Soviet Union's leading dissidents. Offers a revealing look at the miscarriage of justice in the USSR, including the outlandishly severe punishments meted out for minor offenses and the continuing punishment of "offenders" even after their prison terms had ended.

1992. Azbel, Mark: *Trapped in the Soviet Union* (translated from the Russian and edited by Grace P. Forbes). Boston: Houghton Mifflin, 1981. 513 p.

Memoir of a Soviet Jewish *refusenik* who requested permission to leave the Soviet Union in 1972. Offers a glimpse into the life of Jews who could no longer remain in the Soviet Union but who -- since they were not permitted to emigrate -- had no place to live: they literally existed in limbo.

1993. Berger, Joseph: *Shipwreck of a generation: the memoirs of Joseph Berger*. London: Harvill, 1971. 286 p.

1994. Butman, Hillel: *From Leningrad to Jerusalem: the gulag way* (translated from Russian by Stefani Hoffman). Berkeley, CA: Benmir Books, 1990. 320 p.

Memoir of the 1970 attempt to gain free emigration for Soviet Jewry by an aborted effort to skyjack an Aeroflot airliner. Butman was a police investigator who was fired in 1960 for Zionist activities. Thereafter he -- and other members of the Leningrad Zionist underground -- planned the desperate skyjacking to focus attention on the plight of Soviet Jewry. Foiled by the KGB, a Soviet court gave harsh sentences to all the plotters. Massive protests throughout the world in response to this action led to the Soviets opening emigration during the remainder of the decade. Butman himself left the USSR in 1979 and settled in Jerusalem.

> # 972. Cholawski, S.: *Soldiers from the ghetto.*

1995. Eberstadt, Fernanda: "Siberian holiday." *Commentary*, v. 77 # 2 (February, 1984): 37-46.

1996. Harper, Samuel N.: *The Russia I believe in: the memoirs of Samuel Northrup Harper, 1902-1941* (ed. by Paul V. Harper). Chicago: Chicago University Press, 1945. 278 p.

1997. Kuzichkin, Vladimir: *Inside the KGB: my life in Soviet espionage* (translated from Russian by Thomas B. Beattie). New York: Pantheon Books, 1990. 406 p.

Memoir of a KGB resident (agent) in Teheran from 1977 until his defection in 1982. Offers an important corrective to those who attributed an almost super-human efficiency to the KGB, noting the agency's near constant infighting and partisanship.

1998. Kopelev, Lev: *The education of a true believer.* London: Wildwood House, 1981. 328 p.

Memoir by a Russian Jewish dissident who began his public career as a Communist official. Kopelev took part in the brutal *kolkhozization* program of the early 1930s. Describes his personal experience within a historical context. In the post-Stalin era Kopelev came to doubt communism, and in 1977 he was expelled from the Communist party. Of special interest is Kopelev's discussion of the nationalities problem. Although he identifies himself as Jewish he also denies any feeling of connectedness to Jewry in either the religious or nationalist sense. His rejection of emigration reflects the orientation of a serious portion of Soviet Jewry in the late 1970s, but appears in subsequent years to be a minority opinion.

1999. Krivitsky, Walter: *In Stalin's secret service: an exposé of Russia's secret policies by the former chief of the Soviet intelligence in Western Europe* (preface by William J. Hood). Frederick, MD: University Publications of America, 1985. 273 p.

Reprinted edition of Krivitsky's memoirs of service in the GRU, originally published in 1939. Krivitsky, a Ukrainian Jewish Communist, defected to the West in 1938 because of his qualms regarding the Stalinist purges. Initially Krivitsky sought asylum in the United States, but he later agreed to help British intelligence, thereby signing his own death warrant. Exposed by a Soviet mole, he was found murdered in Washington, DC in 1940. Krivitsky's book is based on his testimony at the Dies Committee (The House Unamerican Activities Committee) and created a major stir when first published.

2000. Levchenko, Stanislav: *On the worng side: my life in the KGB*. Washington, DC: Pergamon, 1988. 244 p.

Levchenko was a senior KGB officer in Washington who defected to the U.S. in 1979.

2001. Lvov, Arkady: "To my son -- on leaving Russia." (translated from Russian by Gloria D. Sosin). *Midstream*, v. 26 # 7 (August/September, 1980): 42-47.

2002. Marchenko, Anatoly: *My testimony* (translated from Russian by Michael Scammell). New York: E. P. Dutton, 1969. 415 p.

Memoir of life in the post-Stalinist *gulags*. Marchenko notes that while the number of prisoners has declined, brutality in the camps has increased. Four types of prisoners are now incarcerated in the *gulag*: reform-minded intellectuals associated with the human rights movement, nationalists seeking the secession of their homelands, religious activists, and common criminals.

2003. Markish, Esther: *The long return* (translated from French by D. J. Goldstein). New York: Ballantine Books, 1978. 293 p.

Memoir by the wife of Peretz Markish, the writer and leader of the Jewish Anti-Fascist Committee who was shot at Stalin's orders on August 12, 1952. More than just her life story, Markish offers a microcosm of Russian Jewish history since 1917.

2004. Navrozov, Lev: "Getting out of Russia." *Commentary*, v. 54 # 4 (October, 1972): 45-53.

2005. Nudel, Ida: *A hand in the darkness: the autobiography of a Refusenik* (translated from Russian by Stefani Hoffman). New York: Warner Books, 1990. 314 p.

Personal story of the woman popularly known as the "guardian angel of the prisoners of conscience." Nudel fought with the Soviet authorities for sixteen years to finaly be allowed to emigrate. During that time, Nudel had to endure harassment by the KGB, an assassination attempt, and exile in Siberia. A moving account of courage, *A hand in the darkness* also provides an intimate portrait of the Jewish *samizdat*.

2006. Penkovsky, Oleg: *The Penkovsky papers* (ed. by Frank Gibney, translated from Russian by P. Deriabin). Garden City, NY: Doubleday, 1965. 412 p.

Deals with the trial of Colonel Oleg Penkovsky, the highest ranking KGB officer to defect to the West. Penkovsky was caught, tried, and executed in 1963. Although the case remains unclear, and the partial transcript of the trial presented in the book hides as much as it reveals, enough interesting material is provided in the included translation of Penkovsky's diary to intrigue all readers.

2007. Ratushinskaya, Irina: "En-route to the *gulag*." *Commentary*, v. 86 # 3 (September, 1988); 35-40.

Memoir of a clebrated Russian poetess arrested and sent to a *gulag* in 1982.

2008. Rosenberg, Suzanne: *A Soviet odyssey*. New York: Oxford University Press, 1988. 212 p.

Memoir by one of only a few women inmates of the Stalinist *gulags* to survive. Despite the ardent bolshevism of her parents and husband, Rosenberg found herself caught up in the purges and was sentenced to five years hard labor because she refused to inform on other family members to the secret police.

2009. Shcharansky, Natan: *Fear no evil: an exhilirating memoir of courage* (Translated from Russian by Stefani Hoffman). New York: Random House, 1988. 437 p.

Memoir of Russian Jewry's best known dissident. Sharansky begins by noting his early, priviledged life as a child prodigy and computer scientist. The Six-day War awakened Sharansky's Jewish identity. Zionism eventually brought Sharansky to Judaism and by the mid-1970s he, his wife Avital, and other Jewish activists had begun a courageous campaign to open the gates of emigration. In 1978 Sharansky was unjustly accused of espionage and was sentenced to thirteen years of hard labor in a Siberian *gulag*. After a massive international campaign, he was freed and allowed to emigrate to Israel in 1986.

2010. Shcharansky, Avital with Ilana Ben-Joseph: *Next year in Jerusalem*. New York: William Morrow, 1979. 189 p.

Emphatic insider's account of Natan Shcharansky's struggle for Jewish emigration, written by his wife. Though the book is not a piece of scholarship, it does provide very important insights into the Shcharanskys activities and Natan's 1978 trial for treason.

2011. Shevchenko, Arkady N.: *Breaking with Moscow*. New York: Alfred A. Knopf, 1985. 378 p.

Controversial memoir by a high ranking Soviet defector. The controversy derives precisely from Sevchenko's defection to the West and his later re-defection to the Soviet Union. Scholars have questioned whether his revelations were real or were part of a policy of willful disinformation concocted by the KGB.

2012. Skrjabina, E.: *Siege and survival: the odyssey of a Leningrader*. Carbondale: Southern Illinois University Press, 1971. 174 p.

Diary and memoir of the 900 day siege of Leningrad by German and Finnish forces during World War II by a survivor of the heroic ordeal.

2013. Talbott, Strobe (ed.): *Khrushchev Remembers*. Boston: Little, Brown & Co., 1970. 639 p.

Memoir by the former Soviet premier, written after he was removed from office in 1964. Central to the memoir is Khrushchev's discussion of the purges of the 1930s. Although many of the sections are clearly disengenuous -- for example, the frequent references to Stalin's antisemitism while Khrushchev repeatedly insists that "Jews be kept in their place" -- the memoir still offers numerous previously unkown insights into Soviet politics.

2014. Trotsky, Leon: *My life: an attempt at an autobiography*. New York: Scribner's / London: Butterworth, 1930. 512 p.

Autobiographical investigation of Russian communism. Although Trotsky concentrates on his personal story, he uses his life as a case study of a Russian revolutionary. Trotsky is especially bitter in his condemnation of Stalin.

2015. Yeremenko, A. I.: *The Arduous beginning* (translated from Russian by Vic Schneierson). Moscow: Progress Publishers, 1966. 329 p.

Somewhat tendentious memoir of Stalin's main field commander in the early part of the Great Patriotic War. Yeremenko magnified his own importance while attempting to place blame for the Red Army's initial failure to stem the Nazi *blitz* on others.

2016. Zhukov, Georgii K.: *The Memoirs of Marshal Zhukov*. New York: Delacorte Press, 1971. 703 p.

Memoirs of the Soviet "general who never lost a battle." Although Zhukov mainly concentrates on defending his and Stalin's reputation against Soviet and Western critics, nevertheless, he also offers important details on the planning that went into the Soviet victory over Nazi Germany on the Eastern Front during World War II.

# Glossary

AEROFLOT: The Soviet National Airlines.

ANONIMKA: Anonymous complaints about the quality of life in the Soviet Union.

ANSCHLUSS: The unification of Austria with Germany that occured on March 13, 1938.

APPARATCHIK(I): Member(s) of the Communist party bureaucracy.

BARBAROSSA, OPERATION: Code name for the German invasion of the Soviet Union on June 22, 1941.

BASMACHI: "Bandits," Soviet term for the Central Asian Muslims who rebelled between 1918 and 1924.

BLACK HUNDREDS: Colloquial name for the Soyuz Russkogo Narodna [Union of the Russian People], a radical right-wing antisemitic party in Tsarist Russia, founded November 1905.

BOLSHEVIK(S): Early name for the Communist party or its members.

BUND: General Jewish Workers Union of Lithuania, Poland, and Russia; Jewish Socialist-nationalist party founded October 7, 1897.

BYULLETEN OPPOSZITSII: Opposition Bulletin; Russian language newspaper published by pro-Trotsky communists in Paris during the 1920s.

CEMA: Council for Mutual Economic Assistance [also abbreviated COMECON]; agency founded in 1949 to coordinate economic activity in the Communist bloc.

CHEKA: Vserossiyskaya Chrezvychaynaya Komissiya po bor'be s Kontrrevolyutsiyey i sabotazhem, All Russian Extraordinary Commission to Combat Counterrevolution and Sabotage; secret police agency established by Lenin in 1917.

COMINFORM: Communist Information Bureau, established in 1947 and disbanded in 1959.

COMINTERN: Communist International, semi-secret agency for the spread of communism founded by Lenin in 1918 and disbanded on Stalin's orders in 1943.

CPSU: Communist Party Soviet Union.

DECEMBRIST(S): Supporter(s) of the failed December 1825 revolution.

DER STÜRMER: Nazi weekly published by Julius Streicher.

DESEDA CIRCLE: Movement for constitional reform in late Tsarist Russia.

DUMA: Parliament established by Tsarist decree in 1905 but which had no real powers.

EDIONACHALIE: Single person management.

EINSATZGRUPPEN: Mobile killing groups comprised of SS personnel tasked with carrying out the Final Solution in occupied

Soviet territories.

EMES: Yiddish language edition of PRAVDA.

GLASNOST: "Openness," an element of Mikhial S. Gorbachev's ideology emphasizing individual responsibility within the Soviet state.

GLAVISKUSSTVO: CPSU Artistic Department in the 1920s

GPU: Gosudarstvennoye Politicheskoye Upravleniye, Main political Directorate of the Army and Navy; security and police service that replaced CHEKA and was later incorporated into the NKVD.

GREAT PATRIOTIC WAR: Term used by the Soviets to designate the Second World War.

GRU: Glavnoye Razvedyvatelnoye Upravleniye, Main Intelligence Directorate of the General Staff; Soviet military intelligence during World War II.

GULAG(S): State security prison system; Soviet term for concentration camp(s) usually located in the vast expanses of Siberia.

HASIDISM: Jewish mystical-pietistic religious movement arising in eighteenth century Eastern Europe.

HASKALAH: Movement for Jewish enlightenment originating in Germany during the eighteenth century.

IZVESTIYA: The Soviet government's official daily newspaper.

JUDENRAT/JUDENRÄTE: Nazi-imposed Jewish community council(s) in Eastern Europe.

KADET(S): Constitutional Democratic party; anti-Marxist, middle-class Russian party that advocated the creation of a constitutional monarchy in Russia.

KAHAL/KEHILLAS: The organized Jewish community, or the council running the community, closed down on Stalin's orders, or decimated by the Nazis.

KARAITE(S): Sectarian Jews (classified by the Nazis as Aryans, and thus spared extermination), largely living in areas of the Soviet Union.

KOLKHOZ(ES): State collective farm(s).

KGB: Komitet Gosudarstvennoi Bezopasnosti, Committee for State Security; secret police agency that replaced the NKVD in 1954.

KOMITET NARODNOGO KONTROLIA: [KNK] CPSU Central Control Commission and Workers' and Peasants' Inspecorate, established by Lenin in 1923.

KOMMANDOSTAB: Special command staff, generally of the SS.

KOMSOMOL: Kommunisticheskii Soyuz Molodozhi, the CPSU youth movement.

KONTROLERY: Early Bolshevik Control Commissions, later organized into the govermental offices of the Soviet Union.

KOUMINTANG: The Nationalist Chinese movement led by Generalissimo Chiang Kai-Shek

KPD: Kommunistche Partei deutschlands, the German Communist Party.

KULAKS: Wealthy farmers owning private estates and employing seasonal laborers. The Kulaks' lands were seized by Lenin after the Bolshevik *putsch*.

MENSHEVIKS: Russian Social Democrats; Marxists who opposed Lenin and the Bolsheviks before 1917.

MGB: Ministerstvo Gosudarstvennoye Bezopasnosti, Ministry of State Security; Soviet secret police agency active from 1946 to 1954.

MLADOROSSY: Young Russians, a quais-fascist party founded by Russian émigrés in Germany in the 1920s.

MUJAHIDEEN: Muslin Guerrillas operating against the Soviets in Afghanistan.

MULLAH(S): Honorific title given to Muslim religious leader(s).

NARODNIKI: "Populists," Russian terrorist group active during the 1870s and 1880s seeking to change the Tsarist system by a policy of selective assassination.

NATO: North Atlantic Treaty Organization; defensive alliance founded by the U.S. and its West European allies in 1949.

NKVD: Narodnyy Komissariat Vnutrennikh Del, People's Commissariat for Internal Affairs; Soviet secret police agency operational between 1934 and 1943. From 1943 to 1946 the NKVD operated as the NKGB.

NOMENKLATURA: "Classification," the list of hierarchical positioning within the Soviet bureaucracy.

NOVY MIR: Permitted opposition journal published by the Union of Soviet writers until closed down by the Brezhnev government in 1970.

OBLAST: Region or Province of the USSR.

OBSHCHINA: Village administrative council in Tsarist Russia.

OCTOBRISTS: Adherents of the October 17, 1905 Manifesto which promised democratic reforms in the Russian empire.

OGAS: State System for the Collecting and Processing Information for Reporting, Planning, and Management of the National Economy.

OGONYOK: Popular weekly published by PRAVDA.

OGPU: Obyedinennoy Gosudarstvennoye Politichskoye Upravleniye, Unified State Political Directorate; secret police agency that replaced CHEKA in 1923.

OKHRANA: Tsarist secret police force created in 1881.

OSOAVIAKHIM: Society of Friends of Defense and Aviation-Chemical Construction; voluntary para-military defense organization founded in 1927.

PAMYAT: Russian antisemitic organization, founded in the mid-1980s.

PERESTROIKA: "Restructuring," the element of Gorbachev's ideology emphasizing the need to reform the Communist party and the USSR.

POCHVENNICHESTVO: Native Soil movement, an off-shoot of the NARODNIKI.

POLITBURO: Politicheskoye Buro; the primary political executive committee of the Communist party.

POMESHCHIKI: Kulaks who continued to reside on their own land as squatters after Lenin nationalized their lands.

PRAGUE SPRING: Common name for the Czechoslovakian reform movement led by Anton Dubcek in 1968.

PRAVDA: Official daily newspaper of the CPSU Central Committee.

PROLETARIAT: The urban working class.

PROLETARSKAYA REVOLUTSIYA: Historical journal on the October Revolution published by the USSR Academy of Sciences during the 1920s and 1930s.

PROTOCOLS OF THE ELDERS OF ZION: Forged antisemitic work purporting to describe a Jewish plot for world domination.

RAZVERTSKA: Bolshevik method of grain procurement.

REFUSENIKS: Jewish activists who were refused emigration permits by the Soviet authorities.

REICHSFÜHRER-SS: Leader of the SS, Heinrich Himmler's title after June 1936.

ROLLBAHN MORD: "Murder Path," slang term used by *Einsatzgruppen* members to describe the beginning of their operations.

RUKH: Ukrainian liberal movement founded in 1989 which supported Gorbachev's reforms.

SALT: Strategic Arms Limitation Talks [Treaties]. Two sets of arms limitation talks held between the U.S. and USSR in the 1970s. The SALT-II treaty was never ratified. In the late 1980s SALT was replaced by the START talks.

SAMIZDAT: The underground publication and distribution of governmentally banned literature.

SHABASHNIKI: Migrant workers.

SHTETL: Small Jewish community in Eastern Europe.

SMERSH: Smert' Shpionam, Death to Spies; Soviet military counter-intelligence agency active between 1943 and 1946.

SOVIET: Council.

SOVIETISH HEIMLAND: "The Soviet Homeland," a Yiddish language monthly published by the Soviet Writers' Union.

SPETSNAZ: Voiska Spetsialnogo Naznacheniya, Special Designation Troops; the Red Army commandos.

SS: Schutzstaffel; Nazi party elite guard.

STAKHANOVITE MOVEMENT: Post-Stalin liberal movement.

START: Startegic Arms Reduction Talks. Arms control talks held between the U.S. and USSR during the 1980s. One result of START was the 1988 INF Treaty that resulted in the elimination of so-called theatre nuclear weapons.

SUBBOTNIKI: Labor battalions created by the BOLSHEVIKS in 1919.

SYNDICALISM: Trade union theory that calls for the control of society by workers' federations.

USSR: Union of Soviet Socialist Republics. Official name: Soyuz Sovyetskikh Sotsialistichestkikh Respublik.

VEKHIST(S): Group of former Marxists who turned to pietistic religious practices in the aftermath of the Revolution of 1905.

VTslK: The All Russian Central Executive Committee of Soviets; quasi-governmental agency that ran the Soviet Union's daily affairs from the October Revolution until July 1918.

WEHRMACHT: The German Army.

YCL: Young Communist League, see KOMSOMOL.

ZEMLYACHESTVO: Village commune comprising all the workers from a single village.

ZEMSTVO(S): Regional govermental agency (or agencies) in Tsarist Russia.

# Author/Title Index

# Subject Index

**About the Editors**

ABRAHAM J. EDELHEIT and HERSHEL EDELHEIT are researchers and writers on the Holocaust and related topics. Among their earlier publications are *Bibliography of Holocaust Literature*, *The Jewish World in Modern Times*, and *A World in Turmoil* (Greenwood Press, 1991).